Learning Rails 5
Rails from the Outside In

J. Mark Locklear
with Barnabas Bulpett and Eric J. Gruber

Beijing · Boston · Farnham · Sebastopol · Tokyo

Learning Rails 5

by J. Mark Locklear and Eric J. Gruber

Printed in the United States of America.

Published by O'Reilly Media, Inc., 1005 Gravenstein Highway North, Sebastopol, CA 95472.

O'Reilly books may be purchased for educational, business, or sales promotional use. Online editions are also available for most titles (*http://oreilly.com/safari*). For more information, contact our corporate/institutional sales department: 800-998-9938 or *corporate@oreilly.com*.

Editor: Allyson MacDonald
Production Editor: Nicole Shelby
Copyeditor: Rachel Monaghan
Proofreader: Charles Roumeliotis

Indexer: Judy McConville
Interior Designer: David Futato
Cover Designer: Randy Comer
Illustrator: Rebecca Demarest

August 2016:   First Edition

Revision History for the First Edition
2016-08-09:   First Release
2017-02-24:   Second Release

See *http://oreilly.com/catalog/errata.csp?isbn=9781491926192* for release details.

978-1-491-92619-2

[LSI]

Table of Contents

Foreword

I came to Rails in 2010. At the time I was doing contract work as a QA engineer in Raleigh, NC. Previous to this I was an out of work software tester. After following my wife to Asheville, NC for a university teaching position I decided I wanted to move from software testing to development work. Asheville is a small market and finding work was tough, so Raleigh was one of my only options. At the time Rails was at version 2.x. Though I was only testing, not developing Rails apps, the learning curve was steep. The process of putting all the pieces of a Rails App in place (GIT, Bundler, Gems, Gemfiles, RVM) was daunting to say the least. "Drinking from a fire hose" was the term we used. I was living and working in Raleigh during the week, and going home to be with my wife on the weekend. This living arrangement gave me lots of time to explore this new framework. I wrote test scripts during the day, and spent my evenings working through Rails tutorials. I owe a debt of gratitude to many of the engineers I worked with on the Entitlement Services team at Red Hat. Specifically, Brenton Leanhardt for his patience and mentoring in learning Ruby and Linux. At the time Rails was only about 5 years old and there were still questions of whether or not Rails was enterprise ready. Those questions have since fallen by the wayside, and Rails is now considered a full-fledged enterprise development platform. Rails is no longer a second-class citizen to Java or PHP, and is arguably at the top of the web framework pecking order.

I began teaching Rails in the Fall of 2014 at Asheville-Buncombe Technical College. By far the biggest hurdle I find my students are faced with in getting started with Rails is setting up the Rails development environment. To begin with Rails is not very Windows friendly. Unless you own a Mac or are a Linux guru you are already a second-class citizen in the Rails world (see "In Defense of Windows" on page 3 in Chapter 1). But, be encouraged. Microsoft is taking steps to make the Rails experience better. That being said, if you want the full Rails development experience you must still own a Mac or use some flavor of Linux. After this, your challenges are not over. Generally, you want to install some kind of version control for Ruby (RVM or RBENV), along with any number of system level packages for Rails. I say all this not to scare you, but to prepare you. Getting your development environment set up can be daunting, but I promise you, it will be worth it. Think of it as a right of passage for Rails development. Once your environment is properly set up you seldom have to revisit it in any sophisticated way, or if you do, you can usually correct whatever problem you are having pretty quickly.

Finally, I want to encourage you to learn Rails, and assure you that you will benefit from this book even if you do not go on to become a Rails developer. I can say this with confidence because Rails has become the gold standard for Model-View-Controller (MVC) architecture in web development. In addition to the general MVC structure, Rails has also created a workflow around migrations, dev ops tasks, REST, GIT, and community support. For all these reasons, even if you do not go on to do great things in Rails, you will encounter some if not all of these challenges in whatever web development platform you choose to work in. By exposing yourself to Rails and its solutions to these challenges you will learn best practices that can be applied to other frameworks and workflows.

— J. Mark Locklear

Preface

Let me tell you why you're here. You're here because you know something. What you know you can't explain, but you feel it. You've felt it your entire life: that there's something wrong in the world. You don't know what it is, but it's there. Like a splinter in your mind, driving you mad. It is this feeling that brought you to me.
—Morpheus, The Matrix

What is wrong in the world? Web development. It is way harder than it has to be.

Everyone cool seems to agree: Ruby on Rails is an amazing way to build web applications. Ruby is a powerful and flexible programming language, and Rails takes advantage of that flexibility to build a web application framework that takes care of a tremendous amount of work for the developer. Everything sounds great!

Except, well... all the Ruby on Rails books talk about this "Model-View-Controller" thing, and they start deep inside the application, close to the database, most of the time. From an experienced Rails developer's perspective, this makes sense—the framework's power lies largely in making it easy for developers to create a data model quickly, layer controller logic on top of that, and then, once all the hard work is done, put a thin layer of interface view on the very top. It's good programming style, and it makes for more robust applications. Advanced Ajax functionality seems to come almost for free!

From the point of view of someone learning Ruby on Rails, however, that race to show off the power of Rails can be extremely painful. There's a lot of seemingly magical behavior in Rails that works wonderfully—until one of the incantations isn't quite right and figuring out what happened means unraveling all that work Rails did. Rails certainly makes it easier to work with databases and objects without spending forever thinking about them, but there are a lot of things to figure out before that ease becomes obvious.

If you'd rather learn Ruby on Rails more slowly, starting from pieces that are more familiar to the average web developer and then moving slowly into controllers and models, you're in the right place. You can start from the HTML you already likely know, and then move more deeply into the many interlinked components of Rails.

 This updated version of *Learning Rails* covers version 5.0. There are substantial changes from earlier versions. Rails itself keeps changing, even in ways that affect beginners.

Who This Book Is For

If you've been working with the Web long enough, you'll know that writing web applications always seems more complicated than it should be. There are lots of parts to manage, along with lots of people to manage, and hopefully lots of visitors to please. Ruby on Rails has intrigued you as one possible solution to that situation.

You may be a designer who's moving toward application development or a developer who combines some design skills with some programming skills. You may be a programmer who's familiar with HTML but who lacks the sense of grace needed to create beautiful design—that's a fair description of one of the authors of this book, anyway. Wherever you're from, whatever you do, you know the Web well and would like to learn how Rails can make your life easier.

The only mandatory technical prerequisite for reading this book is direct familiarity with HTML and a general sense of how programming works. You'll be inserting Ruby code into that HTML as a first step toward writing Ruby code directly, so understanding HTML is a key foundation. (If you don't know Ruby at all, you probably want to look over Appendix A or at least keep it handy for reference.)

Cascading Style Sheets (CSS) will help you make that HTML look a lot nicer, but it's not necessary for this book. Similarly, a sense of how JavaScript works may help. Experience with other templating languages (like PHP, ASP, and ASP.NET) can also help, but it isn't required.

You also need to be willing to work from the command line sometimes. The commands aren't terribly complicated, but they aren't hidden behind a graphical interface either. If you are not comfortable working from the command line this is a nice goal [as a web developer] to work toward. General fluency at the command line is a nice gateway drug to more sofisticated dev ops (development operations) and sys admin (system administrator) skills. While web development and dev ops are very different skill sets, I have never met a good web developer that did not know some dev ops, just as I have never met a good sys admin who did not have some development and coding skills.

Who This Book Is Not For

We don't really want to cut anyone out of the possibility of reading this book, but there are some groups of people who aren't likely to enjoy it. Model-View-Controller purists will probably grind their teeth through the first few chapters, and people who insist that data structures are at the heart of a good application are going to have to wait an even longer time to see their hopes realized. If you consider HTML just a nuisance that programmers have to put up with, odds are good that this book isn't for you. Most of the other Ruby on Rails books, though, are written for people who want to start from the model!

Also, people who are convinced that Ruby and Rails are the one true way may have some problems with this book, which spends a fair amount of time warning readers about potential problems and confusions they need to avoid. Yes, once you've worked with Ruby and Rails for a while, their elegance is obvious. However, reaching that level of comfort and familiarity is often a difficult road. This book attempts to ease as many of those challenges as possible by describing them clearly.

What You'll Learn

Building a Ruby on Rails application requires mastering a complicated set of skills. You may find that—depending on how you're working with it, and who you're working with—you only need part of this tour. That's fine. Just go as far as you think you'll need.

At the beginning, you'll need to install Ruby on Rails. We'll explore different ways of doing this, with an emphasis on easier approaches to getting Ruby and Rails operational.

Next, we'll create a very simple Ruby on Rails application, with only a basic view and then a controller that does a very few things. From this foundation, we'll explore ways to create a more sophisticated layout using a variety of tools, learning more about Ruby along the way.

Once we've learned how to present information, we'll take a closer look at controllers and what they can do. Forms processing is critical to most web applications, so we'll build a few forms and process their results, moving from the simple to the complex.

Forms can do interesting things without storing data, but after a while it's a lot more fun to have data that lasts for more than just a few moments. The next step is setting up a database to store information and figuring out how the magic of the ActiveRecord library in Rails makes it easy to create code that maps directly to database structures—without having to think too hard about database structures or SQL.

Once we have ActiveRecord up and running, we'll explore scaffolding and its possibilities. Rails scaffolding not only helps you build applications quickly, it helps you learn to build them well. The RESTful approach that Rails emphasizes will make it simpler for you to create applications that are both attractive and maintainable. For purposes of illustration, using scaffolding also makes it easier to demonstrate one task at a time, which we hope will make it easier for you to understand what's happening.

Ideally, at this point, you'll feel comfortable with slightly more complicated data models, and we'll take a look at applications that need to combine data in multiple tables. Mixing and matching data is at the heart of most web applications.

We'll also take a look at testing and debugging Rails code, a key factor in the framework's success. Migrations, which make it easy to modify your underlying data structures (and even roll back those changes if necessary), are another key part of Rails's approach to application maintainability.

The next step will be to add some common web applications elements like sessions and cookies, as well as authentication. Rails (with the help of gems for authentication) can manage a lot of this work for you.

We'll also let Rails stretch its legs a bit, showing off its support for Syntactically Awesome Stylesheets (Sass), CoffeeScript scripting, bundle management, and sending email messages.

By the end of this tour, you should be comfortable with working in Ruby on Rails. You may not be a Rails guru yet, but you'll be ready to take advantage of all of the other resources out there for becoming one.

Ruby and Rails Style

It's definitely possible to write Ruby on Rails code in ways that look familiar to programmers from other languages. However, that code often isn't really idiomatic Ruby, as Ruby programmers have chosen other paths. In general, this book will always try to introduce new concepts using syntax that's likely to be familiar to developers from other environments, and then explain what the local idiom does. You'll learn to write idiomatic Ruby that way (if you want to), and at the same time you'll figure out how to read code from the Ruby pros.

We've tried to make sure that the code we present is understandable to those without a strong background in Ruby. Ruby itself is worth an introductory book (or several), but the Ruby code in a lot of Rails applications is simple, thanks to the hard work the framework's creators have already put into it. You may want to install Rails in Chapter 1, and then explore Appendix A before diving in.

Other Options

There are lots of different ways to learn Rails. Some people want to learn Ruby in detail before jumping into a framework that uses it. That's a perfectly good option, and if you want to start that way, you should explore the following books:

- *Programming Ruby*, Fourth Edition by Dave Thomas with Chad Fowler and Andy Hunt (Pragmatic Bookshelf, 2013)
- *The Well-Grounded Rubyist* by David A. Black (Manning, 2014)
- *Learning Ruby* by Michael Fitzgerald (O'Reilly, 2007)
- *The Ruby Programming Language* by David Flanagan and Yukhiro Matsumoto (O'Reilly, 2008)
- *Ruby Pocket Reference* by Michael Fitzgerald (O'Reilly, 2015)
- *Practical Object-Oriented Design in Ruby: An Agile Primer* by Sandi Metz (Addison-Wesley, 2012)
- *Metaprogramming Ruby* by Paolo Perrotta (Pragmatic Programmers, 2010)

You may also want to supplement (or replace) this book with other books on Rails. If you want some other resources, you can explore the following:

- For maximum excitement, try *http://railsforzombies.com/*, a training tool that includes video and exercises. The first few videos are free.
- For the latest Ruby on Rails Screencasts, check out Go Rails (*https://gorails.com*).
- While these videos are out of date (Rails 3), many are still very relevant. Try RailsCasts (*http://railscasts.com*). Ryan Bates's style has been the gold standard for technical screencasts for almost a decade.
- For updates to this book, including screencasts, check out this book's website (*http://learningrails5.com*).
- The Ruby on Rails Tutorial by Michael Hartl provides a faster-moving introduction that covers many more extensions for Rails.
- *Agile Web Development with Rails*, Fourth Edition (Pragmatic Programmers, 2010), by Sam Ruby, Dave Thomas, and David Heinemeier Hansson gives a detailed explanation of a wide range of features.

Ideally, you'll want to make sure that whatever books or online documentation you use cover at least Rails 3.0 (or later). The perpetual evolution of Rails has unfortunately made it dangerous to use a lot of formerly great but now dated material (some of it works, some of it doesn't).

Finally, key resources you should always explore are the Ruby on Rails Guides (*http://guides.rubyonrails.org*), which provide an excellent and well-updated overview for a lot of common topics. Sometimes they leave gaps or demand more background knowledge than beginners have, but they're a wonderful layer of documentation at a level above the basic (though also useful) API documentation (*http://api.rubyonrails.org*).

Rails Versions

The Rails team is perpetually improving Rails and releasing new versions. This book was updated for Rails 5.0 and Ruby 2.2.3.

If You Have Problems Making Examples Work

When you're starting to use a new framework, error messages can be hard, even impossible, to decipher. We've included occasional notes in the book about particular errors you might see, but it seems very normal for different people to encounter different errors as they work through examples. Sometimes it's the result of skipping a step or entering code just a little differently than it was in the book. It's probably not the result of a problem in Rails itself, even if the error message seems to come from deep in the framework. That isn't likely an error in the framework, but much more likely a problem the framework is having in figuring out how to deal with the unexpected code it just encountered.

If you find yourself stuck, here are a few things you should check:

What version of Ruby are you running?
> You can check by entering `ruby -v`. All of the examples in this book were written with Ruby 2.2.3. Versions of Ruby older than 2.x may cause problems for Rails 5.x. Chapter 1 explores how to install Ruby, but you may need to find documentation specific to your operating system and environment.

What version of Rails are you running?
> You can check by running `rails -v`. You might think that you should be able to use the examples here with any version of Rails 5.x, but Rails keeps changing in ways that break even simple code. The examples on *http://bit.ly/learn-rails-5* were writen for Ruby 2.2.3 and Rails 5.0. If you're running a version of Rails other than 5.0, especially an earlier version, you will encounter problems.

Are you calling the program the right way?
> Linux and Mac OS X both use a forward slash, /, as a directory separator, whereas Windows uses a backslash, \. This book uses the forward slash, but if you're in Windows, you may need to use the backslash. Leaving out an argument can also produce some really incomprehensible error messages.

Is the database connected?

By default, Rails expects you to have SQLite up and running, though some installations use MySQL or other databases. If you're getting errors that have "sql" in them somewhere, it's probably the database. All the examples in the this book use SQLite. This is installed with Rails, and usually does not require attention. Check that the settings in *database.yml* are correct, and that the permissions, if any, are set correctly.

Are all of the pieces there?

Most of the time, assembling a Rails application, even a simple one, requires modifying multiple files—at least a view and a controller. If you've only built a controller, you're missing a key piece you need to see your results; if you've only built a view, you need a controller to call it. As you build more and more complex applications, you'll need to make sure you've considered routing, models, and maybe even configuration and gems. What looks like a simple call in one part of the application may depend on pieces elsewhere.

Eventually, you'll know what kinds of problems specific missing pieces cause, but at least at first, try to make sure you've entered complete examples before running them.

It's also possible to have files present but with the wrong permissions set. If you know a file is there, but Rails can't seem to get to it, check to make sure that permissions are set correctly.

Did you save all the files?

Of course this never happens to you. However, making things happen in Rails often means tinkering with multiple files at the same time, and it's easy to forget to save one as you move along. This can be especially confusing if it was a configuration or migration file. Always take a moment to make sure everything you're editing has been saved before trying to run your application.

Are your routes right?

If you can't get a page to come up, you probably have a problem with your routes. This is a more common problem when you're creating controllers directly, as you will be up through Chapter 4, rather than having Rails generate scaffolding. Check *config/routes.rb*.

Is everything named correctly?

Rails depends on naming conventions to establish connections between data and code without you having to specify them explicitly. This works wonderfully, until you have a typo somewhere obscure. Rails also relies on a number of Ruby conventions for variables, prefacing instance variables with @ or symbols with :. These special characters make a big difference, so make sure they're correct.

Is the Ruby syntax right?

> If you get syntax errors, or sometimes even if you get a `nil` object error, you may have an extra space, missing bracket, or similar issue. Ruby syntax is extremely flexible, so you can usually ignore the discipline of brackets, parentheses, or spaces—but sometimes it really does matter.

Is another Rails app running?

> Jumping quickly between programs can be really confusing. In a normal development cycle, you'll just have one app running, and things just work. When you're reading a book, especially if you're downloading the examples, it's easy to start an app, close the window you use to explore it, and forget it's still running underneath. Definitely stop one server before running another while you're exploring the apps in this book.

Are you running the right program?

> Yes, this sounds weird. When you're developing real programs, it makes sense to leave the server running to check back and forth with your changes. If you're testing out a lot of small application examples quickly, though, you may have problems. Definitely leave the server running while you're working within a given example, but stop it when you change chapters or set off to create a new application with the `rails` command.

Did the authors just plain screw up?

> Obviously, we're working hard to ensure that all of the code in this book runs smoothly the first time, but it's possible that an error crept through. You'll want to check the errata, described in the next section, and download sample code, which will be updated for errata at *https://github.com/bbulpett/LR5*.

It's tempting to try Googling errors to find a quick fix. Unfortunately, the issues just described are more likely to be the problem than something else that has clear documentation. The Rails API documentation (*http://api.rubyonrails.org/*) might be helpful at times, especially if you're experimenting with extending an example. There shouldn't be much out there, though, beyond the book example files themselves that you can download to fix an example.

If You Like (or Don't Like) This Book

If you like—or don't like—this book, by all means, please let people know. Amazon reviews (*http://amzn.to/2aTrwMY*) are one popular way to share your happiness (or lack of happiness), or you can leave reviews on this book's O'Reilly page (*http://bit.ly/learn-rails-5*).

There's also a link to errata on the O'Reilly site. Errata gives readers a way to let us know about typos, errors, and other problems with the book. The errata will be visible on the page immediately, and we'll confirm it after checking it out. O'Reilly can also fix errata in future printings of the book and on Safari, making for a better reader experience pretty quickly.

We hope to keep this book updated for future versions of Rails and will also incorporate suggestions and complaints into future editions.

Conventions Used in This Book

The following font conventions are used in this book:

Italic
> Indicates pathnames, filenames, and program names; Internet addresses, such as domain names and URLs; and new items where they are defined.

`Constant width`
> Indicates command lines and options that should be typed verbatim; names and keywords in programs, including method names, variable names, and class names; and HTML element tags.

`Constant width bold`
> Indicates emphasis in program code lines.

`Constant width italic`
> Indicates text that should be replaced with user-supplied values.

 This icon signifies a tip, suggestion, or general note.

 This icon indicates a warning or caution.

Using Code Examples

First let me thank Barnabas Bulpett for his work in creating the sample applications for this book. His tireless work and attention to 12 a.m. emails has ensured the compainion code for the book is flawless. Also, he has created a very helpful *README.md* at the root of each application that includes helpful tips on the functionality of each app.

The code examples for this book, which are available from *http://oreil.ly/Learning Rails5*, come in two forms. One is a set of examples, organized by chapter, with each example numbered and named. These examples are referenced from the relevant chapter. The other form is a dump of all the code from the book, in the order it was presented in the book. That can be helpful if you need a line that didn't make it into the final example, or if you want to cut and paste pieces as you walk through the examples. Hopefully, the code will help you learn.

This book is here to help you get your job done. In general, you may use the code in this book in your programs and documentation. You do not need to contact us for permission unless you're reproducing a significant portion of the code. For example, writing a program that uses several chunks of code from this book does not require permission. Selling or distributing a CD-ROM of examples from O'Reilly books *does* require permission. Answering a question by citing this book and quoting example code does not require permission. Incorporating a significant amount of example code from this book into your product's documentation *does* require permission.

We appreciate, but do not require, attribution. An attribution usually includes the title, author, publisher, and ISBN. For example: "*Learning Rails 5* by J. Mark Locklear, Simon St.Laurent, Edd Dumbill, and Eric J. Gruber. Copyright 2012 Simon St.Laurent, Edd Dumbill, and Eric Gruber, 978-1-449-30933-6."

If you feel your use of code examples falls outside fair use or the permission given above, feel free to contact us at *permissions@oreilly.com*.

O'Reilly Safari

 *Safari* (formerly Safari Books Online) is a membership-based training and reference platform for enterprise, government, educators, and individuals.

Members have access to thousands of books, training videos, Learning Paths, interactive tutorials, and curated playlists from over 250 publishers, including O'Reilly Media, Harvard Business Review, Prentice Hall Professional, Addison-Wesley Professional, Microsoft Press, Sams, Que, Peachpit Press, Adobe, Focal Press, Cisco Press, John Wiley & Sons, Syngress, Morgan Kaufmann, IBM Redbooks, Packt, Adobe Press, FT Press, Apress, Manning, New Riders, McGraw-Hill, Jones & Bartlett, and Course Technology, among others.

For more information, please visit *http://oreilly.com/safari*.

How to Contact Us

Please address comments and questions concerning this book to the publisher:

O'Reilly Media, Inc.

1005 Gravenstein Highway North

Sebastopol, CA 95472

800-998-9938 (in the United States or Canada)

707-829-0515 (international or local)

707-829-0104 (fax)

We have a web page for this book, where we list lectures, errata, examples, and any additional information. You can access this page at *http://learningrails5.com*.

In addition, O'Reilly maintains a page for the book at *http://bit.ly/learn-rails-5*.

To comment or ask technical questions about this book, send email to: *bookquestions@oreilly.com*.

For more information about our books, courses, conferences, and news, see our website at *http://www.oreilly.com*.

Find us on Facebook: *http://facebook.com/oreilly*

Follow us on Twitter: *http://twitter.com/oreillymedia*

Watch us on YouTube: *http://www.youtube.com/oreillymedia*

Acknowledgments

This book was updated to Rails 5 in May 2016. For this revision I would like to thank Barnabas Bulpett for his help, support, and motivation while updating and rewriting the book. Barnabas not only wrote all of the sample book code, but entirely rewrote Chapter 10, in addition to making significant content contributions throughout other chapters. A huge thanks to Natasha Ansari for updating all of the images in the book, in addition to editing and tech review, and thanks also to Aaron Sumner for tech review.

Mark Locklear would like to thank his wife Erica for showing him what true passion is, his daughter Faith for helping him appreciate the simple things in life, and his parents John Pat and Deletha for giving him the ultimate example of hard work and perseverance.

Barnabas Bulpett would like to thank O'Reilly Media and Mark Locklear for giving him the opportunity to provide the example code that accompanies this book. In addition, he wishes thank his two children, Kaya and Moses, for their support and patience through the late nights of work. Barnabas also thanks his father, Thomas Bulpett, for teaching him the value of hard work.

Natasha Ansari would like to thank Barnabas Bulpett for his dedication and hard work and Mark Locklear for showing us that Rails makes sense (kinda).

We'd also like to thank Simon St. Laurent, Edd Dumbill, and Eric J. Gruber for their work on the previous editions of the book.

Finally, thanks to Rachel Monaghan for cleaning up our prose, Nicole Shelby and Melanie Yarbrough for getting this book through production, and Judy McConville for the patient work it takes to build an index.

## CHAPTER 1

Starting Up Ruby on Rails

What we call the beginning is often the end. And to make an end is
to make a beginning. The end is where we start from.
— T. S. Eliot

Before you can use Rails, you have to install it. Even if it's already installed on your computer, you may need to consider upgrading it. In this chapter, we'll take a look at some ways of installing Ruby, Rails, and the supporting infrastructure. Please feel free to jump to whatever pieces of this section interest you and skip past those that don't. Once the software is working, we'll generate the basic Rails application, which will at least let you know if Rails is working. However you decide to set up Rails, in the end you're going to have a structure like that shown in Figure 1-1.

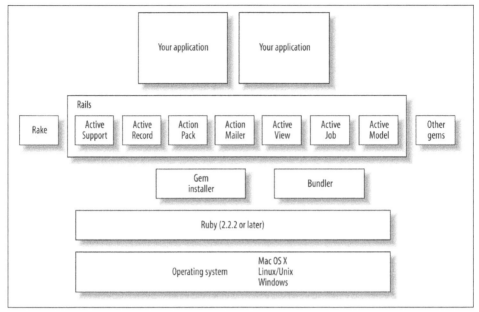

Figure 1-1. The many components of a Rails installation

All of these options are free. You don't need to spend any money to use Rails, unless maybe you feel like buying a nice text editor.

If You Run Windows, You're Lucky

Windows users have two options for getting a basic installation of Rails and supporting tools—everything you need to use this book—far more easily than anyone else: EngineYard's RailsInstaller (*http://railsinstaller.org*) and Bitnami's Ruby Stack (*https://bitnami.com/stack/ruby/installer*). Each of these installers provides all the key components in a one-click installation. Visit the site and download the installer; after that, you should be ready to move ahead to "Starting Up Rails" on page 9.

Really, it's that easy! (Well, except that you may have to tell Windows Defender not to block the port Rails uses to present the site. It's also possible that you'll have to install developer tools on newer versions of Windows.)

Rails on Windows might be considered a bridge to full Rails development. You will find that many gems do not work on Windows, so if you want to take the next step in Rails development, consider moving to OS X or Linux operating systems. Ubuntu is a wonderful OS; a dual-boot environment with Windows is a good way to get started using Linux while not entirely cutting ties with Windows.

As this book was going to print, RailsInstaller included installs for Windows and OS X along with the MySQL database. Bitnami offers installers for Windows, Mac, and Linux, and includes both MySQL and Postgres databases with its install.

In Defense of Windows

When I was planning my first Rails class at Asheville-Buncombe Technical Community College during the summer of 2014, I initially planned to require students to use either Mac or Linux for their Rails environment. If they were Windows users, then I would require they install Virtualbox and Vagrant to run a Linux environment in Windows (still not a bad option, by the way). *By God they WILL get the full Rails development experience!* I told myself. However, after some reflection, I was inclined to change my thinking on this matter. It's foolish for us as Rails apologists to say, "We have this great web development framework. It's fast, flexible, has great support...but sorry, Windows users, you have to use either Mac or Linux to join the club." That's just plain wrong and flies in the face of the inclusivity and diverse nature the Rails community has always embraced.

Getting Started at the Command Line

Installing Rails by hand requires installing Ruby (preferably 2.2.2 or later), installing Gems, and then installing Rails. You will eventually also need to install SQLite, MySQL, or another relational database, though SQLite is already present on OS X and in many Linux distributions.

Ruby comes standard on a number of Linux and OS X platforms. To see whether it's there, and what version it has, enter **ruby -v** at the command prompt. You'll want Ruby 2.2.2 or later, so you may need to update it to a more recent version:

- On OS X, the preinstalled version of Ruby will vary widely depending on your OS X version. The following table summarizes which Ruby versions are included.

OS X version	Ruby version included
Yosemite (10.10) and Mavericks (10.9)	Ruby 2.0.0
Snow Leopard (10.6), Lion (10.7), and Mountain Lion (10.8)	Ruby 1.8.7
Leopard (10.5)	Ruby 1.8.6
Older versions	Ruby 1.8.2

- If you're on Tiger (10.4) or an earlier version of OS X, you'll need to update Ruby itself, a challenge that's beyond the scope of this book. You may want to investigate the Homebrew guide (*http://brew.sh*). For a more comprehensive installation, check out the excellent tutorials from RailsGirls (*http://bit.ly/2aTroNH*). (You should ignore the versions of Rails installed with OS X—they're guaranteed to be out of date. You'll need to update Ruby to version 2.2.2 to use Rails 5.)

- Most distributions of Linux include Ruby, but you'll want to use your package manager to make sure it's updated to 2.2.2. Some, notably Ubuntu and Debian, will name the gem command gem1.9.

- For Windows, unless you're a hardened tinkerer, it's much easier to use RailsInstaller or Bitnami. If you're feeling strong, the one-click RubyInstaller (*http://rubyinstaller.org*) is probably your easiest option, though there are other alternatives, including Cygwin (*http://www.cygwin.com*), which brings a lot of the Unix environment to Windows.

A saner long-term approach to installing Ruby and Rails includes also installing rvm (*https://rvm.io*), the Ruby version manager, which frees you from having to worry about what version of Ruby your system decided it should have as well as giving you better options for managing a clean work environment. (It was created by Wayne E. Seguin, the same person who created RailsInstaller.) If that doesn't seem right to you, you can also find out more on how to install Ruby on a variety of platforms at the Ruby website (*http://www.ruby-lang.org/en/downloads/*).

If rvm isn't for you, you may also want to explore rbenv (*https://github.com/sstephenson/rbenv/*), a much smaller and simpler approach to switching between versions of Ruby.

RubyGems (often just called Gems) is also starting to come standard on a number of platforms and has shipped with OS X versions since Leopard (10.5). However, if you need to install Gems, see the RubyGems User Guide's instructions (*http://guides.ruby gems.org/rubygems-basics/*).

If you use MacPorts, apt-get, or a similar package installer, you may want to use it only to install Ruby, and then proceed from the command line. You certainly can install Gems and Rails with these tools, but Gems can update itself, which can make for very confusing package update issues.

Once you have RubyGems installed, Rails and its many dependencies are just a command away (though the output has grown more verbose with every version of Rails):

```
marklocklear$ gem install rails
Fetching: i18n-0.7.0.gem (100%)
Successfully installed i18n-0.7.0
```

```
Fetching: thread_safe-0.3.5.gem (100%)
Successfully installed thread_safe-0.3.5
Fetching: tzinfo-1.2.2.gem (100%)
Successfully installed tzinfo-1.2.2
Fetching: concurrent-ruby-1.0.2.gem (100%)
Successfully installed concurrent-ruby-1.0.2
Fetching: activesupport-5.0.0.gem (100%)
Successfully installed activesupport-5.0.0
Fetching: rack-2.0.1.gem (100%)
Successfully installed rack-2.0.1
Fetching: rack-test-0.6.3.gem (100%)
Successfully installed rack-test-0.6.3
Fetching: mini_portile2-2.1.0.gem (100%)
Successfully installed mini_portile2-2.1.0
Installing ri documentation for sprockets-rails-3.1.1
Parsing documentation for rails-5.0.0
Installing ri documentation for rails-5.0.0
...
37 gems installed
```

You may need to use sudo, which gives your command the power of the root (administrative) account, if you're working in an environment that requires root access for the installation; otherwise, you can just type **gem install rails**. That will install the latest version of Rails, which may be more recent than 5.0.1, as well as all of its dependencies. **gem install rails** will install the latest official release of Rails, which at present is 5.0.1. It will not install any Rails betas. (To see which version of Rails is installed, enter **rails -v** at the command line.)

You may also need to install the sqlite3 gem, which isn't automatically installed by the Rails gem but is needed for development. That's **gem install sqlite3**.

If you're ever wondering which gems (and which versions of gems) are installed, type **gem list --local**. For more information on gems, just type **gem**, or visit the Ruby Gems website (*http://rubygems.org*).

 You can see the documentation that gems have installed by running the command gem server, and visiting the URL (usually *http://localhost:8808*) that command reports. When you're done, you can turn off the server with Ctrl-C.

Once you have Rails installed, you can create a Rails application easily from the command line. Here's what it looks like in its extended glory, but you don't need to read it every time:

```
marklocklear$ rails new hello01
      create
      create  README.md
      create  Rakefile
```

```
create  config.ru
create  .gitignore
create  Gemfile
create  app
create  app/assets/config/manifest.js
create  app/assets/javascripts/application.js
create  app/assets/javascripts/cable.js
create  app/assets/stylesheets/application.css
create  app/channels/application_cable/channel.rb
create  app/channels/application_cable/connection.rb
create  app/controllers/application_controller.rb
create  app/helpers/application_helper.rb
create  app/jobs/application_job.rb
create  app/mailers/application_mailer.rb
create  app/models/application_record.rb
create  app/views/layouts/application.html.erb
create  app/views/layouts/mailer.html.erb
create  app/views/layouts/mailer.text.erb
create  app/assets/images/.keep
create  app/assets/javascripts/channels
create  app/assets/javascripts/channels/.keep
create  app/controllers/concerns/.keep
create  app/models/concerns/.keep
create  bin
create  bin/bundle
create  bin/rails
create  bin/rake
create  bin/setup
create  bin/update
create  config
create  config/routes.rb
create  config/application.rb
create  config/environment.rb
create  config/secrets.yml
create  config/cable.yml
create  config/puma.rb
create  config/spring.rb
create  config/environments
create  config/environments/development.rb
create  config/environments/production.rb
create  config/environments/test.rb
create  config/initializers
create  config/initializers/application_controller_renderer.rb
create  config/initializers/assets.rb
create  config/initializers/backtrace_silencers.rb
create  config/initializers/cookies_serializer.rb
create  config/initializers/cors.rb
create  config/initializers/filter_parameter_logging.rb
create  config/initializers/inflections.rb
create  config/initializers/mime_types.rb
create  config/initializers/new_framework_defaults.rb
create  config/initializers/session_store.rb
```

```
    create  config/initializers/wrap_parameters.rb
    create  config/locales
    create  config/locales/en.yml
    create  config/boot.rb
    create  config/database.yml
    create  db
    create  db/seeds.rb
    create  lib
    create  lib/tasks
    create  lib/tasks/.keep
    create  lib/assets
    create  lib/assets/.keep
    create  log
    create  log/.keep
    create  public
    create  public/404.html
    create  public/422.html
    create  public/500.html
    create  public/apple-touch-icon-precomposed.png
    create  public/apple-touch-icon.png
    create  public/favicon.ico
    create  public/robots.txt
    create  test/fixtures
    create  test/fixtures/.keep
    create  test/fixtures/files
    create  test/fixtures/files/.keep
    create  test/controllers
    create  test/controllers/.keep
    create  test/mailers
    create  test/mailers/.keep
    create  test/models
    create  test/models/.keep
    create  test/helpers
    create  test/helpers/.keep
    create  test/integration
    create  test/integration/.keep
    create  test/test_helper.rb
    create  tmp
    create  tmp/.keep
    create  tmp/cache
    create  tmp/cache/assets
    create  vendor/assets/javascripts
    create  vendor/assets/javascripts/.keep
    create  vendor/assets/stylesheets
    create  vendor/assets/stylesheets/.keep
    remove  config/initializers/cors.rb
       run  bundle install
Fetching gem metadata from https://rubygems.org/
Fetching version metadata from https://rubygems.org/
Fetching dependency metadata from https://rubygems.org/
Resolving dependencies....
Installing rake 11.2.2
```

```
Using concurrent-ruby 1.0.2
Using i18n 0.7.0
Installing minitest 5.9.0
Using thread_safe 0.3.5
Using builder 3.2.2
Using erubis 2.7.0
Using mini_portile2 2.1.0
Using pkg-config 1.1.7
Using rack 2.0.1
Using nio4r 1.2.1
Using websocket-extensions 0.1.2
Using mime-types-data 3.2016.0521
Using arel 7.0.0
Using bundler 1.12.5
Installing byebug 9.0.5 with native extensions
Installing coffee-script-source 1.10.0
Installing execjs 2.7.0
Using method_source 0.8.2
Using thor 0.19.1
Installing debug_inspector 0.0.2 with native extensions
Installing ffi 1.9.13 with native extensions
Installing multi_json 1.12.1
Installing rb-fsevent 0.9.7
Installing puma 3.4.0 with native extensions
Installing sass 3.4.22
Installing tilt 2.0.5
Installing spring 1.7.2
Installing sqlite3 1.3.11 with native extensions
Installing turbolinks-source 5.0.0
Using tzinfo 1.2.2
Using nokogiri 1.6.8
Using rack-test 0.6.3
Using sprockets 3.6.3
Using websocket-driver 0.6.4
Using mime-types 3.1
Installing coffee-script 2.4.1
Installing uglifier 3.0.0
Installing rb-inotify 0.9.7
Installing turbolinks 5.0.0
Using activesupport 5.0.0
Using loofah 2.0.3
Using mail 2.6.4
Installing listen 3.0.8
Using rails-dom-testing 2.0.1
Using globalid 0.3.6
Using activemodel 5.0.0
Installing jbuilder 2.5.0
Using rails-html-sanitizer 1.0.3
Installing spring-watcher-listen 2.0.0
Using activejob 5.0.0
Using activerecord 5.0.0
Using actionview 5.0.0
```

```
Using actionpack 5.0.0
Using actioncable 5.0.0
Using actionmailer 5.0.0
Using railties 5.0.0
Using sprockets-rails 3.1.1
Installing coffee-rails 4.2.1
Installing jquery-rails 4.1.1
Installing web-console 3.3.1
Using rails 5.0.0
Installing sass-rails 5.0.5
Bundle complete! 15 Gemfile dependencies, 63 gems now installed.
Use `bundle show [gemname]` to see where a bundled gem is installed.
        run  bundle exec spring binstub --all
* bin/rake: spring inserted
* bin/rails: spring inserted
```

This also gets longer and longer with each new version of Rails. Also, the bundle install piece may pause for a long moment.

 Rails application directories are just ordinary directories. You can move them, obliterate them and start over, or do whatever you need to do with ordinary file management tools. Each application directory is also completely independent—the general "Rails environment" just generates these applications.

Starting Up Rails

To start Rails, you'll need to move into the directory you just created—**cd hello01**—and then issue your first command to get the Puma server (which will be described shortly) busy running your application:

```
marklocklear$ rails server
=> Booting Puma
=> Rails 5.0.0 application starting in development on http://localhost:3000
=> Run `rails server -h` for more startup options
Puma starting in single mode...
* Version 3.4.0 (ruby 2.3.0-p0), codename: Owl Bowl Brawl
* Min threads: 5, max threads: 5
* Environment: development
* Listening on tcp://localhost:3000
Use Ctrl-C to stop
```

Rails is now running, and you can watch any errors it encounters through the extensive logging you'll see in this window.

By default, `rails server` binds only to `localhost` at 0.0.0.0 or 127.0.0.1, and the application isn't visible from other computers. Normally, that's a security feature, not a bug, though you can specify an address for the server to use with the `-b` option (and `-p` for a specific port) if you want to make it visible.

For more details on options for using `rails server`, just enter **rails server -h**.

If you now visit *http://localhost:3000*, you'll see the welcome screen shown in Figure 1-2. When you're ready to stop Rails, you can just press Ctrl-C.

Figure 1-2. The Rails welcome page

 You frequently can leave Rails running while coding. In development mode, you can make many changes to your application with the server running, and you won't have to restart the server to see them. If you change configuration, add scopes, or install gems, though, you'll need to restart.

Puma (*http://puma.io*) is written in Ruby and bundled with recent releases of Rails. It's very convenient for Ruby development, with or without Rails. It's an excellent testing server, but unlike earlier versions of Rails that used WEBrick, Puma can also be used in production.

If you've never used Ruby, now would be a good time to explore Appendix A, which teaches some key components of the language inside of a very simple Rails application.

 Depending on how you set up your Rails environment and how you use Bundler, described in Chapter 17, you may need to preface your calls to `rails`, `rake`, and similar mechanisms with `bundle exec` to make sure you're running exactly the version of the tools you expect to be running. If this seems like a lot of extra typing, visit this blog post by Gabe Berke-Williams (*http://bit.ly/2aTrlBk*) to learn about binstubs, a way to avoid this.

Test Your Knowledge

Quiz

1. What's the name of the Ruby application packaging utility and how do you install Rails with it?

2. What is Puma, and why is it included with Rails?

3. Why should you install a particular version of Ruby on your platform when Ruby already comes installed?

Answers

1. RubyGems or just "gems," which is run with the `gem` command, is Ruby's application packager. To install the latest version of Rails and all its dependencies, just type `gem install rails`.

2. Puma is a web server, and allows you to run your application locally for testing and development.

3. Rails 5 only works with Ruby versions 2.2.2 and above.

## CHAPTER 2

Rails on the Web

Is fear preventing you from taking action? Acknowledge the fear,
watch it, take your attention into it, be fully present with it.
—Eckhart Tolle, *The Power of Now*

Now that you have Rails installed, it's time to make Rails do something—not necessarily very much yet, but enough to show you what happens when you make a call to a Rails application, and enough to let you do something to respond when those calls come in. There's a long tradition in computer books of starting out with a program that says "hello" to the programmer. We'll follow that tradition and pursue it a bit further to make clear how Rails can work with HTML. You're welcome, of course, to make Rails say whatever you'd like.

 The work in this chapter depends on the *hello* application created in Chapter 1. If you didn't create one, go back and explore the directions given there. You can also find the files for the first demonstration in *ch02/hello01* of the downloadable code.

Creating Your Own View

Saying "hello" is a simple thing, focused exclusively on putting a message on a screen. To get started, we can post that message using a view including HTML that will get sent to the browser.

Rails actually won't let you create views directly. Its controller-centric perspective requires that views be associated with controllers. While that might seem like a bit of an imposition, it's not too hard to work around.

Creating anything in Rails requires going to the command line. Open a terminal or command window and go to the home directory of your Rails application.

Then type:

```
rails generate controller hello index
```

`rails generate`'s first argument, `controller`, specifies that it should generate code for a controller, in this case named `hello`, the second argument. Finally, including `index` at the end requests a view named index, bound to the hello controller.

Model-View-Controller

"You keep talking about views, controllers, and models. What is all that?"

It's a bit of programmer-speak: Model-View-Controller, or MVC, is an old idea that got its start in the Smalltalk programming world of the 1970s. The *model* is the underlying data structure, specific to the task the program is addressing; *controllers* manage the flow of data into and out of those objects; and *views* present the information provided by those controllers to users.

MVC is an excellent approach for building maintainable applications, as each layer keeps its logic to itself. Views might include a bit of code for presenting the data from the controller, but most of the logic for moving information around should be kept in the controller, and logic about data structures should be kept in the model. If you want to change how something looks, but not change the logic or the data structures, you can just create a new view, without disrupting everything underneath it.

As you see more of Rails, in this book and elsewhere, you'll probably come to appreciate MVC's virtues, though it can seem confusing and constraining at first. Chapter 4 will explain how Rails uses MVC in more detail.

You'll see something like:

```
1   create  app/controllers/hello_controller.rb
2   route  get "hello/index"
3   invoke  erb
4   create    app/views/hello
5   create    app/views/hello/index.html.erb
6   invoke  test_unit
7   create    test/controllers/hello_controller_test.rb
8   invoke  helper
9   create    app/helpers/hello_helper.rb
10  invoke    test_unit
11  invoke  assets
12  invoke    coffee
13  create      app/assets/javascripts/hello.coffee
14  invoke    scss
15  create      app/assets/stylesheets/hello.scss
```

Depending on how your Rails installation worked, it's possible that you'll receive a message requesting that you run `bundle install` first. Run that, and then you should be able to generate controllers (and everything else) without a hitch.

The `create` entries identify directories and files that the generator created itself. You'll see a new controller in line 1, a new *views* directory in line 4, the index file (*index.html.erb*) we requested in line 5, a template for creating tests for that controller in line 7, and a helper in line 9. Lines 13 and 15 create supporting CoffeeScript (which compiles to JavaScript) and Sass (which compiles to CSS) files, respectively. (The *.rb* file extension is the conventional extension for Ruby files; *.erb* is the common extension for Embedded Ruby files.)

If you foul up a `rails generate` command, you can issue `rails destroy` to have Rails try to fix your mistakes. Suggestion: Include the Linux command (`rm -rf app_name`) executed from the parent directory of the app to remove it in case there is a need to start over.

Rails 5.x requires one more step before we can run the application. For the purposes of this exercise, you'll need to visit the *config/routes.rb* file and change the `get` `"hello/index"` line to look like this:

```
get 'hello' => 'hello#index'
```

Now Rails will know where to find your code—don't worry about why quite yet, but the index file is now available to the application. Run `rails server` to get it going, and then take a look at *http://localhost:3000/hello/*. Figure 2-1 shows what Rails created to start with.

Figure 2-1. The generated index file identifies its home

This isn't pretty, but there's already something to learn here. Note that the URL that brought up this page is *http://localhost:3000/hello/*. As the page itself says, though, the file is in *app/views/hello/index.html.erb*. There's a web server running and it's serving files out of the application's directory, but Rails uses its own rules, not the file structure, to decide what gets presented at what URL. For right now, it's enough to know that the name of the controller, hello, will bring up its associated view, which is defined by the *index.html.erb* file.

The initial contents of that file are fairly simple, like those of Example 2-1.

Example 2-1. The default contents of index.html.erb

```
<h1>Hello#index</h1>
<p>Find me in app/views/hello/index.html.erb</p>
```

The Rails designers didn't even give these generated pieces a full HTML document structure. Since the generated code will get replaced anyway, it doesn't matter very much. It's not that Rails doesn't care about the surrounding markup, but rather that the surrounding markup usually comes from layouts, which are covered in the next chapter. For this chapter's purposes, however, the view is enough to work with.

For starters, we'll just modify the file a little bit so that it presents a slightly friendlier hello, as shown in Example 2-2.

Example 2-2. The new contents of index.html.erb

```
<h1>Hello!</h1>
<p>This is a greeting from app/views/hello/index.html.erb</p>
```

If you save that file and then reload, you'll see something like Figure 2-2.

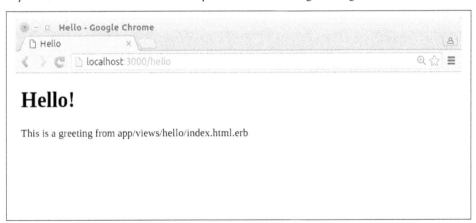

Figure 2-2. A revised greeting

Putting one simple HTML page in the slightly obscure location of a generated HTML page isn't incredibly exciting, but it's a start.

What Are All Those Folders?

You might have noticed the large set of folders Rails created for an application. We'll explore most of these in detail over the course of this book, but for now, here's a quick guide to what's there:

app
> Where you build your application's core. It includes subfolders for controllers, assets (like images, stylesheets, and JavaScript), helpers, models, and views.

config
> Hosts database configuration, URL routing rules, and the Rails environment structures for development, testing, and deployment. You'll also see a *config.ru* file in the main application directory. Rails uses that to start your application, and you shouldn't touch that for now.

db
> Provides a home to scripts used to manage relational database tables.

doc
> Collects documentation generated from Ruby code using RubyDoc. RubyDoc is a documentation generator for Ruby, much like JavaDoc. For a lot more information, see *http://www.ruby-doc.org/*.

lib
> Holds code that doesn't quite fit into the model, view, or controller classifications, typically code that's shared by these components. The *tasks* subdirectory contains Rake tasks for your application, and *assets* holds files that might not logically fit in the *app/assets* folder.

log
> Gathers log data—not just errors, but very rich information on requests, how they were processed, how long it took to process them, and session data from the request.

public
> Contains mostly static HTML and the *favicon.ico* file for your application, as well as things like 404 Not Found error reporting pages.

test
> Contains code—generated at first, but updated by you—for testing your Rails application.

tmp

> The internal home in Rails for session variables, temporary files, cached data, and more.

vendor

> This folder is mostly defunct. In previous versions of Rails it housed plug-ins and gems from outside of Rails itself. Also, if the application has been frozen to a particular version of Rails, that version may be stored here.

Most of the time you'll work in *app* or *test*, with some ventures into *public* to work on the few parts of your application that Rails doesn't control directly.

Adding Some Data

As pretty much every piece of Rails documentation will suggest, views are really meant to provide users with a perspective on data managed by a controller. It's a little strange to run through all this generation and layers of folders just to create an HTML file. To start taking advantage of a little more Rails power, we'll put some data into the controller for *hello* and *hello_controller.rb*, and then incorporate that data into the view.

If you open *app/controllers/hello_controller.rb*, you'll see the default code that Rails generated, like that in Example 2-3.

Example 2-3. A very basic controller that does nothing

```
class HelloController < ApplicationController
  def index
  end
end
```

This is the first real Ruby code we've encountered, so it's worth explaining a bit. The name of the class, `HelloController`, was created by the script generator based on the name we gave, Hello. Rails chose this name to indicate the name and type of the class, using its normal convention for controllers. Controllers are defined as Ruby classes, which inherit (`<`) most of their functionality from the `ApplicationController` class. (You don't need to know anything about `ApplicationControllers` or even classes—at least not yet—so if you don't understand at this point, just enjoy the generated code and keep reading.)

 If you need to learn more about Ruby to be comfortable proceeding, take a look at Appendix A.

def index is the start of the index method (also known as an action), which Rails will call by default when it's asked for a Hello. As you can see, it comes to a nearly immediate end, which is followed by the end for the class as a whole. If we want to make the index method do anything, we'll have to add some logic. For our current purposes, that logic can stay extremely simple. Defining a few variables, as shown in Example 2-4, will let us play with the basic interactions between controllers and views, and allow the view to do a few more interesting things. (Example 2-4 is part of the code in *ch02/hello02*.)

Example 2-4. A basic controller that sets some variables

```
class HelloController < ApplicationController
  def index
    @message="Hello!"
    @count=3
    @bonus="This message came from the controller."
  end
end
```

Variables whose names start with @ are called *instance variables*. They belong to the class that defines them and have the convenient property of being accessible from the associated view.

 When choosing variable names, always be very careful to avoid the enormous list of reserved words (*http://bit.ly/2aTsmcR*).

If you use those names, you may find not only that your programs don't run correctly, but also that the supporting development environment misbehaves in strange and annoying ways.

To actually use those variables, make some changes to the view as in Example 2-5.

Example 2-5. Modifying index.html.erb to use instance variables from the controller

```
<h1><%= @message %></h1>
<p>This is a greeting from app/views/hello/index.html.erb</p>
<p><%= @bonus %></p>
```

There are two new pieces here, highlighted in bold. Each contains the name of one of the instance variables from *hello_controller.rb*, surrounded by the <%= and %> tags. When Rails processes this document, it will replace the <%= … %> with the value inside. You can, of course, create those values from much more complex sources than just a simple variable, but it's easier to see what's happening here in a simple example.

The <% and %> tags are delimiters used by ERb, Embedded Ruby. ERb is part of Ruby and is used extensively in Rails. ERb isn't the only way to generate result views with Rails, but it's definitely the most common.

The result, shown in Figure 2-3, incorporates the variables from `HelloController` into the resulting document.

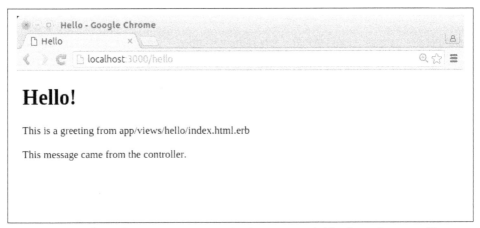

Figure 2-3. Resulting document incorporating instance variables from the controller

If you do a View Source and look at the contents of the HTML body element, shown in Example 2-6, the ERb markup has completely disappeared, replaced by the instance variable values.

Example 2-6. HTML that Rails generated based on Example 2-4 and Example 2-5

```
<h1>Hello!</h1>
<p>This is a greeting from app/views/hello/index.html.erb</p>
<p>This message came from the controller.</p>
```

How Hello World Works

The Hello World programs are actually doing a lot of work, as shown in Figure 2-4, though most of it happens transparently.

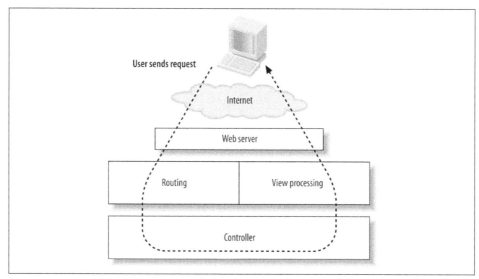

Figure 2-4. Simplified processing path for the Hello World programs

When the code runs, Rails interprets the request for *http://localhost:3000/hello/* as a call to the Hello controller. It has a list of routing rules, managed through the *config/routes.rb* file you can edit—this is just the default behavior. Controllers can have multiple methods, but the default method (just like when you request an HTML file) is index. Rails routing functionality then calls the index method, which sets up some basic variables.

When the controller is done, Rails passes its data to the view in the *app/views/hello* directory. How does it know to go there? Thanks to the magic of naming conventions, that view processing (possibly including layouts) generates an HTML result, which gets sent to the browser.

Rails applications have lots of moving parts, but you can usually look at the parts and guess (or control) what Rails is going to do with them. As you'll see in later chapters, the connections between controllers, models, and databases rely heavily on such naming conventions and default behaviors. The connections that Rails creates in this way won't solve all of your problems all of the time, but they do make it easy to solve a wide variety of problems most of the time. Figure 2-5 shows the pathways Rails built on naming conventions in the view and controller.

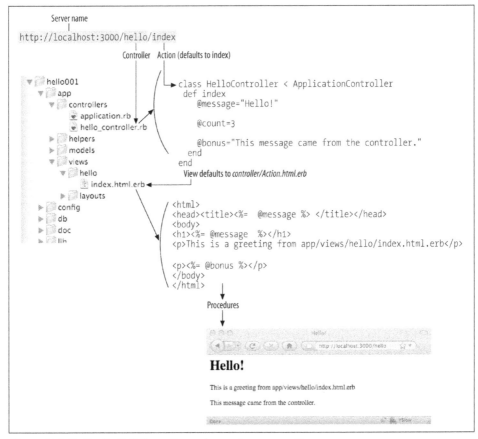

Figure 2-5. Paths Rails follows through naming conventions

 Prior to Rails 3 a security hole allowed content to come up from the controller to the view without checking to see if it included an HTML injection or cross-site scripting (XSS) attack. You had to use h or sanitize to clean up content. Rails 3 and later checks content automatically, simplifying your work and sparing you some typing. If you need to include HTML, you can use the raw method and html_safe property as described in Railscast #204 (*http://bit.ly/2aTs1Xu*) or in "Creating Helper Methods" on page 107 in Chapter 6.

Adding Logic to the View

You can also put more sophisticated logic into the views, thanks to the <% and %> tags. (The opening tag lacks the = sign.) These tags let you put Ruby code directly into your ERb files. We'll start with a very simple example, shown in Example 2-7, that takes advantage of the count variable in the controller. (This example is part of the *ch02/hello03* code sample.)

Example 2-7. Modifying index.html.erb to present the @bonus message as many times as @count specifies

```
<h1><%= @message %></h1>
<p>This is a greeting from app/views/hello/index.html.erb</p>

<% for i in 1..@count %>
  <p><%= @bonus %></p>
<% end %>
```

The count variable now controls the number of times the bonus message appears because of the for...end loop, which will simply count from 1 to the value of the count variable.

The for loop is familiar to developers from a wide variety of programming languages, but it's not especially idiomatic Ruby. Ruby developers would likely use a times construct instead, such as:

```
<% @count.times do %>
  <p><%= @bonus %></p>
<% end %>
```

Depending on your fondness for punctuation, you can also replace the do and end with curly braces, as in:

```
<% @count.times {  %>
  <p><%= @bonus %></p>
<% } %>
```

As always, you can choose the approach you find most comfortable, though brackets and for loops aren't considered the standard idiom.

The loop will run three times, counting up to the value the controller set for the count variable. As a result, "This message came from the controller." will appear three times, as shown in Figure 2-6.

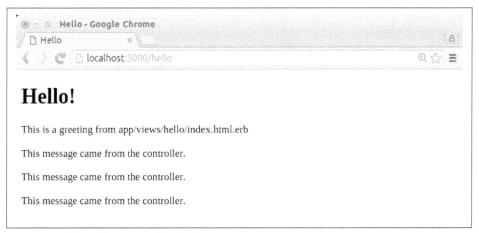

Figure 2-6. The Hello page after the loop executes

It's not the most exciting page, but it's the foundation for a lot more work to come.

 If you want to comment out ERb lines, you can just insert a # symbol after the <%. For example <%#= @message %> would do nothing, because of the #.

Test Your Knowledge

Quiz

1. What is the difference between <% and <%=?
2. How much logic should you put in your ERb files?
3. How does Rails know what controller goes with what view, if you don't tell it?
4. Which method can you use to insert HTML that comes to the view from the controller?

Answers

1. When you use <%=, Rails will insert the return value of the code you've used into the document. If you use <%, nothing will be added to the document.
2. In general, you should put as little logic into your ERb files as possible. You may need to put some logic there to make sure that users get the right presentation of

the information you're sharing or to build an interface for them to work with it. However, you should avoid putting much else there.

3. Once you've turned on the default routing rule, Rails maps controllers to views through naming conventions, unless your code specifies otherwise.

4. The `raw` method will let you include markup directly. This is dangerous, so use it sparingly!

## CHAPTER 3

Adding Web Style

*My mission in life is not merely to survive, but to thrive; and to do so with some passion,
some compassion, some humor, and some style.*
—Maya Angelou

The application presented in Chapter 2 is pretty appalling, visually. You're not likely
to want to present pages that look like that to your visitors, unless they're fond of the
early 1990s retro look. Rails provides a number of features that will help you make
your views present results that look the way you think they should look, and do so
consistently.

 This chapter will explore Rails features for supporting CSS and
HTML, but it can't be an HTML or CSS tutorial. If you need one of
those, try *Learning Web Design* (O'Reilly, 2012) by Jennifer Niederst
Robbins or David Sawyer McFarland's *CSS: The Missing Manual*
(O'Reilly, 2015).

I Want My CSS!

Figure 3-1, the result of the last chapter's coding, is not exactly attractive.

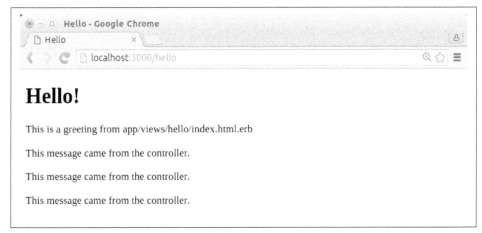

Figure 3-1. The Hello page after the loop executes

Even this fairly hopeless page, however, can be improved with the bit of CSS shown in Example 3-1. We could put this stylesheet right into the *index.html.erb* file as an internal `style` element, or add it to *app/assets/stylesheets/application.css*.

Example 3-1. A simple stylesheet for a simple page

```
body { font-family:sans-serif;
     }

h1 {font-family:serif;
    font-size: 24pt;
    font-weight: bold;
    color:#F00 ;
    }
```

Better CSS would of course be a good idea, but this will get things started. It might make sense to call Example 3-1 *hello.css*, but with asset management (discussed in Chapter 17), it makes more sense for now to put it into the *hello.scss* Rails created when you generated the controller. This is actually a Sass file, which will get a lot more attention in Chapter 16. For now, just add the CSS to the file, making it look like Example 3-2.

Example 3-2. Adding CSS to the SCSS file

```
// Place all the styles related to the Hello controller here.
// They will automatically be included in application.css.
// You can use Sass (SCSS) here: http://sass-lang.com/

body { font-family:sans-serif;
     }
```

```
h1 {font-family:serif;
    font-size: 24pt;
    font-weight: bold;
    color:#F00 ;
    }
```

The result, combining the HTML generated by the view with the newly linked style-sheet, is shown in Figure 3-2. It's not beautiful, but you now have control over styles.

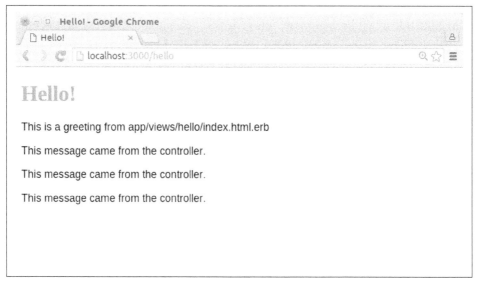

Figure 3-2. A very slightly prettier "Hello!" using CSS

So Rails will now pick up that CSS, but how does it know?

How did the stylesheet get linked from the head element? Chapter 2 mentioned that the surrounding HTML document structure came from a layout. Layouts are stored in *app/views/layouts*, and in this case, we'll be using the default *application.html.erb* file, which gets applied when there aren't any more specific layouts for a view. (You can find all of these files in *ch03/hello04*.) Its initial contents include an HTML5 DOC TYPE declaration, a basic HTML document structure, and some links to additional components, as shown in Example 3-3.

Example 3-3. The application.html.erb file created by Rails

```
<!DOCTYPE html>
    <html>
    <head>
      <title>Hello01</title>
        <%= stylesheet_link_tag application, media: all,
```

```
                        data-turbolinks-+track => true %>
    <%= javascript_include_tag application, data-turbolinks-track => true %>
      <%= csrf_meta_tags %>
  </head>
  <body>

  <%= yield %>

  </body>
  </html>
```

While the title might be a surprise, this code was generated in the very first iteration of Hello samples, so that's what's in use. You can certainly change it.

More important, however, are the stylesheet_link_tag, javascript_include_tag, csrf_meta_tag, and yield. The first is the key piece needed for setting styles, the next is for JavaScript, the next avoids cross-site request forgery (CSRF), and finally, the yield is where the content from your view will go, as the HTML generated with that layout (Example 3-4) shows.

Example 3-4. HTML generated by the application.html.erb file

```
<!DOCTYPE html>
    <html>
    <head>
      <title>Hello01</title>
      <link href="/assets/application.css?body=1" media="all" rel="stylesheet"
      type="text/css" />
    <link href="/assets/hello.css?body=1" media="all" rel="stylesheet"
    type="text/css" />
      <script src="/assets/jquery.js?body=1" type="text/javascript"></script>
      <script src="/assets/jquery_ujs.js?body=1" type="text/javascript"></script>
      <script src="/assets/hello.js?body=1" type="text/javascript"></script>
      <script src="/assets/application.js?body=1" type="text/javascript"></script>
        <meta content="authenticity_token" name="csrf-param" />
      <meta content="HENkZLxuUaswIRUh9tV7w1SZpuE24dZWVjSKf6TRuR8=" name="csrf-token" />
    </head>
    <body>

    <h1>Hello!</h1>
    <p>This is a greeting from app/views/hello/index.html.erb</p>
    <p>This message came from the controller.</p>
    <p>This message came from the controller.</p>
    <p>This message came from the controller.</p>


    </body>
    </html>
```

The application is using the default layout, so why not grab all the possibly relevant stylesheets? If you look more closely, though, it's including */assets/hello.css*, which doesn't exist. Manually visiting *http://localhost:3000/assets/hello.css* brings up Example 3-5.

Example 3-5. CSS generated from the hello.css.scss file

```
/* line 4, .../ch03/hello04/app/assets/stylesheets/hello.css.scss */
        body {
          font-family: sans-serif;
        }

/* line 6, .../ch03/hello04/app/assets/stylesheets/hello.css.scss */
        h1 {
          font-family: serif;
          font-size: 24pt;
          font-weight: bold;
          color: #F00;
        }
```

That's the CSS, all right, with some extra debugging information to indicate where it came from. Fortunately, these comments only appear when you run the application in development mode, and will disappear in production mode.

There's more, though. Because the default link is to `"application"`, not `"hello"`, there is also a link to */assets/application.css*. There is an *application.css* file, which looks like Example 3-6.

Example 3-6. Original contents of the application.css file

```
/*
 * This is a manifest file that'll be compiled into application.css, which
 * will include all the files listed below.
 *
 * Any CSS and SCSS file within this directory, lib/assets/stylesheets,
 * vendor/assets/stylesheets, or any plugin's vendor/assets/stylesheets directory
 * can be referenced here using a relative path.
 *
 * You're free to add application-wide styles to this file and they'll appear at the
 * bottom of the compiled file so the styles you add here take precedence over
 * styles defined in any other CSS/SCSS files in this directory. Styles in
 * this file should be added after the last require_* statement.
 * It is generally better to create a new file per style scope.
 *
 *= require_tree .
 *= require_self
 */
```

If you actually load *http://localhost:3000/assets/application.css*, however, you'll see that those require statements have compiled *hello.css* into the resulting file (see Example 3-7).

Example 3-7. CSS generated from the application.css file

```
body {
  font-family: sans-serif; }

h1 {
  font-family: serif;
  font-size: 24pt;
  font-weight: bold;
  color: #F00; }
/*
 * This is a manifest file that'll be compiled into application.css, which will
 * include all the files listed below.
 *
 * Any CSS and SCSS file within this directory, lib/assets/stylesheets,
 * vendor/assets/stylesheets, or any plugin's vendor/assets/stylesheets directory
 * can be referenced here using a relative path.
 *
 * You're free to add application-wide styles to this file and they'll appear at the
 * bottom of the compiled file so the styles you add here take precedence over
 * styles defined in any other CSS/SCSS
 * files in this directory. Styles in this file should be added after the last
 * require_* statement.
 * It is generally better to create a new file per style scope.
 *
 */
```

The API documentation doesn't explain why you should want two copies of the same CSS delivered to the browser, but perhaps it helps with debugging when CSS comes from multiple sources. In production mode, this compilation goes further, requiring you to precompile your assets before running the application, and references only one resulting stylesheet.

The layout file also creates a few links to JavaScript files (which this code doesn't currently use), something that looks like it must have come from the csrf_meta_tag, and the content generated by the view where the yield used to be.

A lot of sites use the same general structure—headers, stylesheets, and often navigation—across many or all pages. While you certainly could create a copy of the layout file for every controller your application uses, that would violate a core principle of Rails: Don't Repeat Yourself, or DRY. Much of the time, it'll make much more sense to create a layout that acts as the default for your entire application, and only create different layouts for the cases where you actually need them.

For simple applications and for getting started, this works wonderfully. There are, of course, more precise ways of specifying both layouts and stylesheets.

What's That Yield?

It kind of makes sense that a layout would yield control to a more specific template and then pick up again, but a `yield` has a more specific meaning in Ruby, one you'll doubtless see more often as you work with it.

Ruby programmers like to play with *blocks*. Blocks are nameless chunks of code, usually contained in curly braces ({}). Many Ruby methods can accept, in addition to the usual parameters, a block of code. When `yield` appears, that block of code gets executed. In this case, the block that gets called is the result of the controller and view template processing, and so the proper content gets inserted into the layout.

Specifying Stylesheets

You can make Rails include only the stylesheets you want with a little extra work on the `stylesheet_link_tag`. Instead of the `stylesheet_link_tag "application"` element in *application.html.erb* shown in Example 3-3, you can just write:

```
<%= stylesheet_link_tag 'hello' %>
```

When Rails processes the document, it will convert that into something like:

```
<link href="/assets/hello.css?body=1" media="screen"
rel="Stylesheet" type="text/css" />
```

This keeps Rails from including everything you might or might not want from *assets/ stylesheets*. If that isn't quite what you had in mind, you can pass `style sheet_link_tag` more detailed parameters:

```
<%= stylesheet_link_tag hello, media: "all", type: "text/css" %>
```

This will produce:

```
<link href="/assets/hello.css?body=1" media="all" rel="Stylesheet"
type="text/css" />
```

What happened there? What are all of those strange variables with colons after them followed by quoted text? They're *named parameters* for the `stylesheet_link_tag` method. The names with colons in front are called *symbols*, which is a bit confusing.

It's easiest to read the colon as meaning "the thing named" and the `=>` as "has the value of." This means that the thing named `media` has the value of `all`, the thing named `type` has the value of `text/css`, and so on. The `stylesheet_link_tag` method assembles all of these pieces to create the final `link` element.

Creating a Layout for a Controller

As you develop your application, different components will likely have different looks, and relying on a single layout for the entire application will make less and less sense. It's easy to create a layout that works with a specific view, separating the document structure and supporting resources from the presentation logic without falling back to a generic application-wide layout.

Creating a specific layout for your particular controller is simple—just create a layout with the name of your controller plus *.html.erb* in the *app/views/layouts* folder. If Rails finds a layout with the name of the controller (and hasn't been told to use another layout in code), it uses it. If it can't find one, it defaults to *application.html.erb*. (This approach is demonstrated in *ch03/hello05*.) The naming conventions Rails follows to decide on a layout are shown in Figure 3-3.

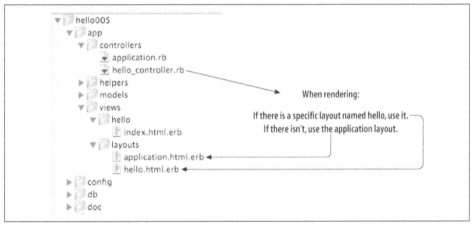

Figure 3-3. Deciding which layout to use, based on naming conventions

To demonstrate how this works, copy *application.html.erb* to *hello.html.erb* and modify it slightly to see the difference, as shown in Example 3-8. (This is included in *ch03/hello05*.)

Example 3-8. Slightly modified layout for hello.html.erb

```
<!DOCTYPE html>
<html>
<head>
  <title><%= @message %></title>
  <%= stylesheet_link_tag application, media: all, data-turbolinks-track => true %>
  <%= javascript_include_tag application, data-turbolinks-track => true %>
  <%= csrf_meta_tags %>
</head>
<body>
```

```
<p>(using hello layout)</p>
<%= yield %>

</body>
</html>
```

The (using hello layout) text just gives us a visible marker to see that content is coming from the *hello.html.erb* layout. (It'll go away immediately after this example.) When opened in the browser, the layout and view will combine to produce the HTML shown in Example 3-9, which displays as Figure 3-4.

Example 3-9. Combining a layout and a view produces a complete result

```
<!DOCTYPE html>
<html>
    <head>
        <title>Hello!</title>
        <link href="/assets/application.css?body=1" media="all" rel="stylesheet"
        type="text/css" />
      <link href="/assets/hello.css?body=1" media="all" rel="stylesheet"
        type="text/css" />
        <script src="/assets/jquery.js?body=1" type="text/javascript"></script>
        <script src="/assets/jquery_ujs.js?body=1" type="text/javascript"></script>
        <script src="/assets/hello.js?body=1" type="text/javascript"></script>
        <script src="/assets/application.js?body=1" type="text/javascript"></script>
        <meta content="authenticity_token" name="csrf-param" />
        <meta content="HENkZLxuUaswIRUh9tV7w1SZpuE24dZWVjSKf6TRuR8="
        name="csrf-token" />
    </head>
    <body>
        <p>(using hello layout)</p>
        <h1>Hello!</h1>
        <p>This is a greeting from app/views/hello/index.html.erb</p>
        <p>This message came from the controller.</p>
        <p>This message came from the controller.</p>
        <p>This message came from the controller.</p>


    </body>
</html>
```

There's another piece here worth noting, highlighted in Example 3-9. The title element contains the same content—coming from the @message variable—as the original view did. The layout has access to all of the same variables as the view. If you were creating a layout that was going to be used for many different controllers, you might want to choose a more specific variable name for that piece, say @page_title, and make certain that all of your controllers support it.

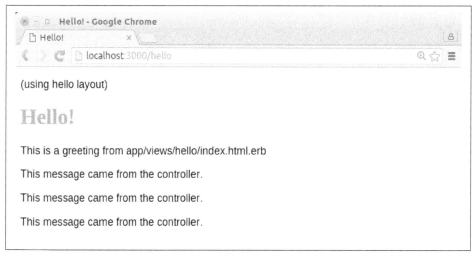

Figure 3-4. Applying a layout to a view

Choosing a Layout from a Controller

Left to its own devices, Rails assumes that each view has a layout file associated with it by the naming convention or uses the default for the application. There are many cases, though, where groups of related views share a common layout, but that layout isn't necessarily the application default. It's much easier to manage that common layout from a single file rather than having to change a layout for every controller every time the design changes.

The simplest way to make this work is to have controllers specify what layout they would like to use. If standardization is your main purpose, adding a layout declaration like that shown in Example 3-10 (included in *ch03/hello06*) will work.

Example 3-10. Specifying a layout choice in a controller

```
class HelloController < ApplicationController

  layout "standard_layout"

  def index
    @message="Hello!"
    @count=3
    @bonus="This message came from the controller."
  end
end
```

Instead of looking for *app/views/layouts/hello.html.erb* to be the layout, Rails will now look for *app/views/layouts/standard_layout.html.erb*.

The `layout` call needs to happen outside of a method definition, on its own, or you will get mysterious `undefined method 'layout'` errors. It's not that `layout` is undefined, exactly, but that it must be in the right place.

The `layout` call can also take `nil` (for no layout) or a symbol as a method reference. If there is a method reference, that method will determine which layout is used. Example 3-11 shows what this might look like.

Example 3-11. Choosing a layout based on program calculations

```
class HelloController < ApplicationController

  layout :admin_or_user

  def index
    ...
  end

  private

  def admin_or_user
    if admin_authenticated
      "admin_screen"
    else
      "user_screen"
    end
  end
end
```

In this case, `layout` took a reference to the `admin_or_user` method, which returned either the `admin_screen` layout or the `user_screen` layout as its choice depending on the value of the `admin_authenticated` variable (whose value is calculated somewhere else).

One other feature of `layout` is worth noting, though we're not ready to use it yet. If your application can return, say, XML or RSS instead of HTML, you may want to be able to turn off your HTML layout in cases where it won't be wanted. You might say:

```
layout "standard_layout", except: :rss
layout "standard_layout", except: [:rss, :xml, :text_only]
```

The first one uses the layout except when RSS has been requested, while the second uses the layout except for requests for RSS, XML, and text formats. You could also work the opposite way, saying to use the layout only for HTML:

```
layout "standard_layout", only: :html
```

You can also select a layout (or no layout) using the `render` function. (You may want to do this if your controller includes multiple actions that need their own layouts.)

Sharing Template Data with the Layout

Layouts and view templates share the same information from the controller, but there may be times when a view template should include information that needs to be embedded in the layout. This might be navigation particular to different areas of a site, personalization, or some kind of status bar, for instance, that shows the user how far they've gone through a particular task.

Example 3-12 shows a modified template (included in *ch03/hello07*) that creates a numbered list HTML fragment that the layout in Example 3-13 will include separately—actually, *before* it includes the main template output. The structure created by the `<% content_for(:list) do %>` code in Example 3-12 is called upon by the `<%= yield :list %>` tag in Example 3-13.

Example 3-12. index.html.erb with newly added HTML structure for separate inclusion

```
<h1><%= @message %></h1>
<p>This is a greeting from app/views/hello/index.html.erb</p>

<% for i in 1..@count %>
  <p><%= @bonus %></p>
<% end %>

<% content_for(:list) do %>
  <ol>
  <% for i in 1..@count %>
    <li><%= @bonus %></li>
  <% end %>
  </ol>
<% end %>
```

Example 3-13. Layout template with added yield, exposing the list from Example 3-12

```
<!DOCTYPE html>
    <html>
    <head>
      <title><%=@message%></title>
      <%= stylesheet_link_tag "application" %>
      <%= javascript_include_tag "application" %>
      <%= csrf_meta_tag %>
    </head>
    <body>
```

```
<%= yield :list %>
<!--layout will incorporate view-->
<%= yield %>

</body>
</html>
```

The result, shown in Figure 3-5, isn't exactly beautiful, but it demonstrates that a template can create content that a layout can include anywhere it likes.

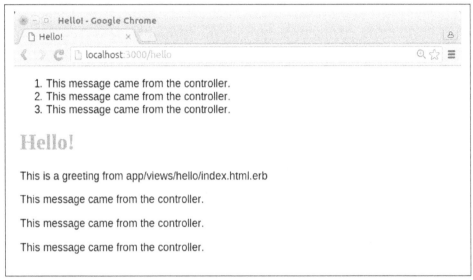

Figure 3-5. Layout including content created as a separate piece by a template

Always remember that this works because the template has executed before the layout adds its own ideas. You can communicate from the template to the layout but not from the layout to the template.

Setting a Default Page

Before we move on to more "serious" concerns about developing applications, there's one question that web developers always seem to ask about 15 minutes into their first Rails experience: how do I set a default page for the application?

To do this, you'll need to enter an extra line in the *config/routes.rb* file. Add the following line at the bottom:

```
root to: "hello#index"
```

Save the file and restart your server. You should see something like Figure 3-6.

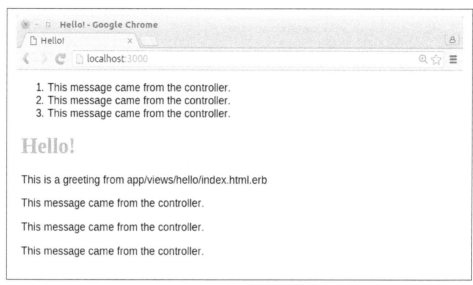

Figure 3-6. Accessing a controller by default, when the URL doesn't specify one

Don't worry if this edit seems mysterious. You'll learn more about how routing works starting in Chapter 4, with a lot more detail to come in Chapter 15.

Test Your Knowledge

Quiz

1. Where would you put your CSS stylesheet, and how should you connect it to your view?

2. How does Rails know which layout to apply to a particular view?

3. What does that `yield` thing do?

4. How do I send data from the view template to the layout?

Answers

1. Stylesheets go in the *assets/stylesheets* directory, and you (or Rails) connect them to your views (or layouts) by putting a call to `stylesheet_link_tag` in the head element.

2. By default, Rails will apply the layout in *app/views/layout/application.html.erb* to all of your views. However, if there is a layout file in *app/views/layout/* that has the same name as a view, Rails will use that instead.

3. The `yield` method hands control to a different block of code, one that was passed with parameters. Rails often handles this quietly, making it easy to share data between, for example, layouts and views.

4. The layout has access to all of the same variables the view uses. You don't need to do anything special to pass variables to the layout, even if you want the layout to apply them early in your HTML document.

## CHAPTER 4

Managing Data Flow: Controllers and Models

*Remove all the traffic lights, yellow lines, one-way systems, and road markings,
and let blissful anarchy prevail. I imagine it would produce a kind of harmony.*
—Sadie Jones

Sadie Jones's advice notwithstanding, Rails does not share her affection for blissful anarchy. It's time to meet the key player in Rails applications. Controllers are the components that determine how to respond to user requests and coordinate responses. They're at the heart of what many people think of as "the program" in your Rails applications, though in many ways they're more of a switchboard. They connect the different pieces that do the heavy lifting, providing a focal point for application development. The model is the foundation of your application's data structures, which will let you get information into and out of your databases.

 Controllers are important, certainly a "key player," but don't get too caught up in them. When you're coming from other development environments, it's easy to think that controllers are the main place you should put application logic. As you get deeper into Rails, you'll likely learn the hard way that a lot of code you thought belonged in the controller really belonged in the model, or sometimes in the view.

Getting Started, Greeting Guests

Controllers are Ruby objects. They're stored in the *app/controllers* directory of your application. Each controller has a name, and the object inside of the controller file is called *name*Controller.

Demonstrating controllers without getting tangled in all of the other Rails components is difficult, so for an initial tour, the application will be incredibly simple. (You can see the first version of it in *ch04/guestbook01*.) Guestbooks were a common (if kind of annoying) feature on early websites, letting visitors "post messages" so that the site's owner could tell who'd been there. (The idea has since evolved into more sophisticated messaging, like Facebook's Timeline.)

 If you've left any Rails applications from earlier chapters running under `rails server`, it would be wise to turn them off before starting a new application. Remember, you can stop the server using Ctrl-C.

To get started, create a new Rails application, as we did in Chapter 1. If you're working from the command line, type:

```
rails new guestbook
```

Rails will create the usual pile of files and folders. Next, you'll want to change to the *guestbook* directory and create a controller:

```
cd guestbook
rails generate controller entries
    create  app/controllers/entries_controller.rb
    invoke  erb
    create   app/views/entries
    invoke  test_unit
    create   test/controllers/entries_controller_test.rb
    invoke  helper
    create   app/helpers/entries_helper.rb
    invoke    test_unit
    invoke  assets
    invoke    coffee
    create     app/assets/javascripts/entries.coffee
    invoke    scss
    create     app/assets/stylesheets/entries.scss
```

If you then look at *app/controllers/entries_controller.rb*, which is the main file we'll work with here, you'll find:

```
class EntriesController < ApplicationController
end
```

This doesn't do very much. However, there's an important relationship in that first line. Your `EntriesController` inherits from `ApplicationController`. The `ApplicationController` object lives in *app/controllers/application_controller.rb*, and it also doesn't do very much initially, but if you ever need to add functionality that is shared by all of the controllers in your application, you can put it into the `ApplicationController` object.

To make this controller actually do something, we'll add a method. For right now, we'll call it `sign_in`, creating the very simple object in Example 4-1.

Example 4-1. Adding an initial method to an empty controller

```
class EntriesController < ApplicationController
  def sign_in
  end
end
```

We'll also need a view, so that Rails has something it can present to visitors. You can create a *sign_in.html.erb* file in the *app/views/entries/* directory, and then edit it, as shown in Example 4-2.

You can also have Rails create a method in the controller, as well as a basic view at the same time that it created the controller, by typing:

```
rails generate controller entries sign_in
```

You can work either way, letting Rails generate as much (or as little) code as you like.

Example 4-2. A view that lets users see a message and enter their name

```
<h1>Hello <%= @name %></h1>
<%= form_tag action: 'sign_in' do %>
   <p>Enter your name:
   <%= text_field_tag 'visitor_name', @name %></p>

   <%= submit_tag 'Sign in' %>

<% end %>
```

Example 4-2 has a lot of new pieces to it because it's using *helper methods* to create a basic form. Helper methods take arguments and return text, which in this case is HTML that helps build your form. The following particular helpers are built into Rails, but you can also create your own:

- The `form_tag` method takes the name of our controller method, `sign_in`, as its `:action` parameter.
- The `text_field_tag` method takes two parameters and uses them to create a form field on the page. The first, `visitor_name`, is the identifier that the form will use to describe the field data it sends back to the controller, while the second is default text that the field will contain. If the user has filled out this form previously, and our controller populates the `@name` variable, it will list the user's name. Otherwise, it will be blank.

- The last helper method, `submit_tag`, provides the button that will send the data from the form back to the controller when the user clicks it.

Once again, you'll need to enable routing for your controller. You'll need to edit the *config/routes.rb* file. Add the following lines at the top of the file inside the do block:

```
get 'entries/sign_in' => 'entries#sign_in'
post 'entries/sign_in' => 'entries#sign_in'
```

If you start up the server and visit *http://localhost:3000/entries/sign_in*, you'll see a simple form like Figure 4-1.

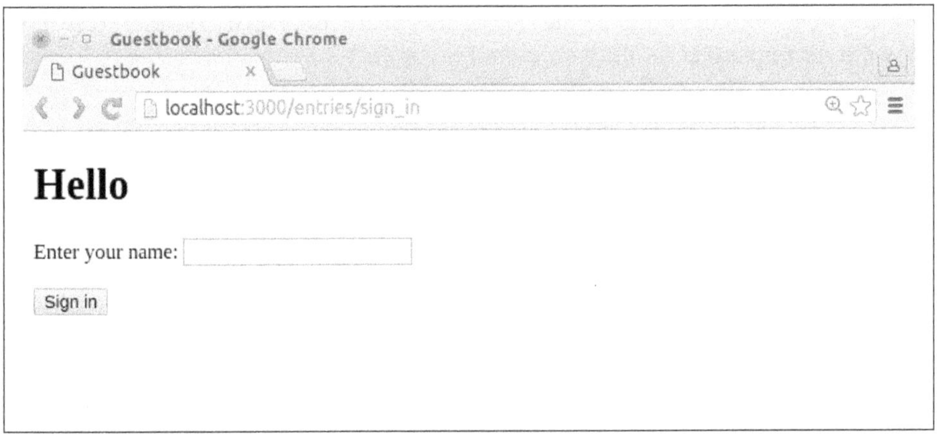

Figure 4-1. A simple form generated by a Rails view

Now that we have a way to send data to our controller, it's time to update the controller so that it does something with that information. In this very simple case, it just means adding a line, as shown in Example 4-3.

Example 4-3. Making the sign_in method do something

```
class EntriesController < ApplicationController
  def sign_in
    @name = params[:visitor_name]
  end
end
```

The extra line gets the `visitor_name` parameter from the request header sent back by the client and puts it into `@name`. (If there wasn't a `visitor_name` parameter, as would be normal the first time this page is loaded, `@name` will just be blank.)

If you enter a name into the form, you'll now get a pretty basic hello message in return, as shown in Figure 4-2. The name will also be sitting in the form field for another round of greetings.

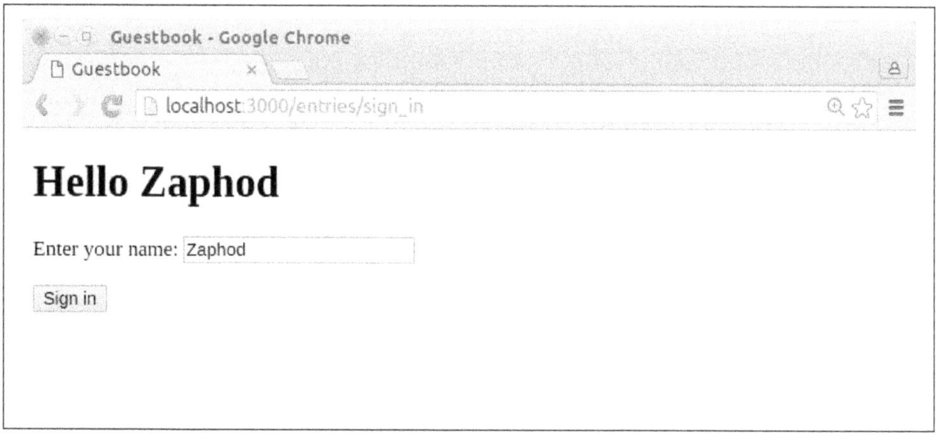

Guestbook - Google Chrome

Guestbook ×

localhost:3000/entries/sign_in

Hello Zaphod

Enter your name: Zaphod

Sign in

Figure 4-2. A greeting that includes the name that was entered

> If, instead of Figure 4-2, you get a strange error message about "wrong number of arguments (1 for 0)," check your code carefully. You've probably added a space between `params` and `[`, which produces a syntax error whose description isn't exactly clear.

The controller is now receiving information from the user and passing it to a view, which can then pass more information.

There is one other minor point worth examining before we move on, though: how did Rails convert the *http://localhost:3000/entries/sign_in* URL into a call to the `sign_in` method of the `entries` controller? If you look in the *config* directory of your application, you'll find the *routes.rb* file, which contains the rules we enabled for choosing what gets called when a request comes in:

```
get 'entries/sign_in' => 'entries#sign_in'
post 'entries/sign_in' => 'entries#sign_in'
```

In this case, the URL *entries/sign_in* maps the controller to an action separated by a #; in this example *entries* is the controller and *sign_in* is the action (see Figure 4-3). Also, notice we have two separate entries, one for `get` and another for `post`. We will talk more about these in Chapter 5, but our `get` route allows us to make a request for data, and our `post` route allows us to send data to that same route.

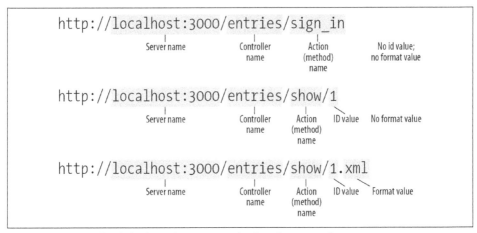

Figure 4-3. How the default Rails routing rules break a URL down into component parts to decide which method to run

You can also see your routes by typing **rails routes** from the command line. This gives you a slightly more compact version and shows how Rails interpreted the *routes.rb* file.

Application Flow

The Rails approach to handling requests, shown in Figure 4-4, has a lot of moving parts between users and data.

Rails handles URL processing instead of letting the web server pick which file to execute in response to the request. This allows Rails to use its own conventions, called *routing*, for deciding how a request gets handled, and it allows developers to create their own routing conventions to meet their applications' needs.

The router sends the request information to a controller. The controller, centralizing the logic for responding to different kinds of requests, decides how to handle the request. The controller may interact with a data model (or several), and those models will interact with the database if necessary. The person writing the controller never has to touch SQL, though, and even the person writing the model should be able to stay away from it.

Once the controller has gathered and processed the information it needs, it sends that data to a view for rendering. The controller can pick and choose among different views if it needs to, making it easy to throw an XML rendering on a controller that was originally expecting to be part of an HTML-generating process. You could offer several different kinds of HTML—basic, Ajax, or meant for mobile—from your applications if necessary. Rails can even, at the developer's discretion, generate basic views automatically, a feature called *scaffolding*. Scaffolding makes it extremely easy to get started on the data management side of an application without getting too hung up on its presentation.

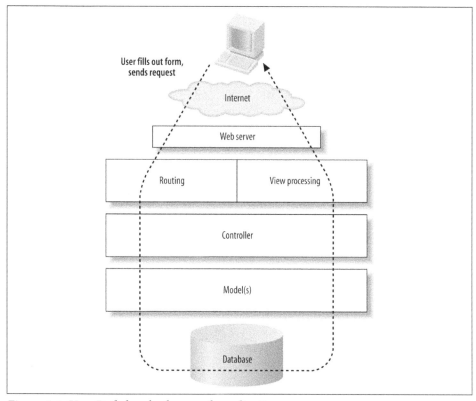

Figure 4-4. How Rails breaks down web applications

The final result comes from the view, and Rails sends it along to the user. The user, of course, doesn't need to know how all of this came to pass—she just gets the final view of the information, which hopefully is what she wanted.

Now that you've seen how this works in the big picture, it's time to return to the details of making it happen.

Keeping Track: A Simple Guestbook

Most applications will need to do more with data—typically, at least, they'll store the data and present it back as appropriate. It's time to extend this simple application so that it keeps track of users who have stopped by, as well as greeting them. This requires using models. (The complete application is available in *ch04/guestbook02*.)

As Chapter 5 will make clear, in most application development, you will likely want to create your models by letting Rails create a scaffold, since Rails won't let you create a scaffold after a model with the same name already exists. Nonetheless, understanding the more manual approach will make it much easier to work on your applications in the long run.

Connecting to a Database Through a Model

Keeping track of visitors will mean setting up and using a database. This should be easy when you're in development mode, as Rails now defaults to SQLite, which doesn't require explicit configuration. (When you deploy, you'll still want to set up a database, typically MySQL or Postgres, as discussed in Chapter 20.) To test whether SQLite is installed on your system, try issuing the command **sqlite3 -help** from the command line. If it's there, you'll get a help message. If not, you'll get an error, and you'll need to install SQLite.

Once the database engine is functioning, it's time to create a model. Once again, it's easiest to use `generate` to lay a foundation, and then add details to that foundation. This time, we'll create a simple model instead of a controller and call the model entry:

```
$rails generate model entry
    invoke  active_record
    create    db/migrate/20110221152951_create_entries.rb
    create    app/models/entry.rb
    invoke    test_unit
    create      test/models/entry_test.rb
    create      test/fixtures/entries.yml
```

For our immediate purposes, two of these files are critical. The first is *app/models/ entry.rb*, which is where all of the Ruby logic for handling a person will go. The second, which defines the database structures and thus needs to be modified first, is in the *db/migrate/* directory. It will have a name like *[timestamp]_create_entries.rb*, where [timestamp] is the date and time when it was created. It initially contains what's shown in Example 4-4.

Example 4-4. The default migration for the entry model

```
1  class CreateEntries < ActiveRecord::Migration
2    def change
3      create_table :entries do |t|
4
5        t.timestamps
6      end
7    end
8  end
```

There's a lot to examine here before we start making changes. First, note on line 1 that the class is called `CreateEntries`. The model may be for an entry, but the migration will create a table for more than one entry. Rails names tables (and migrations) using the plural form can handle most common English irregular pluralizations. (In cases where the singular and plural would be the same, you end up with an *s* added for the plural, so deer become deers and sheep become sheeps.) Many people find this natural, but other people hate it. For now, just go with it—fighting Rails won't make life any easier.

Also on line 1, you can see that this class inherits most of its functionality from the `Migration` class of ActiveRecord. ActiveRecord is the Rails library that handles all the database interactions. (You can even use it separately from Rails, if you want to.)

The action begins on line 2 with the `change` method. Rails used to have separate `self.up` and `self.down` methods, one to build tables and one to take them down, but Rails 3.1 got smarter. It's smart enough to understand how to run `change` backward to roll back the migration—effectively it provides you with "undo" functionality automatically.

This example takes the slow route through creating a model so you can see what happens. In the future, if you'd prefer to move more quickly, you can also add the names and types of data on the command line, as you will do when generating scaffolding in Chapter 5.

The `change` method operated on a table called `entries`. Note that the migration is not concerned with what kind of database it works on. That's all handled by the configuration information. You'll also see that migrations, despite working pretty close to the database, don't need to use SQL—though if you really want to use SQL, it's available.

Storing the names people enter into this very simple application requires adding a single column:

```
create_table :entries do |t|
  t.string :name
  t.timestamps
end
```

The new line refers to the table (`t`) and creates a column of type `string`, which will be accessible as `:name`.

In older versions of Rails, that new line would have been written:

```
t.column :name, string
```

The old version still works, and you'll definitely see migrations written this way in older applications and documents. The new form is a lot easier to read at a glance, though.

The t.timestamps line is there for housekeeping, tracking "created at" and "updated at" information. Rails also will automatically create a primary key, :id, for the table. Once you've entered the new line (at line 4 of Example 4-4), you can run the migration with:

```
$ rails db:migrate
(in /Users/simonstl/rails/guestbook) //you will have a different path here
==  CreateEntries: migrating ========================================
-- create_table(:entries)
   -> 0.0021s
==  CreateEntries: migrated (0.0022s) ===============================
```

 Previous to Rails 5, commands like db:migrate were Rake tasks, so you would run rake db:migrate to migrate the database. When to use rails and when to use rake was a source of confusion for many Rails newcomers, so now all commands can be run with the rails command.

In this case, the db:migrate task runs all of the previously unapplied change (or self.up) migrations in your application's *db/migrate/* folder. db:rollback gives you an undo option for the previous command by running the change methods backward (or the self.down methods if present).

Now that the application has a table with a column for holding names, it's time to turn to the *app/models/entry.rb* file. Its initial contents are very simple:

```
class Entry < ApplicationRecord
end
```

The Entry class inherits from ApplicationRecord, which in turn inherits from the ActiveRecord library's Base class, but has no functionality of its own. Previous to Rails 5 all models inherited directly from ActiveRecord, but now models inherit from ApplicationRecord, which is located in *app/models/application_record.rb*.

```
class ApplicationRecord < ActiveRecord::Base
  self.abstract_class = true
end
```

You can see this class simply inherits from ActiveRecord::Base, and also is set as an abstract class, which, if you are familiar with object-oriented programming, means the class can only be inherited from and not instantiated. This allows for a single point of entry for your models.

Remember that the names in your models also need to stay away from the list of reserved words presented at Ruby Magic (*http:// bit.ly/2aTsMjj*) or Reserved Words in Ruby on Rails (*http://bit.ly/ 2aTt4Xz*). Don't worry, Rails won't let you shoot yourself in the foot. If you attempt to name a model using a reserved word, Rails will give you a friendly warning.

Connecting the Controller to the Model

As you may have guessed, the controller is going to be the key component transferring data that comes in from the form to the model, and then it will be the key component transferring that data back out to the view for presentation to the user.

Storing data using the model

To get started, the controller will just blindly save new names to the model, using the code highlighted in Example 4-5.

Example 4-5. Using ActiveRecord to save a name

```
class EntriesController < ApplicationController
  def sign_in
    @name = params[:visitor_name]
    @entry = Entry.create({:name => @name})
  end
end
```

The preceding highlighted line combines three separate operations into a single line of code, which might look like:

```
@entry = Entry.new
@entry.name = @name
@entry.save
```

The first step creates a new variable, `@entry`, and declares it to be a new `Entry` object. The next line sets the `name` property of `@entry`—effectively setting the future value of the column named "name" in the entries table—to the `@name` value that came in through the form. The third line saves the `@entry` object to the table. There is nothing special about the `@entry` variable name. There is no special connection to that variable and `Entry.create`. We could have said `@foo = Entry.create`, and as long as we were consistant with our variable name, it would be OK.

In web development, saving values directly to the database like this is not considered a security risk or a poor practice. Chapter 5 will cover strong parameters and whitelisting of database values. Production applications should use the practices set forth in Chapter 5, but for the purposes of seeing how models and controllers interact, what we are doing here will suffice.

The `Entry.create` approach assumes you're making a new object, takes the values to be stored as named parameters, and then saves the object to the database.

 Both the `create` and the `save` methods return a boolean value indicating whether or not saving the value to the database was successful. For most applications, you'll want to test this and return an error if there was a failure.

These are the basic methods you'll need to put information into your databases with ActiveRecord. (There are many shortcuts and more elegant syntax, as Chapter 5 will demonstrate.) This approach is also a bit too simple. If you visit *http://localhost:3000/entries/sign_in/*, you'll see the same empty form that was shown in Figure 4-1. However, because `@entry.create` was called, an empty name will have been written to the table. The log data that appears in the server's terminal window shows:

```
(0.1ms)  begin transaction
  SQL (87.3ms)  INSERT INTO "entries" ("created_at", "name", "updated_at")
  VALUES (?, ?, ?) [["created_at", Mon, 20 Feb 2012 16:18:14 UTC +00:00],
  ["name", nil],["updated_at", Mon, 20 Feb 2012 16:18:14 UTC +00:00]]
```

The `nil` is the problem here because it really doesn't make sense to add a blank name every time someone loads the form without sending a value. On the bright side, we have evidence that Rails is putting information into the entries table, and if we enter a name, say "Preston," we can see the name being entered into the table:

```
(0.1ms)  begin transaction
  SQL (0.6ms)  INSERT INTO "entries" ("created_at", "name", "updated_at")
  VALUES (?, ?, ?)  [["created_at", Mon, 20 Feb 2012 16:18:48 UTC +00:00],
  ["name", "Preston"], ["updated_at", Mon, 20 Feb 2012 16:18:48 UTC +00:00]]
```

It's easy to fix the controller so that NULLs aren't stored—though as we'll see in Chapter 7, this kind of validation code really belongs in the model. Two lines, highlighted in Example 4-6, will keep Rails from entering a lot of blank names.

Example 4-6. Keeping blanks from turning into permanent objects

```
class EntriesController < ApplicationController
  def sign_in
    @name = params[:visitor_name]
    unless @name.blank?
```

```
      @entry = Entry.create({:name => @name})
    end
  end
end
```

Now Rails will check the `@name` variable to make sure that it has a value before putting it into the database. `unless @name.blank?` will test for both nil values and blank entries. (`blank?` is a Rails method extending Ruby's `String` objects.)

If you want to get rid of the NULLs you put into the database, you can run `rails db:rollback` and `rails db:migrate` (or `rails db:migrate:redo` to combine them) to drop and rebuild the table with a clean copy. In this case, you should stop the server before running `rails` and restart it when you're done.

```
== CreateEntries: reverting ====================================================
  -- drop_table(:entries)
     -> 0.0012s
== CreateEntries: reverted (0.0013s) ===========================================

== CreateEntries: migrating ====================================================
  -- create_table(:entries)
     -> 0.0015s
== CreateEntries: migrated (0.0016s) ===========================================
```

If you want to enter a few names to put some data into the new table, go ahead. The next example will show how to get them out.

Retrieving data from the model and showing it

Storing data is a good thing, but only if you can get it out again. Fortunately, it's not difficult for the controller to tell the model that it wants all the data or for the view to render it. For a guestbook, it's especially simple, as we just want all of the data every time.

Getting the data out of the model requires one line of additional code in the controller, highlighted in Example 4-7.

Example 4-7. A controller that also retrieves data from a model

```
class EntriesController < ApplicationController
  def sign_in
    @name = params[:visitor_name]
    if !@name.blank? then
      @entry = Entry.create({:name => @name})
    end

    @entries = Entry.all
  end
end
```

The `Entry` object includes a `find` method (`Entry.all`); like `new` and `save`, it is inherited from its parent `ActiveRecord::Base` class without any additional programming.

Next, the view, still in *views/entries/sign_in.html.erb*, can show the contents of that array to the site's visitors so they can see who's come by before, using the added lines shown in Example 4-8.

Example 4-8. Displaying existing users with a loop

```
<h1>Hello <%= @name %></h1>

<%= form_tag action: 'sign_in' do %>
    <p>Enter your name:
    <%= text_field_tag 'visitor_name', @name %></p>

    <%= submit_tag 'Sign in' %>
<% end %>
<p>Previous visitors:</p>
<ul>
<% @entries.each do |entry| %>
  <li><%= entry.name %></li>
<% end %>

</ul>
```

The loop here iterates over the `@entries` array, running as many times as there are entries in `@entries`. `@entries`, of course, holds the list of names previously entered, pulled from the database by the model that was called by the controller in Example 4-7. For each entry, the view adds a list item containing the `name` value, referenced here as `entry.name`. The result, depending on exactly what names you entered, will look something like Figure 4-5.

It's a lot of steps, yes, but fortunately you'll be able to skip a lot of them as you move deeper into Rails. Building this guestbook didn't look very much like the "complex-application-in-five-minutes" demonstrations that Rails promoters like to show off, but now you should understand what's going on underneath the magic. After the apprenticeship, the next chapter will get into some journeyman fun. Also, after refreshing the page, look in the logs, and you'll see that Rails is actually making a SQL call to populate the `@entry` array:

```
Entry Load (0.4ms)  SELECT "entries".* FROM "entries"
```

This is from the `@entries = Entry.all` line we added to our controller earlier.

Figure 4-5. The guestbook application, now displaying the names of past visitors

---

Looking Under the Hood

Every now and then, you may find something missing or need to see what exactly is coming into your view. Rails includes a number of useful pieces that, while you should never use them in production code, can help you see the data Rails is providing to your view.

To see everything Rails is sending, add this to your view:

```
<%= debug(assigns) %>
```

The results are both overwhelming and kind of repetitive, but you can hunt through there for useful pieces. For just the parameters that came in from a request, use:

```
<%= debug(params) %>
```

Other arguments to debug that might be useful in certain situations are base_path, controller, flash, request, response, and session.

Finding Data with ActiveRecord

The find method and its relatives are common in Rails, usually in controllers. It's constantly used as find(id) to retrieve a single record with a given id, while the similar all method retrieves an entire set of records. There are four basic ways to call find, and then a set of options that can apply to all of those uses. You can also give all of these commands a try in the Rails console before you use them in your code. You can enter the Rails console by typing **rails c** in your terminal window. We will talk more about the console in Chapter 11, but give it a try with the following finder methods and sample output.

id

The find method is frequently called with a single id, as in find(*id*), but it can also be called with an array of ids, like find (*id1, id2, id3, …*) in which case find will return an array of values. Finally, you can call find ([*id1, id2*]) and retrieve everything with id values between *id1* and *id2*.

```
2.2.2 :003 > Entry.find 1
  Entry Load (0.2ms)  SELECT  "entries".* FROM "entries"
  WHERE "entries"."id" = ? LIMIT 1  [["id", 1]]
=> #<Entry id: 1, name: "Henry",
created_at: "2015-10-03 21:48:02",
updated_at: "2015-10-03 21:48:02">
```

all

Calling the all method—Entry.all, for example—will return all the matching values as an array.

```
2.2.2 :001 > Entry.all
  Entry Load (0.7ms)  SELECT  "entries".* FROM "entries"
=> #<ActiveRecord::Relation [#<Entry id: 1,
name: "Henry", created_at: "2015-10-03 22:07:31",
updated_at: "2015-10-03 22:07:31">, #<Entry id: 2,
name: "Rhoda", created_at: "2015-10-03 22:07:43",
updated_at: "2015-10-03 22:07:43">,
#<Entry id: 3, name: "Allen",
created_at: "2015-10-03 22:07:47",
updated_at: "2015-10-03 22:07:47">, #<Entry id: 4,
name: "Mary", created_at: "2015-10-03 22:07:51",
updated_at: "2015-10-03 22:07:51">, #<Entry id: 5,
name: "Pollie", created_at: "2015-10-03 22:07:55",
updated_at: "2015-10-03 22:07:55">]>
```

first

Calling first—Entry.first, for example—will return the first matching value only. If you want this to raise an error if no matching record is found, add an exclamation point, as first!.

```
2.2.2 :002 > Entry.first
  Entry Load (0.2ms)  SELECT  "entries".* FROM "entries"
  ORDER BY "entries"."id" ASC LIMIT 1
=> #<Entry id: 1, name: "Henry",
created_at: "2015-10-03 22:07:31",
updated_at: "2015-10-03 22:07:31">
```

last

Calling last—Entry.last, for example—will return the last matching value only. Just as with first, if you want this to raise an error if no matching record is found, add an exclamation point, as last!.

```
2.2.2 :003 > Entry.last
  Entry Load (0.2ms)  SELECT  "entries".* FROM "entries"
  ORDER BY "entries"."id" DESC LIMIT 1
 => #<Entry id: 5, name: "Pollie",
 created_at: "2015-10-03 22:07:55",
 updated_at: "2015-10-03 22:07:55">
```

The options, which have evolved into chainable methods, give you much more control over what is queried and which values are returned. All of them actually modify the SQL statements used to query the database and can accept SQL syntax, but you don't need to know SQL to use most of them. This list of options is sorted by your likely order of needing them:

where

The where method lets you limit which records are returned. If, for example, you set:

```
2.2.2 :004 > Entry.where(name: "Pollie")
  Entry Load (0.2ms)  SELECT "entries".* FROM "entries"
  WHERE "entries"."name" = ?  [["name", "Pollie"]]
 => #<ActiveRecord::Relation [#<Entry id: 5,
 name: "Pollie", created_at: "2015-10-03 22:07:55",
 updated_at: "2015-10-03 22:07:55">]>
```

then you would only see records where the name has a value of Pollie.

order

The order method lets you choose the order in which records are returned, though if you're using first or last it will also determine which record you'll see as first or last. The simplest way to use this is with a field name or comma-separated list of field names:

```
2.2.2 :005 > Entry.order(:name)
  Entry Load (0.3ms)  SELECT "entries".* FROM "entries"
  ORDER BY "entries"."name" ASC
 => #<ActiveRecord::Relation [#<Entry id: 3,
 name: "Allen", created_at: "2015-10-03 22:07:47",
 updated_at: "2015-10-03 22:07:47">, #<Entry id: 1,
 name: "Henry", created_at: "2015-10-03 22:07:31",
 updated_at: "2015-10-03 22:07:31">, #<Entry id: 4,
 name: "Mary", created_at: "2015-10-03 22:07:51",
 updated_at: "2015-10 03 22:07:51">, #<Entry id: 5,
 name: "Pollie", created_at: "2015-10-03 22:07:55",
 updated_at: "2015-10-03 22:07:55">, #<Entry id: 2,
```

```
name: "Rhoda", created_at: "2015-10-03 22:07:43",
updated_at: "2015-10-03 22:07:43">]>
```

By default, the order will sort in ascending order, so the option just shown would sort by :name values in ascending order. We might also pass in a second sort field value:

```
2.2.2 :005 > Entry.order(:name, :city)
```

Using :city as a second sort field would first sort by :name, then by :city. If you want to sort a field in descending order, just put desc after the field name:

```
2.2.2 :014 > Entry.order(name: "desc")
```

This will return the names sorted in descending order.

limit

The limit option lets you specify how many records are returned. If you wrote:

```
2.2.2 :016 > Entry.limit 3
  Entry Load (0.2ms)  SELECT  "entries".*
  FROM "entries" LIMIT 3
 => #<ActiveRecord::Relation [#<Entry id: 1,
 name: "Henry", created_at: "2015-10-03 22:07:31",
 updated_at: "2015-10-03 22:07:31">,
 #<Entry id: 2, name: "Rhoda",
 created_at: "2015-10-03 22:07:43",
 updated_at: "2015-10-03 22:07:43">,
 #<Entry id: 3, name: "Allen",
 created_at: "2015-10-03 22:07:47",
 updated_at: "2015-10-03 22:07:47">]>
```

you receive only the first three records back. (You'll probably want to specify order to ensure that they're the ones you want.)

offset

The offset option lets you specify a starting point from which records should be returned. If, for instance, you wanted to retrieve the next three records after a set you'd retrieved with limit, you could specify:

```
2.2.2 :017 > Entry.limit(3).offset(2)
  Entry Load (0.2ms)  SELECT  "entries".*
  FROM "entries" LIMIT 3 OFFSET 2
 => #<ActiveRecord::Relation [#<Entry id: 3,
 name: "Allen", created_at: "2015-10-03 22:07:47",
 updated_at: "2015-10-03 22:07:47">,
 #<Entry id: 4, name: "Mary",
 created_at: "2015-10-03 22:07:51",
 updated_at: "2015-10-03 22:07:51">,
 #<Entry id: 5, name: "Pollie",
```

```
        created_at: "2015-10-03 22:07:55",
        updated_at: "2015-10-03 22:07:55">]>
```

readonly
> The `readonly` option retrieves records so that you can read them, but cannot make any changes.

group
> The `group` option lets you specify a field that the results should group on, like the SQL `GROUP BY` clause.

lock
> `lock` lets you test for locked rows.

joins, include, select, *and* from
> These options let you specify components of the SQL query more precisely. You may need them as you delve into complex data structures, but you can ignore them at first.

Rails also offers *dynamic finders*, which are methods it automatically supports based on the names of the fields in the database. If you have a `given_name` field, for example, you can call `find_by_given_name(name)` to get the first record with the specified *name*, or `find_all_by_given_name(name)` to get all records with the specified *name*. These are a little slower than the regular `find` method but may be more readable.

 Rails also offers an elegant way to create more readable queries with scopes, which you should explore after you've found your way around.

Test Your Knowledge

Quiz

1. Where would you put code to which you want all of your controllers to have access?

2. How do the default routes decide which requests to send to your controller?

3. What does the `change` method do in a migration?

4. What three steps does the `create` method combine?

5. How do you test to find out whether a submitted field is blank?

6. How can you retrieve all of the values for a given object?

7. How can you find a set of values that match a certain condition?

8. How can you retrieve just the first item of a set?

Answers

1. Code in the `ApplicationController` class, stored at *app/controllers/application_controller.rb*, is available to all of the controllers in the project.

2. The default routes assume that the controller name follows the first slash within the URL, that the controller action follows the second slash, and that the ID value follows the third slash. If there's a dot (.) after the ID, then what follows the dot is considered the format requested.

3. The `change` method is called when Rails runs a migration. The code explains what to create moving forward, but Rails can also run it backward. It usually creates tables and fields.

4. The `create` method creates a new object, sets its properties to those specified in the parameters, and saves it to the database.

5. You can test to see whether something is blank using an `if` statement and the `blank?` method, as in:

```
if @name.blank? then
   something to do if blank
end
```

6. To retrieve all values for a given object, use `.all`.

7. To retrieve a set of values, use `.where(conditions)`.

8. To get the first of a set, use `.first`. You may need to set an `:order` parameter to make sure that your understanding of "first" matches that of Rails.

## CHAPTER 5

Accelerating Development with Scaffolding and REST

Truth forever on the scaffold, wrong forever on the throne.
—James Russell Lowell

The example in the previous chapter contained the key components you need to work with Rails and began to demonstrate how they work together. Rails is more than just a set of components, however—it's a tightly knit package that includes tools to get you started more quickly. Rails can even teach you some best practices while making your work easier.

A First Look at Scaffolding

So, how do Rails developers build applications more quickly? One key piece of the puzzle is scaffolding. Instead of building a detailed controller and view, you can let Rails put up an interface to your data. In most cases, the scaffolding will be temporary, something you build on and replace, but in some cases, the scaffolding may be enough to do what you need. The scaffolding also provides an excellent way to see what the creators of Rails think is a good way to accomplish common tasks.

To get started, create a new application named *guestbook*:

```
$ rails new guestbook
```

Then change to that directory:

```
$ cd guestbook
```

And then create a model and supporting scaffolding with a single command from the command line. (You can also find all of these files in *ch05/guestbook03*.)

```
$ rails generate scaffold Person name:string
  invoke  active_record
  create    db/migrate/20120220162923_create_people.rb
  create    app/models/person.rb
  invoke    test_unit
  create      test/models/person_test.rb
  create      test/fixtures/people.yml
  invoke  resource_route
   route  resources :people
  invoke  scaffold_controller
  create    app/controllers/people_controller.rb
  invoke    erb
  create      app/views/people
  create      app/views/people/index.html.erb
  create      app/views/people/edit.html.erb
  create      app/views/people/show.html.erb
  create      app/views/people/new.html.erb
  create      app/views/people/_form.html.erb
  invoke    test_unit
  create      test/controllers/people_controller_test.rb
  invoke    helper
  create      app/helpers/people_helper.rb
  invoke      test_unit
  invoke    jbuilder
  create      app/views/people/index.json.jbuilder
  create      app/views/people/show.json.jbuilder
  invoke  assets
  invoke    coffee
  create      app/assets/javascripts/people.coffee
  invoke    scss
  create      app/assets/stylesheets/people.scss
  invoke  scss
  create    app/assets/stylesheets/scaffolds.scss
```

This command makes Rails do a lot of different things. First, examine the initial line:

```
rails generate scaffold Person name:string
```

It tells Rails to generate scaffolding, based around a model named `Person`, whose content is a `name` that is a `string`. If the model has more pieces to it—and most will—you can just keep listing the different data fields and their types.

Given this information, Rails goes on to create:

- A data migration to establish the tables needed for the model
- A model (with accompanying tests and fixtures for the tests)
- A new route that will map user requests to the controller
- A controller to send data among the different components
- Four views (index, edit, show, and new), in addition to a supporting partial form (*_form.html.erb*) that reduces code duplication

- Tests for the controller
- An empty file for helper methods
- A CoffeeScript file for scripting the pages
- Two stylesheets, people and scaffold, for all of those views

You'll need to run the migration file with **rails db:migrate**, and then you can run **rails server** to fire up the application. Visit *http://localhost:3000/people*, and you'll see something like Figure 5-1.

Figure 5-1. The index page of the newly generated application

While Figure 5-1 lacks the "Hello" of the application built in the previous chapter, and the form field to enter your name isn't right on the first page, it's still basically the same idea. You can see who visited, and you can enter new names. If you click on the "New Person" link, you'll see the screen in Figure 5-2, which lets you enter a new name.

Figure 5-2. Entering a new name

When you enter a name and click the "Create person" button, you'll see a page representing the newly created person, as shown in Figure 5-3. (The URL, though it points to a single person, still uses the plural form, *people*, as the record is one of a set.)

Figure 5-3. A newly created person

There are two options here. Clicking Edit will let you change the name (as shown in Figure 5-4), while clicking Back returns you to the original (index) page—only now you'll see the name in a table, as shown in Figure 5-5.

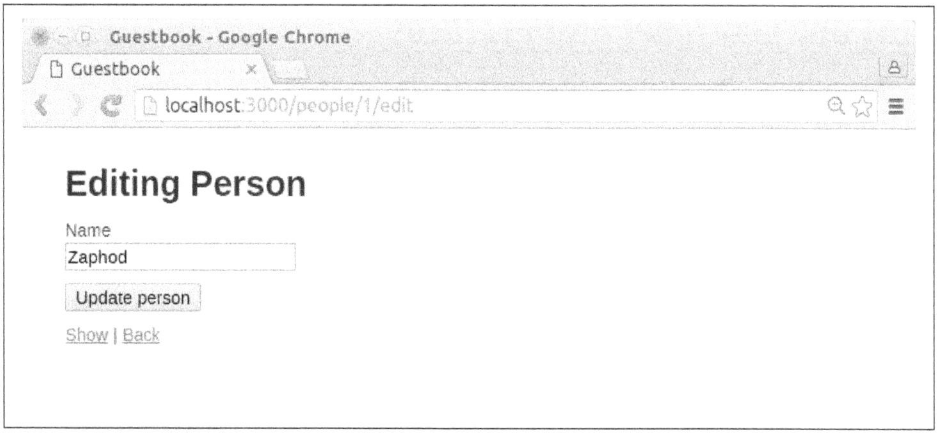

Figure 5-4. Updating an existing person

Figure 5-5. The new list of people, with options for modifying them

It's not quite as simple as the application built by hand in the previous chapter, but much of it is actually identical. The migration file looks just like the one created by hand (plus or minus some whitespace), and the model has exactly as much new code in it as the one built by hand.

The scaffolding's action takes place in the single line added to the routing file, in a controller that needs a careful explanation, and in the views, which don't do very much that you haven't already seen before. To understand why this controller works the way it does, though, there's another story that needs to be told. Fortunately, it's a RESTful story.

REST and Controller Best Practices

REST is an approach to building web applications that takes as much advantage of the underlying structure of the Web as possible. This makes a lot of things more comfortable:

- Users will find that the applications work as they'd like in their web browsers. They can bookmark pages and come back to them, and the URLs are actually meaningful.

- Network administrators can use all their preferred techniques for managing web traffic without worrying about disrupting an application.

- You, of course, get the greatest benefits. REST-based architecture is a very neat fit with the Rails MVC approach and makes it easier to keep track of which code does what where. Rails is also set up to make it extremely easy for you to use REST, supporting a number of ways for you to say, "I'd like this to behave REST-fully."

REST doesn't create new techniques so much as dusts off old techniques and encourages developers to use them as they were designed to be used. Of course, even early in the Web's development, developers hacked and slashed their way into a different style of programming, so there are some adjustments to make. Fortunately, Rails makes it easy to adjust and opens new horizons in doing so.

REST stands for REpresentational State Transfer, which describes what happens but isn't the most immediately meaningful explanation.

Websites and Web Applications

Web developers have historically used two HTTP methods to get information into and out of sites: GET and POST. On the surface, GET used the "data fits into the query string" approach, whereas POST used the "we have a nice clean URL with data elsewhere" approach. There's more to it than that, though.

Much of the Web is read-only, and for those applications, GET worked very smoothly. Browser caches and proxy servers could check once in a while to see if a page had changed. For many applications, where POSTs were used to add new data and GETs were used to see that data, things weren't much more complicated. Unfortunately, though, the reliance on GET and POST overloaded those methods and created some problems.

For GET, the most obvious problem was that URLs became very large very quickly as more and more data was exchanged. Beyond that, though, were some other creative issues:

- Proxy servers generally treated a GET request as an opportunity to cache information and reduce the amount of traffic needed next time. This could lead to sensitive data stored on a not-necessarily-secure proxy server and could also create some strange problems around the proxy server checking whether the result had changed when another request came through with the same data.

- Some applications used links containing GET requests to ask for changes in data —even deletions. (Think *http://example.com/doIt/?action=delete.*) As the quest for speed became more important, developers came up with browser extensions that prefetched information from links in the document…and activated these actions without the user expecting it. Oops.

The general rule with GET has become "make sure that none of your GET requests do anything dangerous." GET requests are supposed to be *idempotent*, yielding the same result even when issued multiple times. No GET request changes the results of the next GET request to the same resource, for example.

 PUT and DELETE requests are also supposed to be idempotent— PUTting the same thing repeatedly yields the same data that was PUT, while DELETE-ing the same thing repeatedly yields the same nothingness. HEAD requests, which are basically a GET returning headers only, are also idempotent.

POST had a simpler problem that could be avoided through careful programming, and a harder problem that was largely political:

- Pretty much nothing created with POST was bookmarkable unless the receiving application immediately created a redirect to something reflecting the result of the POST. Entire applications were often written so that users could bookmark only the front page. For internal applications this might be tolerable, but all these POST requests also blocked search engines, which pretty much only used GET.

- Once it became clear that using GET for heavy lifting created problems, POST wound up carrying nearly all of the data transfers from users to the server and then pretty much all purely computer-to-computer transfers. XML-RPC, SOAP, and most discussions of "web services" really meant "HTTP POST to a given URL" when they said "Web."

The old way of working with the Web mostly worked, but it clearly had some dark corners and plenty of room for improvement. As it turned out, all the pieces needed for that improvement already existed.

PATCH is the primary HTTP method for updates. PUT means resource creation or replacement at some given URL, while PATCH allows full and partial updates. PATCH is not idempotent.

Toward a Cleaner Approach

Although developers had become accustomed to using just these two methods, and browsers had given them the greatest support, HTTP had more pieces to offer than just GET and POST. The two most important of these are PUT and DELETE, which combine with GET and POST to give HTTP a complete set of verbs for manipulating data.

HTTP also has a HEAD method, which is kind of a GET-lite frequently used to check on the freshness of cached data, and OPTIONS and TRACE. Rails uses HEAD.

How can you manage data with just POST, GET, PUT, and DELETE?

As it turns out, it's a familiar question for many programmers, who often work with the cheerfully named CRUD model, which stands for create, read, update, and destroy. If you've worked with SQL, you're already familiar with INSERT, SELECT, UPDATE, and DELETE. That basic set of verbs manages practically everything we do with databases, and the art of using SQL is about skillfully combining those generic verbs with specific data to accomplish the tasks you need to accomplish.

While CRUD is relatively easy to understand and implement, it's far from the only or best way to implement REST-based applications. However, CRUD is definitely the fastest way to get started using REST in Rails and is often a substantial improvement over less structured options.

In Rails, this is typically described as show, create, update, and destroy, as you saw in the links in Figure 5-5. You'll also see that pattern in the controller Rails creates as part of the scaffolding. *Working this way requires a shift in the way developers think about controllers* and about writing web applications generally.

The example created in the previous chapter treated the controller as a container for actions or verbs. You could, if you wanted, write an entire Rails application in a single controller with a method for every action it offers the user and views to match. Those methods would then work with a variety of models, getting information into and out of the application. If that became too large of a mess, you could use a number of con-

---

trollers to group different methods, though there would be lots of ways to group them.

The example built with scaffolding takes a very different approach. The publicly available verbs are standardized—each controller implements the same verbs. Instead of being a container for a wide variety of actions, the controller becomes a standardized piece connecting a data model to the Web: a noun.

This maps perfectly to the way that REST expects the Web to work. Our familiar URLs (or uniform resource identifiers—URIs—as REST prefers to call them) connect the client to a *resource* on the server. These resources are the nouns that the HTTP verbs work on, and the controller makes sure that those standardized verbs work in predictable ways on the data models underneath.

REST offers one last bonus. "Resources" are information, not necessarily information frozen into a particular representation. If a user wants the same information in JSON instead of HTML, the resource should (if you're being nice, and Rails is nice by default) be able to provide the information as JSON. By using the RESTful features of Rails, you're not just creating a website, but a resource that other applications can interact with. This also makes it much easier to create Ajax applications on top of Rails and to build mashups. Effectively, it's what a rich interpretation of "web services" should have meant in the first place.

 Thinking too hard about resources can lead to some complicated philosophical irritations. The authors have learned through painful experience that trying to sort out the proper relationship of XML namespaces to the resources that identify them is infinitely complicated, as is interpreting the meaning of a fragment identifier (*#id*) in any situation where the same resource can produce multiple data representations.

The answer to these irritations is simple: don't think about them. If you find yourself going down the resource philosophy rathole, step back and focus on something more practical. These issues can create the occasional practical problem, but generally they sit quietly unless stirred up.

Examining a RESTful Controller

Rails scaffolding is a very conscious implementation of REST, an example generally worth emulating and extending. Even in cases where browser limitations keep REST from working as simply as it should, Rails fills the gaps so that you can focus on building your application, not on corner cases. The simple one-field application shown earlier is enough to demonstrate the principles that Rails has used to generate the scaffolding.

Opening the *app/controllers/people_controller.rb* file reveals Example 5-1. It defines seven methods, each prefaced with a sample of the HTTP request that should call it. This chapter will explore each method individually, but take a moment to explore the whole thing and get a feel for what's going on, and how these methods are similar and different.

Example 5-1. A RESTful controller created as part of Rails scaffolding

```ruby
class PeopleController < ApplicationController
  before_action :set_person, only: [:show, :edit, :update, :destroy]

  # GET /people
  # GET /people.json
  def index
    @people = Person.all
  end

  # GET /people/1
  # GET /people/1.json
  def show
  end

  # GET /people/new
  def new
    @person = Person.new
  end

  # GET /people/1/edit
  def edit
  end

  # POST /people
  # POST /people.json
  def create
    @person = Person.new(person_params)

    respond_to do |format|
      if @person.save
        format.html { redirect_to @person, notice:
          'Person was successfully updated.' }
      else
        format.html { render :new }
        format.json { render json: @person.errors, status: :unprocessable_entity }
      end
    end
  end

  # PATCH/PUT /people/1
  # PATCH/PUT /people/1.json
  def update
    respond_to do |format|
```

```
      if @person.update(person_params)
        format.html { redirect_to @person, notice:
          'Person was successfully created.' }
        format.json { render :show, status: :ok, location: @person }
      else
        format.html { render :edit }
        format.json { render json: @person.errors, status: :unprocessable_entity }
      end
    end
  end

  # DELETE /people/1
  # DELETE /people/1.json
  def destroy
    @person.destroy
    respond_to do |format|
      format.html { redirect_to people_url,
      notice: 'Person was successfully destroyed.' }
      format.json { head :no_content }
    end
  end

  private
    # Use callbacks to share common setup or constraints between actions.
    def set_person
      @person = Person.find(params[:id])
    end

    # Never trust parameters from the scary internet,
    #only allow the whitelist through.
    def person_params
      params.require(:person).permit(:name)
    end
end
```

How can this scaffold support seven methods when REST only has four verbs? If you look closely, the first four methods are all based on GET requests for slightly different things:

- The index method answers GET requests for a listing of all the available data.

- The show method answers GET requests to display a single record from the dataset.

- The new method answers GET requests for a form to create a new record. (It doesn't actually create a record directly—note the use inside the method of new but not save.)

- The edit method answers GET requests for an editable version of a single record from the dataset, gathering its components and sending them out as a form.

The other three methods are the other three REST verbs:

- The `create` method responds to POSTs that send new data to create a new record. If it can create it, the method then redirects to a page showing the new record.

- The `update` method responds to PUTs that send data modifying an existing record. Like `create`, it tests whether the change was successful and redirects.

- The `destroy` method responds to DELETEs, obliterating the requested record.

Figure 5-6 illustrates the processing paths these seven methods support and how they're reached.

Because not all browsers directly support PUT and DELETE in forms, Rails uses a hidden field approach to support them as you'll see in the next chapter.

All of these methods reach the controller thanks to the line the generator added to the top of *config/routes.rb*:

```
resources :people
```

Unlike `match`, which defined a simple routing by fragmenting the URL, `resources` expects a particular set of routes reflecting RESTful expectations. If you want to see the full set of routes it created, run `rails routes`. You'll see something like:

```
$ rails routes
       Prefix Verb   URI Pattern                Controller#Action
       people GET    /people(.:format)          people#index
              POST   /people(.:format)          people#create
   new_person GET    /people/new(.:format)      people#new
  edit_person GET    /people/:id/edit(.:format) people#edit
       person GET    /people/:id(.:format)      people#show
              PATCH  /people/:id(.:format)      people#update
              PUT    /people/:id(.:format)      people#update
              DELETE /people/:id(.:format)      people#destroy
```

That's a lot of new pieces from one line of code, but don't worry—the basic handling for all of those pieces has already been created for you.

When you see `people#index`, it refers to the `index` action of the `people` controller. Older versions of `rails routes` used to report this more verbosely, as `{:action=>"index", :controller=>"peo ple"}`.

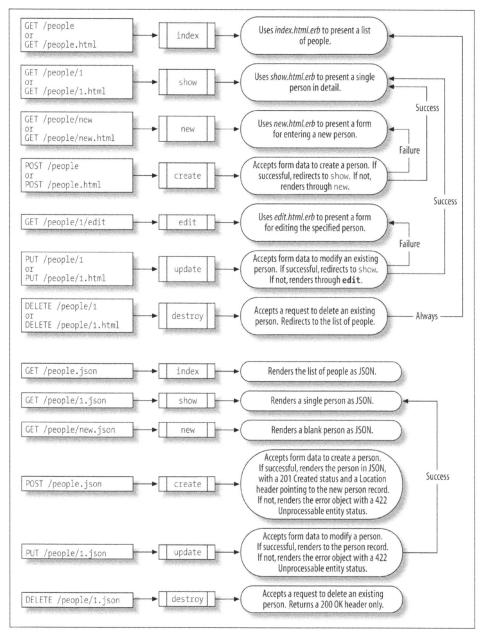

Figure 5-6. The many paths through a REST-based resource

If your applications stay simple enough, these methods will take care of most of your needs for getting information from views to models and back again. You're welcome to skip the next section and jump to the end of the chapter if you'd prefer to work on getting things built immediately, but there's much more to learn from these simple bits of code if you're interested. They are an excellent guide to the basics of getting things done in Rails.

index: An Overview of Data

Example 5-2 contains the `index` method, the most likely starting point for a visitor exploring the data.

Example 5-2. The index method shows all the records in HTML or JSON

```
# GET /people
# GET /people.json
def index
  @people = Person.all
end
```

As the comments indicate, this responds to requests for *people* or for *people.json*. Just as Example 4-7 did it makes a call to the `Person` model's `find` method, passing it the parameter `:all` to indicate that it should return everything, using the abbreviated syntax `Person.all` to do so. While the controller does not explicitly say it, this method can return the information as JSON, not just as HTML.

 If you want to return XML, you'll want to explore the `to_xml` method.

The default scaffold tests for HTML and JSON, though other formats, like XML, are available. This controller will, depending on what the client wants, either use the standard HTML-generating view for a response or generate a JSON file from the `@people` object. Figure 5-7 shows how a JSON response might look in the browser.

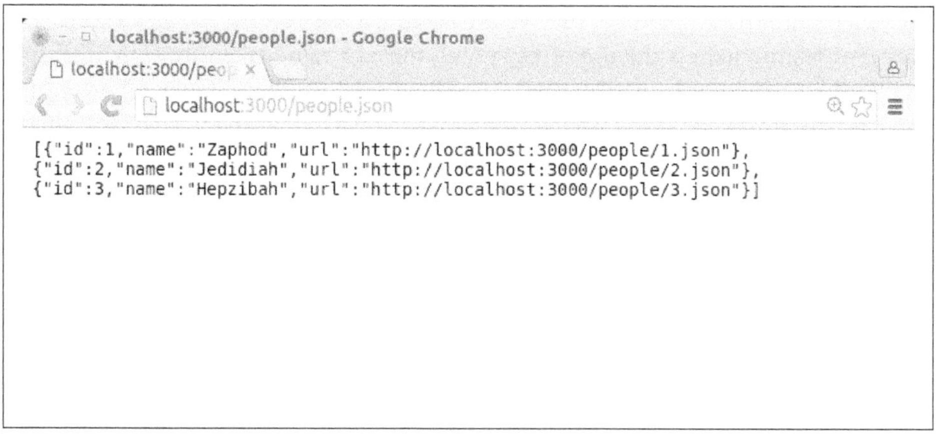

Figure 5-7. A JSON response listing people

show: Just One Row of Data and the Before Filter

Example 5-3 contains the show method, the most likely starting point for a visitor exploring the data.

Example 5-3. The show method extracts one row of data to display

```
# GET /people/1
# GET /people/1.json
def show
end
```

However, this action introduces us to something new in Rails. The action is pretty plain compared to the previous index action. But don't be fooled. If we look back to the top of our people controller, we see the line of code shown in Example 5-4.

Example 5-4. Before action that calls set_person method

```
before_action :set_person, only: [:show, :edit, :update, :destroy]
```

This line tells Rails, before you do anything, run the set_person method on the show, edit, update, and destroy actions only. If we look at the bottom of the controller, we see the code shown in Example 5-5.

Example 5-5. The set_person method called by the before action

```
# Use callbacks to share common setup or constraints between actions.
    def set_person
      @person = Person.find(params[:id])
    end
```

This method finds a single `Person` record based on the ID that is passed to it. The only new feature here is the use of `find` with the `:id` value taken from the parameters. Rails's routing will populate the `:id` value based on the number following the controller name in the URL, whether or not a format is specified. The `:id` value is central to the Rails RESTful processing approach, as resources have controller names that identify their source and `:id` values that let users and developers focus more tightly on specific records.

 For more information on before, after, and around filters in Rails, check out the Ruby on Rails guides (*http://bit.ly/2aTtJIj*).

new: A Blank Set of Data Fields

Example 5-6 contains the `new` method, which presents a form users can fill out to add data to the database.

Example 5-6. The new method collects data structure information and sends it to a form

```
# GET /people/new
def new
  @person = Person.new
end
```

The `new` method highlights the strength of Rails in working flexibly with data structures. The call to `Person.new` creates a new blank data structure based on the `Person` model, but Rails uses that data structure in an unusual way. This controller will simply pass it to the view in *new.html.erb*, without ever having to consider questions like, "What is the schema for this data?" The controller is spared the problem of worrying about the structures that come through the model and can simply pass them on to the next level of Rails components.

Remember, the `new` method creates a blank data structure, but it doesn't actually do anything to the database; it only exists in memory. The blank structure created here will be used as a template for the view to do its work and then thrown away. The actual changes to the database will come when the `create` method receives data for a new record, and it will populate and save a new record.

edit: Hand Me That Data, Please

The `edit` method, shown in Example 5-7, is the last of the GET-based methods, and the simplest.

Example 5-7. The edit method collects a record to send it out for user editing

```
# GET /people/1/edit
def edit
end
```

Similar to the show method we discussed earlier, edit makes use of the before action to retrieve a single Person record and passes it on to the view, which will populate a form with the data and let the user make changes. Like new, edit itself doesn't make any changes. The actual changes to the data will come in through the update method.

create: Save Something New

The create method, shown in Example 5-8, is extremely busy relative to its peers, doing a lot of things other methods haven't done before.

Example 5-8. The create method saves an incoming record to the database

```
# POST /people
# POST /people.json
def create
  @person = Person.new(person_params)

  respond_to do |format|
    if @person.save
      format.html { redirect_to @person, notice:
        'Person was successfully created.' }
      format.json { render :show, status: :created, location: @person }
    else
      format.html { render :new }
      format.json { render json: @person.errors, status: :unprocessable_entity }
    end
  end
end
```

The first thing that the create method does is create a new Person object based on the person_params method. The person_params method is found near the bottom of the controller and is a way of whitelisting parameters that are sent to the model. This is a security practice to help prevent accidentally allowing users to update sensitive model attributes.

> For more information on strong parameters in Rails, check out the Ruby on Rails guides (*http://bit.ly/2aRZ8Yz*).

The scaffolding forms, as the next chapter will demonstrate, return the data neatly packaged so that Rails doesn't have to inspect every field. It can move through as a unit.

The `respond_to` method is a feature of ActionController, a wrapper that lets you create responses in various formats while building on the same data. The format object comes to the controller through Rails routing, typically identifying that a particular request wants a response in HTML or JSON format. How does Rails know what the client wants? Through the HTTP `Accept` header and through the file extension on the URL. (In the routing files, you'll frequently see `:format` to pick up the file extension.)

The `respond_to do |format|` block also does much more here. It opens with:

```
if @person.save
```

This does two things. First, it attempts to save the record to the database through the `Person` model. Second, `@person.save` returns a `true` or `false` value that the `if` statement will process to determine what it should send back to the user.

If it's `true`—that is, the save was successful—the application uses the `:notice` functionality (described in the next chapter, where you can see what it connects to) to let the user know the operation was a success.

Then, if the request wanted HTML back, it redirects the user to the `show` method for the new `@person` object, using the `redirect_to` helper method. (`redirect_to` understands the routing table and can reliably send the visitor to the right place.) If the request wanted JSON back, it executes a more complicated rendering:

```
render json: @person, status: :created, location: @person
```

As it was for `index` and the other methods, the JSON will be generated based on the `@person` object. The HTTP response will also include a `201 Created` status header and identify its location as where the `@person` object can be shown. (`200 OK` is the normal header, though `404 Not Found` is probably the header most people recognize.)

The response if there's an error—`@person.save` returned `false`—is to report back to the user, sending the incoming data to another copy of the form for creating people:

```
else
  format.html { render action: "new" }
  format.json { render json: @person.errors, status: :unprocessable_entity }
end
```

If an HTML response has been requested, the user will just get a blank field for a new entry attempt. If a JSON response was requested, the sender will get a little more information back—a `422 Unprocessable Entity` message and the errors from the `@person` object.

Put This Updated Record In

The `update` method, shown in Example 5-9, is much like the `create` method except that it responds to a PUT instead of a POST and updates a record instead of creating one.

Example 5-9. The update method changes a record and saves the result

```
# PATCH/PUT /people/1
# PATCH/PUT /people/1.json
def update
  respond_to do |format|
    if @person.update(person_params)
      format.html { redirect_to @person,
        notice: 'Person was successfully updated.' }
      format.json { render :show, status: :ok, location: @person }
    else
      format.html { render :edit }
      format.json { render json: @person.errors, status: :unprocessable_entity }
    end
  end
end
```

The request will include an ID value in the URL that the Rails router will send as `:id` to the controller. Like a POST request, it will also come with parameters, which in this case will represent the updated data.

The key line here is:

```
    if @person.update(person_params)
```

While the `create` method used `new` to create a fresh record from the parameters that arrived with the form, the `update` method uses the `set_person` before action to get the record that is to be changed based based on `:id`, and then the `update` action uses the `update` method called on `@person` to try changing those values to the parameters from the form. The value returned by `update` determines whether it sends back successful responses or an error message.

The successful response to a JSON `update` is notably different from the successful response to a JSON `create`—instead of sending the new JSON document, all that the updater gets is HTTP headers, created with the `head` method, indicating a `204 No Content` response. (HTTP responses in the 200 range are successful; 204 just means that there isn't a message beyond success.)

Destroy It

The final method is `destroy`, shown in Example 5-10, which responds to HTTP DELETE requests.

Example 5-10. The destroy method removes a Person record

```
# DELETE /people/1
# DELETE /people/1.json
def destroy
  @person.destroy
  respond_to do |format|
    format.html { redirect_to people_url, notice:
      Person was successfully destroyed. }
    format.json { head :no_content }
  end
end
```

One notable aspect of this code is that it contains absolutely nothing that will ask the sender to reconsider. Make certain that your view code asks users if they really truly mean it *before* you call this method. (The views generated by the scaffolding do ask, fortunately.)

Destroying a record is a two-step process. First, Rails locates the object to destroy using the `set_person` before action, and then it issues a call to that object's `destroy` method. Unlike `save` or `update`, the `destroy` method is just assumed to have happened. Since there isn't actually a record to show, the response uses a redirect to the main list of entries as its HTML response and a blank "No content" as its JSON response.

If you'd like to experiment with some much more powerful scaffolding, you might want to explore ActiveScaffold (*http://bit.ly/ 2aTtttb*). It goes far beyond the basics Rails provides, into Ajax and a higher level of automation.

Now that you've seen how all of these pieces work, it's time to do more creative things with the pieces. The next chapter will examine how to do a lot more with forms and data models and how to use the controller to connect them.

Micro-Applications

While Rails is well equipped to handle the creation of large-scale web applications quickly, it has another powerful side that's less frequently discussed. Thanks to scaffolding and Rails's transparent use of SQLite, you can quickly and easily build smaller applications with Rails, keeping track of whatever information you'd like.

Even with a single table, it's easy to build things like address lists, infinitely expandable glossaries, expense trackers, and so on. With the multimodel approaches you'll learn in Chapter 9, you'll be able to build more sophisticated applications that manage a lot more data but still don't require huge amounts of effort to build or run. Add the authentication features in Chapter 14, and you can even share your applications with some friends with free cloud hosts like Heroku.

Most people think of applications scaling up, but the ability to scale down comfortably makes it a lot easier to experiment with Rails development and to solve some of the minor data-handling problems life presents. "Web scale" is any scale, including small scale.

Escaping the REST Prison

While REST is extremely powerful, developers used to working in other environments may be cursing at this point, wondering whether they really need to build every part of their application according to this weird new paradigm.

Don't worry: you don't have to. You could, if you wanted, stick with the GET/POST approach shown in earlier chapters. Rails doesn't enforce RESTfulness.

However, you may want to explore a combination of approaches. If a page is only ever going to be reached with GET, use a simple controller and view or even a static page where appropriate. If a page needs to manage more sophisticated data input and output, then use REST to simplify that process. In a more complex application, it might make sense to use REST for cases where data is coming in or being edited and to use simpler controllers for situations where the application is just presenting information.

The remainder of this book is going to use the combination approach. REST is just too convenient for getting structured data in and out of a website to ignore, but when REST isn't necessary, there's no need to let it dominate.

(And, of course, the simple approach Rails takes to REST isn't entirely loved by the REST world either, but making Rails substantially more RESTful would take some major redesign.)

Test Your Knowledge

Quiz

1. How many files does Rails create in response to a single `script/generate scaffold` request?

2. In REST, how do HTTP GET, PUT, POST, and DELETE map to the "CRUD" of create, read, update, and destroy?

3. What does *idempotent* mean?

4. How do you make sure a result can be bookmarked?

5. Why do four basic REST functions end up making seven different methods in the controller?

6. What does `resources :people` mean?

7. How do you specify responses in different formats?

8. How does an ID value connect to a specific resource?

9. What happens if you send a Rails application a chunk of JSON?

Answers

1. Rails creates a lot of files in response to a `script/generate scaffold` request, though some of them may exist already. It will create index, show, new, and edit view files, as well as one with the name of the object specified. It will also create a model, test, test fixture, migration, controller, test controller, and helper class, and add a route to the routing table, plus stylesheets and scripts. So, the answer is usually 17.

2. GET maps to read. POST maps to create. PUT maps to update. DELETE maps to destroy.

3. *Idempotent* means that you can call the same method as many times as you want and still get the same result. A GET request should be idempotent, and no matter how many GET requests you make, none of those GET requests will change what is returned on the next call.

4. The easiest way to make sure that something can be bookmarked is to make it consistently accessible through a GET request to a particular URL. (Making this work with other request methods often means presenting their results as a redirect to a GET. That way the results are bookmarkable, and the transaction only happens once.)

5. The four REST methods map neatly to create, read, update, and delete for a single resource, but there are a few other operations needed to make the application more usable to humans. All of them use GET. The `index` method shows a listing of all the resources available. The `new` method provides a form you can use to create a new resource. The `edit` method provides a form you can edit to modify an existing resource. Those forms then call the `create` and `update` methods, respectively.

6. `resources :people` creates a huge collection of routes that connect specific URLs to the REST methods for working with `:people` objects.

7. You can provide replies in different formats using the `respond_to do |format|` call inside of a controller.

8. By default, Rails uses REST-based routing to connect to resources whose primary key matches the ID value provided in the URI.

9. If you send the JSON as part of a POST or PUT, Rails will check the JSON to see if it matches what Rails expects for the data structure that should go there. If it doesn't match, it will reply with an error. If it does match, it will create a new record based on the data (POST) or modify an existing record (PUT).

CHAPTER 6

Presenting Models with Forms

In many cases, the user interface to a program is the most important part for a commercial company: whether the programs works correctly or not seems to be secondary.
—Linus Torvalds

The previous chapter showed how Rails makes it easy to create simple applications using scaffolding, but a key aspect of Rails scaffolding is that it isn't meant to be permanent. This doesn't necessarily mean that you'll tear it down completely and start over, but it usually means that you'll at least make substantial improvements to make it more attractive. This is especially important where information is coming in from users. While Rails scaffolding provides basic functionality, you're very likely going to want to improve on the forms it creates.

More Than a Name on a Form

To demonstrate a reasonably complete set of HTML form features, the application needs to support more than one data field and needs to support fields in a variety of types. Rails, because it works with a wide variety of databases, supports a narrower set of types than each of those databases. The types of fields that Rails supports through ActiveRecord include:

```
:string
:text
:integer
:float
:decimal
:datetime
:timestamp
:time
:date
```

```
:binary
:boolean
```

The `:string` type is generally limited to 255 characters, whereas `:text` can hold longer data. The `:integer`, `:float`, and `:decimal` types all hold numbers, although integers may not have a fractional part to the right of the decimal point. The `:date time`, `:timestamp`, `:time`, and `:date` types hold the classically complicated combination values used to represent dates and times. The `:binary` type can hold unstructured binary data, often called BLOBs (binary large objects). (You'll need to decide how you want to handle binary data—just stuffing it into a database isn't always the right answer.) Finally, the `:boolean` is the simplest type, accepting only the values of `1` and `0`, equal to `true` and `false`.

HTML forms offer a variety of ways to enter data that doesn't map one-to-one to the data types Rails uses:

- Text fields (normal, hidden, and password)
- Text areas
- Checkboxes
- Radio buttons
- Selection lists (including multiple selections and grouped selections)
- File uploads
- Other buttons (submit, reset)

To demonstrate how these pieces work with ActiveRecord data types, we'll create an application with the following data fields:

Ordinary strings
Name, secret, country, email

Long strings
Description

Boolean
"Can we send you email?"

Numbers
An integer for specifying graduation year, a floating-point number for body temperature, and a decimal for price

Dates and times
The user's birthday and a favorite time of day

File uploads deserve separate coverage, so we will explore them in Chapter 8 in the section "Adding a Picture by Uploading a File" on page 131.

Yes, these choices are somewhat whimsical, but they'll provide a framework in which to explore how Rails supports data types and how you can build on that support.

Generating HTML Forms with Scaffolding

Although this application is approaching the point beyond which much generated code becomes more of a hassle than a help, it makes sense to create one last round of scaffolding, replacing the application from the previous chapter. After this, we'll work within the same application for a while, as this kind of tearing down and rebuilding is only a good idea at the very beginning of a project.

To get started, create a new application. Move or rename the old guestbook application to get it out of the way, and then run `rails new guestbook`. Then, run the following clunky mess from the command line at the top level of the newly created application:

```
rails generate scaffold Person name:string secret:string country:string
email:string description:text can_send_email:boolean graduation_year:integer
body_temperature:float price:decimal birthday:date favorite_time:time
```

This kind of long list of data structures in the scaffolding is annoying. It's hard to type, and what's worse, if you find that you made a mistake after you've already modified the generated code, you have a painful choice.

You can either rerun the scaffolding generation and lose all your changes to the logic, or you can modify the migration, the model, and the views by hand. Rails scaffolding generators just overwrite the old code—there's no support for more subtle fixes.

Neither of these is a fun way to fix a typo, so remember: when you first generate scaffolding, it's easier to get things right the first time. This doesn't mean you need to get everything right all at once—no one ever does—but adding new features to code is generally much more fun than fixing a typo. It may be easiest to set up the command in a text editor and then paste it in after checking it carefully. (You can also find the resulting files for this particular command in *ch06/guestbook04*.)

Before going further, examine the `change` method in the migration this created in *db/migrate/*_create_people.rb*, shown in Example 6-1. (It won't actually be *_create_people.rb*—the * will be replaced by a timestamp.)

Example 6-1. Creating a richer table with many data types from a migration

```
def change
  create_table :people do |t|
    t.string :name
    t.string :secret
    t.string :country
    t.string :email
    t.text :description
    t.boolean :can_send_email
    t.integer :graduation_year
    t.float :body_temperature
    t.decimal :price
    t.date :birthday
    t.time :favorite_time

    t.timestamps
  end
end
```

As requested, Rails created a structure containing many fields of various types. For now, this will do for a demonstration, though eventually there will be change in the data model that requires change to the migration. Run **rails db:migrate**, and the migration will build the database table for the application.

The model Rails created is simple:

```
class Person < ApplicationRecord
end
```

Next, it's time to look at the form that Rails created for making new people, *app/views/people/new.html.erb*, shown in Example 6-2.

Example 6-2. The new.html.erb file contains very little

```
<h1>New person</h1>

<%= render 'form', person: @person %>

<%= link_to 'Back', people_path %>
```

Using `<%= render 'form' %>`, Rails put the meat of the form into a *partial*, a separate file that can be included by reference. Partials are great for avoiding some kinds of repetition, offering a flexible means of sharing consistent pieces of pages across your application. Chapter 8 will cover a few additional options that might help you do even better at avoiding repetition. The Rails naming conventions mean that form will get interpreted as *_form.html.erb*, which is shown in Example 6-3.

Example 6-3. The _form.html.erb file supports basic input functionality

```erb
<%= form_for(@person) do |f| %>
  <% if @person.errors.any? %>
    <div id="error_explanation">
      <h2><%= pluralize(@person.errors.count, "error") %>
      prohibited this person from being saved:</h2>
      <ul>
      <% @person.errors.full_messages.each do |message| %>
        <li><%= message %></li>
      <% end %>
      </ul>
    </div>
  <% end %>

<div class="field">
  <%= f.label :name %>
  <%= f.text_field :name %>
</div>
<div class="field">
  <%= f.label :secret %>
  <%= f.text_field :secret %>
</div>
<div class="field">
  <%= f.label :country %>
  <%= f.text_field :country %>
</div>
<div class="field">
  <%= f.label :email %>
  <%= f.text_field :email %>
</div>
<div class="field">
  <%= f.label :description %>
  <%= f.text_area :description %>
</div>
<div class="field">
  <%= f.label :can_send_email %>
  <%= f.check_box :can_send_email %>
</div>
<div class="field">
  <%= f.label :graduation_year %>
  <%= f.text_field :graduation_year %>
</div>
<div class="field">
  <%= f.label :body_temperature %>
  <%= f.text_field :body_temperature %>
</div>
<div class="field">
  <%= f.label :price %>
  <%= f.text_field :price %>
</div>
<div class="field">
```

```
  <%= f.label :birthday %>
  <%= f.date_select :birthday %>
</div>
<div class="field">
  <%= f.label :favorite_time %>
  <%= f.time_select :favorite_time %>
</div>
<div class="actions">
  <%= f.submit %>
</div>
<% end %>
```

There are some useful new features in the highlighted parts. First, almost at the top of the form is a section that shows any validation errors in the data fields, an interface component you'll want to consider carefully as you develop richer data. (Do you want to present error messages at the top? Mixed in with the form? Both?)

The form_for method sets up an f variable that the other methods here will rely on for context. Because it is so central to form building with Rails, it is described in depth in the next section.

The :description, which is intended to be a longer piece of text, gets a textarea to contain it:

```
<%= f.text_area :description %>
```

Similarly, the boolean :can_send_email gets a checkbox:

```
<%= f.check_box :can_send_email %>
```

Most of the numbers, except graduation_year, get plain text_fields, but the date and time are handled differently:

```
<%= f.date_select :birthday %>
...
<%= f.time_select :favoriteTime %>
```

Rails has its own set of controls for handling the always-thorny problem of entering dates and times. They might not be exactly the approach you prefer, but for now, they're the default. Start up the server, and visit *http://localhost:3000/people/new*. As you can see in Figure 6-1, they're easily the most intricate form control Rails generates by default, but using a series of drop-down boxes to specify a date and time isn't most people's idea of fun. Replacing them isn't simple, though.

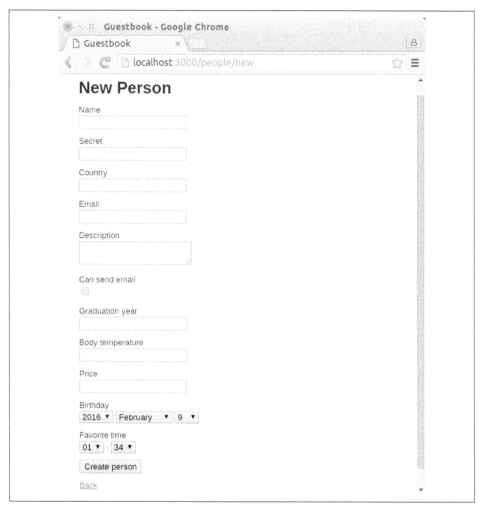

Figure 6-1. Basic form generated by Rails scaffolding

Figure 6-1 is a foundation for a form, but it's also a challenge. Users generally want something that is more exciting than this and more helpful.

 To create especially helpful forms, you'll likely want to use Java-Script or CoffeeScript, as explored in Chapter 18. However, even without client-side programming, there are lots of opportunities for improvement beyond what's shown here.

Form as a Wrapper

The form_for helper method sets up the entire form, creating the HTML form element but also providing context for all of the fields in the form. The form_for
method is a bit sneaky too. Both the *new.html.erb* view and the *edit.html.erb* view use
form_for the same way:

```
<%= form_for(@person) do |f| %>
...
<% end %>
```

However, the generated form element looks very different, depending on what exactly
is in @person. If @person is just an empty object structure, form_for will work on the
assumption that this is to create a new object. If @person actually contains data, however, form_for will assume that its form is editing that object and create a different-
looking form element, plus a hidden field to enable the REST capabilities of Rails.

When given an empty @person object, form_for prepares for a new person:

```
<form class="new_person" id="new_person" action="/people" accept-charset="UTF-8"
method="post">
<input name="utf8" type="hidden" value="✓" /><input type="hidden"
name="authenticity_token" value="zMV6S9pwJzSiQrEm3EvCeyxy26..." />
```

Note that the action goes to people, generically. The class and id reflect a new person, and the method is simply post.

When given an @person object with content, however, form_for switches to editing a
person:

```
<form class="edit_person" id="edit_person_1" action="/people/1"
accept-charset="UTF-8" method="post">
<input name="utf8" type="hidden" value="✓" />
<input type="hidden" name="_method"
value="patch"/> <input type="hidden" name="authenticity_token" value="3cWZ..." />
```

The action now goes to a URL that includes the ID of the object being edited, and the
class and id attributes change values. The method stays at post—but the hidden
input with the name _method almost immediately after the form is there to indicate
that it should really be treated as a patch. (As Chapter 5 noted, browsers don't all support the HTTP verbs PATCH and DELETE, so this input element is designed to help
Rails get around that, using POST but indicating that it should be treated differently.)

The REST capabilities of Rails make form_for seem extra smart, but if you're not creating forms explicitly for a RESTful environment, you need to know a few more
things about this method. form_for understands Rails routing and will choose its
attributes accordingly.

The `form_for` method is part of ActionView's `FormHelper` module, and the way that Rails's RESTful scaffolding uses it relies quite completely on its default behavior. Rails takes `@person` as its one clue to what you want and treats it as a much more complex call to `form_for`. The `form_for` object can take more arguments:

A type

Instead of just listing `@person` and letting `form_for` guess at the structure we intended, this could have specified `:person` as the type, followed by the `@person` object.

A URL

The `:url` named parameter lets you specify a URL for the action attribute. It's unlikely that you'll just point directly to a URL unless it's one outside of your Rails application. More typically, you'll ask Rails to create a URL that points to a controller in your application, something like `:url => { :action => "cele brate" }`.

HTML attributes

The scaffolding populated the `form` element's `method`, `class`, and `id` attributes automatically, but if you wanted to specify an `id` of `special_form`, a `class` of `my_form`, and a `method` of `put`, you could specify:

```
html: { id: 'special_form', class: 'my_form', method: 'put' }
```

Combined into one, somewhat strange call, this could look like:

```
<%= form_for :person, @person, :url => { action: "celebrate" },
 html: { id: 'special_form', class: 'my_form',
 method: 'put' } do |f| %>
```

The `form_for` method also sets up the variable `f`, which provides the context all of the other fields will need to do their work, letting you use a shorter form to call their helper methods. (You don't have to call this variable `f`, but it's a conveniently short, while still memorable enough, name.)

 Rails also supports `:remote` and `:builder` for creating unobtrusive JavaScript hooks and specifying a `FormBuilder`.

Also, Rails has created an `input` element named `authenticity_token`, which is based on the session ID. Rails uses this internally to minimize cross-site request forgery (CSRF) attacks, as discussed in Chapter 20. This only gets used for PUT, POST, and DELETE requests—GET requests should all be safe by design (if, of course, you designed your application so that GET requests just return information—not change it).

 If other developers want to script your Rails application from the outside, they certainly can—that's what the JSON side of REST is for.

Finally, you should know that you can create forms in Rails applications without using `form_for`. You can, of course, create HTML forms by hand. Rails also offers the `form_tag` method for creating forms as well as a set of form field helper methods (also ending in `_tag`) if you want to create forms programmatically, but aren't binding them directly to a model.

Creating Text Fields and Text Areas

The Rails scaffolding included only two kinds of text fields in the body of the form:

```
<%= f.text_field :name %>
...
<%= f.text_area :description %>
```

Creating a field using `text_field` results in a single-line form field, generating HTML like:

```
<input id="person_name" name="person[name]" size="30" type="text" />
```

The `text_area` results aren't much more complicated, though they support rows and columns rather than just a size in characters:

```
<textarea cols="40" id="person_description" name="person[description]"
rows="20"></textarea>
```

Both of these use a convention to come up with an `id` attribute, one that could be handy if you need to apply stylesheets. Both also use a convention to create the `name` attribute, *type[property]*, which you'll need to know if you want to create HTML forms by hand that feed into Rails controllers. The rest is fairly generic—a size of 30 characters for the `text_field` and 40 columns by 20 rows for the `text_area`.

If you want to add more attribute values to your `text_area` or `text_field`, or change the default values, you can just add named parameters. For example, to change the size of the description to 30 columns by 10 rows, you could write:

```
<%= f.text_area :description, cols: 30, rows: 10 %>
```

This will generate:

```
<textarea cols="30" rows="10" name="person[description]"
  id="person_description"></textarea>
```

That same approach works for any attribute you want to add or modify, though you should definitely be cautious about modifying the `name` attribute, which the Rails controller will use to figure out which data maps to which object property.

There are two other options for text fields that Rails supports. You've already seen Rails use the first, hidden fields, for things like the `authenticity_token` field and the `_method` hack, but both of those just kind of happened. If you want to create an explicit hidden field, use the `hidden_field` method, like:

```
<%= f.hidden_field :graduation_year %>
```

The graduation year value will be included in the page but not visibly:

```
<input type="hidden" name="person[graduation_year]"
  id="person_graduation_year" />
```

Since we've hidden the `graduation_year` field, go ahead and comment out or remove the associated label from the line just above the field reference. (Hidden fields are probably not what you want in forms creating new objects, but you may find other uses for them elsewhere in your applications.)

The other type of text field is useful mostly for passwords and related tasks. You can create a password field using the `password_field` method. In this example, it would be good for hiding the `secret` field, as in:

```
<%= f.password_field :secret %>
```

which generates:

```
<input id="person_secret" name="person[secret]" size="30" type="password" />
```

That input field will put up asterisks for each character entered, hiding the value of the field from shoulder-surfing wrongdoers.

You can use `text_area`, `text_field`, and the other form-field-generator methods without the `f` context object at the start of them. If you want to do that, you need to specify an object directly in the call, though, as the first argument. That would look like:

```
<%= text_area :person, :description %>
```

instead of:

```
<%= f.text_area :description %>
```

You can use either version within a `form_for` tag, which is very helpful when you need to mix code from multiple sources.

If you're looking through the Rails API documentation and wondering why what they describe looks a bit different from what you're writing, this may be the cause of the disconnect.

Labels

Rails and its scaffolding support a common feature of HTML that makes forms feel much more professional: labels. When labels are explicitly connected to the fields, clicking on the label shifts focus to the field. It gives users a bigger target to hit and simplifies accessibility as well.

Labels are easy. To make the headline "Name" associate with the field right below it, the scaffolding code uses:

```
<div class="field">
  <%= f.label :name %><br>
  <%= f.text_field :name %>
</div>
```

The generated HTML contains a bit of extra information the browser uses to make the association:

```
<div class="field">
  < label for="person_name">Name </label><br>
  <input type="text" name="person[name]" id="person_name" />
</div>
```

If you click on the word "Name," focus will shift to the field for entering a name just below it.

If you want the label to say something other than the name of the field, just add a string as the second argument, as in:

```
<%= f.label :name, 'Your name' %>
```

This will generate:

```
<label for="person_name">Your Name</label><br>
```

The label method is a nice feature, but at the same time, it seems as if there's a good deal of repetition going on in this code, something you'll see how to fix in Chapter 8.

Creating Checkboxes

Checkboxes are mostly simple. They can be checked or not checked, and Rails maps their contents to a boolean value transparently. This simple request for a checkbox:

```
<%= f.check_box :can_send_email %>
```

yields this bit of HTML:

```
<div class="field">
  <label for="person_can_send_email">Can send email</label><br>
  <input name="person[can_send_email]" type="hidden" value="0" />
  <input type="checkbox" value="1" name="person[can_send_email]"
  id="person_can_send_email" />
</div>
```

That's a little more complicated than expected, though. Why is there a second input element of type hidden? It's another Rails workaround, providing a default value in case the checkbox isn't checked:

> The HTML specification says unchecked check boxes are not successful, and thus web browsers do not send them. Unfortunately this introduces a gotcha: if an Invoice model has a paid flag, and in the form that edits a paid invoice the user unchecks its check box, no paid parameter is sent.... To prevent this the helper generates an auxiliary hidden field before the very check box. The hidden field has the same name and its attributes mimic an unchecked check box.[1]

If the checkbox is checked, that value will go through. If not, the value of the hidden input with the same name will go through.

The check_box method has a few more tricks to offer. As was possible with the text fields, you can specify additional attributes—perhaps class for CSS styling?—with named parameters:

```
<%= f.check_box :can_send_email, class: email %>
```

This will produce a checkbox with a class attribute of email:

```
<div class="field">
  <label for="person_can_send_email">Can send email</label><br>
  <input name="person[can_send_email]" type="hidden" value="0" />
  <input class="email" type="checkbox" value="1" name="person[can_send_email]"
  id="person_can_send_email" />
</div>
```

---

1 From the API doc (*http://bit.ly/2aTtZah*).

You can also specify that the box should be checked if you want, which will override the value that comes into the form from the underlying object. Use this with caution:

```
<%= f.check_box :can_send_email, {class: email, checked: checked} %>
```

Notice that there are now curly braces around the arguments that specify attributes. They aren't strictly necessary, but checkboxes allow for some additional arguments where they will be necessary, even if there is only one attribute given a value. More precisely, you can also specify return values in place of 1 and 0 if you'd like, if your code is set up to support them:

```
<%= f.check_box :can_send_email, {class: 'email'}, "yes", "no" %>
```

This will generate:

```
<div class="field">
  <label for="person_can_send_email">Can send email</label><br>
  <input name="person[can_send_email]" type="hidden" *value="no"* />
  <input class="email"
  type="checkbox" value="yes" name="person[can_send_email]"
  id="person_can_send_email" />
</div>
```

For most of the helper functions that create form components, the options hash is the last argument, and you can just list the named parameters for the attribute values at the end, without the braces around them. However, because checkboxes have the arguments for checked and unchecked values *after* the options hash, you need to specify the attributes in the middle, in curly braces, if you specify values for checked and unchecked. Ruby will give you strange errors if the braces are missing and the values appear at the end. (If you don't specify values for checked and unchecked, you can just include named parameters without the braces as usual.)

 If you're using Rails's built-in boolean type to store data from your checkboxes, don't specify values for checked and unchecked. The default 1 and 0 are correct for this situation, and Rails won't know what to do with other values (unless, of course, you provide code for processing them).

Creating Radio Buttons

Creating radio buttons is a little more complicated and not something that the scaffolding will do for you. Just as when you create radio buttons in HTML, radio buttons in Rails are created as independent objects, united only by a naming convention. Radio buttons are often effectively used for small selection lists, so this example will focus on the country field, offering just a few options.

For the first round, we'll just create some linked buttons by brute force, as shown in Example 6-4.

Example 6-4. Asking Rails to create a specific list of linked radio buttons

```
<fieldset>
  <legend>Country</legend>
    <%= f.radio_button :country, 'USA' %> <%= f.label "person_country_usa",
    "USA" %><br>
    <%= f.radio_button :country, 'Canada' %> <%= f.label "person_country_canada",
    "Canada" %><br>
    <%= f.radio_button :country, 'Mexico' %> <%= f.label "person_country_mexico",
    "Mexico" %><br>
</fieldset>
```

This will generate the result shown in Figure 6-2.

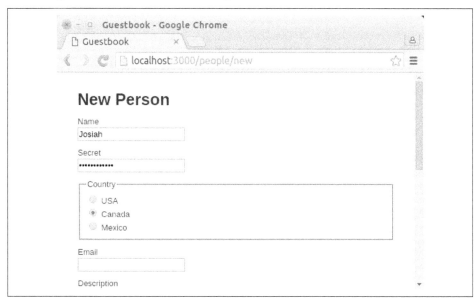

Figure 6-2. Simple radio buttons added to a Rails-based form

The HTML this created is pretty simple:

```
<fieldset>
  <legend>Country</legend>
  <input id="person_country_usa" name="person[country]" type="radio"
value="USA" />
  <label for="person_country_usa">USA</label><br>
  <input id="person_country_canada" name="person[country]" type="radio"
  value="Canada" />
  <label for="person_country_canada">Canada</label><br>
  <input id="person_country_mexico" name="person[country]" type="radio"
  value="Mexico" />
  <label for="person_country_mexico">Mexico</label><br>
</fieldset>
```

If the underlying :country object had had a value that matched any of these, Rails would have added a checked="checked" attribute to the input element. Since it's a new object, none of these is checked by default and users have to check one themselves.

You probably won't always want to specify each of the buttons and its label by hand in the view template. Creating a set of radio buttons from a hash isn't difficult and makes it easier for a controller to specify what should appear in a view. Example 6-5 creates a hash (this should normally come from the controller), sorts it, and then uses it to create a set of four radio buttons.

Example 6-5. Creating a sorted set of linked radio buttons from a hash

```
<% nations = { 'United States of America' => 'USA', 'Canada' => 'Canada',
  'Mexico' => 'Mexico', 'United Kingdom' => 'UK' }%>

<fieldset>
  <legend>Country</legend>
  <% list = nations.sort
  list.each do |x| %>
    <%= f.radio_button :country, x[1] %>
    <label for="<%= ("person_country_" + x[1].downcase) %>">
    <%= x[0] %></label><br>
  <% end %>
</fieldset>
```

The first line creates a nations hash. The long names act as keys to shortened country names as values. Why? Well, if you think about how radio buttons work, human users are selecting the keys (the long names) that lead to the values (the short names) that we actually send to the computer. (This will also make it much easier to change the radio buttons into a selection list later.)

Within the area that previously listed radio buttons explicitly, there is Ruby code that sorts the hash into an array, using sort. Then list.each loops over the array, running once for each object in the array. In this case, because the hash had two values, the x array that comes out of the loop contains the key, indexed at 0, and the value, indexed at 1. The next line puts the key, x[0], into the value of the radio button and uses the longer name, x[1], for the label, using the f.radio_button method to create the actual markup.

Figure 6-3 shows the resulting radio buttons. The generated HTML underneath them looks like:

```
    <fieldset>
      <legend>Country</legend>
        <input type="radio" value="Canada" name="person[country]"
        id="person_country_canada" />
          <label for="person_country_canada"> Canada</label><br>
```

```
<input type="radio" value="Mexico" name="person[country]"
id="person_country_mexico" />
  <label for="person_country_mexico"> Mexico</label><br>
<input type="radio" value="UK" name="person[country]"
id="person_country_uk" />
  <label for="person_country_uk"> United Kingdom</label><br>
<input type="radio" value="USA" name="person[country]"
id="person_country_usa" />
  <label for="person_country_usa"> United States of America</label><br>
</fieldset>
```

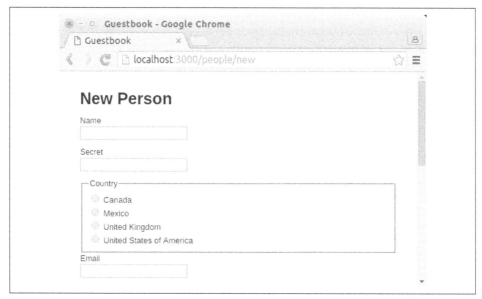

Figure 6-3. Radio buttons generated from a sorted hash

Of course, you won't usually generate radio buttons by declaring a hash explicitly. Radio buttons and selection lists are both typically used in Rails to connect one data model to another. Chapter 9 will get into greater detail about how multiple models work.

Creating Selection Lists

Selection lists are, in many ways, like radio buttons on a larger scale. Rather than filling a screen with radio buttons, a list lets you hide the options except during that critical time when you're actually making a selection. Showing radio buttons for over 190 countries would take up a huge amount of screen real estate. Selection lists offer a much more compact but still convenient way for users to make choices.

Rails has a number of helper methods for creating selection lists, but the simplest place to start is the select method. In its most basic form, select takes two arguments: the attribute that populates it and a set of choices. Choices can be represented in a number of different ways, from a simple array of strings to a hash or other more complex set of values.

Using an array of strings, the call to create a selection list might look like:

```
<%= f.label :country %><br>
<%= f.select :country, [ ['Canada', 'Canada'],
                         ['Mexico', 'Mexico'],
                         ['United Kingdom', 'UK'],
                         ['United States of America', 'USA'] ]%>
```

This uses a two-dimensional array, in which the display values come first, and the values that go to the server come second. Under the HTML result shown in Figure 6-4, this generates:

```
<p>
  <label for="person_country">Country</label><br>
  <select name="person[country]" id="person_country">
  <option value="Canada">Canada</option>
  <option value="Mexico">Mexico</option>
  <option value="UK">United Kingdom</option>
  <option value="USA">United States of America</option></select>
</p>
```

Figure 6-4. A selection list created from an array of strings

You can also set a default choice for your selections by adding a `selected` named parameter:

```
<%= f.select :country, [ ['Canada', 'Canada'],
  ['Mexico', 'Mexico'],
  ['United Kingdom', 'UK'],
  ['United States of America', 'USA'] ],
  :selected => 'USA'%>
```

This generates the same markup, except that the `option` element for USA now looks like:

```
<option selected="selected" value="USA">
United States of America</option></select>
```

(Rails normally sets :selected to the current value of the field.) You can also use select with a hash, instead of specifying the array. Example 6-6 shows how this looks much like it did for the radio buttons in Example 6-5.

Example 6-6. Creating a sorted selection list from a hash

```
<% nations = { 'United States of America' => 'USA', 'Canada' => 'Canada',
                'Mexico' => 'Mexico', 'United Kingdom' => 'UK' }%>
<p>
  <%= f.label :country %><br>
  <% list = nations.sort %>
  <%= f.select :country, list %>
</p>
```

Rails also offers a number of specific selection fields, including one for time zones (time_zone_select). Additionally, if you decide that you want to get really fancy, you can create multilevel selection lists with option_groups_from_collec tion_for_select. You can also create selection lists that let users choose multiple values by setting the :multiple option to true.

Dates and Times

Rails also provides support for basic date and time entry, as was shown in the form generated by the scaffolding. The scaffolding started out with:

```
<div class="field">
  <%= f.label :birthday %><br>
  <%= f.date_select :birthday %>
</div>
<div class="field">
  <%= f.label :favorite_time %><br>
  <%= f.time_select :favorite_time %>
</div>
```

And these generated the neat-looking but very inconvenient selection lists shown in Figure 6-5.

Figure 6-5. The Rails default approach of using selection lists for dates and times

Besides the date_select and datetime_select methods, Rails also offers time_select and has a variety of helper methods for individual pieces of dates and times. Rails offers some options that can make these interfaces more customizable, but picking days off a 31-item selection list or minutes off a 60-item list is pretty much always going to be a less-than-fun user experience. You'll probably want to turn to more attractive date and time interfaces from JQuery libraries or revert to simple text boxes, but in case you have an application where you want to use these methods, the options for them include:

:start_year

> By default, Rails sets the start year to five years before the current date. You can specify an earlier (or later) date if you need to, by specifying :start_year => *value*.

:end_year

> Rails also sets the end year to five years after the current date. Again, you can specify a later (or earlier) date by specifying end_year: *value*.

:use_month_numbers

> If you'd prefer to have the months listed by numbers rather than by names, set use_month_numbers: true.

:discard_day

> Some date applications don't need days. You can set discard_day: true to simply not include the day field. You can also do the same with :discard_month or :discard_year, and for times and datetimes, you can do the same with :discard_hour, :discard_minute, and :discard_seconds.

:disabled

> Setting disabled: true tells Rails to show the date, but doesn't allow change. The values will appear in gray. (It works for other fields as well.)

`:include_blank`

Setting `include_blank: true` tells Rails to include a blank choice at the top of each selection list, so users don't have to specify every single component of a date.

`:include_seconds`

Specifying `include_seconds: true` adds a field for seconds to times and date-times.

`:order`

Using the `order` option lets you specify the sequence for the different components of the date or time. You list the components as an array, such as `order: [:month, :day, :year]`.

Creating Helper Methods

So far, this chapter has shown you how to use a number of the helper methods that come with Rails. You can also create your own helper methods. There are lots of good reasons to do so:

Less repetition

You can come closer to the Rails DRY (Don't Repeat Yourself) ideal if you can combine multiple pieces into a single invocation.

More readable code

You can see more obviously which pieces of your code are actually doing the same work when they call the same method, instead of perpetually reinventing the wheel.

More consistency

The same code used in multiple places will rarely stay identical.

Sharing across views

Multiple views within an application can reference the same helper methods.

Creating helper methods might not be your very first priority in creating an application, but once you have a basic idea of what you want to create in your views, it's a good idea to start assembling common tasks into helper methods.

Within the application directory structure, helper methods go into the *app/helpers* directory. At this point, the guestbook application will have two files there: *application_helper.rb* and *people_helper.rb*.

The first helper method will take the Example 6-5 code for generating radio buttons from a hash. Example 6-7 shows what's left when this is reduced to a call to the but tons helper method.

Example 6-7. Creating a sorted set of linked radio buttons from a hash with a helper method

```
<% nations = { 'United States of America' => 'USA',
'Canada' => 'Canada', 'Mexico' =>
'Mexico', 'United Kingdom' => 'UK' }%>

<%= buttons(:person, :country, nations) %>
```

The buttons method is in the *people_helper.rb* file, the contents of which are shown in Example 6-8.

Example 6-8. A helper method for creating a sorted set of linked radio buttons from a hash

```
1    module PeopleHelper
2
3      def buttons(model_name, target_property,button_source)
4          html=''
5          list = button_source.sort
6          html << '<fieldset><legend>Country</legend>'
7          list.each do |x|
8            html << radio_button(model_name, target_property, x[1])
9            html << (x[0])
10           html << '<br>'
11         end
12         html << '</fieldset>'
13         return html.html_safe
14     end
15
16   end
```

There's a lot going on in the `buttons` method. It's contained by the `PeopleHelper` module, which was originally empty in the version created by the scaffolding. Lines 2 through 15 are all new additions. This version of `buttons`, defined starting on line 3, looks more like the older version of the helper functions, taking a model name as its first argument, then the targeted property, and then the source from which the radio buttons will be created.

Because the helper function isn't in the view, there isn't any ERb markup here. Instead, the helper function builds a string, starting in line 4. Often, the first declaration of the string includes the first tag, but as the radio buttons don't have a containing element, this starts with the empty string. Line 5 adds the `legend` element. Lines 5 and 6 are the same logic for sorting the hash as was used in the original code from Example 6-4, but the contents of the loop, in lines 8 to 10, are very different.

Lines 8 through 10 all append something to the `html` variable, using the `<<` operator. Line 8 appends radio button markup created through Rails's `radio_button` helper.

Line 9 appends the text the user will see, and line 10 appends a `<br />` tag, putting a line break between the buttons. Rails developers often avoid mixing explicit markup with code, preferring to use `content_tag` or other helper methods—but you can use markup here if you think it's appropriate.

Line 12 just closes the loop over the hash, but line 13 is a bit unusual. Explicit return statements aren't necessary in Ruby methods unless you're returning multiple results or want to break at an unexpected time. Ruby will assume that the last variable you touched is the return value. However, using `return` is a good way to avoid surprises, and if you feel like writing briefer code, you can leave off `return` and just write `html` there. The `.htmlsafe` marks the returned string as OK for Rails to include without escaping it.

 By using `.htmlsafe` (or the `raw` method), you're taking complete responsibility for ensuring that the content of that string isn't going to cause problems. In this case, where all of the content came from the application itself, it is safe—but be *very* careful about flagging things that do include user-provided content.

If you leave off line 13 completely, however, you'll have an unpleasant surprise, shown in Figure 6-6. It looks like `html` was the last variable touched in line 9, but the `each` loop block, which closes in line 10, is actually considered the last thing touched. The value of the block is the underlying array, which shows up to yield this unfortunate result.

```
Country
[["Canada", "Canada"], ["Mexico", "Mexico"], ["United Kingdom", "UK"], ["United States of America", "USA"]]
```

Figure 6-6. Instead of radio buttons, an all-too-visible array

A more sophisticated helper method, shown in Example 6-9, could check the list of items to select from, and decide whether to represent it as radio buttons or a list, depending on length. It adds an extra `if` statement, highlighted in the code. This may or may not be a level of smarts you want to build into your helper methods, but it certainly demonstrates how custom helper methods can assemble just a little more logic for your views.

Example 6-9. A helper method that chooses between radio buttons and selection lists

```
module PeopleHelper
  def button_select(model_name, target_property, button_source)
    html=' '
    list = button_source.sort
    if list.length < 4
```

```
    html << '<fieldset><legend>Country</legend>'
    list.each {|x|
      html << radio_button(model_name, target_property, x[1])
      html << (x[0])
      html << '<br>'
    }
    html << '</fieldset>'
  else
    html << ' <label for="person_country">Country</label><br>'
    html << select(model_name, target_property, list)
  end
  return html.html_safe
 end
end
```

You'll need to change the call from buttons to button_select in *form.html.erb*, too:

```
<% nations = { United States of America => USA, Canada => Canada,
Mexico => Mexico, United Kingdom => UK }%>

<%= button_select(:person, :country, nations) %>
```

Test Your Knowledge

Quiz

1. How many properties and data types can you specify in a call to rails generate scaffold?

2. Where does Rails actually specify the data types for properties?

3. What is the difference between the form_for method and the form_tag method explored earlier?

4. How do you add HTML attributes to the HTML generated by the Rails helper methods?

5. Why does the check_box helper create an extra hidden form field?

6. How do you specify which option in a selection box is the default?

7. Where should you put helper methods you create?

8. Why would you use a partial?

Answers

1. As many as your operating system will let you put on a single command line. They get inconvenient quickly—if you want to add a huge number, you may want

to edit that command line in a text editor and make sure it's right before putting it in.

2. The only place that the data types are specified *in Rails* is in the migrations. Once the migrations build the database, Rails gets its understanding of the data types from the database. (This is very different from Java development, for example.)

3. The `form_for` method creates an entire environment with context based on an `ActiveRecord` class that other helper methods can use to create their own fields within the form. The `form_tag` method is mostly about wrapping the form in an appropriate form tag. The helpers called inside of `form_tag` are on their own.

4. You can generate HTML attributes using named parameters put inside of a parameter named `:html`, such as `html: { id: person_form, class: generic_form }` or you can just pass the parameters directly, without wrapping them in the `:html => { … }`.

5. The `input` element with a `hidden` type is there to ensure that a value is returned to the Rails application if the checkbox isn't checked.

6. You specify a default value with the `:selected` named parameter.

7. Helper methods go in the *app/helpers* directory. Helpers that should be available across the entire application go into *application_helper.rb*, while helpers that apply to a specific view go into files named *viewname_helper.rb*.

8. Partials let you put code that would otherwise repeat across your application into a single convenient location. They're a perfect example of Rails's support for its "Don't Repeat Yourself" mantra.

## CHAPTER 7

Strengthening Models with Validation

The logic of validation allows us to move between the two limits
of dogmatism and skepticism.
    —Paul Ricoeur

At this point, you have most of the ingredients needed to create simple web applications in Rails, provided you're willing to stick to a single database table. There's one large problem remaining: users (and programs connecting through web services) don't always put in the data you want them to put in. Making your application work reliably requires checking information as it comes in and interacting with users so that they know how to get it right.

As you'll see throughout this chapter, Rails expects all data validation to happen in the model layer and provides tools that make it easy to do there. If you find yourself putting data-checking code into the views or the controllers, pause for a moment—you're quite likely doing something wrong.

The one probable exception is if you're adding warnings for users working in your forms via JavaScript, avoiding a round trip to the server, but you should never rely on those to limit your data to the correct types. All that work should do is give users more information more rapidly.

Without Validation

You might think, since the examples in Chapter 6 defined data types, that Rails will be doing some basic content checking—ensuring that numeric data actually includes numbers, for example.

Nope. Rails and the Rails scaffolding give you places where you can add validation code, but absolutely none of it is built in. The easiest way to see what happens is to try putting in bad data, as shown in Figure 7-1.

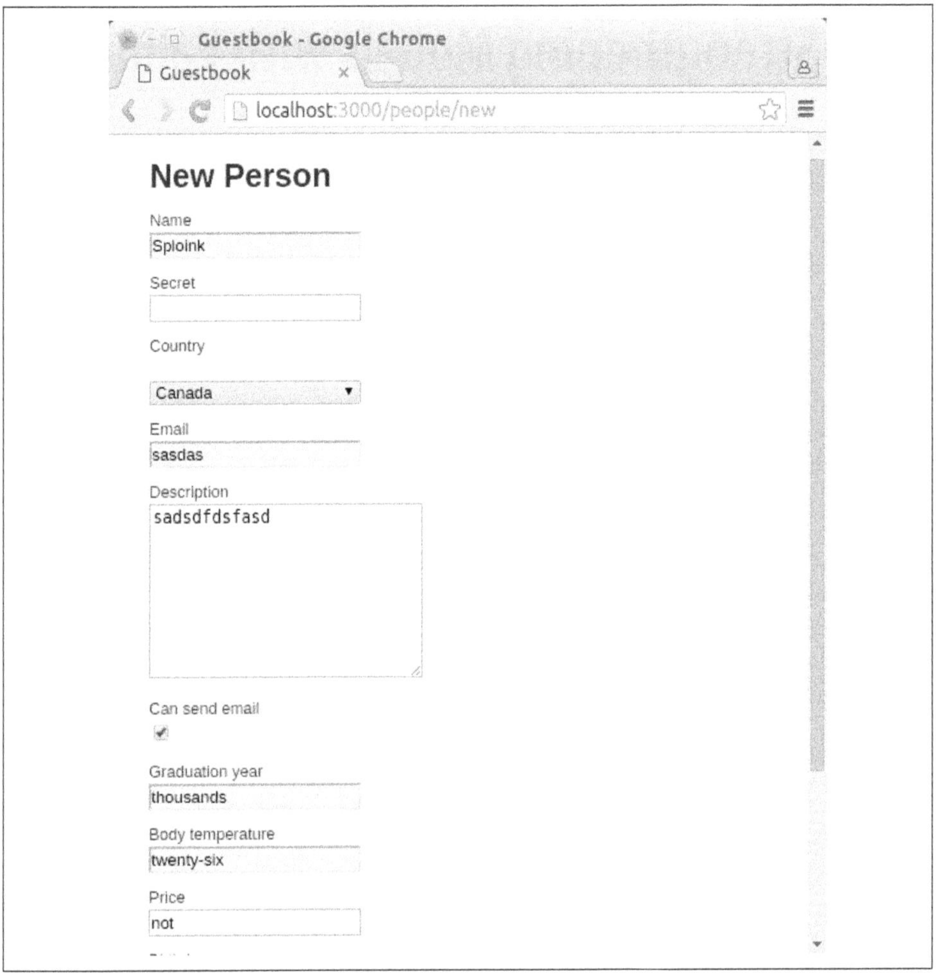

Figure 7-1. Entering bad data into a form

The text fields might not be the data you want, but at least they're text. The boolean value and the dates are constrained to a few choices by the interface design already—you can't choose bad data. The form control for Graduation won't let you keep text in it, though it doesn't understand "thousands," either. However, "twenty-six," and "not" aren't numbers. But Rails doesn't care—it accepts those strings and converts them to a number: 0 (zero), as shown in Figure 7-2.

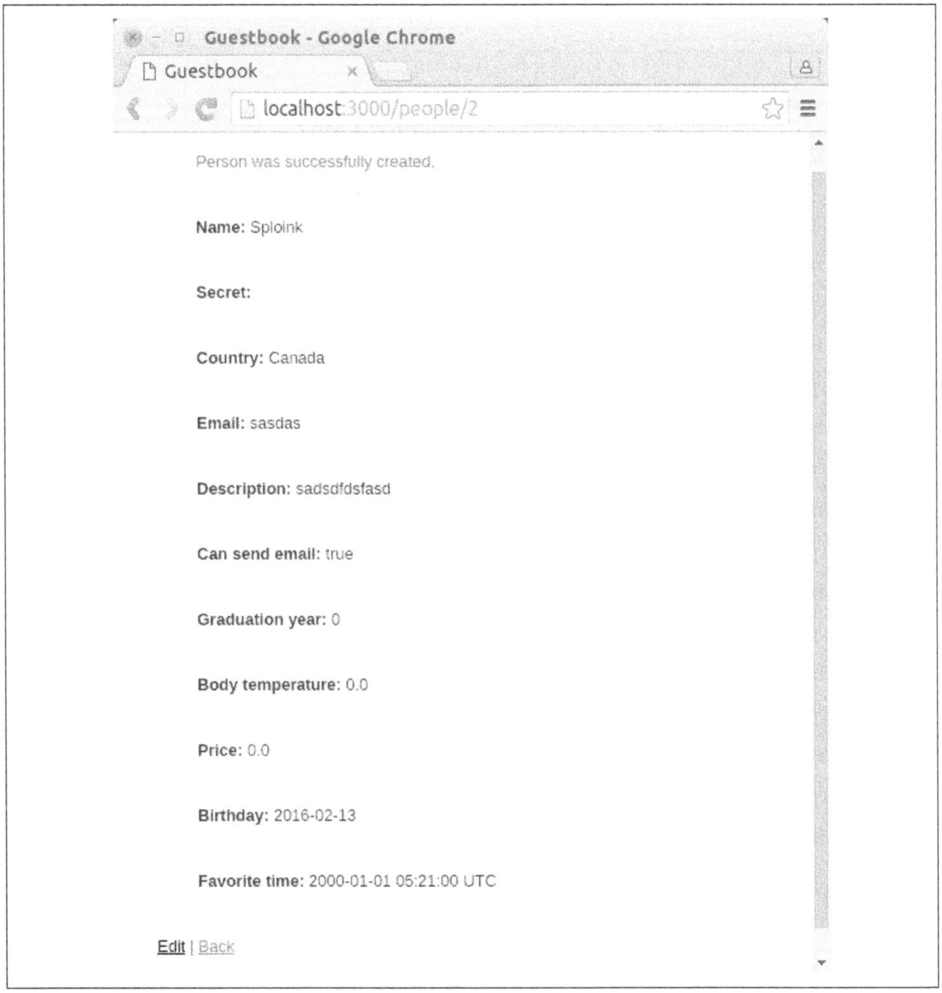

Figure 7-2. Nonnumeric data converted to zeros in a "successful" creation

You can see what happened by looking at the data that scrolled by in the `rails server` window when the request went in. You don't need a detailed understanding of SQL to find the problem—looking at the data going in will show it. Example 7-1 lists the data going into the Rails app and then shows the SQL INSERT with the data moving out from the Rails app to the database.

Example 7-1. Rails console when data is inserted into the database

```
Started POST "/people" for 127.0.0.1 at 2012-02-20 12:18:15 -0500
Processing by PeopleController#create as HTML
  Parameters: {"utf8"=>"✓",
"authenticity_token"=>"A/Z8vCOlXzYSDJarLutojHjzpUIrhcQ5mhGCLgIFL4w=",
```

```
"person"=>{"name"=>"Sploink", "secret"=>"", "country"=>"Canada",
"email"=>"sasdas",
"description"=>"true", "can_send_email"=>"1", "graduation_year"=>"",
"body_temperature"=>"twenty-six",
"price"=>"not", "birthday(1i)"=>"2012", "birthday(2i)"=>"2",
"birthday(3i)"=>"20",
("person"=>{"name"...)
"favorite_time(1i)"=>"2012", "favorite_time(2i)"=>"2",
"favorite_time(3i)"=>"20",
"favorite_time(4i)"=>"17", "favorite_time(5i)"=>"16"},
"commit"=>"Create Person"}
   (0.1ms)  begin transaction
  SQL (53.1ms)  INSERT INTO "people" ("birthday", "body_temperature",
  "can_send_email",
"country", "created_at", "description", "email", "favorite_time",
"graduation_year",
"name", "price", "secret",
 "updated_at") VALUES (?, ?, ?, ?, ?, ?, ?, ?, ?, ?, ?, ?, ?)
[["birthday", Mon, 20 Feb 2012],
["body_temperature", 0.0], (["body_temperature"...]) ,
["can_send_email", true], ["country", "Canada"],
["created_at", Mon, 20 Feb 2012 17:18:16 UTC +00:00],
["description", "true"],
 ["email", "sasdas"], ["favorite_time", Mon,
20 Feb 2012 17:16:00 UTC +00:00], ["graduation_year", nil], (["graduation...]),
["name", "Sploink"], ["price",
#BigDecimal:102e79d68,0.0,9(9)>], (["price"...]) , ["secret", ""],
["updated_at", Mon, 20 Feb 2012 17:18:16 UTC +00:00]]
   (4.8ms)  commit transaction
Redirected to http://localhost:3000/people/1
Completed 302 Found in 79ms (ActiveRecord: 58.0ms)
```

The parameters are complicated by the many pieces of incoming dates that use a
naming convention to identify their parts, but it's clear that "twenty-six" and "not"
went into the Rails application. In the SQL command going to the database, both
price and body_temperature went in as 0.0.

Between receiving the data and sending it to the database, Rails converted those values to numbers. The strings became zero (0.0), since they weren't actually numeric.
Fixing this problem will require spending some time in the model, developing barri-
ers that check incoming data and stop it if the data doesn't match your application's
requirements.

The Original Model

The *person.rb* file has been lurking in the *models* directory since the application was
created. You might expect it to contain a list of fields for each person, defining data
types and such. Instead, it looks like Example 7-2.

Example 7-2. The foundation of all Rails models

```
class Person < ApplicationRecord
end
```

That's pretty barren! The connections between Rails and the database are running purely on naming conventions. The Rails migration set up the database, as Example 6-1 demonstrated, and that's where all the data type information went. Perhaps it's even disturbingly quiet, as most object-oriented programming includes some specific information about object properties in the class definition that creates the object.

The minimalist approach Rails takes to model classes, however, lets you focus on the pieces you need to contribute to the model. Having the definitions elsewhere may mean that you sometimes have to look around to figure out what you're working on —especially if you're modifying code someone else wrote—but it also makes a clean slate truly clean.

The Power of Declarative Validation

You could write code that tests each property's value as it arrives, and there may be times when you need to do that, but Rails offers a simpler approach that works for the vast majority of cases: *declarative validation.* (You can find the complete example shown here in *ch07/guestbook05.*)

Instead of checking to see if a value is present, for instance, you can just write:

```
# the name is mandatory
validates_presence_of :name
```

The `validates_presence_of` declaration activates the internal Rails validation tools, which can automatically block the addition of a record that's missing a name and report an error to the user, as shown in Figure 7-3.

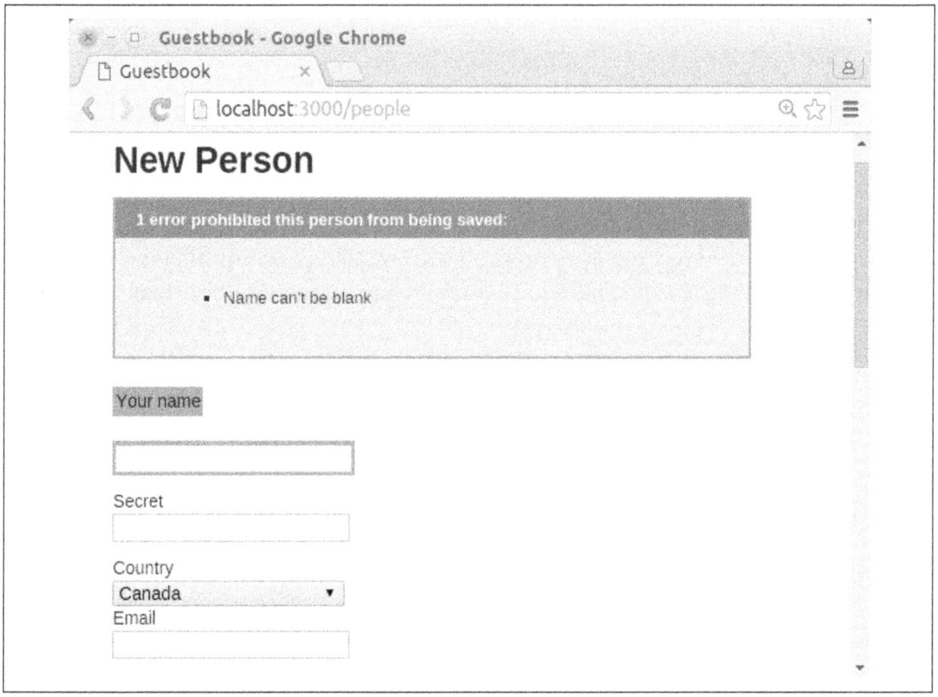

Figure 7-3. Failing a simple validation

How did the model reach through the controller, all the way into the view, and make that happen? It's worth walking back through once to trace the path Rails took. Example 7-3 shows the HTML that generated those messages.

Example 7-3. Model errors reported in HTML from the view

```
<form class="new_person" id="new_person" action="/people" accept-charset="UTF-8"
method="post"><input name="utf8" type="hidden" value="✓" /><input type="hidden"
name="authenticity_token" value="QkN0ldeGb9D0TA8W9=" />
  <div id="error_explanation">
    <h2>1 error prohibited this person from being saved:</h2>

  <ul>
    <li>Name can't be blank</li>
  </ul>
</div>

  <div class="field">
  <div class="field_with_errors"><label for="person_name">Name</label></div><br>
  <div class="field_with_errors"><input type="text" value="" name="person[name]"
id="person_name" /></div>
  </div>
```

```
<div class="field"> <label for="person_secret">Secret</label><br>
<input type="text" value="" name="person[secret]" id="person_secret" /> </div>
```

The first piece, the `error_explanation` div, came from this code in the view (or partial):

```
<% if person.errors.any? %>
  <div id="error_explanation">
    <h2><%= pluralize(person.errors.count, "error") %> prohibited this person
    from being saved:</h2>

    <ul>
    <% person.errors.full_messages.each do |message| %>
      <li><%= message %></li>
    <% end %>
    </ul>
  </div>
<% end %>
```

Rails inserted the `fieldWithErrors` div around the name field through the usual field creation method in the view (or partial):

```
<%= f.text_field :name %>
```

This kind of automatic error presentation is another reason it's a good idea to use the built-in Rails methods for creating fields, rather than handcoding your own HTML in them.

The controller also took part in the action. If you look back at the `PeopleControl ler`'s `create` method, you'll see:

```
# POST /people
# POST /people.json
def create
  @person = Person.new(person_params)

  respond_to do |format|
    if @person.save
      format.html { redirect_to @person, notice: Person was successfully
      created. }
      format.json { render :show, status: :created, location: @person }
    else
      *format.html { render :new }
      *format.json { render json: @person.errors, status:
      :unprocessable_entity }
    end
  end
end
```

If the controller has an error, `@person.save` will fail, returning `false`. If the request is for HTML, the controller will render a new copy of the form for creating a new person entry. All of the error information will pass through to that view automatically. If it is a JSON request, it will also report back the errors.

 One major benefit of putting validation in the model is that your validation will apply to any effort to change your data—whether it came from users over the Web, from programs accessing your application through REST-based web services, or from something you built into the program yourself.

Now that we've seen how the errors flow out from the model to the view, it's time to examine how to set up the validation declarations that make it all happen.

Managing Secrets

While we'd like visitors to enter their names, it's usually best not to be too picky about names because they come in so many varieties. On the other hand, the `:secret` field is rife with opportunities for demanding expectations. Along the way, this example will demonstrate how you can use multiple validations on the same field in sequence.

Customizing the Message

The `:secret` field needs to be present. Sometimes, though, it's worth telling a user why a particular mistake matters rather than just insisting, "*field_name* can't be blank." Rails makes that easy to do by letting you specify a `message:` to go with your validation. If the validation fails, the user sees the `:message`. The following code adds a message to the test for `:secret`'s presence:

```
# secret is also mandatory, but let's alter the default Rails message to be
# more friendly
  validates_presence_of :secret,
    message: "must be provided so we can recognize you in the future"
```

If the user leaves the `:secret` field blank, he'll see a custom error message as shown in Figure 7-4.

Even if the user provides a `:secret`, though, not all `:secrets` are created equal. Another set of validations will test the actual content of `:secret`, as shown here:

```
# ensure secret has enough letters, but not too many
  validates_length_of :secret, in: 6..24

# ensure secret contains at least one number
  validates_format_of :secret, with: /[0-9]/,
    message: "must contain at least one number"

# ensure secret contains at least one upper case
  validates_format_of :secret, with: /[A-Z]/,
```

```
    message: "must contain at least one upper case character"

# ensure secret contains at least one lower case
  validates_format_of :secret, with: /[a-z]/,
    message: "must contain at least one lower case character"
```

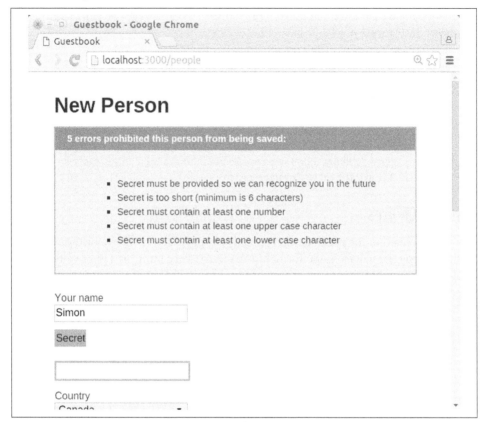

Figure 7-4. A custom error message sent to the user

The first of these validations tests the length of :secret, making sure that it lies between a 6-character minimum and a 24-character maximum:

```
validates_length_of :secret, in: 6..24
```

Rails is smart enough that if a user enters a secret that's too short, it will report back that:

```
Secret is too short (minimum is 6 characters)
```

And it will do the same for the maximum. There probably isn't any need to customize the :message. However, the next three validations use the power of regular expressions. *Regular expressions*, or *regexes*, are compact but powerful patterns that Rails will test against the value of `:secret`. If the testing of `:secret` against the regular expression specified in `:with` returns `true`, then the validation passes and all is well. If it fails the test, then the specified message will go out to the user.

All of these tests will be performed in sequence, and the user will see an error message reflecting all the tests that failed. For example, a blank `:secret` will yield the full set shown in Figure 7-4.

 Regular expressions are a complex subject you can study to nearly infinite depth. Appendix C can get you started. Mike Fitzgerald's *Introducing Regular Expressions* (O'Reilly, 2012) is a much deeper but still gentle introduction. Jeffrey Friedl's *Mastering Regular Expressions* (O'Reilly, 2006) is pretty much the classic overview of the field, but Tony Stubblebine's *Regular Expression Pocket Reference* (O'Reilly, 2007) is a concise guide to the capabilities and syntax in different environments.

Limiting Choices

The form created in the previous chapter only supported four values for the `:country` field. Limiting the values in the form, however, isn't very limiting. Other values could come in from other forms or, more simply, from a JSON request using the REST interface. If we want to limit the values it can have, the data model is the place to do that:

```
# the country field is a controlled vocabulary: we must check that
# its value is within our allowed options
  validates_inclusion_of :country, in: ['Canada', 'Mexico', 'UK', 'USA'],
    message: "must be one of Canada, Mexico, UK or USA"
```

The `validates_inclusion_of` method requires an `in:` parameter that lists the possible choices as an array, and in this case `message:` specifies what the user will see if it fails. There's also a `validates_exclusion_of` method that's very similar, but flunks if the value provided matches one of the specified values.

Testing Format with Regular Expressions

Regular expressions are useful for ensuring that `:secret` contained certain patterns, but sometimes you want to make sure that a field actually matches a pattern. The `:email` field is a good candidate for this, even though the simple regular expressions used to check email addresses are hard to read if you haven't spent a whole lot of time with regular expressions:

```
# email should read like an email address; this check isn't exhaustive,
# but it's a good start
  validates_format_of :email,
```

```
with: /\A([^@\s]+)@((?:[-a-z0-9]+\.)+[a-z]{2,})\Z/i,
  message: "doesn't look like a proper email address"
```

The `validates_format_of` method takes a field to check and a regular expression for the `:with` parameter. You'll want to provide a `:message` parameter since Rails won't know how to turn the regular expression into meaningful explanations for ordinary web application users.

Seen It All Before

Validation isn't always about the specific content of a field coming in. Sometimes it's about how incoming data compares to existing data. The simplest and probably most common comparison is that for uniqueness. You don't want multiple users to have the same username or multiple objects to have the same supposedly unique identifier, for example.

You could write some code that checks all of the entries in your existing database to make sure that the new entry is unique, but Rails is happy to do that for you:

```
# how do we recognize the same person coming back? by their email address
# so we want to ensure the same person only signs in once
  validates_uniqueness_of :email, case_sensitive: false,
    message: "has already been entered, you can't sign in twice"
```

The `case_sensitive:` property lets you specify whether textual values should be compared so that differences in case matter. The default value is `true`, but as email addresses are not case-sensitive, `false` is a better option here. The `message:` is useful for explaining just what happened.

By default, `validates_uniqueness_of` checks `:email` only against the other values in the same database column. If you wanted to ensure that data was unique across multiple columns, the `:scope` property would let you do that. For instance, to check `:email` against `:email` plus `:name` against `:name` and `:secret` against `:secret`, you could write:

```
validates_uniqueness_of :email, case_sensitive: false,
    scope: [:name, :secret],
    message: "has already been entered, you can't sign in twice"
```

Using `:scope` makes more sense in more complicated applications with multiple unique identifiers. This kind of combining of multiple fields into a single scope is similar to the concept of a compound key in many databases.

Numbers Only

While many fields accept any text the user wants to provide, applications tend to prefer 4.1 to "four and one-tenth" for numeric fields. By default, as Figure 7-2 showed, Rails doesn't check that only numeric data goes into numeric fields. When the user puts text data into the database, the type conversion will yield a zero—probably not what's appropriate most of the time. Of course, though, Rails lets you check this easily, along with a lot of details that you may need to support your particular use of numbers. The :graduation_year field, for example, comes with a lot of constraints as well as some openness. That's easy to check using validates_numericality_of:

```
# Graduation year must be numeric, and within sensible bounds.
# However, the person may not have graduated, so we allow a
# nil value too. Finally, it must be a whole number (integer).
  validates_numericality_of :graduation_year, allow_nil: true,
     greater_than: 1920, less_than_or_equal_to: Time.now.year,
     only_integer: true
```

The first parameter here actually relaxes constraints. Specifying allow_nil: => true allows the value to stay blank. Only nonblank values will have their value checked.

 allow_nil: is available for all of the validates methods. You'll want to use it wherever you don't mean to place demands on users.

The next two parameters are a verbose way of saying > and <=. A set of parameters for testing numbers is offered by the validates_numericality_of method:

equal_to
    Tests that the value being validated is equal to the value provided in the parameter.

even
    Tests that the value is an even number (dividing by 2 yields no remainder).

greater_than
    Tests that the value being validated is greater than the value provided in the parameter.

greater_than_or_equal_to
    Tests that the value being validated is greater than or equal to the value provided in the parameter.

less_than
    Tests that the value being validated is less than the value provided in the parameter.

less_than_or_equal_to
    Tests that the value being validated is less than or equal to the value provided in the parameter.

odd
   Tests that the value is an odd number (dividing by 2 yields a remainder of 1).

`only_integer`
   Tests that the value being validated is an integer, with no fractional part.

The named parameters have values. For the methods that make comparisons, the value is the argument against which the incoming value will be compared. These can be simple values or method calls, such as `:less_than_or_equal_to =>` `Time.now.year`. For the boolean tests (`even`, `odd`, `only_integer`), the value specifies whether or not the test counts for validation, and the default value for all of them is `false`.

The next two fields, `:body_temperature` and `:price`, are also numbers, with relatively simple validations:

```
# Body temperature doesn't have to be a whole number, but we ought to
# constrain possible values. We assume our users aren't in cryostasis.
validates_numericality_of :body_temperature, allow_nil: true,
  greater_than_or_equal_to: 60,
  less_than_or_equal_to: 130, only_integer: false

validates_numericality_of :price, allow_nil: true,
  only_integer: false
```

A Place on the Calendar

You could test date components individually, but more typically, you'll want to test whether or not the date falls within a given range. Rails makes this easy with the `vali` `dates_inclusion_of` method, already examined previously, and its inverse, `validates_exclusion_of`:

```
# Restrict birthday to reasonable values, i.e., not in the future and not
# before 1900
validates_inclusion_of :birthday,
  in: Date.civil(1900, 1, 1) .. Date.today,
  message: "must be between January 1st, 1900 and today"
```

The `:in` parameter actually takes a list of possible values (an enumerable object, technically), and in this case, the definition creates a list of values between January 1, 1900 (thanks to the `Date.civil` method), and today's date (thanks to the `Date.today` method).

Testing for Presence

The `allow_nil:` parameter noted earlier lets you say that things don't need to be present, but there are also times when the *only* validation you want to perform is to make certain that a given field contains a value. In this case, `validates_presence_of` is extremely convenient:

```
# Finally, we just say that favorite time is mandatory.
# While the view only allows you to post valid times, remember
# that models can be created in other ways, such as from code
# or web service calls, so it's not safe to make assumptions
# based on the form.
validates_presence_of :favorite_time
```

As the comment reminds you, while an HTML form can make some explicit demands of users, you should avoid writing code that assumes that all data will be coming in through the form. With REST-based approaches, a lot of your objects may arrive or be changed through JSON (or maybe XML, if you set that up) sent over HTTP.

Beyond Simple Declarations

The tests just shown are valuable but also limited. They test a single value against a limited set of possibilities and don't allow interactions among different values. While Rails makes it easy to do easy things, it fortunately also makes it fairly easy to do more complicated things. (You can find these more complicated examples in *ch07/ guestbook06*.)

Test It Only If

One of the simplest tests is to require a validation if, and only if, another condition is met. The `:if` parameter, available on every test, lets you define those conditions. (There's a corresponding `:unless` parameter that works similarly but in the opposite direction.) The easiest way to use `:if` is to point it at a method that returns a boolean value. That way your code can stay readable, and you can put whatever complications are involved in the test into a more maintainable and testable separate method.

This example uses the value of the `:can_send_email` field to determine whether the `:description` field must have a value. Neither is a field that would typically need much validation, but they can easily be treated as connected:

```
# if person says can send email, then we'd like them to fill their
# description in, so we understand who it is we're sending mail to
validates_presence_of :description, if: :require_description_presence?

# we define the supporting condition here
def require_description_presence?
  self.can_send_email
end
```

The `validates_presence_of` method will only perform its test if the condition specified by the `:if` parameter returns `true`. The `:if` parameter's value comes from the require_description_presence? method, which in this case simply returns the value of can_send_mail.

 Two small things to note about the require_description_pres ence? method: first, its name ends in a question mark, which is an easy way to flag that a method returns a boolean value. Second, it doesn't seem to do anything—but Ruby returns the value of the last thing touched, so the value of self.can_send_email becomes the return value. (And self here and throughout is optional, more a verbal tic for reminding the programmer of what's being called than a necessary part of the program.)

Do It Yourself

While Rails's built-in validation is very helpful for a broad range of data checking, there are always going to be times when it's just not enough. For example, while Rails can check the length of a string in characters, you might want to count words instead.

Performing such checks requires two steps. First, you need to create a call to your method using validate, which should point to readily identifiable methods that contain your custom logic. To indicate that validation failed, use self.errors.add, as shown in Example 7-4. This will tell Rails that there is an error and which field it applies to, as well as give you a chance to add a message to the user.

Example 7-4. Custom validation with validate and self.errors

```
validate :description_length_words

def description_length_words
  # only do this validation if description is provided
  unless self.description.blank? then
    # simple way of calculating words: split the text on whitespace
    num_words = self.description.split.length
    if num_words < 5 then
      self.errors.add(:description, "must be at least 5 words long")
    elsif num_words > 50 then
      self.errors.add(:description, "must be at most 50 words long")
    end
  end
end
```

When you perform validation this way, you do more work but gain some control. The unless self.description.blank? line is necessary because you can't just specify allow_nil => true. This is because allow_nil is a parameter of the validate method, not a general test in Ruby, so your description_length_words method does not have access to it. Similarly, there aren't any automatically generated messages. You have to provide them. And finally, of course, you're responsible for all of the validation logic itself.

 Rails also offers a `validates_each` method that can help you create more descriptively named validations. For more, see the APIdock discussion of this method (*http://bit.ly/2aTyr9a*).

Test Your Knowledge

Quiz

1. How much type checking does Rails do against the types you specified in your migrations?

2. What happens when a validation error is reported?

3. How do you customize the error notifications users see when their data doesn't match up to your validator's expectations?

4. How do you test the detailed syntax of user-entered data to make sure it matches a particular pattern?

5. If there's more than one error reported by the validator methods, what does Rails do?

6. How do you specify if something may be either valid or blank?

7. How do you specify that a value has to be outside of a particular range?

8. How can you specify that a validation applies only if another value in the form has a particular value?

Answers

1. Rails does no type checking by default. It just coerces the data that came in to the matching type, and if it doesn't match, too bad. You have to provide explicit validation code for every field you create.

2. Validation errors block the saving of records. The model sends the data back through the controller to the view, adding messages about what is wrong with the data, so the view can display them.

3. The `:message` named parameter lets you provide a specific notification. Rails will do some notifying by default in basic cases, but you're generally wise to add your own messages.

4. The `validates_format_of` method lets you test against regular expressions, or you can write your own more complicated tests by extending validation through the `validate` method.

5. Rails will report all of the messages from all of the validating methods to the user and highlight all of the fields with errors. It won't save the data to the database until it is submitted again and passes validation.

6. You can allow blank entries by specifying `allow_nil: => true` as an attribute on your validation. That permits the field to either have a correct value or no value at all.

7. The `validates_exclusion_of` method lets you make sure a value is outside of a given range.

8. The `:if` parameter lets you define conditions where validation applies.

## CHAPTER 8

Improving Forms

No one is an artist unless he carries his picture in his head before painting it, and is sure of his method and composition.

—Claude Monet

Now that you can safely get information between your users and your applications, it's time to examine some ways to do it better. Here are a few more features to explore:

- Supporting file uploads, a common website feature that steps outside of the simple form field to database column mapping

- Designing form builders, which makes it easier to create forms that look the way you think they should, not the way Rails does it by default

Once you've figured out these pieces, you'll have a reasonably complete understanding of the options Rails offers for creating classic web applications. Ajax still lies ahead, but the basics are still useful for a wide variety of situations.

Adding a Picture by Uploading a File

Since we're building a collection of people, it might be nice to know what they look like. Adding file uploads to Rails applications requires making changes in several different places:

- The form for creating and editing a person needs a file upload field.

- The model representing person data needs to handle the file data.

- A new migration needs to add a field for the file extension, because pictures come in different formats.

- The view that shows a person should display the picture too.

One key piece of a Rails application is missing here: the controller. The controller doesn't actually need to do anything more than it is already doing: passing data between the view and the model. One more piece of data, even a big chunk like a photo file, isn't going to make a difference to that default handling. (You can find the complete files for this example in *ch08/guestbook07*.)

 This chapter will show how to handle uploaded files directly. There are some gems, notably paperclip and carrierwave, that can handle uploaded files for you. The example here is to show you how to handle uploads and manage files.

File Upload Forms

The simplest step seems to be adding the file upload field to the form, in *app/views/people/_form.html.erb*:

```
<div class="field">
  <%= f.label :photo %><br />
  <%= f.file_field :photo %>
</div>
```

Well, almost. Including a file upload changes the way an HTML form is submitted, changing it to a multipart form. For creating a new person, this means shifting from an HTML result that looks like:

```
<form action="/people" method="post">
```

to a result that looks like:

```
<form action="/people/" enctype="multipart/form-data" method="post">
```

Adding the enclosure type means that Rails will know to look for an attachment after the main body of form field data has arrived.

That means a little more work on the `form` tag, created by the `form_for` method in our partial, *_form.html.erb*. In the old form, before the upload was added, it looked like:

```
<%= form_for(@person) do |f| %>
```

In the new form, it has a few more pieces:

```
<%= form_for(@person, html: { multipart: true }) do |f|  %>
```

Fortunately, updating this one form partial takes care of changes needed both to create a record with the upload and to edit one.

Model and Migration Changes

Adding a photo requires somewhat more effort than adding another ordinary field to the application, mostly because it (usually) doesn't make sense to store potentially large chunks of media data like photos directly in a database. For this demonstration, it makes much better sense to store the photo in the filesystem, renamed to match the ID of the person it goes with.

There's still one catch that requires accessing the database, though: photo files come in lots of different formats, and there's little reason to restrict users to a single format. That will require keeping track of which file extension is used for the uploaded file by storing the extension in the database. Doing that will require creating a migration, in addition to adding a lot of logic to the model. The combination of filesystem and database use is shown in Figure 8-1.

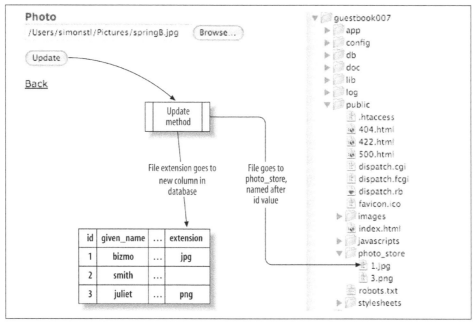

Figure 8-1. Uploading a file into the public directory, with metadata stored in the database

A migration for an extension

Chapter 10 will explore migrations in much greater depth, but this migration is relatively simple. Rails will apply migrations in the sequence of their filenames with the opening number being the critical piece. The *db/migrate* folder already contains a migration whose name ends in *_create_people.rb*, defining a CreatePeople class. To make it easy for us to figure out what's going on, the next migration will contain an

AddPhotoExtensionToPerson class. Following the same naming convention, this will be a timestamp followed by _add_photo_extension_to_person.rb. To create the migration file, enter:

```
rails generate migration add_photo_extension_to_person
```

 For more detail on creating migrations by hand, see Chapter 10. This one is simple enough that you can probably follow along without the full tutorial, though.

The newly generated migration won't have much in it, but you need to add details. There doesn't need to be very much inside this migration, as it only creates (and destroys, if necessary) one field, :extension, of type :string:

```
class AddPhotoExtensionToPerson < ActiveRecord::Migration
  def change
    add_column :people, :extension, :string
  end
end
```

When this migration is run, it will add a new column to the :people table that will be used to store :extension data. If rolled back, it deletes that column.

To run the migration, just run **rails db:migrate** as usual. When you use this command, Rails will find the new migration file, determine that it hasn't run it yet, and add the column to the existing :people table, as requested:

```
== 2 AddPhotoExtensionToPerson: migrating =========================
-- add_column(:people, :extension, :string)
   -> 0.0757s
== 2 AddPhotoExtensionToPerson: migrated (0.0759s) ===============
```

You'll also need to add :photo to the list of accepted parameters in *app/controllers/people_controller.rb*. The new migration doesn't take care of that detail for you.

```
...
def person_params
    params.require(:person).permit(:name, :secret, :country, :email,
    :description, :can_send_email, :graduation_year, :body_temperature,
    :price, :birthday, :favorite_time, :photo)
end
```

Leave that off, and you'll get lots of "Can't mass-assign protected attributes: photo" messages.

Extending a model beyond the database

Data storage issues should all be handled in the model. Normally, Rails will save any properties that come into the model that have names corresponding to columns in the corresponding database table.

 Behind the scenes, ActiveRecord keeps track of which tables contain which columns and uses that information to generate a lot of code automatically. In development mode, it checks tables and generates code constantly, which is part of why development mode is slow but extremely flexible.

However, the migration just shown didn't create a column that would map to `:photo`, just one for `:extension`. This is deliberate. Because these photos will be stored as files outside of the database, Rails *shouldn't* handle them automatically. Explicit model code, in *app/models/person.rb*, will have to do that. Fortunately, Rails has an easy (and declarative) way to make sure the code for storing the photo runs after the rest of validation has happened, with its `after_save` callback method:

```
# after the person has been written to the database, deal with
# writing any image data to the filesystem
  after_save :store_photo
```

Unfortunately, Rails doesn't have a built-in `store_photo` method. That requires coding.

 The `after_save` method is one of several callback methods supported by ActiveRecord. Note that there are after and before methods for `create`, `destroy`, `save`, `update`, `validation`, `validation_on_create`, and `validation_on_update`. If you need to tweak ActiveRecord's data handling, these can be valuable tools.

`store_photo`, the last method in the `Person` class, will call on some other methods that also need to be written, but it's probably still easiest to look at `store_photo` first before examining the methods on which it depends:

```
private

# called after saving, to write the uploaded image to the filesystem
def store_photo
  if @file_data
    # make the photo_store directory if it doesn't exist already
    FileUtils.mkdir_p PHOTO_STORE
    # write out the image data to the file
    File.open(photo_filename, 'wb') do |f|
      f.write(@file_data.read)
    end
```

```
    # avoid repeat-saving
    @file_data = nil
  end
end
```

First, note that this method comes after the private keyword, making it invisible outside of the model class to which it belongs. Controllers and views shouldn't be calling store_photo directly. Only other methods within the same model should be able to call it. (It's not required that you make this method private, but it makes for cleaner code overall.)

 Anything that appears after the private keyword will be treated as private, so if you have other public code (like the next few methods), be sure to put it above this line in the file.

Within the method itself, the first line, if @file_data, is simple—if there is actually data to be stored, then it's worth proceeding. Otherwise, this isn't necessary. Then there's a call to Ruby's file-handling classes, creating a directory for the photos. (This causes no harm if the directory already exists.) The next few lines open a file whose name is specified by *photo_filename*; write the data to it, and close it. At the end, store_photo sets @file_data to nil to make sure the file doesn't get stored again elsewhere in the application.

This takes care of saving the file, which is the last thing done as the model finishes up its work on a form submission, but more details get attended to earlier, paving the way for saving the file. The photo= method takes care of a few details when a submission arrives:

```
# when photo data is assigned via the upload, store the file data
# for later and assign the file extension, e.g., ".jpg"
def photo=(file_data)
  unless file_data.blank?
    # store the uploaded data into a private instance variable
    @file_data = file_data
    # figure out the last part of the filename and use this as
    # the file extension. e.g., from "me.jpg" will return "jpg"
    self.extension = file_data.original_filename.split('.').last.downcase
  end
end
```

The def for this method looks a bit unusual because it takes advantage of a Rails convention for writing to model attributes. Writing def photo=(file_data) creates a method that grabs the file_data content for :photo, which Rails creates based on the contents of the file_field from the HTML form. It defines what happens when person.photo is assigned a value. That file_data content gets moved to an

---

`@file_data` instance variable that is private to the model but is accessible to any of the methods within it. (`@file_data` is what `store_photo` referenced, for instance.)

The `photo=` method also handles the one piece of the filename that will get stored in the database—the file extension. It gets the original name, splits off the piece after the last ".," and lowercases it. (You don't have to be this draconian, but it does make for simpler maintenance.) Note that `photo=` just assigns a value to the `extension` variable of the current `Person` object. ActiveRecord will save that value automatically as it maps to the `:extension` column created by the migration.

The next few pieces are filename housekeeping:

```
# File.join is a cross-platform way of joining directories;
# we could have written "{Rails.root}/public/photo_store"
PHOTO_STORE = File.join Rails.root, 'public', 'photo_store'

# where to write the image file to
  def photo_filename
    File.join PHOTO_STORE, "#{id}.#{extension}"
  end

# return a path we can use in HTML for the image
  def photo_path
    "/photo_store/#{id}.#{extension}"
  end
```

`PHOTO_STORE` provides the application with a path to this Rails application's *public* directory where static files can go. The `photo_filename` method gets called by `store_photo` when it needs to know where the photo file should actually go on its host machine's filesystem. You can see that instead of preserving the original filename, it uses the `id`—the primary key number for this `Person`—when it creates a name for the photo. This may seem like overkill, but it has the convenient virtue of avoiding filename conflicts. Otherwise, if multiple people had uploaded *me.jpg*, some of them would be surprised by the results.

The `photo_path` method handles filename housekeeping for views that need to display the image. It's unconcerned with where the file exists in the server's filesystem and focuses instead on where it will appear as a URL in the Rails application. Again, `photo_path` uses the `id` to create the name. Its one line, a string, actually *is* the return value.

There's another housekeeping function that supports the view. Not everyone will necessarily have a photo, and broken image icons aren't particularly attractive. To simplify dealing with this, the model includes a `has_photo` method that checks to see if there's a file corresponding to the `id` and `extension` of the current record:

```
# if a photo file exists, then we have a photo
def has_photo?
  File.exists? photo_filename
end
```

Remember, Ruby will treat the last value created by a method as its return value—in this case, the response to `File.exists?`. This returns `true` if there is a file corresponding to the `id` and `extension`, and `false` if there isn't.

Showing it off

The last piece that the application needs is a way to show off the picture. That's a simple addition in the *show.html.erb* view:

```
<p>
  <strong>Photo:</strong>
    <% if @person.has_photo? %>
      <%= image_tag @person.photo_path %>
    <% else %>
      No photo.
    <% end %>
</p>
```

The `has_photo?` method from the model lets the view code decide whether or not to create an `img` element for the photo. If there is one, it uses the model's `photo_path` method for the `src` attribute, pointing to the file in the *public* directory's *photo_store* directory. If not, there's plain text with the message "No photo" rather than a broken image icon.

Results

It's time to try this code. Running `rails server` fires up the application, which at first glance looks very similar to earlier versions, as shown in Figure 8-2. (And yes, displaying everyone's "secret" isn't very secret, but we'll get to a much better solution in Chapter 14.)

If you click the "New Person" link or go to edit an existing record, you'll see a new field for the photo, shown in Figure 8-3.

When a photo is uploaded, it is stored in the application's *public* directory, in a *photo_store* directory, as shown in Figure 8-4. Note that there is a skipped number— only records that actually have photos leave any trace here.

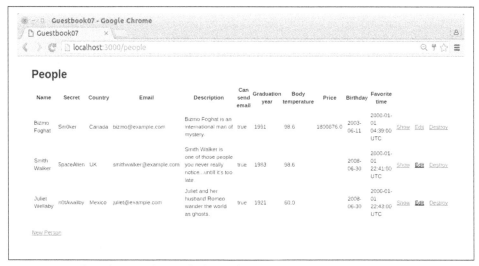

Figure 8-2. A list of users who might have photos

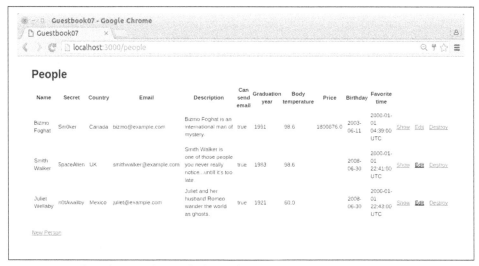

Figure 8-3. A file field in the person form

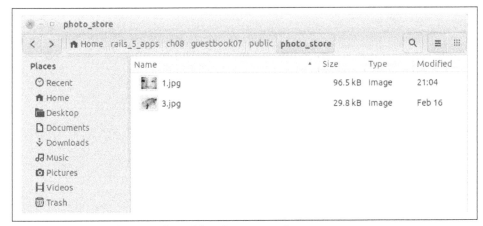

Figure 8-4. Stored photos in the public/photo_store directory

Showing a page for a record that includes a photo yields the photo embedded in the page as shown in Figure 8-5. (Note that at present there aren't any constraints on photo size. You could constrain it, but you'll have to install a graphics library, configure it, and connect it to Ruby and Rails.)

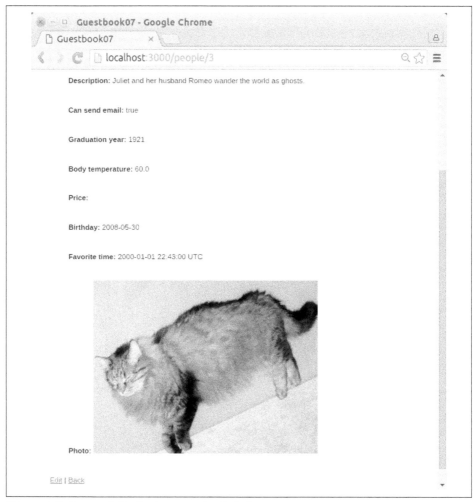

Description: Juliet and her husband Romeo wander the world as ghosts.

Can send email: true

Graduation year: 1921

Body temperature: 60.0

Price:

Birthday: 2008-05-30

Favorite time: 2000-01-01 22:43:00 UTC

Photo:

Edit | Back

Figure 8-5. A record displaying an uploaded photo

Records that don't have an associated photo just get the "No photo" message shown in
Figure 8-6.

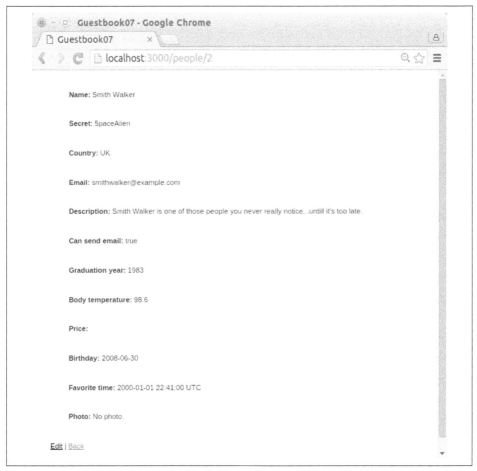

Figure 8-6. A record unadorned with a photo—but spared a broken image icon

This isn't quite a simple process, but multimedia usually stretches frameworks built around databases. Rails is flexible enough to let you choose how to handle incoming information and work with the filesystem to develop a solution that fits. (And if this isn't quite the right solution for you, don't worry—many people are working out their own solutions to these issues and sharing them.)

> It is possible for programs treating your application as a REST-based web service to send photos as multipart/form-data. However, Rails's default approach to generating JSON responses won't give them an easy way to retrieve the photos unless the programs understand the `photo_store/id.extension` convention.

Standardizing Your Look with Form Builders

While Rails scaffolding is a convenient way to get started, you may have noticed that it's pretty repetitive and not especially attractive. Some of this can be fixed with judicious use of CSS, but Rails supports more permanent fixes through the use of *form builders*. Creating form builders is an opportunity to define how your data will be presented to users and how they'll interact with that data. Form builders also let you create abstractions that keep programmers out of the visual details of your application while still giving them full access to views.

The basic concepts behind form builders are simple, though you can use them to create complex and intricate components. You can use form builders in multiple ways, starting from simple wrapping of your own special types and developing through more complex ways to change the ways forms are written.

 You can also combine form builders with Ruby metaprogramming to create your own terse yet descriptive syntaxes for creating forms, but metaprogramming is *way* beyond the scope of this book. If you encounter an application with view code that looks nothing like you expected, though, that may be what's going on.

Supporting Your Own Field Types

Chapter 6 showed how Rails supported a variety of data types by default, including a more complicated (if not very user-friendly) set of controls for entering dates. While the built-in set of widgets is helpful, you're definitely not limited to it. You can build reusable form components that match your needs more precisely.

This can be very useful when you have components that take the same limited set of values. Chapter 6 showed a helper method for creating drop-down lists or radio buttons depending on the number of choices, culminating in Example 8-1.

Example 8-1. A helper method that chooses between radio buttons and selection lists

```
module PeopleHelper
  def button_select(model_name, target_property, button_source)
    html=''
    list = button_source.sort

    if list.length < 4
      html << '<fieldset><legend>Country</legend>'
      list.each {|x|
        html << radio_button(model_name, target_property, x[1])
        html << (x[0])
        html << '<br>'
      }
```

```
      html << '</fieldset>'
    else
      html << ' <label for="person_country">Country</label><br>'
      html << select(model_name, target_property, list)
    end
    return html.html_safe
  end

end
```

Rather than create a generic helper method whose focus is on the kind of HTML it generates, it can be more appealing to create a form builder method whose focus is on data that's appropriate for a given model. Linking the HTML specifically to a given model makes it vastly easier to keep interfaces consistent. Example 8-2, included in *ch08/guestbook08*, shows a form builder method, country_select, that is designed specifically for use with the :country field.

Example 8-2. A form builder, stored in app/helpers/tidy_form_builder.rb, providing a method more tightly bound to the expectations of the :country field

```
class TidyFormBuilder < ActionView::Helpers::FormBuilder

# our country_select calls the default select helper with the
# choices already filled in
  def country_select(method, options={}, html_options={})
    select(method, [['Canada', 'Canada'],
                    ['Mexico', 'Mexico'],
                    ['United Kingdom', 'UK'],
                    ['United States of America', 'USA']],
                  options, html_options)
  end
end
```

Note that form builders, which go in the *app/helpers* directory, all inherit from the ActionView::Helpers::FormBuilder class. The methods inside the class will then be made available to views that specify that they want to use this helper.

The country_select method is built using the select helper method already explored in Chapter 6. It takes a method parameter, options, and html_options like the select method does. What does the method parameter do? You probably think of the method as the field—:name, for example. You can see how much more tightly bound country_select is to :country—it wouldn't be of much use for any other field unless you have, say, different kinds of fields expecting the same list of countries. The result is a select field seeded with the choices you've deemed acceptable for country.

Note that the `options` and `html_options` arguments are simply passed through. Preserving them offers developers more flexibility when they go to apply your form builder in different situations.

Calling the form builder requires two things. First, the view has to reference the `Tidy FormBuilder`, and then it has to actually call `country_select`. Unlike helper classes, where a naming convention is enough to connect supporting code with the view, form builders require an explicit call. (You will likely use the same builder for multiple views in any case, as `:country` might turn up in a lot of different contexts.)

As was the case for the multipart form, calling the builder means adding a `:builder` parameter to the `form_for`:

```
<%= form_for(@person, html: { multipart: true },
  builder: TidyFormBuilder) do |f| %>
```

Rails will know to look for `TidyFormBuilder` in */app/helpers/tidy_form_builder.rb*. Actually, calling the method is pretty simple. Just replace:

```
<p>
    <%= f.label :country %><br />
    <%= f.select (:country, [ ['Canada', 'Canada'],
                     ['Mexico', 'Mexico'],
                     ['United Kingdom', 'UK'],
                     ['United States of America', 'USA'] ]) %>
  </p>
```

with:

```
<div class="field">
  <%= f.label :country %><br />
  <%= f.country_select :country %>
</div>
```

The results will be identical, but the logic around the `country` object is much better encapsulated, and just plain easier to use, in the builder version.

Adding Automation

The Rails helper methods are certainly useful, but they tend to map directly to HTML markup. When you have multiple related markup components for a single field, code can start to feel messy very quickly. That's true even when they're as simple as an input field with a label, like this from the scaffolding:

```
<p>
    <%= f.label :name %><br />
    <%= f.text_field :name %>
  </p>
```

Multiply that by a hundred fields, and there's a lot of repetitive code around. Remember, the Rails mantra is "Don't Repeat Yourself" (DRY), and there's a huge opportunity to avoid repetition here.

Although it's kind of a separate task from the country selector, this can also happen easily inside of the TidyFormBuilder, as shown in *ch08/guestbook09*. In fact, it's easy for it to take place there because methods in the builder can use the same names as the helper methods and subclass them, adding the extra functionality needed to simplify the view code. About the only tricky part is making sure that your subclassed methods use the same signature—list of parameters—as the originals, which just means checking the Rails API documentation:

```
def text_field(method, options={})
  ...
end
```

The text_field method takes a method parameter. The options array is the usual set of options. Once the signature is set up, the single line of code inside combines a label with a call to the original method to create a return value. Add this to *tidy_form_builder.rb*:

```
def text_field(method, options={})
  label = label_for(method, options) + super(method, options)
end
```

Calling super, in the second half of this line, means to call the original text_field method, which gets passed the method and options objects. The first half of the line calls another method, however, adding the label. The label_for method is declared at the end of the TidyFormBuilder class and is private, as it is for internal use only:

```
private

def label_for(method, options={})
  label(options.delete(:label) || method).safe_concat("<br />")
end
```

The label method is the same as usual and is concatenated to a <br /> tag. Note first that you can't just use the usual + for concatenation. Because of Rails's defenses against cross-site scripting, you have to use the safe_concat method. Otherwise, Rails will escape the < and >, and you'll have a mess on your form.

If you find that you can't use .safe_concat on a string, check to make sure that you control its contents. If yes, call .html_safe on the string. It will become an ActiveSupport::SafeBuffer object, and the .safe_concat method will be available.

There's also something tricky going on in the arguments to label:

```
  options.delete(:label) || method)
```

This looks for an option named :label, letting you specify label text for the field through a :label parameter. Accessing the :label value through delete seems strange, but delete does two things: it removes the :label parameter from the options array, which will keep it from passing through to the super call, and it also returns the :label parameter's value, if there is one. If there isn't a :label, the || will fall through to method, which will create a label with the default—the internal name of the field.

The call to create a field is now much simpler. In *_form.html.erb*, we can now replace:

```
<div class="field">
  <%= f.label :name, 'Your name' %><br>
  <%= f.text_field :name %>
</div>
```

with:

```
<%= f.text_field :name %>
```

The other methods, with more complex signatures, need a bit more code, but it's the same basic logic, as these demonstrate:

```
def time_select(method, options = {}, html_options = {})
   label_for(method, options) + super(method, options, html_options)
end

def select(method, choices, options = {}, html_options = {})
   label_for(method, options) + super(method, choices, options, html_options)
end

def check_box(method, options = {}, checked_value = "1", unchecked_value = "0")
   label_for(method, options) + super(method, options, checked_value,
unchecked_value)
end
```

And again, the calls to create a select list and a checkbox become simpler:

```
<%= f.check_box :can_send_email %>
```

```
<%= f.time_select :favorite_time %>
```

There's one last bit to notice. Remember how country_select calls the select method? It now calls the method that provides the label. That means that you can simplify:

```
<p>
  <%= f.label :country %><br />
  <%= f.country_select :country %>
</p>
```

to:

```
<p>
<%= f.country_select :country %>
</p>
```

The next step will reduce this even further, while making it easier to style and manipulate the resulting HTML.

Integrating Form Builders and Styles

All of those `<div class="field">` and `</div>` tags are calling out for simplification, but there's another opportunity here: to add further information to the form that will help users fill it out properly. The `WrappingTidyBuilder`, included in *ch08/guestbook10*, is much like the prior `TidyBuilder`, including its `country_select` method and its methods for providing labels. It goes in *app/helpers/wrapping_tidy_form_builder.rb*. It also, however, takes advantage of the work it's putting into wrapping to add some extra information to fields that are required. This requires a few extra components:

- A `:required` option specified in calls from the view
- A `wrap_field` method that puts the opening and closing tags around the label and form fields
- Calls to `wrap_field` from the other methods
- A bit of extra code in the `label` method that adds a textual indicator that a field is required
- Support for the new wrapper in a CSS stylesheet used for pages built with these methods
- Linking that CSS stylesheet to your application through an addition to the layout file

The `:required` option is specified in calls to the form builder's methods, if desired:

```
<%= f.text_field :name, required: true %>

<%= f.password_field :secret, required: true %>

<%= f.country_select :country, required: true %>
```

`required:`, in this code, is only about how the field should be presented. Specifying whether a field should genuinely be required is better done in the model validation described in Chapter 7.

The `wrap_field` method, like the `label_for` method, comes after `private` in the code, making it callable only within the class or subclasses. It's not very complicated, choosing what value to use for the class attribute based on the contents of the `:required` option:

```
def wrap_field(text, options={})
field_class = "field"
if options[:required]
field_class = "field required"
end
"<div class=
'#{field_class}'>".html_safe.safe_concat(text).safe_concat("</div>")
end
```

By default, `class`, which gives CSS stylesheets a hook for formatting the `div`, will just contain "field." It's a form field. If `:required` is `true`, however, it will have the value "field required." The `class` attribute can contain multiple values separated by spaces, so this means that the stylesheet can format this `div` as both a form field and as required.

The other methods need to call `wrap_field`, which makes them slightly more complicated. Therefore, the following:

```
def text_field(method, options={})
    label = label_for(method, options) + super(method, options)
end
```

grows to become this:

```
def text_field(method, options={})
 wrap_field(label = label_for(method, options) + super(method, options), options)
end
```

Looking through the parentheses, this means that `wrap_field` gets called with the text generated by the older methods, along with the options that it also needs to explore.

This wrapping happens for all of the public methods in `WrappingTidyBuilder` with one important exception: `country_select`. Why? Because `country_select` already calls `select`, which will do the wrapping for it.

Connecting a field option to CSS styling is a good idea, but there's one problem: not every browser uses CSS. Remember Lynx, the text-only web browser? It's still out there, and so are a lot of different browsers that don't use CSS. Some are screen readers, while others are simplified browsers for cell phones and other devices. To address that possibility, modifying `label_for` will add an asterisk to required fields, using the same logic that `wrap_field` had used:

```
def label_for(method, options={})
  label = label(options.delete(:label) || method)
  if options[:required]
    label.safe_concat(" <span class='required_mark'>*</span>")
  end
  label.safe_concat("<br />")
end
```

If the `required:` option is set to `true`, this means that the label will have an extra `<span class='required_mark'>*</span>` appended after the label and before the `<br />` break between the label and the field.

You'll need to connect this builder to the view in */app/views/people/_form.html.erb* in its `form_for` declaration:

```
<%= form_for(@person, html: { multipart: true },
      builder: WrappingTidyFormBuilder) do |f| %>
```

The last piece needed is a stylesheet. The stylesheet itself will go into the *assets/style-sheets/* directory, most reasonably appended to the already-generated *people.scss*. From there, it will be accessible to your application.

Four styles are defined. One is for the field, another for the label inside the field, another for the asterisk in the `required_mark`-classed span, and a last one for the fields marked `required`:

```
/* styles for our forms */

div.field {
  margin-top: 0.5em;
  margin-bottom: 0.5em;
  padding-left: 10px;
}

div.field label {
  font-weight: bold;
}

div.field span.required_mark {
  font-weight: bold;
  color: red;
}

/* draw attention to required fields */

div.required {
  padding-left: 6px;
  border-left: 4px solid #dd0;
}
```

So, what does all this look like? Figure 8-7 gives you a sense of what's happened. Note the bars along the left edge of the required fields (yellow on the screen) and the red asterisks after their labels.

The first time through, this seems like a lot of work. And the first time through, it is. The good news, however, is that once you've done this, all that work is easy to reuse. You can change the stylesheet without having to go back to the layout. You can change the `wrap_field` method to do whatever you like. Once the infrastructure is built, it's much easier to change the details or to assign different details to different people working on a project without fear of collision.

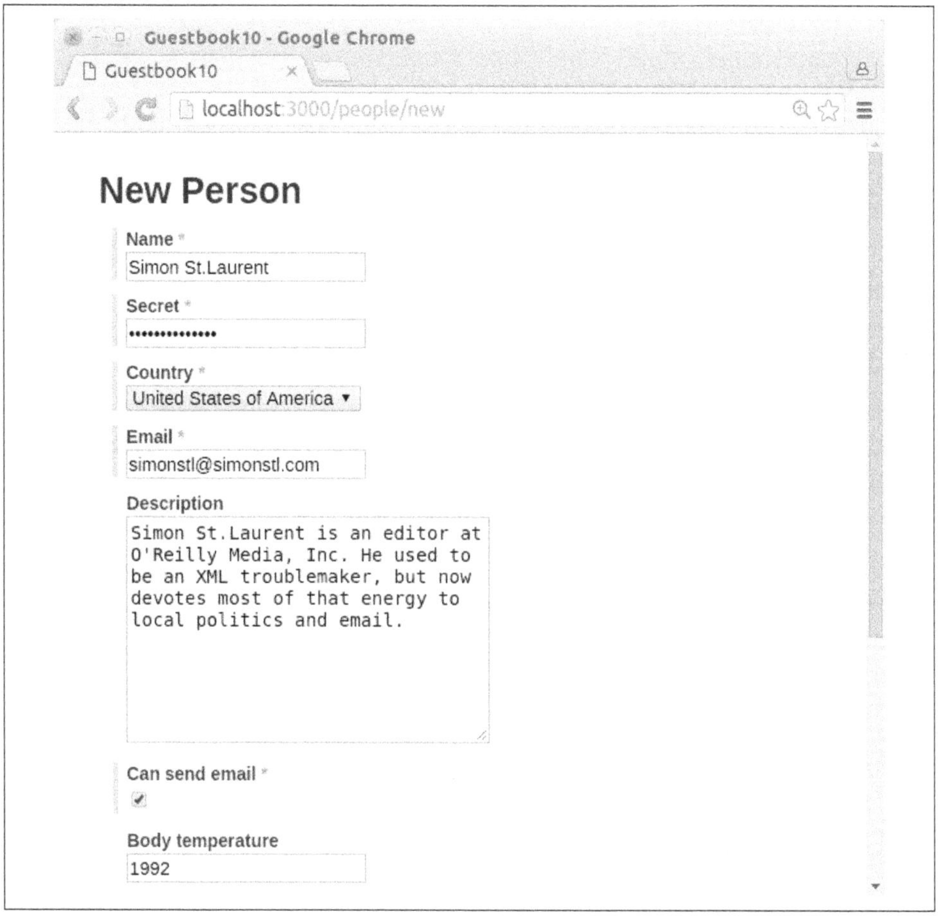

Figure 8-7. Extra formatting created through a form builder and CSS

Test Your Knowledge

Quiz

1. How much change did the controller need to handle file uploads?
2. What goes into a migration when you add a field to a table?
3. How do you make methods invisible (and uncallable) outside of their class?
4. Are form builders for binding presentation to a specific piece of your model, or for supporting more general form construction?

5. Do builders map to controllers automatically?

6. Why (and when) are form builders worth the extra trouble of creating them?

Answers

1. The controller needed no change at all. All of the changes were in the views, to enable users to upload and display the file, and in the model, to handle the file when it arrived and when it was needed.

2. A migration that adds a field needs an `add_column` call defining the field in the `change` method.

3. Placing method definitions after the `private` keyword makes them usable only within the class.

4. They can be used for both general form construction and the creation of reusable components tightly bound to a particular model. You can even mix the two approaches in the same class.

5. No. Helper methods can bind to controllers through naming conventions, but using form builders requires adding a `:builder` argument to your `form_for` call.

6. Form builders are a great idea when they let you avoid repeating yourself. Used properly, they can make it easy for an application to look consistent even if many different developers are working on different parts of the project.

## CHAPTER 9

Developing Model Relationships

Much of what I do in my job is think about whether relationships we see in data are causal, as opposed to just reflecting correlations.
—Emily Oster

Everything you've done so far has been in the context of an application with one and only one table. That's actually enough power to run a lot of different projects from contact managers to time-series data collection. However, you'll quickly find that most of the projects for which it's worth creating a web application require more than just one table. Fortunately, Rails makes that easy, giving you the tools you need to create multiple tables and manage even complex relationships between them.

 If you don't know much about databases, now is a good time to visit Appendix B. Up to this point, it's been possible to largely forget that there was a relational database underneath the application except for some mechanics. From this point on, you'll need to understand how tables work in order to understand how Rails models work. (You still don't need to understand SQL, however.)

Working with multiple tables is, on the surface, pretty simple. Every Rails model maps to a table, so working with multiple tables just means working with multiple models. The hard part is managing the relationships between the tables—which in Rails demands managing the relationships between models.

Most of the steps for working with multiple models are the same as for working with single models, just done once for each table. Once the models are created, though, the real work begins. Some of it can be done easily and declaratively, while other parts require thinking ahead and writing your own code. This chapter marks the point where Rails itself can't directly support the operations suggested by your data models, and so there's a lot of coding to do. While the scaffolding still provides a helpful supporting framework, there's a lot of editing to do on models, migrations, routes, controllers, and views.

 Once again, it's important to emphasize how much easier it is to create a Rails application from scratch rather than trying to build it on top of an existing database. If you're trying to retrofit an old database with a shiny new Rails interface, odds are good that you need a much more advanced book than this one. You'll need to learn what goes on behind the scenes, not just how Rails works when all is well.

Connecting Awards to Students

The guestbook example of the previous few chapters isn't the best foundation on which to demonstrate a multitable application, so it's time to change course. If you'd like to get an overview of the structures this chapter will create, these structures will be the same as those introduced in Appendix B, using students, awards, and courses. (The first version of them can be found in *ch09/students01*.)

Start by creating a new application:

```
rails new students
```

Then **cd students**, and create a `student` model and the usual related scaffolding:

```
rails generate scaffold student given_name:string middle_name:string
family_name:string date_of_birth:date grade_point_average:decimal
start_date:date
```

Then create a second model, `award`, and its scaffolding:

```
rails generate scaffold award name:string year:integer student_id:integer
```

The students application now contains two models, one for students and one for awards. Students will receive awards, and awards will be connected to students, but Rails doesn't know that yet. The `rails generate` command gives a hint of this because it includes a `student_id` field, an integer that will connect to the (unspecified but automatic) `id` field of the students model.

 Though we won't use it in this chapter, check out the use of *references* when generating a model. It adds a `belongs_to` association in addition to an index in the migration. See this Ruby on Rails guide on migration (*http://bit.ly/2aTzE0a*) for more information.

Establishing the Relationship

To tell Rails about the connections between the two models, you need to modify the models. In *app/models/student.rb*, add the following between the `class` line and the end:

```
# a student can have many awards
has_many :awards
```

And in *app/models/award.rb*, add:

```
# every award is linked to a student, through student_id
belongs_to :student
```

These two declarations establish a relationship between the two models. Student records have awards—students don't have to have awards, but they can have many of them. Awards, however, for the purposes of this example, are always linked to students.

 Technically, `has_many` and `belongs_to` are method names. They just happen to look like declarations, and it's a lot easier to think of them that way.

Now Rails knows about the connections between the models. What is it going to do to support that relationship, and what's still up to you?

Rails doesn't add automatic checking or validation to ensure that the relationships between objects work. It doesn't require, for example, that every award have a valid `student_id`. It doesn't change the scaffolding that was already built. Establishing the connection in the model is just the first step toward building the connection into your application.

Rails does provide some help in doing that, though. With these declarations, Rails adds methods to your classes, making it much easier for a `student` object to work with its `award` objects and for an `award` object to work with its `student` objects. You can find a complete listing of the methods added in the API documentation for `has_many` and `belongs_to`. For now, it probably makes sense to show how the association can help.

You'll need to run `rails db:migrate` and `rails server` to start the app. Once it's running, visit *http://localhost:3000/students/new* to create a student record, which you can then link to from an awards record.

Supporting the Relationship

There is only one reference to a possible connection in the original forms created by the scaffolding: a field (which was specified when you created the awards), meant to hold the `student_id`, on the forms for entering and editing awards (*http://localhost: 3000/awards/new*), shown in Figure 9-1.

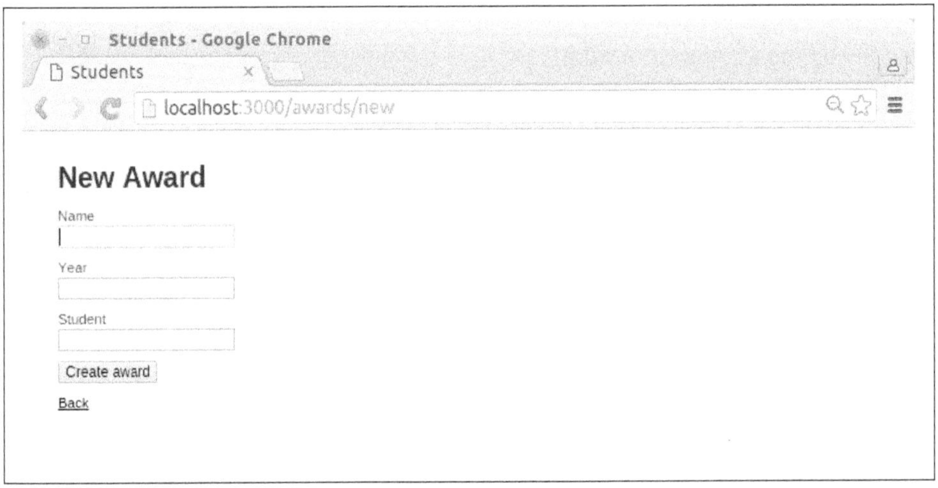

Figure 9-1. A basic awards form, where you can enter student numbers if you happen to know them

As it turns out, while you can enter numbers corresponding to student IDs in the student field (if you know them, figuring them out from the URLs for student records), there isn't any constraint on the numbers that go there. Awards can go to nonexistent students. It's easy to improve the situation, though, by adding a `select` field to the *app/views/awards/_form.html.erb* partial:

```
<div class="field">
<%= f.label :student_id %><br/>
<%= f.select :student_id, Student.all.order(:family_name,:given_name).collect
{|s|[(s.given_name + " " + s.family_name), s.id]} %>
</div>
```

The highlighted piece there might seem indigestible, but it's a fairly common way to create select lists based on related collections. The `select` method needs a field to bind to—`:student_id`—as its first parameter. The second parameter is a collection for the list to display. `Student` gets an object referring to the `students` model. The `all` method, which you've encountered before in *show.html.erb* templates, retrieves the list of all (`:all`) student records, sorted by family name and then given names (thanks to the `:order` method).

The find method doesn't quite finish the work, though. You could stop here if you were content to list object reference information in the select field. To show something a little more meaningful, however—both to the human user and to the program interpreting what comes back from the form—you need to specify both what gets displayed in the select field and the value that will get sent back.

That's where the collect method is useful. It takes a block as an argument ({}). The |s| is a very brief way of saying that Ruby should loop through the collection of students and put each row into a variable named s. On each iteration of the loop, the block will return an array, contained in [and]. Each of those arrays, which will become lines in the select list, will have two values. The first is the name of the student, which Ruby generates by concatenating its given_name to a space and its family_name. That value will be displayed to the user. The second is the id value for the student, and that value will be what comes back from the form to the server.

All of that work creates the simple form shown in Figure 9-2, with its drop-down box for students.

Figure 9-2. An awards form that minimizes guesswork about students

When the user submits this form, Rails gets back a "1" identifying the student's id (at least it will if the students table looks like Figure B-1 in Appendix B). That will go in the student_id field in the table. A "1" will be puzzling for humans, though. To fix that, in *app/views/awards/*, in *show.html.erb*, replace:

```
<%= @award.student_id %>
```

with:

```
<%= @award.student.given_name %> <%= @award.student.family_name %>
```

and in *index.html.erb*, replace:

```
<%= award.student_id %>
```

with:

```
<%= award.student.given_name %> <%= award.student.family_name %>
```

Note that the @award variable (just award in *index.html.erb*) suddenly has a new method. Of course it understood student_id—that's a field defined by the original rails generate command. But the student method, and its methods given_name and family_name, are new. Those features are the result of Rails recognizing the belongs_to declaration and providing a more convenient notation for getting to the specific student that this particular award belongs_to.

While using student is great, there's one problem with the code just shown—it keeps repeating itself to combine given_name and family_name. There's a way to avoid that and to simplify most of this code. In the model for student (in *app/models/student.rb*), add a method called name that returns a simpler form:

```
def name
  given_name + " " + family_name
end
```

Like the methods representing database fields, the name method will be available from awards, as in:

```
<%= @award.student.name %>
```

or:

```
<%= f.select :student_id, Student.all.collect {|s| [s.name, s.id]} %>
```

You'll now get the cleaner-looking result shown in Figure 9-3 for a little less work.

The name method creates what is often called an *attribute* on the model, acting as a method for retrieving its value. If you want to create attributes that can be assigned values, the convention would suggest a name like name=, along the lines of the photo= method described in "Extending a model beyond the database" on page 135.

Awards are now connected to students, but there still isn't any enforcement of that connection, just a form field that makes it difficult to enter anything else. Even with the form, though, there are corner cases—someone could, for example, delete a student after the form had been sent to a user. Or, more likely, a REST request could send JSON with a bad student_id—fixing up the view hasn't changed anything in the model.

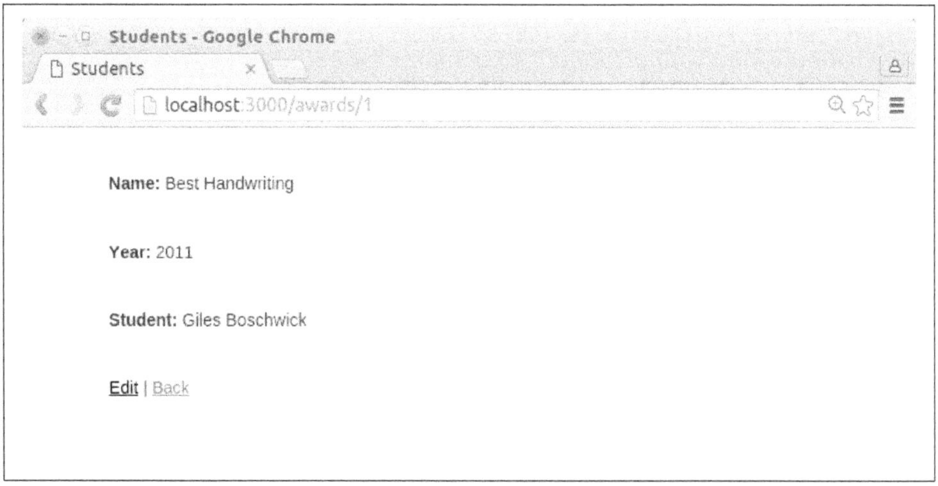

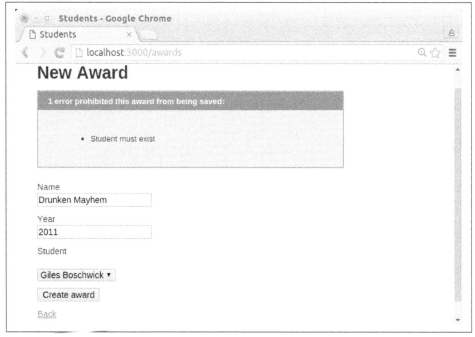

Figure 9-3. Showing a record with a name instead of a student ID number

Rails ensures the existence of a student ID before saving an award. If you try to save an award record with a student that doesn't exist, you'll get a message like that shown in Figure 9-4. (Note that because the student was deleted, his or her name isn't available in the select list, and Giles Boschwick comes up again.)

Figure 9-4. Enforcing the existence of students for every award

Connecting Students to Awards

So, awards now have a basic understanding of the student records to which they connect. What can student records do with awards?

Removing Awards When Students Disappear

Although in reality you might want to keep award listings around when students leave, for demonstration purposes it's worth considering the problem of orphaned records. Rails checks that a corresponding student record exists at the time the award record is created, but once the record has been created, validation doesn't notice, for example, if the student is deleted. Keeping award records in sync with student records requires something more active.

Rails makes it very easy to make sure that when student records are deleted, the corresponding awards records are also deleted. You just need to add an option to the has_many declaration in *app/models/student.rb*:

```
has_many :awards, dependent: :destroy
```

This is powerful and easy, but beware: those deletions will take place without any further confirmation. Once the user agrees to delete a student record, all of the awards records connected to that student will also disappear.

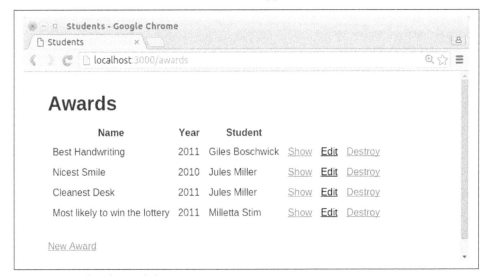

Figure 9-5. A brief awards list

Counting Awards for Students

While adding the awards list to the main list of students could get really verbose, it does make sense to add a count of awards received to the list of students. If you add

---

the set of awards listed in Figure B-3 of Appendix B, you'll have an awards list like that shown in Figure 9-5.

Adding a count of these awards to the students list that's in *app/views/students/index.html.erb* is simple. There needs to be a new column for awards, so at the end of the first row (in the first `tr` element), add:

```
<th>Awards</th>
```

And then, after:

```
<td><%= student.start_date %></td>
```

add:

```
<td><%= student.awards.count %></td>
```

Just as every `award` object now has a `student` object because of `belongs_to`, every `student` object has an `awards` object, thanks to the `has_many` declaration. Getting a count of awards for that student is as simple as specifying `count`. Figure 9-6 shows the results of these additions.

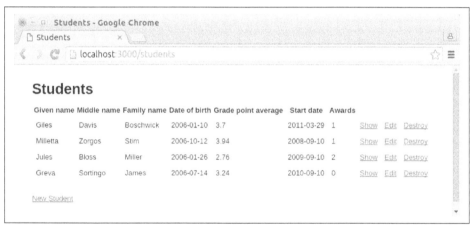

Figure 9-6. A students list complete with count of awards

You'll probably want to format them more beautifully, but the basic data is there. It also makes sense to add a list of awards to each of the individual student views, so that users can see what students have won as they review the records. Thanks to the `awards` method, it isn't difficult to add an awards table to *app/views/students/show.html.erb*:

```
<h3>Awards</h3>
<table>
  <tr>
    <th>Name</th>
    <th>Year</th>
```

```
        <th>Student</th>
      </tr>

  <% @student.awards.each do |award| %>
    <tr>
      <td><%= award.name %></td>
      <td><%= award.year %></td>
      <td><%= award.student.name %></td>
    </tr>
  <% end %>
  </table>
```

In the view, the `@student` variable contains the current student. Running a `for` loop over the collection returned by `@student.awards`, which contains only the awards for the current student, lets you put the information about the awards into a table. You'll get a result like that shown in Figure 9-7.

Figure 9-7. A student record with awards listed

Nesting Awards in Students

The connections between students and awards are workable, but the way that the two models are handled by the web application doesn't reflect their actual roles in the data models. Depending on your application and your preferences, this may be perfectly acceptable. There is, however, a better way to represent the awards model that more clearly reflects its relationship to students, implemented in *ch09/students02*.

The models will stay the same, and the views will stay almost the same. The main things that will change are the routing and the controller logic. Chapter 13 will explain routing in much greater depth, but for now, it's worth exploring the ways that routing can reflect the relationships of your data models.

If the work involved in creating a nested resource seems overwhelming, don't worry. It's not mandatory Rails practice, though it is certainly a best practice. Unfortunately, it's just complicated enough that it's hard to automate—but maybe someday this will all disappear into a friendlier rails generate command.

Changing the Routing

Near the top of the *config/routes.rb* file are the lines:

```
resources :awards
resources :students
```

Delete them, and replace them with:

```
resources :students do
  resources :awards
end
```

The nested code reflects a nested resource relationship.

You'll still be able to visit *http://localhost:3000/students/*, but *http://localhost:3000/awards/* will return an error. The routing support that the link_to methods expected when the original scaffolding was built has been demolished. The views in the *app/views/awards* directory are now visible only if users go through students, and this change of position requires some changes to the views.

Instead of the old URLs, which looked like:

```
http://localhost:3000/awards/2
```

the URLs to awards now follow a more complicated route:

```
http://localhost:3000/students/3/awards/2
```

That added students/3 reflects that the award with the id of 2 belongs to the student with the id of 3.

Changing the Controller

While changing the routing is a one-line exercise, the impact on the awards controller is much more complicated. Most of it reflects the need to limit the awards to the specified student. Example 9-1 shows the new controller with all changes bolded and commented. Most of the changes simply add the student object as context.

Example 9-1. Updating a controller to represent a nested resource

```
class AwardsController < ApplicationController
  before_action :get_student
  before_action :set_award, only: [:show, :edit, :update, :destroy]

  # GET /awards
  # GET /awards.json
  def index
    @awards = @student.awards
    # was @awards = Award.all
  end

  # GET /awards/1
  # GET /awards/1.json
  def show
  end

  # GET /awards/new
  def new
    @award = @student.awards.build
    # was @award = Award.new
  end

  # GET /awards/1/edit
  def edit
  end

  # POST /awards
  # POST /awards.json
  def create
    @award = @student.awards.build(award_params)
    # was @award = Award.new(award_params)

    respond_to do |format|
      if @award.save
        format.html { redirect_to student_awards_url(@student),
        notice: 'Award was successfully created.' }
        # was format.html { redirect_to @award,
        # notice: 'Award was successfully created.' }
        format.json { render :show, status: :created, location: @award }
      else

      and
```

```ruby
def update
  respond_to do |format|
    if @award.update(award_params)
      format.html { redirect_to student_awards_url(@student),
      notice: 'Award was successfully updated.' }
      # was format.html { redirect_to @award,
      # notice: 'Award was successfully updated.' }
      format.json { render :show, status: :ok, location: @award }
    else
      format.html { render :edit }
      format.json { render json: @award.errors, status: :unprocessable_entity }
    end
  end
end

# DELETE /awards/1
# DELETE /awards/1.json
def destroy
  @award.destroy
  respond_to do |format|
    format.html { redirect_to (student_awards_path(@student)),
    notice: 'Award was successfully destroyed.' }
    format.json { head :no_content }
  end
end

private
  # get_student converts the student_id given by the routing
  # into an @student object, for use here and in the view
  def get_student
    @student = Student.find(params[:student_id])
  end

  # Use callbacks to share common setup or constraints between actions.
  def set_award
    @award = @student.awards.find(params[:id])

    # @award = Award.find(params[:id])
  end

  # Never trust parameters from the scary internet,
  # only allow the whitelist through.
  def award_params
    params.require(:award).permit(:name, :year, :student_id)
  end
end
```

Most of these changes, in some form or another, convert a reference to awards generally to a reference to an award that applies to a particular student. You'll see some naming inconsistencies as that context forces different syntax: Award.all simply disappears, new becomes `build`, and `awards_url` becomes `student_awards_url`. These new, different methods are created automatically by Rails thanks to the routing changes made earlier. Eventually these shifts will feel normal to you.

The new `AwardsController` uses one new technique. It starts with a `before_action`, a call to code that will get executed before everything else does. In this case, the `before_action` calls the `get_student` method, which helps reduce the amount of repetition in the controller. The controller will receive the `student_id` value from routing, taking from the URL. Practically all of the time, though, it makes more sense to work with the corresponding `Student` object. The `get_student` method takes the `student_id` and uses it to retrieve the matching object and place it in the `@student` variable. That simplifies the methods in the controller and will also be used in the views.

 It's not hard to imagine a circumstance in which users want a complete list of awards and students. You can still provide one—it's just an extra step beyond the nested resource, requiring its own routing, controller method, and view.

Changing the Award Views

If users visit the new URLs at this point, they'll get some strange results. Rails routing originally defined one set of methods to support the old approach, and not only the results but also the method names and parameters need to change.

In the old version of *app/views/awards/index.html.erb*, the Show/Edit/Destroy links looked like Example 9-2, while the updated version looks like Example 9-3. Updates are marked in bold.

Example 9-2. Code for displaying awards before nesting by student

```
<p id="notice"><%= notice %></p>

<h1>Awards</h1>

  <table>
    <thead>
      <tr>
        <th>Name</th>
        <th>Year</th>
        <th>Student</th>
        <th colspan="3"></th>
      </tr>
    </thead>

    <tbody>
```

```erb
  <% @awards.each do |award| %>
    <tr>
      <td><%= award.name %></td>
      <td><%= award.year %></td>
      <td><%= award.student.name %></td>
      <td><%= link_to 'Show', award  %></td>
      <td><%= link_to 'Edit', edit_award_path(award) %></td>
      <td><%= link_to 'Destroy', award, method: :delete,
        data: { confirm: 'Are you sure?' } %></td>
    </tr>
    <% end %>
  </tbody>
</table>

<%= link_to 'New Award', new_award_path %>
```

Example 9-3. Displaying the awards on a student-by-student basis

```erb
<p id="notice"><%= notice %></p>

<h1> Awards for <%= @student.name %></h1>

<% if !@student.awards.empty? %>
  <table>
    <thead>
      <tr>
        <th>Name</th>
        <th>Year</th>
        <th>Student</th>
        <th colspan="3"></th>
      </tr>
    </thead>

    <tbody>
      <% @awards.each do |award| %>
        <tr>
          <td><%= award.name %></td>
          <td><%= award.year %></td>
          <td><%= award.student.name %></td>
          <td><%= link_to 'Show', [ @student, award ] %></td>
          <td><%= link_to 'Edit', edit_student_award_path( @student, award ) %></td>
          <td><%= link_to 'Destroy', [ @student, award ], method: :delete,
            data: { confirm: 'Are you sure?' } %></td>
        </tr>
      <% end %>
    </tbody>
  </table>

  <br>
<% else %>
  <p><%= @student.given_name %> hasn't won any awards yet.</p>
<% end %>
```

```
<%= link_to 'New Award', new_student_award_path(@student) %> |
<%= link_to 'Back', @student %>
```

In the new version, Example 9-3, the additional information about the student informs nearly every interaction. The headline (h1) has acquired the name of a specific student, rather than just being "Awards" generally. There's extra logic—the if and else statements—to make sure that awards are only displayed for students who have awards, presenting a polite message for students without awards.

The largest changes, however, are in the logic that creates links. The Show and Destroy links change arguments, from just award to [@student, award], reflecting the additional information link_to will need to create a proper link. The links for Edit and New Award call a different method, new_student_award_path, which will work through the nested resource routing to generate a link pointing to the right place. Given an argument for both a student and an award, it will generate a link to edit that award; given just a student argument, it will generate a link to create a new award for that student.

There's also a new Back link that goes back to the student's page. That's completely new navigation, necessary because of the extra context this page now has. Figure 9-8 shows what all of this looks like for Jules Miller with his two awards, while Figure 9-9 shows the result for Milletta Stim, who hasn't won any yet.

Figure 9-8. The awards list, scoped to a particular student

Figure 9-9. The awards list, when the student doesn't have any awards yet

The changes to *show.html.erb* are smaller, turning the links from:

```
<%= link_to Edit, edit_award_path(@award) %> |
<%= link_to Back, awards_path %>
```

to:

```
<%= link_to Edit, edit_student_award_path(@student, @award) %> |
<%= link_to Back, student_awards_path(@student) %>
```

The information displayed is the same, and context has little effect except on the links. Everything still looks like Example 9-3 except that the URL is different, and you'd see a different link in the status bar if you rolled over Edit or Back.

There are also some minor changes to *new.html.erb* and *edit.html.erb*. Both of them get new headlines:

```
<h1>New Award for <%= @student.name %></h1>
```

and:

```
<h1>Editing Award for <%= @student.name %></h1>
```

Yet again, the links at the bottom change (though only the second line applies to *new.html.erb*):

```
<%= link_to Show, [@student, @award] %> |
<%= link_to Back, student_awards_path(@student) %>
```

In *_form.html.erb*, the form_for call changes from:

```
<%= form_for(@award) do |f| %>
```

to:

```
<%= form_for([@student, award]) do |f| %>
```

You should also delete the `:student_id` selector.

Given an array of arguments instead of a single argument, `form_for` can automatically adjust to get the routing right for its data. The rest of the form fields look the same except that the `select` call to create the picklist for students disappears completely, as that information comes from context.

Figure 9-10 shows the form for entering a new award in use, and Figure 9-11 shows the form for editing an existing award.

Figure 9-10. Entering a new award for a particular student

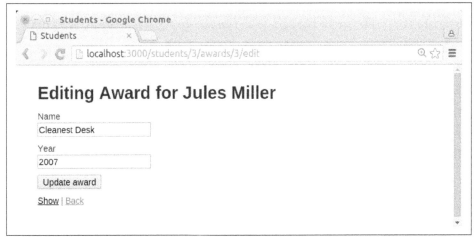

Figure 9-11. Editing an award—note the disappearance of the select box

Connecting the Student Views

There's one last set of things to address: adding links from the student views to the awards views. Awards used to have their own independent interface, but now they're deeply dependent on students. There are only two places where adding links makes clear sense, though: in the index listing and in the view that shows each student.

In *show.html.erb*, add a link to the awards for the student between Edit and Back with:

```
<%= link_to 'Awards', student_awards_path(@student) %> |
```

As shown in Figure 9-12, that'll give you a path to the awards for a student. (You might drop the existing list of awards there, too.)

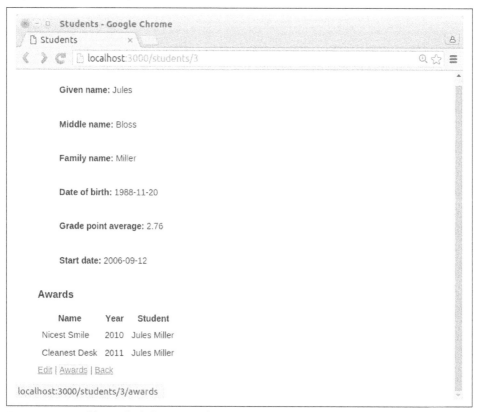

Figure 9-12. Adding a link from a student to a student's awards

That may actually be all the interface you want, but sometimes it's easier to look at a list of students and click on an Awards button for them. To add that, you need to add a column to the table displayed in *index.html.erb*. Between the links for Edit and Destroy, add:

```
<td><%= link_to 'Awards', student_awards_path(student) %></td>
```

The result will look like Figure 9-13. If users click on the Awards links, that will bring them to pages like Figures 9-8 and 9-9.

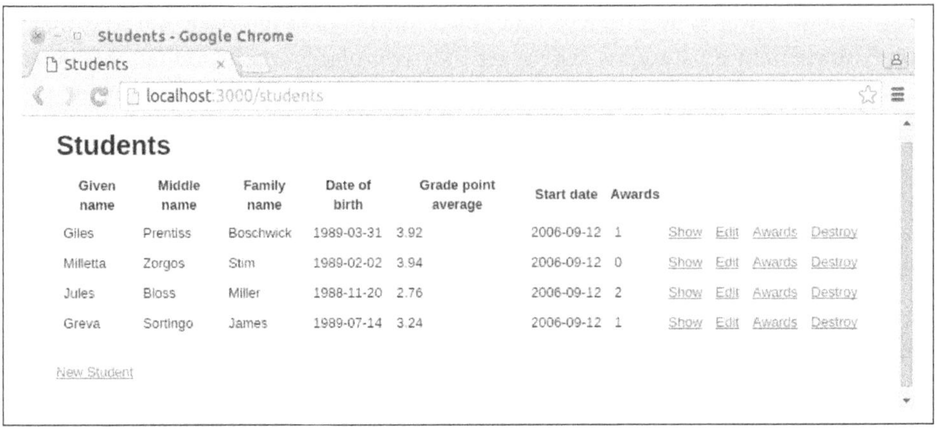

Figure 9-13. Student listing with connection to awards for each

Is Nesting Worth It?

Shifting awards from having their own interface to an interface subordinate to students was a lot of work. It's fairly clear why nesting resources is the "right" approach in Rails—it makes the has_many/belongs_to relationship explicit on every level, not just in the model. The work in the routing and the controller establishes the changes necessary for both the regular web user interface and the RESTful web services interface to work this way. The views, unfortunately, take some additional effort to bring in line, and you may have had a few ideas of your own while reading this about how you'd like them to work.

In the abstract, nesting is a great idea, but at the same time, it requires a lot of careful work to implement correctly in the views layer. That work may or may not be your first priority, though if you're going to nest resources, it's easier done earlier in the implementation process rather than later.

If you've built nested resources, you may find situations where you need to build additional interfaces. Sometimes the supposedly subordinate model is the main one people want to work with. In the awards example, most of the time people might want to know what awards a student has received or add an occasional award, and the nested interface will work just fine. However, if lots of awards are given out across an entire school at the end of the year, and one person has the task of entering every award into the system, that person might want a more direct interface rather than walking through the nesting. This situation could be addressed with an extra view that looked more like the ones earlier in the chapter.

Whether or not you decide to nest your own resources, you now have the information you need to do so, and you'll know what you're working with should you encounter Rails applications built using nested resources.

Many-to-Many: Connecting Students to Courses

The other frequent relationship between tables or models is many-to-many. A student, for example, can be taking zero or more courses, while a course can have zero or more students. (Students with zero courses might not yet have registered for anything, while courses with zero students might be awaiting registration or just unpopular.)

The relationship between the two is equal from a modeling standpoint, so there won't be any need for nested resources, just a lot of connections. As usual, it makes sense to move up from the database through models to controllers and views to produce the code in *ch09/students03*. And also as usual, while Rails provides you with a foundation, you're still going to need to add a lot to that foundation.

 Remember, don't name a table "classes," or you will have all kinds of strange Rails disasters because of name conflicts. "Courses" is a safer option.

Creating Tables

Building a many-to-many relationship requires creating tables—not just a single table, but a many-to-many relationship that will require adding two tables beyond the student table already in the application. One will be the actual course list, and the other the table that joins courses to students, as shown in Figure B-5 of Appendix B. Creating the course list—which will need a full set of scaffolding—is simple:

```
rails generate scaffold course name:string
```

Creating the join table requires an extra few steps. Start by creating a migration:

```
rails generate migration CreateCoursesStudents
```

Doing this will create a migration file in *db/migrate* with a name that ends in *create_courses_students.rb*. Unfortunately, when you open it, all you'll see is:

```
class CreateCoursesStudents < ActiveRecord::Migration
  def change
    create_table :courses_students do |t|
    end
  end
end
```

Once again, you've reached the boundaries of what autogenerated code will do for you for the present. Creating the connecting table will require coding the migration directly. A simple approach, building just on what you've seen in previous generated migrations, looks like:

```
class CreateCoursesStudents < ActiveRecord::Migration
  def change
    create_table :courses_students, id: false do |t|
      t.integer :course_id, null: false
      t.integer :student_id, null: false
    end
      end
end
```

All of this depends on meeting the Rails expectations for naming conventions. The table name is the combination of the two models being joined in alphabetical order, and the fields within the table are id values for each of the other models.

There is one performance-related issue to consider here. Rails has used the id value for tables as its main approach for getting data into and out of them rapidly. The id value, which you don't have to specify, is automatically indexed. If you want your application to be able to move through the many course_id and student_id values in this table, however, you'll need to add an index, as in:

```
class CreateCoursesStudents < ActiveRecord::Migration
  def change
    create_table :courses_students, id: false do |t|
      t.integer :course_id, null: false
      t.integer :student_id, null: false
    end

    # Add index to speed up looking up the connection, and ensure
    # we only enroll a student into each course once
    add_index :courses_students, [:course_id, :student_id], unique: true
  end
end
```

Indexes will be explained in greater detail in Chapter 13. Before moving on to the next steps, run **rails db:migrate** to build your tables.

Connecting the Models

Like has_many and belongs_to, has_and_belongs_to_many is a declaration that goes in the model. In *app/models/student.rb*, add:

```
# a student can be in many courses, a course can have many students
has_and_belongs_to_many :courses
```

And in *app/models/course.rb*, add:

```
# a student can be in many courses, a course can have many students
  has_and_belongs_to_many :students
```

That's all you need to do to establish the connection. Rails will automatically—thanks to naming conventions—use the `courses_students` table you built to keep track of the connections between students and courses.

You may find it useful to add some convenience methods to the model, depending on what you need in your interfaces. In the `students` model, it makes sense to add some logic that answers basic questions and returns some information that Rails won't provide automatically. These build, of course, on the `courses` object that Rails did add to the model. First, in the student model (*student.rb*), a convenience method checks to see whether a given student is enrolled in a specified course:

```
def enrolled_in?(course)
  self.courses.include?(course)
end
```

The `enrolled_in?` method uses the `include?` method of `courses` to check whether a particular course is included in the list. If it is, then the student is enrolled, and `include?` and `enrolled_in?` will both return `true`. Otherwise, they return `false`.

> The `enrolled_in?` convenience method will get called many times as the number of courses grows, executing the same query repeatedly. For now, its clarity is probably more important than its performance, but as you get more familiar with how Rails interacts with databases, you will want to optimize this method for better performance.

A similarly useful convenience method returns the list of courses that a student is not yet enrolled in, making it easy to create logic and forms that will let him or her enroll:

```
def unenrolled_courses
  Course.all - self.courses
end
```

This one-liner does some tricky set arithmetic. First, it calls `Course.all` to get a full list of all the courses available. Then it calls `self.courses` to get a list of the courses that already apply to this particular student. Finally, it does subtraction—set subtraction—removing the courses in `self.courses` from the full list. The `-` doesn't just have to mean subtracting one number from another.

> The `has_and_belongs_to_many` relationship is somewhat controversial; some developers may prefer a `has_many :through` relationship, creating the intermediate table by hand.

Adding to the Controllers

Many-to-many relationships don't demand the kinds of controller change that nested resources did. You don't need to change method calls inside of the generated code, but you may want to add some further methods to support functionality for both courses and students. While the added methods in the models focused on data manipulation, the methods in the controllers will add logic supporting interfaces to that data. The basic RESTful interfaces will remain, and the new interfaces will supplement them with some extra functionality specific to the combination of the two models.

In *app/controllers/courses_controller.rb*, the currently simple application only needs one extra method:

```
# GET /courses/1/roll
def roll
  @course = Course.find(params[:id])
end
```

Add this after the `destroy` method at the end of the controller, but before the `private` keyword. The `roll` method, which will need a *roll.html.erb* view, will just provide a list of which students are in a given course for roll call. The `:id` parameter will identify which course needs a list.

There's more to add in *app/controllers/students_controller.rb*, as we need a way to add students to and remove them from courses. First, though, it makes sense to create a means of listing which courses a student is in:

```
# GET /students/1/courses
def courses
  @student = Student.find(params[:id])
  @courses = @student.courses
end
```

As the `:get_student` method did for awards, the `courses` method takes an `id` value given it by the routing and turns it into an object—in this case a pair of objects, representing a given student and the courses he or she is taking.

The next two methods are pretty different from the controller methods the book has shown so far. Instead of passing data to a view, they collect information from the routing and use it to manipulate the models and then redirect the user to a more ordinary page with the result. The first, `course_add`, takes a `student_id` and a single `course_id` and adds the student to that course:

```
# POST /students/1/course_add?course_id=2
# (note no real query string, just
# convenient notation for parameters)

def course_add
```

```
#Convert ids from routing to objects
@student = Student.find(params[:id])
@course = Course.find(params[:course])

unless @student.enrolled_in?(@course)
  #add course to list using << operator
  @student.courses << @course
  flash[:notice] = 'Student was successfully enrolled'
else
  flash[:error] = 'Student was already enrolled'
end

redirect_to action: "courses", id: @student
end
```

The course_add method uses the enrolled_in? method defined earlier in the model to check if the student is already in the course. If not, it adds the appropriate course object to the list of courses for that student and reports that all went well using flash[:notice]. If the student was already enrolled, it blocks the enrollment and reports the problem using flash[:error]. Then it redirects to a list of courses for the student, which will show the flash message as well as the list.

The remove method, for demonstration purposes, is a little bit different. It accepts a list of courses to remove the student from. It then tests the list to see if the student was actually enrolled and deletes the record connecting the student to the course if so. It also logs the removal to the info log of the application and then redirects to the same page as course_add, listing the courses for a student:

```
# POST /students/1/course_remove?courses[]=
def course_remove

  #Convert ids from routing to object
  @student = Student.find(params[:id])

  #get list of courses to remove from query string
  course_ids = params[:courses]

  if course_ids.any?
    course_ids.each do |course_id|
      course = Course.find(course_id)
      if @student.enrolled_in?(course)
        logger.info "Removing student from course #{course.id}"
        @student.courses.delete(course)
        flash[:notice] = 'Course was successfully deleted'
      end
    end
  end
  redirect_to action: "courses", id: @student
end
```

Adding Routing

Making those controllers work requires telling Rails that they exist and how they should be called. Again, Chapter 13 will explain routing in greater depth, but you can add extra methods to an existing REST resource through its `:member` named parameter. To add the `roll` method to the routing the scaffolding created, add a `member` to *config/routes.rb*:

```
resources :courses do
  member do
    get :roll
  end
end
```

For students, there are more methods, so the `member` list is a bit more complicated, though generally similar:

```
resources :students do
  resources :awards

  member do
    get :courses
    post :course_add
    post :course_remove
  end

end
```

At this point, Rails knows how to find the extra methods. All that's left is adding support for them to the views.

Supporting the Relationship Through Views

Cementing the relationship between students and courses requires giving users access to the functionality provided by the controllers and models. This can happen on several levels—application-wide navigation, showing counts in related views, and view support for the newly created controllers.

Establishing navigation

The views created by the scaffolding give basic access to both the students and the courses, but there's no user-interface connection or even a navigation connection between them. A first step might add links to both the student pages and the course pages, letting users move between them. As this is moving toward navigation for the application and as it will get used across a lot of different pages, it makes sense to create a navigation partial for easy reuse.

To do that, create a new file, *app/views/application/_navigation.html.erb*. (You'll need to create the *application* directory.) Its contents are simple, creating links to the main lists of students and courses:

```
<p>
  <%= link_to "Students", students_path %> |
  <%= link_to "Courses", courses_path %>
</p>

<hr>
```

You could reference this partial from every view, but that's an inconvenient way to reference a partial that was meant to reduce the amount of repetition needed in the first place. Instead, add it to the layout for the entire app in *app/views/layouts/application.html.erb*. In each file, insert the boldfaced code below the body tag:

```
<body>

<%= render 'navigation' %>

<%= yield %>
```

Every page in the application will now have links to the Students and Courses main index page, as shown in Figure 9-14.

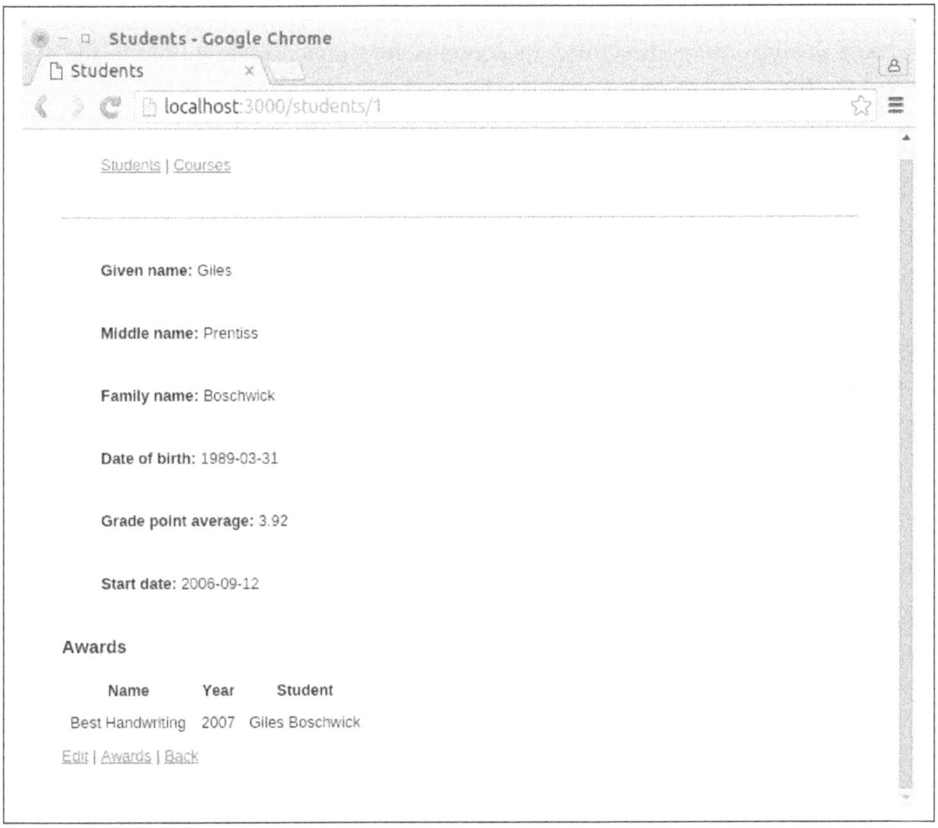

Figure 9-14. Navigation links to Students and Courses

Showing counts

The index page for students, *app/views/students/index.html.erb*, currently lists a count for awards, and you can add a count for courses the same way. You need to insert a heading, `<th>Courses</th>`, in the first tr element, just before `<th>Awards</th>`:

```
<th>Courses</th>
```

and then insert:

```
<td><%= student.courses.count %></td>
```

just before the count of awards. Figure 9-15 shows what this looks like, though the header names are abbreviated a bit to make the table fit better. Note that there aren't any students in courses yet—the interface for adding them hasn't yet been built.

Figure 9-15. Students list showing course counts

Although the *app/views/courses/index.html.erb* file has less in it, you can add
`<th>Enrolled</th>` in the first `tr` element:

```
<th>Enrolled</th>
```

and insert:

```
<td><%= course.students.count %></td>
```

Figure 9-16 shows the courses list, which hasn't been shown previously, though the
RESTful interface made it easy to add the courses used in Appendix B.

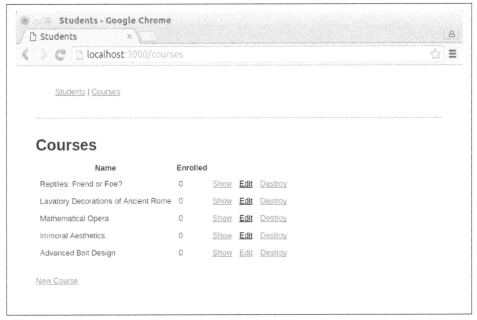

Figure 9-16. Course list showing enrollment counts

Again, no one is registered for any courses yet, so adding that functionality is a natural next step.

Enrolling students in courses

The critical piece for connecting students to courses is, of course, the form for adding courses to students. That form could be linked from the main list if you wanted, but for now, we'll update the *app/views/students/show.html.erb* form, so that it acts as the gateway to a student's awards and courses. There are two pieces to this. First, add a list of courses perhaps in place of the awards list:

```
<p>
  <strong>Courses:</strong>
  <% if !@student.courses.empty? %>
    <%= @student.courses.collect {|c| link_to(c.name, c)}.join(", ").html_safe %>
  <% else %>
    Not enrolled on any courses yet.
  <% end %>
</p>
```

This is much more compact than the table of awards. The `if` checks to see whether the student is registered for any courses. If so, it builds a compact list of courses using the `collect` method. If not, it just says so.

Second, add a link in the cluster of `link_to` calls at the bottom of the file:

```
<%= link_to 'Edit', edit_student_path(@student) %> |
<%= link_to 'Courses', courses_student_path(@student) %> |
<%= link_to 'Awards', student_awards_path(@student) %> |
<%= link_to 'Back', students_path %>
```

Also, when adding a table cell in this manner, the colspan attribute of the final <th>
tag (inside the <thead></thead> markup block) needs to be changed from "3" to "4"
to accommodate the new link. Bear in mind that where the navigation partial called
courses_url, this calls courses_student_path with a specific student. That will take
the user to a page such as *http://localhost:3000/students/1/courses*—which hasn't been
created yet. To create that page, create a *courses.html.erb* file in the *app/views/students*
directory. Example 9-4 shows one possible approach to creating a form for registering
and unregistering students from courses.

*Example 9-4. A courses.html.erb view for registering and removing students from
courses*

```
<h1><%= @student.name %>'s courses</h1>

<% if @courses.length > 0 %>
 <%= form_tag(course_remove_student_path(@student)) do %>
 <table>
  <thead>
    <tr>
       <th>Course</th>
       <th>Remove?</th>
    </tr>
  </thead>

  <tbody>
  <% for course in @courses do %>
    <tr>
      <td><%= course.name %></td>
      <td><%= check_box_tag "courses[]", course.id %></td>
    </tr>
  <% end %>
  </tbody>
 </table>
  <br />

  <%= submit_tag 'Remove checked courses' %>
  <% end %>
<% else %>
  <p>Not enrolled in any courses yet.</p>
<% end %>

<h2>Enroll in new course</h2>

<% if @student.courses.count < Course.count then %>
  <%= form_tag(course_add_student_path(@student)) do %>
```

```
        <%= select_tag(:course,
          options_from_collection_for_select(@student.unenrolled_courses,
            :id, :name)) %>
        <%= submit_tag 'Enroll' %>
    <% end %>
<% else %>
    <p><%= @student.name %> is enrolled in every course.</p>
<% end %>

<p><%=link_to "Back", @student %></p>
```

This view contains two forms. Unlike most of the previous forms, these are created with the form_tag rather than the form_for method because they aren't bound to a particular model. The first form appears if the student is already enrolled in any courses, allowing the user to remove them from those courses. The second form appears if there are courses that the student hasn't yet enrolled in. (More sophisticated program logic might set a different kind of limit.) Each of the forms connects to a controller method on students—course_remove for the first one and course_add for the second.

The form for removing courses uses a list of checkboxes generated from the list of courses, while the form for adding them uses the somewhat more opaque but very powerful options_from_collection_for_select method. This helper method takes a collection—here, the list of courses returned by @student.unenrolled_courses, and two values. The first, :id, is the value to return if a line in the select form is chosen, and the second, :name, is the value the user should see in the form.

Figure 9-17 shows the page before a student has registered for any courses, while Figure 9-18 shows the confirmation and removal options available once the student has signed up for his first course.

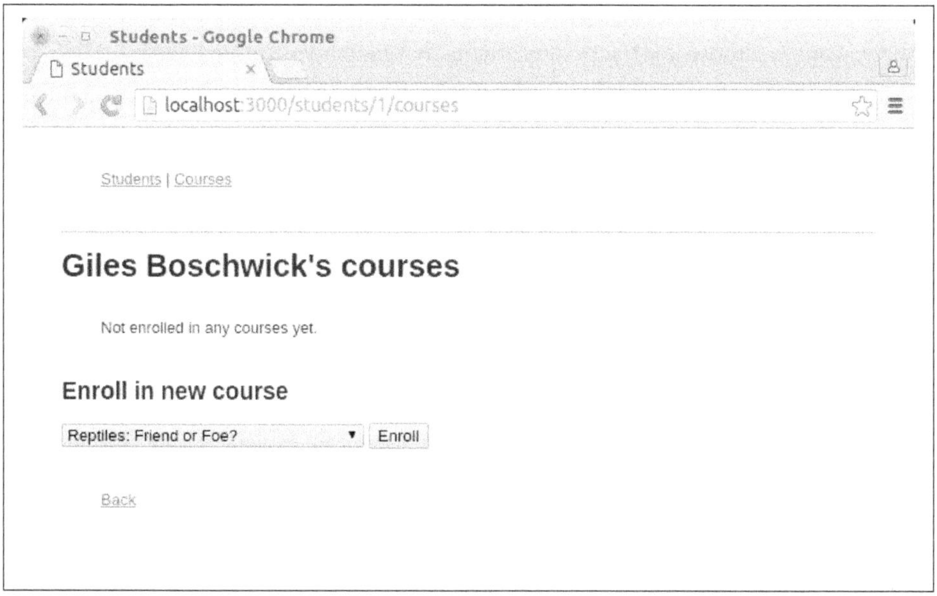

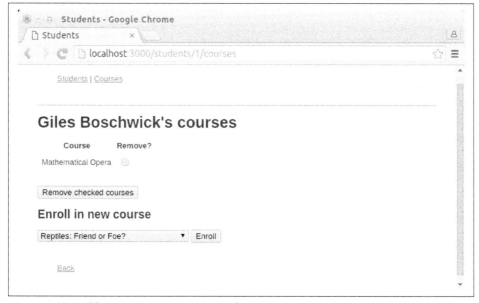

Figure 9-17. *Adding courses, the first time around*

Figure 9-18. *Adding or removing courses after a student has signed up*

The checkboxes will create the parameters for course_remove and are a good choice when you want to operate on multiple objects at once. The select box is much slower and produces the results needed for the single-parameter `course_add`. You will, of course, want to choose interface components that match your users' needs.

There's one last component in need of finishing: the view that corresponds to the `roll` method on the courses controller. In *app/views/courses/show.html.erb*, add this link between the scaffolding's `link_to` calls for Edit and Back:

```
<%= link_to 'Roll', roll_course_path(@course) %> |
```

That will add the link shown in Figure 9-19, which will let users get to the list of students.

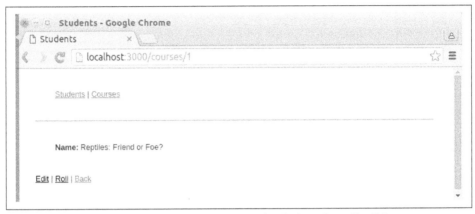

Figure 9-19. A (very brief) course description with a link to the roll call list

The actual roll call list code, shown in Example 9-5, and belonging in *app/views/courses/roll.html.erb*, is another simple table.

Example 9-5. Generating a roll call list through the connections from courses to students

```erb
<h1>Roll for <%= @course.name %></h1>

<% if @course.students.count > 0 %>
  <table>
    <thead>
    <tr>
      <th>Student</th>
      <th>GPA</th>
    </tr>
    </thead>
    <tbody>
    <% @course.students.each do |student| %>
      <tr>
        <td><%= link_to student.name, student %></td>
        <td><%= student.grade_point_average %></td>
      </tr>
    <% end %>
```

```
    </tbody>
  </table>
<% else %>
  <p>No students are enrolled.</p>
<% end %>

<p><%= link_to "Back", @course %></p>
```

The list of students is accessible from the `@course` object that the `roll` method in the controller exposed. That method didn't have anything specific to do with students, but because the students for the course are included in the `course` object, all of their information is available for display in the table as shown in Figure 9-20. The links that `link_to` generated let you go directly to the student's record, making it easy to modify students who are in a particular course.

Figure 9-20. A roll call that connects to records for students in the class

What's Missing?

At this point, you should be starting to get a sense of what's involved in building a real Rails application. These examples really just scratch the surface both of what's necessary and of what's possible.

While the students and courses application has gone much further into Rails than previous applications, it's still largely built on the scaffolding. The connections between course and student interfaces could be deepened. The new methods, while certainly functional, don't follow the same clean architectural lines that their RESTful predecessors had, taking a more direct path to getting things done. And finally, they don't offer the same JSON-in/JSON-out functionality of their RESTful predecessors.

There are also a few more relationships you can explore as you get further into Rails development. The `has_and_belongs_to_many` relationship can be used, for example, to connect a table to foreign keys in the same table, creating a *self-referential* join. There's also `has_many :through`, which lets you connect one table to another through an intermediate table, rather than directly with a foreign key. And finally, there's `has_one`, which is much like `has_many` but limits itself to one connection.

Which of those opportunities are priorities for you depends on the needs of your own application. You may have related tables that need only occasional connections, or tables whose connections aren't modified directly by users. A JSON-based API may be central for you, or it may be a pointless luxury that the RESTful scaffolding already overindulges in. Your allegiance to REST may not yet be that firm in any event.

There's always more you could do, but at this point, you have the basics you need to build real applications. The next few chapters will give you additional tools and techniques, and there's always more to learn, but congratulations! You now know most of what needs to be done to build an application.

Test Your Knowledge

Quiz

1. Where do you specify data relationships?

2. How much effort does Rails put into enforcing relationships between models?

3. What does the `collect` method do?

4. How can you check to see whether a related record exists?

5. Why would you want to go to the trouble of creating a nested resource?

6. When would you use a `before_action`?

7. What does `form_for` do when it is passed an array for its first argument?

8. What two columns are needed in a join table?

9. Why would you want to index the columns of a join table?

10. Where do you tell Rails about new methods you've added to the scaffolding?

Answers

1. Relationships are specified in models. The models on both sides of any given relationship must identify how they relate to the other model. For example, a `has_many` relationship in one model should be matched by a `belongs_to` relationship in another model.

2. Rails doesn't put any effort into enforcing relationships between models. If you have constraints to impose, you need to create code that checks and enforces them.

3. The `collect` method iterates over a collection and gathers the results from a block. It's an easy way to turn a list of data into a `select` list, for instance.

4. You could check for a related record with `find`, but in most validation contexts, it's easier to use the `validates_existence_of` gem. (If you want to check for a related *valid* record, then Rails's built-in `validates_associated` will work.)

5. Nested resources have some programming aesthetic appeal, but they're also useful for making relationships explicit and easily enforceable.

6. `before_actions` are useful anytime you have code that should run in advance of all of the other methods being called. It might be initialization code, or code that tests that certain conditions have been met.

7. The `form_for` method uses the first argument to establish the target for the form's results. If the first argument is a single object, it will create a URL pointing to that object. If the first argument is an array containing more than one object, it assumes that the first object contains the second and generates a URL reflecting a nested resource relationship.

8. A join table needs a column to store `id` values for each of the two models it connects. By Rails conventions, these columns are named *model*_id. A column linking to students, for example, should be `student_id`.

9. Indexing both of the columns in a join table will give you much better response times than leaving them unindexed.

10. You'll need to add information about new methods in the *routes.rb* file and create views for them as well.

## CHAPTER 10

Managing Databases with Migrations

To improve is to change; to be perfect is to change often.
—Winston Churchill

Winston Churchill's quote is quite applicable in the case of migrations. Part of the goal of migrations is to track changes to your database over time. Migrations might seem strange at first, but over time they'll become a very ordinary part of your work, whether you generate them automatically or customize them by hand. The Rails approach to managing data structures is very different from the traditional separation of database design from programming. While Rails still maintains a separate toolkit for defining data structures, that toolkit attempts to improve on the traditional SQL data definition language (DDL) by wrapping DDL in Ruby code.

Migrations are something of a world of their own in the Rails environment, but they are still recognizably Rails, built into the same development process. Migrations are all written in Ruby code using a fairly small set of conventions. This book has used migrations throughout—you can't write much of a Rails application without them—but until the last chapter, and then only once, those migrations were generated with Rails's inventive scripts. Once you move past those scripts, migrations are a little more difficult, but still not that complicated.

The details of migrations may not be your first priority. You can safely skip this chapter and come back to it if database and data structure management seem like good reading for a really rainy day.

What Migrations Offer You

Migrations are part of Rails's general effort to separate developers from direct contact with databases. From a Rails perspective, databases are kind of a "giant hash in the sky," a conveniently persistent storage system for data that shouldn't need much direct attention. While it's good to have a general idea of the database structures underneath your application and to know what tables and rows are, so you can communicate with people outside of Rails development, in many ways Rails itself represents a revolt against database culture in web programming. (Rails apps still largely run on relational databases; however, NoSQL options such as MongoDB are widely used as well.)

Migrations reflect the approach Rails takes to databases. Rails expects database structures to grow and change as the application itself grows and changes. There need not be a large planning meeting at the start of a project to lay out database structures and responsibility for maintaining them—responsibility for the database lies with the same programmers who are writing the rest of the code. Those programmers will make changes as and when they see fit.

As a result, migrations are effectively lists of changes. Each migration is a set of instructions that applies to the results of the previous migration. The first migration creates the first table and probably some rows and columns, and later migrations can create their own tables or modify existing tables.

Also, because programmers can (and do) make mistakes, migrations are designed to be reversible. As long as you take care to be certain your migrations are reversible, migrations offer an incredibly flexible approach that lets you make changes to your database whenever and wherever necessary. (Some operations, of course, can't be reversed. We'll discuss some of those later in the chapter.)

Because Rails works hard at staying independent of any given database implementation, migrations also offer you a convenient technique for creating your application using one database for development or testing and yet another for deployment. They also offer developers a way to deploy improvements even after an application's live version has been released on a production server. However, patching live databases supporting real users can still be a scary proposition.

It's generally a good idea to stick to migrations when managing databases for use with Rails. You may know a lot about MySQL, SQLite, PostgreSQL, Oracle, or whatever database engine you've chosen and be able to tweak your application's database for better performance. Everything will go along fine—until Rails discovers that its migrations' opinion of what your database contains is different from what is actually there.

You may have an especially hard time rolling back migrations as a result, and it'll require careful work to transfer the work you did in the database to the live production environment as well.

You certainly *can* work on your databases directly. Sometimes that will be necessary, especially if you're trying to retrofit Rails to a previously existing database. It's very important, however, to be cautious about doing that until you're completely confident in how these interactions work.

Migration Basics

Migrations are maintained in files stored in the *db/migrate* folder. Each file contains one more or less discrete set of changes to the underlying database. Unlike most of the code you write, migrations are not automatically run when you start up Rails; instead, they wait for an explicit command or `rails db:migrate`.

Migration Files

To create the most basic of Rails migration files, we again harness the power of the `generate` command:

```
rails generate migration empty_migration
```

This simple command will generate an empty migration file in the *db/migrate* directory. However, the filename may look a bit peculiar—something like *20151110005156_empty_migration.rb* (as you can see in *ch10/migrationTester/db/migrate*). The first part of the filename is an exact timestamp of the moment the migration file was generated. The second portion is the name of the migration we provided in the command. You can use `CamelCase` if preferred; Rails will understand and convert the name to `underscores_between_words` format.

A migration is simply pure "vanilla" Ruby. While you could create migration files by hand, you should probably stick to using `generate`. Among other things, this will make life easier by correctly appending the timestamp to the filenames. You can edit those files afterward as needed. Many `generate` calls will create migrations as part of their work toward creating a model and supporting infrastructure, but if you just want to create a blank migration, enter the command **rails generate migration** **NameOfMigration**, where *NameOfMigration* is a reasonably human-comprehensible description of what the migration is going to do. (Again, for the name, you can use CamelCase or underscores_between_words.) Your result, depending on the name you give it, will look something like Example 10-1.

Example 10-1. An empty migration file, fresh from rails generate

```
class EmptyMigration < ActiveRecord::Migration
  def change
  end
end
```

All migrations are descended from `ActiveRecord::Migration`. The `change` method is the heart of the migration. Everything created in this method should vanish when the migration is *rolled back*, leaving the database structure in the same state it had before the migration was run (more on the *rollback* task in the next section).

 As always, the `rails generate` command has smarts and surprises. If you name a migration along the lines of `AddAgeToPeople` and specify `age:integer`, Rails will create a migration that adds a field named `age` to the `people` table, sparing you some typing. (It also works the other way with migrations whose names begin with `Remove`.)

Migrations created as part of a scaffolding generation generally use the `change` method. At the time of this writing, the `change` method supports the following definitions, which Rails knows how to "reverse" should the migration be rolled back:

add_column

add_foreign_key

add_index

add_reference

add_timestamps

change_column_default (must supply a :from and :to option)

change_column_null

create_join_table

create_table

disable_extension

drop_join_table

drop_table (must supply a block)

enable_extension

remove_column (must supply a type)

remove_foreign_key (must supply a second table)

remove_index

remove_reference

remove_timestamps

rename_column

rename_index

rename_table

That's quite a list, and it includes those methods most commonly used by Rails developers. If you go beyond these, however, you'll need to use the self.up and self.down methods instead of change. These methods are fairly easy to understand. We'll explore an example later in this chapter using the popular change_column method.

 While you'll obviously be paying attention when writing your applications, and the generators shouldn't create problems, there's one situation that might still bite you: an unsaved file you're editing. If you think you've made changes and run the migration forward, but didn't save the file, and then save the file and roll the migration back…

Unfortunately, fixing it really depends on what exactly you did. Just be careful to make sure that you've saved all of your files when editing migrations before running them.

Running Migrations Forward and Backward

You apply migrations to the database using the appropriate Rails command. You can run rails --tasks to see the ever-growing list of tasks Rails supports, and most of the database-related tasks are prefixed with db:. While you're learning Rails, there are only three tasks that you really need to know, and two more you should be aware of:

db:migrate

You'll run rails db:migrate frequently to update your database to support the latest tables and columns you've added to your application. If you run your application and get lots of strange missing or nil object errors, odds are good that you forgot to run rails db:migrate. It also updates the *db/schema.rb* file, which is a one-stop description of your database.

`db:rollback`

If you made changes, but they didn't quite work out, `rails db:rollback` will let you remove the last migration applied. If you want to remove multiple migrations, you can specify `rails db:rollback STEP=n`, where *n* is the number of migrations you want to go back. Be careful—when Rails deletes a column or table, it discards the data. It also updates the *db/schema.rb* file, which is a one-stop description of your database.

`db:drop`

If things have gone really wrong with your migrations, `rails db:drop` offers you a "throw it all away and start over" option, obliterating the database you've built —and all its data.

`db:reset`

Using `rails db:reset` is a little different from using `rails db:drop`—it obliterates the database and then builds a new one using the *db/schema.rb* file, reflecting the last structure you'd created.

`db:create`

The `rails db:create` command tells the database to create a new database for your application without requiring you to learn the internal details of whatever database system you're using. (You must, of course, have the right permissions to create that database.)

Most of the time, `rails db:migrate` will be your primary interaction with `rails`. When you run it, it will show information on each migration it runs, as shown in Example 10-2, using the migrations from the previous chapter. (The start of each migration is bolded to make it easier to review the output.)

Example 10-2. Output from Migration, for a set of four migrations

```
$ rails db:migrate
== 20151202015608 CreateStudents: migrating =====================================
-- create_table(:students)
   -> 0.0022s
== 20151202015608 CreateStudents: migrated (0.0023s) ===========================

== 20151202015643 CreateAwards: migrating =======================================
-- create_table(:awards)
   -> 0.0015s
== 20151202015643 CreateAwards: migrated (0.0016s) =============================

== 20151202015725 CreateCourses: migrating ======================================
-- create_table(:courses)
   -> 0.0013s
== 20151202015725 CreateCourses: migrated (0.0014s) ===========================
```

```
== 20151202015800 CreateJoinTableCourseStudent: migrating =====================
== 20151202015800 CreateJoinTableCourseStudent: migrated (0.0000s) ============
```

The timing information may be more than you need to know, but you can see what got called in what migration. If something goes wrong, it will definitely let you know.

 Rails will happily let you perform operations on multiple tables from within a single migration. Eventually, that may be an attractive option, but when you're first starting out, it's usually easier to figure out what's going on, especially what's going wrong, when each migration operates only on a single table.

Inside Migrations

The easiest way to familiarize yourself with migrations is (as is often the case with Rails) to examine what Rails puts in them with `rails generate`. In Chapter 9, we created a `students` model with:

```
rails generate scaffold student given_name:string middle_name:string
family_name:string date_of_birth:date grade_point_average:decimal
start_date:date
```

This command generates many files, but the migration it created went into *db/20151108225528_create_students.rb* and contained the code shown in Example 10-3.

Example 10-3. Code for setting up a table, created with a change method

```
class CreateStudents < ActiveRecord::Migration
    def change
        create_table :students do |t|
          t.string :given_name
          t.string :middle_name
          t.string :family_name
          t.date :date_of_birth
          t.decimal :grade_point_average
          t.date :start_date

          t.timestamps
      end
    end
end
```

Working with Tables

Migrations can be plain and empty or more robust. By convention, migrations that create new tables start their names with "create." The following migration would build a migration with an empty table called "Books."

```
rails generate migration CreateBook
```

This produces a file (*db/migrate/20151110012135_create_book.rb*) with the following code:

```
class CreateBook < ActiveRecord::Migration
  def change
    create_table :books do |t|
    end
  end
end
```

The columns may then be added within the `create_table` method, as just shown, with the `t.` prefix.

 There isn't any listing here for an `id` value even though Rails uses `id`s for practically everything. Rails will automatically add an `id` to tables you create with `create_table` unless you specify the `id: false` option.

Just as columns can be added to a migration generated with scaffolding, these attributes can also be specified when you are generating a simple table like the preceding one. The following command generates the Books table with some basic columns:

```
rails generate migration CreateBookWithColumns title:string author:string
isbn:integer price:float published_date:date
```

which produces the migration file shown in Example 10-4 (*db/migrate/20151117015213_create_book_with_columns*).

Example 10-4. Another example of code for setting up a table with the change method

```
class CreateBookWithColumns < ActiveRecord::Migration
  def change
    create_table :book_with_columns do |t|
      t.string :title
      t.string :author
      t.integer :isbn
      t.float :price
      t.date :published_date
    end
  end
end
```

Data Types

As noted earlier, Rails supports 11 data types directly:

```
:string

:text

:integer

:float

:decimal

:datetime

:timestamp

:time

:date

:binary

:boolean
```

You can create each of these types by calling its name after the `t.` prefix. In Example 10-3, `t.string :given_name` creates a column in the `:students` table of type `string` that's named `given_name`. And `t.date :date_of_birth` creates a column in the `:students` table of type `date` that's named `date_of_birth`.

`t.timestamps` is not the same as `t.timestamp`. It is unique, a convenience method Rails uses to manage creation and modification times as `created_at` and `updated_at` columns. (You can remove timestamps with `t.remove_timestamps`.)

Each of the data types can accept named parameters as well:

- All of them accept `default: value`, though the results may not be what you expect since this doesn't pass through to the model. New models won't have the default value; users won't see them, and they'll be overwritten by whatever the users enter even if it's nothing.

- All types also accept `null: true|false` where the boolean value identifies whether or not a null value is acceptable. Set this to `false` to limit the column to nonnull values.

- `:string`, `:text`, `:binary`, and `:integer` types accept `limit: size`. The `size` is the permitted length of the value in characters or bytes.

- The `:decimal` data type also accepts `:precision` and `:scale` parameters. The `:precision` parameter specifies how many digits the number can have while the `:scale` parameter specifies how many of those digits appear after the decimal point.

Before a migration is run, named parameters can be added to columns depending on their data type. For example, you might edit the preceding migration to read as follows:

```
class CreateBookWithColumns < ActiveRecord::Migration
  def change
    create_table :book_with_columns do |t|
      # entries will be limited to 100 characters and cannot be
      # left empty
      t.string :title, limit: 100
      # entries will be limited to 45 characters
      t.string :author, limit: 45
      # entries will be limited to 13 characters
      t.integer :isbn, limit: 13
      # entries will follow the format "xxxx.xx"
      t.decimal :price, precision: 6, scale: 2
      # this sets the default value to today's  date. However,
      # this is not automatically persisted to the model and will be overwritten
      # with user-entered data.
      t.date :published_date, default: Date.today
    end
  end
end
```

This migration (*db/migrate/20151117015213_create_book_with_columns*) builds upon the last section where we created the Books table. We see here how a slightly more elaborate migration file can provide more specific column definitions as well as some basic constraints for the columns.

 Always specify :precision and :scale if your application might move across different databases like the common case of SQLite in development and MySQL in production. Different databases treat :decimal slightly differently, but specifying these parameters will minimize surprises.

You may find it useful to express these constraints in the migration for implementation in the database layer, but in most cases, you'll probably find it easier to establish these in the model layer with the validations discussed in Chapter 7. (Sometimes specifying :precision and :scale is recommended for :decimal types because of database incompatibilities, however.)

 You can, if necessary, create custom types specific to a given database. If you really, truly are certain you want to do that, study the config.active_record.schema_format setting that's in the *config/ environment.rb* file. In general, though, while it's nice to know that you *can* do this, you usually *shouldn't*.

Working with Columns

When you're first starting out, most of your data structure creation will be whole tables at a time. Once you've established your application, however, new ideas are bound to flow. You'll probably create some new tables, but you'll also create or remove columns within your existing tables. Conveniently, migrations support the `add_column` and `remove_column` methods.

Once the application has been established, table columns may still be added, removed, or changed with a standalone migration. Migrations that add to existing tables start their names with "add." For instance, if the Books table created in the previous section needed to specify the language in which books are written, simply create a migration with `rails g migration AddLanguageToBooks language:string`, which creates the following file (*20151119000940_add_language_to_book.rb*):

```
class AddLanguageToBook < ActiveRecord::Migration
  def change
    add_column :books, :language, :string
  end
end
```

We've already used migrations that add a column to an existing table. As you'll recall, Chapter 8 used a migration to add a column for file extensions:

```
class AddPhotoExtensionToPerson < ActiveRecord::Migration
  def change
    add_column :people, :extension, :string
  end
end
```

The first argument for `add_column` is the table to add the column to. The second argument is the name of the column, and the third argument is the type. You can add extra options, as discussed in "Data Types" on page 198, if you want named parameters following the type. Also note that `add_column` is a reversible method meaning that `rails db:rollback` can cleanly remove the new column.

But what if a column is deemed unnecessary further along in development? Perhaps other migrations have been made on top of the one that created the unwanted column. Thankfully, Rails provides us another means to remove it using the `remove_column` method. A command such as the following will do the trick: `rails g migration RemovePublished_dateFromBooks published_date:date`. The following file is created (*201511190001942_remove_published_date_from_books.rb*):

```
class RemovePublishedDateFromBooks < ActiveRecord::Migration
  def change
    remove_column :books, :published_date, :date
  end
end
```

There are also "plural" versions of these methods—add_columns and remove_col umns—to speed up the alteration of multiple columns at once.

Similarly, existing columns can easily be changed. For example, if the price of books were to skyrocket, you could create a migration with rails g migration alter_col umn_books_price. This will generate a migration file with an empty change method. However, change_column is one of the "irreversible" methods of Rails. Therefore (as stated in "Migration Files" on page 193), we need to provide an up method wherein the column may be redefined as well as a down method that tells Rails how to roll it back (*20151119004306_alter_column_books_price.rb*):

```
class AlterColumnBooksPrice < ActiveRecord::Migration
  def self.up
    # Change the price column to accept 7 digits
    change_column :books, :price, precision: 7, scale: 2
  end

  def self.down
    #Revert the price column back to 6 digits
    change_column :books, :price, precision: 6, scale: 2
  end
end
```

Here, the changes to be implemented when we're running rails db:migrate will be placed within the self.up method. The self.down method tells Rails how we want these changes to be *undone* if and when we roll back the migration. For this example, we'll just return the column to its original state.

There is a multitude of instance methods and transformations available for ActiveRecord migrations. More information can be found in the Ruby on Rails guides (*http://bit.ly/2aTBJZO*) and APIdock (*http://bit.ly/2aTAIBk*).

Indexes

Indexes (or *indices* if you prefer) speed up information retrieval, but slow down writes because the index also has to be updated. By default, the only column Rails tells the database to index is the id column, which it references constantly. If you have other columns that you'll be searching regularly, notably columns in join tables, you'll definitely want to learn about add_index and remove_index. The many-to-many example in Chapter 9 used them in a migration for building the join table between courses and students:

```
class CreateJoinTableCourseStudent < ActiveRecord::Migration
  def change
    create_join_table :courses, :students do |t|
      t.index [:course_id, :student_id], unique: true
      t.index [:student_id, :course_id], unique: true
    end
```

```
    end
  end
```

After this migration's change method has created the `courses_students` table, it calls the `add_index` method. The first argument is always the table to receive the index. The second argument can either be the column to be indexed or an array listing columns. You could have indexed each of the columns in the preceding `add_index` method with two calls:

```
add_index :courses_students, :course_id, unique: true
add_index :courses_students,:student_id, unique: true
```

However, calling the `add_index` method with a two-component array created a different kind of index, indexing the values of each column to the other. For a join table, that's the most efficient approach.

You can also specify two options. The first, `:unique`, indicates whether all values in the column have to be unique. The examples just shown set it to `true`, but if you're indexing content other than `id` values, the default of `false` may be more appropriate. (More typically, these kinds of constraints are applied in Rails rather than the database at the model level.) You can also name the index through the `:name` parameter.

If you reverse this with `rails db:rollback`, rails will call the `remove_index` method *first* and then the `drop_table` method.

Let's look at another example based on the Books table in the previous section. Perhaps this table could also use an index to speed the search of volumes by their ISBNs. We could have easily implemented this by adding `add_index` to the migration used to create the table:

```
class CreateBookWithColumnsAndIndex < ActiveRecord::Migration
  def change
    create_table :book_with_columns do |t|
      t.string :title
      t.string :author
      t.integer :isbn
      t.float :price
      t.date :published_date
    end

    add_index :book_with_columns, :isbn
  end
end
```

The `add_index` method (and its counterpart, `remove_index`) is quite versatile in that it can be added to virtually any migration, even by itself in a "standalone" migration. Indexes may also be created via the addition of a boolean `index` modifier within a column definition. For example, the following migration adds a column to store a "slug" (human-readable ID) for posts in a blog application:

```
class AddSlugToPosts < ActiveRecord::Migration
  def change
    add_column :posts, :slug, :string, index: true
  end
end
```

This simple migration was created with the command `rails g migration AddSlug` `ToPosts`. Then, in the text editor, the `index: true` modifier is added to the new column's parameter list. Remember that indexes should always be added only *after* their respective tables and columns already exist. This way, you can remove the index without error by using the `rails db:rollback` command.

Other Opportunities

Migrations offer many other possibilities for creative database manipulation, advanced development, and general trouble causing. Additionally, the `ActiveRe` `cord::ConnectionAdapters::SchemaStatements` class, which contains most of the methods useful for creating migrations, offers a wide variety of other options you may want to explore. Many, like `rename_column` and `rename_table`, have fairly obvious functionality. Here's the list of what's out there:

    add_belongs_to

    add_column

    add_foreign_key

    add_index

    add_index_options

    add_index_sort_order

    add_reference

    add_timestamps

    assume_migrated_upto_version

    change_column

    change_column_default

    change_column_null

    change_table

    column_exists?

    columns

    columns_for_distinct

    create_alter_table

```
create_join_table
create_table
create_table_definition
drop_join_table
dump_schema_information
foreign_key_column_for
foreign_key_name
foreign_keys
index_exists?
index_name
index_name_exists?
index_name_for_remove
initialize_schema_migrations_table
native_database_types
options_include_default?
quoted_columns_for_index
remove_belongs_to
remove_column
remove_columns
remove_foreign_key
remove_index
remove_index!
remove_reference
remove_timestamps
rename_column
rename_column_indexes
rename_index
rename_table
rename_table_indexes
table_alias_for
table_exists?
```

```
type_to_sql

update_table_definition

validate_index_length!
```

With each version of Rails, this list changes, and it should be noted that some of these methods are seldom actually used. Nonetheless, it is clear that there are a great many tasks, from managing database connections to renaming a simple column that can be automated through Rails migrations. Good references on the usage of these methods can be found in the Rails ActiveRecord documentation and at APIdock (*http:// apidock.com/rails*).

One final method, not listed here, is worth noting: execute. The execute method lets you issue SQL commands to the database. If you're really fond of SQL, that may be something you want to explore, though it's probably not the best option for your first few outings with Rails. Just know that the execute method is *not* reversible. Thus, it must be defined in a self.up block. You must also explicitly tell Rails how to roll it back within self.down. Also be aware that the practice of executing raw SQL within a migration violates *convention over configuration*, an important tenet of Rails development. Nearly anything a SQL statement could accomplish can be done with the above Rails transformations.

Test Your Knowledge

Quiz

1. How do you run migrations forward?

2. How do you create a new migration?

3. When must you use the self.up and self.down methods instead of a change method in a migration?

4. What should the self.down method do in a migration?

5. What Rails data type should you use to represent currency values?

6. How do you add a new field to a record?

Answers

1. With the `rails db:migrate` command.

2. To keep in line with the Rails timestamp-based naming convention, it's best to use `rails generate migration NameOfMigration`, and then edit the resulting file in the *db/migrate* directory.

3. Migrations created with the `change` method are *reversible*, meaning that they can be reversed with `rails db:rollback` just as easily as they were created with `rails db:migrate`. Some of the less common transformations, however, are *not* reversible. You must write these migrations using `self.up` and `self.down`.

4. The `self.down` method defines what should happen if the migration is rolled back with `rails db:rollback`. The tables, column, and indexes created in `self.up` need a corresponding removal process in `self.down`. If you used the `change` method, however, you do not need a `self.down` method.

5. The `:decimal` type is the most precise way to keep track of money. It can keep track of cents to the right of the decimal point and will contain values with a fixed number of decimal places much more accurately than `:float`.

6. New fields get created with `add_column`, as "fields" are represented as columns and the records that contain them as rows.

## CHAPTER 11

Debugging

You should rather be grateful for the weeds you have in your mind,
because eventually they will enrich your practice.
—Shunryu Suzuki, *Zen Mind, Beginner's Mind*

When you're first starting out in Rails, it's easy to wonder what exactly is going on at any given moment. Web applications by their very nature are tricky to debug, as so much happens before you see an answer. Fortunately, Rails includes tools to figure out what's going wrong while applications are running. Debugging tools keep evolving, but there's a basic set you should understand from the beginning.

Creating Your Own Debugging Messages

I'm sure it was facetious, but an old programmer once told me that "the real reason the PRINT statement was invented was for debugging." While it may not be aesthetically pleasing to dump variable values into result screens, it's often the easiest thing to do in early development. All controller instance variables are available to the view, so if you want to see what they contain, you can just write something like:

```
<%= @student %>
```

to display the contents of @student. However, if the object has much complexity and isn't just a string, it will insert something like:

```
#<Student:0x21824f8>
```

into the HTML for the page. All you'll see is the #.

Rails does, however, offer a way to make this more useful. The DebugHelper class offers a helper method named debug. While it won't magically debug your programs, it will present these kinds of messages in a slightly prettier form as YAML (Yet

Another Markup Language). Instead of `<%= @student %>`, for example, you could write `<%= debug(@student) %>`. The debug method would give you:

```
--- !ruby/object:Student
raw_attributes:
  given_name: Milletta
  middle_name: Zorgos
  family_name: Stim
  date_of_birth: '2011-02-02'
  grade_point_average: 3.94
  start_date: '2016-09-12'
  id: 2
  created_at: '2016-02-29 01:08:41.860338'
  updated_at: '2016-03-03 01:44:12.709368'
attributes: !ruby/object:ActiveRecord::AttributeSet
  attributes: !ruby/object:ActiveRecord::LazyAttributeHash
    types:
      id: &5 !ruby/object:ActiveModel::Type::Integer
        precision:
        scale:
        limit:
        range: !ruby/range
          begin: -2147483648
          end: 2147483648
          excl: true
      given_name: &1 !ruby/object:ActiveModel::Type::String
        precision:
        scale:
        limit:
      middle_name: *1
      family_name: *1
      date_of_birth: &2 !ruby/object:ActiveRecord::Type::Date
        precision:
        scale:
        limit:
      grade_point_average: &4 !ruby/object:ActiveModel::Type::Decimal
        precision:
        scale:
        limit:
      start_date: *2
      created_at: &6 !ruby/marshalable:ActiveRecord::AttributeMethods::Time...
        :__v2__: []
        []: &3 !ruby/object:ActiveRecord::Type::DateTime
          precision:
          scale:
          limit:
      updated_at: &7 !ruby/marshalable:ActiveRecord::AttributeMethods::Time...
        :__v2__: []
        []: *3
    values:
      id: 2
      given_name: Milletta
```

```
      middle_name: Zorgos
      family_name: Stim
      date_of_birth: '2011-02-02'
      grade_point_average: 3.94
      start_date: '2016-09-12'
      created_at: '2016-02-29 01:08:41.860338'
      updated_at: '2016-03-03 01:44:12.709368'
additional_types: {}
materialized: true
delegate_hash:
    given_name: !ruby/object:ActiveRecord::Attribute::FromDatabase
      name: given_name
      value_before_type_cast: Milletta
      type: *1
      original_attribute:
      value: Milletta
    middle_name: !ruby/object:ActiveRecord::Attribute::FromDatabase
      name: middle_name
      value_before_type_cast: Zorgos
      type: *1
      original_attribute:
      value: Zorgos
    family_name: !ruby/object:ActiveRecord::Attribute::FromDatabase
      name: family_name
      value_before_type_cast: Stim
      type: *1
      original_attribute:
      value: Stim
    date_of_birth: !ruby/object:ActiveRecord::Attribute::FromDatabase
      name: date_of_birth
      value_before_type_cast: '2011-02-02'
      type: *2
      original_attribute:
      value: 2011-02-02
    grade_point_average: !ruby/object:ActiveRecord::Attribute::FromDatabase
      name: grade_point_average
      value_before_type_cast: 3.94
      type: *4
      original_attribute:
      value: !ruby/object:BigDecimal 36:0.394E1
    start_date: !ruby/object:ActiveRecord::Attribute::FromDatabase
      name: start_date
      value_before_type_cast: '2016-09-12'
      type: *2
      original_attribute:
      value: 2016-09-12
    id: !ruby/object:ActiveRecord::Attribute::FromDatabase
      name: id
      value_before_type_cast: 2
      type: *5
      original_attribute:
      value: 2
```

```
        created_at: !ruby/object:ActiveRecord::Attribute::FromDatabase
          name: created_at
          value_before_type_cast: '2016-02-29 01:08:41.860338'
          type: *6
          original_attribute:
        updated_at: !ruby/object:ActiveRecord::Attribute::FromDatabase
          name: updated_at
          value_before_type_cast: '2016-03-03 01:44:12.709368'
          type: *7
          original_attribute:
  new_record: false
  active_record_yaml_version: 1
```

If you need to take a quick look at what's happening and see it on the page where it's happening, this can be a useful technique.

Raising Exceptions

Sometimes you want to know what a variable looks like inside of a controller before data is reaching your page. There's an easy way to abuse Ruby's mechanism for raising exceptions, `raise`, which will show you that information. This only works in development mode, but then, it's really a better idea to do debugging in development rather than production.

To use this clumsy but sometimes useful mechanism, just add a `raise` in your code—in this case, in *app/controllers/award_controller.rb*:

```
# GET /awards/1
# GET /awards/1.json
def show
  raise @award.to_yaml
end
```

When you go to show an award, you'll get a YAML dump like the one shown in Figure 11-1. It shows you all the information in the `award` variable.

You can also constrain your exceptions by combining them with `if` statements and similar conditionals, though if you do this, be especially careful to take them out when you're done using it. It's easy to forget about an exception you raise only occasionally, and users who encounter it in a production environment will only see a "We're sorry, but something went wrong" message.

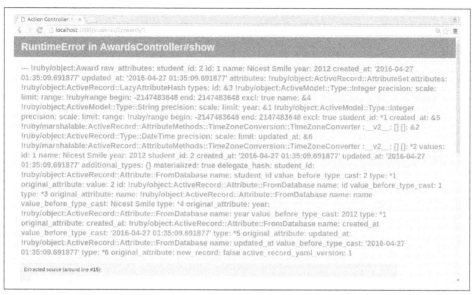

Figure 11-1. *The ugly but helpful result of a deliberately raised exception*

Logging

You may not have thought of it this way, but you've been working with Rails logs since the first time you entered `rails server`. All of that information flowing by is the development log. You can find all of it in the *log* directory of your application, stored in the *development.log* file. (There are also *test.log* and *production.log* files there for use when your application runs in test or development mode, as described in the next chapter.)

While Rails is certainly generous with the information that it sends to the log in development mode, that sheer volume can make it hard to find things. It may also not be sending what you want to see. If you want to send something specific to the log, use the `logger` object in your model, controller, or view. In a model or controller, this would look like:

```
logger.info 'This is a message to send to the log'
```

One piece of information that is logged and is worth pointing out is timing information. You'll find lines in the log like:

```
Completed in 0.01451 (68 reqs/sec) | Rendering: 0.00775 (53%) |
DB: 0.00093 (6%) | 200 OK
```

That tells you how fast the whole thing was completed, how long the view processing (rendering) took, and how long the database processing (DB) took. The last entry on the line is the HTTP response. You should note that Rails can probably execute the code much faster when in production; during development, it's loading, reloading, and logging a lot of extra information.

 The asset pipeline can be noisy in the console. Check out the Quiet Asset gem (*https://github.com/evrone/quiet_asset*) to reduce the amount of asset information displayed in the development log.

Working with Rails from the Console

Rails is so thoroughly web-facing that it can be difficult to imagine working with it from the command line, but it does indeed offer `rails console`. When you run `rails console` rather than `rails server`, Rails starts up a special environment using the Interactive Ruby Shell (irb) instead of firing up a web server. This shell has the full context of your application, so you can load data from your databases, play with models, and generally take a look around.

 You can, if you want, have `rails console` and `rails server` running at the same time in different windows.

The console shell lets you interact with your application from the command line with the full powers of Ruby at your disposal. Most Ruby books include a lot more detail about irb, some even running all of their examples there, but in Rails it's good mostly for playing with models and testing methods.

To get started, try running **`rails console --sandbox`** in one of your applications, say the final students/courses application from Chapter 9. You'll see something like:

```
$ rails console --sandbox
Loading development environment in sandbox (Rails 5)
Any modifications you make will be rolled back on exit
ruby-2.3.0 :001 >
```

If you actually want to make changes to your database, you can leave off the `--sandbox` option (which can be abbreviated `-s`). For the first few visits, it feels safer to know that none of the changes made from the console will last beyond the console session. Everything gets rolled back once the session ends.

To start actually working with some data, load an object into a variable. Rails will not only load the object, it will also show all the details of the underlying fields. (It always shows the return value.)

```
ruby-2.3.0 :001 > s=Student.find(2)
Student Load (26.2ms)
SELECT "students".* FROM "students" WHERE "students"."id" = ?
LIMIT 1
  [["id", 2]] => #<Student id: 2, given_name: "Milletta", middle_name: "Zorgos",
  family_name: "Stim", date_of_birth: "2007-02-02", grade_point_average:
#<BigDecimal:1010c1f00,0.394E1,18(18)>, start_date: "2012-09-12",
  created_at: "2012-02-20 21:10:34", updated_at: "2012-02-20 21:10:34">
```

The model included something that isn't shown here, though: a simpler name method. You can call that from the console, too:

```
ruby-2.3.0 :002 > s.name
=> "Milletta Stim"
```

All of the methods on the model are available to you here. In fact, if you're going to be working with one object for a long time, you can create a new irb console session that's in the context of that object. This lets you call methods and explore without constantly prefacing method names with the variable you used:

```
ruby-2.3.0 :003 > irb s
ruby-2.3.0 :001 > name
 => "Milletta Stim"
ruby-2.3.0 :002 > cList=courses
 Course Load (0.2ms)
 SELECT "courses".* FROM "courses" INNER JOIN "courses_students"
 ON "courses"."id" = "courses_students"."course_id" WHERE "courses_students".
 "student_id" = 2
 => [#<Course id: 1, name: "Reptiles: Friend or Foe?", created_at: "2012-02-20
22:03:47", updated_at: "2012-02-20 22:03:47">, #<Course id: 5, name: "Advanced
Bolt Design", created_at: "2012-02-20 22:04:28",
updated_at: "2012-02-20 22:04:28">]
```

When you're done working inside of this object, just type **quit** or **exit**, and you'll get an exit message like:

```
ruby-2.3.0 :004 > exit
 =>
<IRB::Irb: @context=<IRB::Context:0x00000103021080>, @signal_status=:IN_EVAL,
 @scanner=#<RubyLex:0x0000010301dd18>>
```

This means you are no longer in the object.

You can, of course, change the values in your objects as well:

```
> s.middle_name='Zorgas'
=> "Zorgas"
```

(If you get an error about "undefined local variable," you're probably still in the irb session, not the main console.) If you want to see what values have changed—before you save them—you can use the y method (for YAML, a convenient data exchange format):

```
ruby-2.3.0 :005 > y s
--- !ruby/object:Student
attributes:
  id: 2
  given_name: Milletta
  middle_name: Zorgas
  family_name: Stim
  date_of_birth: 2007-02-02
  grade_point_average: 3.94
  start_date: 2012-09-12
  created_at: 2012-02-20 21:10:34.268306 Z
  updated_at: 2012-02-20 21:10:34.268306 Z
=> nil
```

You can also call the save method:

```
> s.save
  (0.2ms)  SAVEPOINT active_record_1
  (0.1ms)  RELEASE SAVEPOINT active_record_1
=> true
```

The reported return value is true, so the save succeeded. If you're using the sandbox, when the sandboxed session ends, this will be rolled back:

```
> exit
  (0.6ms)  rollback transaction
```

The console also provides two convenience objects you may want to use on their own. The first, helper, gives you instant access to all of the helper methods in your application. If you want to test out a method with a set of arguments, just call the method from helper, as in this call to number_to_human_size:

```
> helper.number_to_human_size 1092582135
=> "1.02 GB"
```

The other convenience object, app, gives you access to your full application context, including the routing table. This lets you do things like test your routing with:

```
ruby-2.3.0 :008 > app.url_for :action=>"index", :controller=>"courses"
=> "http://www.example.com/courses"
ruby-2.3.0 :009 > app.url_for :action=>"new", :controller=>"courses"
=> "http://www.example.com/courses/new"
```

You can also test named routes, which are ubiquitous in RESTful development, but first you need to activate access to the methods that present them with:

```
> include Rails.application.routes.url_helpers
```

Then you can do things like:

```
> new_course_path
=> "/courses/new"
```

You can also call your controllers using the app object, using the `app.get`, `app.post`, `app.put`, and `app.delete` methods from `ActionController::Integration::Ses sion`. The results of these may not be exactly what you expect. For example:

```
> app.get "/students/2"
  Student Load (0.3ms)
  SELECT "students".* FROM "students" WHERE "students"."id" = ?
LIMIT 1  [["id", "2"]]
   (0.2ms)  SELECT COUNT() FROM "courses" INNER JOIN "courses_students" ON
"courses"."id" = "courses_students"."course_id"
  WHERE "courses_students"."student_id" = 2 Course Load (0.1ms)
  SELECT "courses". FROM "courses" INNER JOIN
"courses_students" ON "courses"."id" = "courses_students"."course_id" WHERE
"courses_students"."student_id" = 2
  Award Load (0.2ms)
  SELECT "awards".* FROM "awards" WHERE "awards"."student_id" = 2
  Student Load (0.2ms)
  SELECT "students".* FROM "students" WHERE "students"."id" = 2
LIMIT 1
 => 200
```

You see all the queries executed in processing the request, but the result is 200. The 200 just means that the request was processed successfully and some kind of response produced. A 404 would be the classic "Not Found" error, meaning that Rails couldn't find an action matching that path, and 500 would be a more severe error. You can take a closer look at what happened by asking the app object for the parameters:

```
> app.controller.params
 => <ActionController::Parameters {"controller"=>"students", "action"=>"show",
 "id"=>"2"} permitted: false>
```

This breakdown makes it clear how the routing interpreted the request and called the controller. You can also get to the response itself, though the presentation isn't quite beautiful:

```
> app.response.body
 => "<!DOCTYPE html>\n<html>\n<head>\n  <title>Students
</title>\n  <link href=\"/assets/application.css?body=1\" media=\"all\"
rel=\"stylesheet\" type=\"text/css\" />\n<link href=\"/assets/awards.css?body=1\"
media=\"all\" rel=\"stylesheet\" type=\"text/css\" />\n<link
href=\"/assets/courses.css?body=1\" media=\"all\" rel=\"stylesheet\"
type=\"text/css\" />\n<link href=\"/assets/scaffolds.css?body=1\"
media=\"all\" rel=\"stylesheet\" type=\"text/css\" />\n<link
href=\"/assets/students.css?body=1\" media=\"all\" rel=\"stylesheet\"
type=\"text/css\"
/>\n  <script src=\"/assets/jquery.js?body=1\" type=\"text/javascript\">
</script>\n<script src=\"/assets/jquery_ujs.js?body=1\" type=\"text/javascript\">
</script>\n<script
src=\"/assets/awards.js?body=1\" type=\"text/javascript\">
</script>\n<script src=\"/assets/courses.js?body=1\"
type=\"text/javascript\"></script>\n<script
src=\"/assets/students.js?body=1\" type=\"text/javascript\">
```

```
</script>\n<script src=\"/assets/application.js?body=1\"
  type=\"text/javascript\"></script>\n
<meta content=\"authenticity_token\" name=\"csrf-param\" />\n<meta
content=\"NsFJ0fxytqtTBWclpgI8elq1jRI1BMq/3ir9SOcFr9Y=\" name=\"csrf-token\" />
\n</head>\n<body>\n\n<p>\n<a
href=\"http://www.example.com/students\">Students</a> |\n<a
href=\"http://www.example.com/courses\">Courses</a>\n</p>\n
<hr />\n\n<p id=\"notice\"></p>\n\n<p>\n
<b>Given name:</b>\n  Milletta\n</p>\n\n<p>\n
<b>Middle name:</b>\n  Zorgas\n</p>\n\n<p>\n
<b>Family name:</b>\n  Stim\n</p>\n\n<p>\n
<b>Date of birth:</b>\n  2007-02-02\n</p>\n\n<p>\n
<b>Grade point average:</b>\n  3.94\n</p>\n\n<p>\n
<b>Start date:</b>\n  2012-09-12\n</p>\n\n<p>\n
<b>Courses:</b>\n  <a href="/courses/1">
Reptiles: Friend or Foe?</a>, <a href="/courses/5">
Advanced Bolt Design</a>\n</p>\n\n<h3>Awards</h3>\n
<table>\n<tr>\n<th>Name</th>\n<th>Year</th>\n
<th>Student</th>\n</tr>\n<tr>\n<td>Cleanest
Fingernails</td>\n<td>2012</td>\n<td>Milletta
Stim</td>\n</tr>\n</table>\n\n<a href=\"/students/2/edit\">
Edit</a> |\n<a href=\"/students/2/courses\">Courses</a> |
\n<a href=\"/students/2/awards\">Awards</a> |\n<a
href=\"/students\">Back</a>\n\n\n</body>\n</html>\n"
```

You can also see all of the header information, doubtlessly more than you explicitly set:

```
> app.headers
=> {"Content-Type"=>"text/html; charset=utf-8", "X-UA-Compatible"=>"IE=Edge",
"ETag"=>"\"7c67a2f2af604f6aa3d6835da2f17189\"", "Cache-Control"=>"max-age=0,
private, must-revalidate", "Set-Cookie"=>"_students_session=BAh7B0kiD3Nlc3Np
faWQGOgZFRkkiJWUxNGNiOTEwZGU1Njg3N2Q4MGE4MzZmQGVlMjRhNTc2BjsAVEkiEF9jc3JmX3R
BjsARkkiMU5zRkowZnh5dHF0VEJXY2xwZ0k4ZWxxMWpSSTFCTXEvM2lyOVNPY0ZyOVk9BjsARg%3
-e0da5ba86394465cd6cc1eb3e4edfd66b5146057; path=/; HttpOnly",
"X-Request-Id"=>"065e57b0ece745589221fd734ccbe693",
"X-Runtime"=>"0.168976", "Content-Length"=>"2022"}
```

If you're working from the console and making changes to the code at the same time, there's one more key command you'll want to know: reload!. The Rails console isn't as instantly adapting, even in development mode, as its web interfaces. When you issue the reload! command, the console will reload your updated application code and use it. There's just one thing to watch out for, though: if you've created objects already, they'll still be using the old code. You'll need to tear them down and replace them if you want to test them out with the new code.

The console is a great place to "get your hands dirty" and play with code directly. It lets you tinker with your application much more directly than is easily possible through the web interface. However, it definitely has some limitations. It'll probably take a while to grow comfortable using it—the error messages are often cryptic. It's obviously not a great place to experiment with interfaces. It's very easy to enter a typo and not figure it out before something important has changed or broken.

Most importantly, though, the console is outside of your main application flow. Testing in the console is not usually testing the way the application really works. Not only that, it's not a structured set of tests so much as poking around to see what happens. While the console is useful, it's definitely not your only or best choice for making sure your application behaves correctly.

Debug and Debugger

The console is fun for tinkering and can be extremely useful for trying things out, but it's a completely separate process from the way you (and your users) normally run Rails applications.

If you'd rather do your debugging within a normal web-served Rails, the most common current approach uses the Rails debugger. Previous versions of Rails required a separate gem install, but Rails 5 comes with the debugger already installed via the byebug gem in your Gemfile. The debug method will return an HTML <pre> tag that renders an object in YAML format. Notice what happens when we add the debug statement to the following show view:

```
...
<p id="notice"><%= notice %></p>
<%= debug @student %>
<p>
  <strong>Given name:</strong>
  <%= @student.given_name %>
</p>
...
```

The preceding code displays this:

```
--- !ruby/object:Student
raw_attributes:
  id: 1
  given_name: john
  middle_name: mark
  family_name: locklear
  date_of_birth: '2015-11-05'
  grade_point_average: 3
  start_date: '2015-11-05'
  created_at: '2015-11-05 17:16:07.098952'
  updated_at: '2015-11-05 17:16:07.098952'
  ...
```

Adding debug statements can be helpful, but there are times when simply printing variables is not enough to find the root cause of a problem. When you need to actually dig into source code, the debugger is your best option. It is helpful not just for debugging, but also for learning about Rails source code, and where methods are being called from.

Add the debugger call in one of the controller methods. For a test, modify the `create` method in *app/controllers/students_controller.rb* (as is done in *ch11/students05*) so that it looks like:

```
def create
  @student = Student.new(student_params)
  debugger
  respond_to do |format|
    if @student.save
      format.html
        { redirect_to @student, notice: Student was successfully created. }
      format.json { render :show, status: :created, location: @student }
    else
      format.html { render :new }
      format.json
        { render json: @student.errors, status: :unprocessable_entity }
    end
  end
end
```

Visit *http://localhost:3000/students/new*, enter a new student, and click the "Create student" button. You'll see something like Figure 11-2.

The most important part of Figure 11-2 is the status bar at the lower left: "Waiting for localhost...". That's unusual, unless you've accidentally put an infinite loop into your application. If you check the logs in the window where you ran `rails server`, you'll see that it's waiting for your input at a (byebug) prompt:

```
[24, 33] in ch11/students05a/app/controllers/students_controller.rb
   24:    # POST /students
   25:    # POST /students.json
   26:    def create
   27:      @student = Student.new(student_params)
   28:      debugger
=> 29:      respond_to do |format|
   30:        if @student.save
   31:          format.html { redirect_to @student, notice: Student was... }
   32:          format.json { render :show, status: :created, location: ... }
   33:        else
(byebug)
```

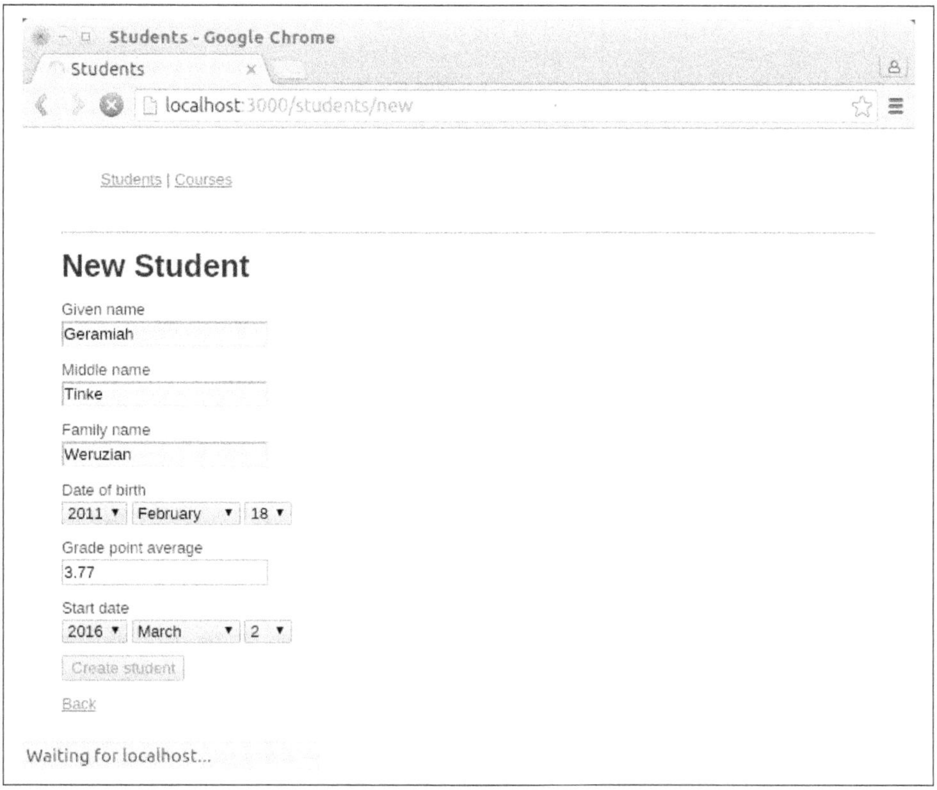

Figure 11-2. Waiting for a response because the debugger kicked in

The line above the prompt is the next statement to be executed, if you type next. Unsurprisingly, it's the line right after debugger. If you type list, you can see where you are in the context of your source code:

```
(byebug) list

[34, 43] in ch11/students05a/app/controllers/students_controller.rb
   34:         format.html { render :new }
   35:         format.json { render json: @student.errors... }
   36:       end
   37:     end
   38:   end
   39:
   40:   # PATCH/PUT /students/1
   41:   # PATCH/PUT /students/1.json
   42:   def update
   43:     respond_to do |format|
```

To see a list of the available commands, type **help**. The main ones you'll need at first to move through code are:

- next (or step) to move forward to the next line
- cont to leave the debugger and let the program continue
- quit to leave the debugger *and* shut down Rails

Following code for any extended period will likely drop you into the Rails framework code, which may be confusing at first. You'll want to enter your debugger commands and other breakpoints close to where you think problems exist or patiently wait for Rails to get out of your way.

While you're in the debugger, you will probably want to inspect variables, which you can do with the p (or pp) command:

```
(byebug) p @student
#<Student id: nil, given_name: "Adolph", middle_name: "Lorenz", family_name:
    "Dial", date_of_birth: "1922-12-12", grade_point_average:
    #<BigDecimal:20de0d8,0.4E1,8(8)>,
    start_date: "2015-11-16", created_at: nil, updated_at: nil>
```

If you want a prettier view of the data or if you're just more comfortable in irb, you can jump into irb and tinker as you like. When you're done working in irb, type **exit** or **quit** to be returned to the debugger shell. (When you enter irb, the prompt changes to >>, and when you exit, it returns to (byebug).) For example, the following session goes into irb to print the @student object as YAML, using the y command explored earlier:

```
(byebug) irb
(byebug) y @student
--- !ruby/object:Student
attributes:
  id:
  given_name: Adolph
  middle_name: Lorenz
  family_name: Dial
  date_of_birth: 1922-12-12
  grade_point_average: 4.0
  start_date: 2015-11-16
  created_at:
  updated_at:
nil

(byebug) exit
/Users/simonstl/Documents/RailsOutIn/current/code/ch11/students001d/app/
controllers/students_controller.rb:62
respond_to do |format|
(byebug)
```

In development mode, Rails will reload your files for every request before you get into the debugger, but if you want the debugger to reload your files for every step, you can issue the command `set autoreload`. It will go much more slowly, but sometimes that's OK for delicate surgery.

For much more detail on using the Ruby debugger with Rails, check out the ever-improving Debugging Rails Applications Guide (*http://edgeguides.rubyonrails.org/ debugging_rails_applications.html*).

Test Your Knowledge

Quiz

1. What's the easiest way to present debugging information in a Rails view?
2. Where can you find information about how quickly different aspects of a request were handled?
3. How can you test routing from the console?
4. How do you tell your program to support the Ruby debugger?
5. How do you let your program continue when you exit the Ruby debugger?

Answers

1. The `debug` method makes it easy to present the complete contents of an object in a mostly readable YAML representation.
2. Rails includes a lot of timing information in its development log, which is available both in the terminal window for `rails server` and in the *log/development.log* file.
3. You can test simple routes by calling `app.url_for`. If you need to test named routes, type **include Rails.application.routes.url_helpers** and then try calling the path methods.
4. You don't! In Rails 5 debugging is turned on by default due to the addition of the byebug gem in the `:development` group.
5. When you use the `cont` command, rather than the `quit` command, the debugger lets Rails get back to what it was doing. The `quit` command exits the debugger and shuts down the application.

## CHAPTER 12

Testing

> *Failures, repeated failures, are finger posts on the road to achievement.*
> *One fails forward toward success.*
> —C. S. Lewis

Testing can spare you much of the work you learned to do in the previous chapter, replacing spot-check debugging with more structured and thorough repetitive testing. Ruby culture places a high value on testing, and Ruby and Rails have grown up with agile development methods where testing is assumed to be a normal part of development. While testing is a complicated subject worthy of a book or several, it's definitely worthwhile to start including tests early in your project development, even while you're still learning the Rails landscape.

Rails provides a number of facilities for creating and managing tests. This chapter will explore its basic testing setup and note some options for building more advanced test platforms. (Examples for this chapter are in *ch12/students06*.)

As you get deeper into Rails culture, you'll find many people using other testing frameworks, notably RSpec, Cucumber, and Capybara, with Factory Girl managing fixtures. It's probably easiest, though, to start by understanding the foundations provided in Rails itself and then moving on when you need more sophisticated features or a particular approach.

Test Mode

Up to this point, all the code in this book has been run in development mode. Rails supports three different environments for running applications. Each of them has its own database, as well as its own settings:

Development

Development is the default mode. In development mode, Rails loads and reloads code every time a request is made, making it easy for you to see changes without a cache getting in the way. It's also typical to use SQLite as the database, as Rails isn't going to be working at high speed anyway.

Test

Test mode runs like production mode, without reloading code, and has its own database so that tests can run against a consistent database. You could use a fancier database for test mode (and might want to if you suspect strange database interactions), but for getting started, the default of SQLite is fine.

Production

Production mode maximizes the efficiency of Rails. It doesn't reload code, enabling it to cache the program and run much faster. Logging is much briefer and error messages are shortened, as giving users a complete stack trace probably isn't helpful. It also does more automatic and directed caching of results, sparing users a wait for the same code to run again.

You can switch among the three modes by using the -e option of `rails server`:

```
rails server -e test
```

The settings for all three modes are in the *config* directory. The *environment.rb* file contains default configuration settings used by all three modes, but the *environments* directory contains *development.rb*, *production.rb*, and *test.rb* files whose settings override those in *environment.rb*.

The *database.yml* file contains the database connection settings for all three modes. By default, it specifies SQLite databases named *db/development.sqlite3*, *db/test.sqlite3*, and *db/production.sqlite3*. As you get closer to deploying applications, you'll want to consider other possible database installations, particularly for production, but for now, these defaults are fine. It's time, though, to set up a database for testing.

If you would like to follow along with this chapter and write code, you can use the */ch09/students03/* app as a starting point. Now would be a good time to make a copy of the *students03* app, the bundle, and migrate.

Testing the Students App

We'll begin by sanity-checking your existing models and controllers, and the associated tests that Rails created for you. To run model tests, run the following at the console inside your app:

```
rails test:models
```

For controller tests, run:

```
rails test:controllers
```

Finally, if you would like to run any specific test file, you can run:

```
rake test TEST=test/controllers/courses_controller_test.rb
```

In the preceding case we ran the courses controller test, but you can run any specific model or controller test by inserting the filepath after TEST=.

Before running these tests, be sure to run `rails db:migrate`. The model tests should not display any errors (because there aren't any), but right off the bat, our controller tests fail. If we look at the errors, we can see each one has a `no route matches...` error. This is because the default controller tests include tests for each of seven RESTful routes in Rails. However, if you recall, those routes are not available for the awards controller. For now we won't worry about these failures, as they will be addressed later in the chapter.

Setting Up a Test Database with Fixtures

Automated testing needs a stable database environment in which to do its work. The contents of the development database will—and should—change on a regular basis as you tinker and experiment to see just how well everything works. This is wonderful for a human development process, but that level of change is dreadful when a computer is testing an application. Once the testing framework is told which value to check for, it can't choose another value because it knows someone else was playing with the data. In fact, if previous tests change the data, the order in which tests are conducted could itself become an issue, masking some bugs and falsely reporting others.

Rails provides this stable environment two ways. First, as noted earlier, it maintains a separate test environment, complete with its own database. Second, the testing environment expects that developers will define stable data, called *fixtures*, for use in that database. Every time a new test is run, the database is reset to that stable set of data. It's a slow way to do things, but it's extremely reliable.

Fixtures are written in YAML. You don't need to know much about YAML to use and create them, however—though you should definitely be aware that whitespace is significant. Rails, in fact, has been creating fixtures in addition to the scaffolding all along. If you check the *test/fixtures* directory of the courses and students application, you'll see files named *awards.yml*, *courses.yml*, and *students.yml*. Their contents aren't particularly exciting, though, as Example 12-1 demonstrates.

Example 12-1. The students.yml fixture file created by Rails

```
# Read about fixtures at
# http://api.rubyonrails.org/classes/ActiveRecord/FixtureSet.html

one:
  given_name: MyString
  middle_name: MyString
  family_name: MyString
  date_of_birth: 2015-11-08
  grade_point_average: 9.99
  start_date: 2015-11-08

two:
  given_name: MyString
  middle_name: MyString
  family_name: MyString
  date_of_birth: 2015-11-08
  grade_point_average: 9.99
  start_date: 2015-11-08
```

Each field has a value, set by the Rails generator to reflect its type, and there are two records, but you may want something more reflective of the data your application is likely to contain, like Example 12-2.

Example 12-2. A more realistic, though still brief, students.yml fixture

```
#test/fixtures/students.yml
magnum:
  given_name: Thomas
  middle_name: Sullivan
  family_name: Magnum
  date_of_birth: 1945-01-29
  grade_point_average: 2.92
  start_date: 1988-09-12

rick:
  given_name: Orville
  middle_name: Wilbur
  family_name: Richard
  date_of_birth: 1943-07-23
  grade_point_average: 3.94
  start_date: 1988-09-12

tc:
  given_name: Theodore
  middle_name:
  family_name: Calvin
  date_of_birth: 1939-12-18
  grade_point_average: 3.76
  start_date: 1988-09-12
```

It's up to you whether you'd like the data to echo the development database, but somewhat meaningful data can be useful when you're trying to find your way through results, especially failures.

If you try to run tests based on the generated fixtures and your migrations set constraints on which fields can be null, you'll get a lot of mysterious errors. In SQLite, they suggest that your database and all of its tables are missing—even though they're not. When you're using MySQL, the error message at least narrows things down to fields, but that still doesn't explain why there's a problem.

The scaffold fixtures may work for testing incredibly simple applications, but most of the time you'll be much better off defining your own fixtures carefully.

There's more you can do in upgrading fixtures than improving readability, however. The fixtures Rails created don't know very much about relationships between models because the fixtures were generated before you told Rails about the relationship. So, for example, the generated fixture for awards looks like Example 12-3.

Example 12-3. The generated awards.yml fixture, without much real data

```
one:
  name: MyString
  year: 1
  student_id: 1

two:
  name: MyString
  year: 1
  student_id: 1
```

Rails knows that `student_id` is a number and gives it a value of 1, which should connect to a student, although as you might have noticed in Example 12-1, the *students.yml* fixture didn't include `id` values. The database might start its `id` count at 1, or it might not.

Fixture data isn't validated before it's loaded into the database. While this might conceivably offer more testing flexibility, you should never assume that fixture data will validate against the model until you've made certain that it does.

Example 12-4 shows a better way to create this fixture, taking advantage of the names in the *student.yml* file that was shown in Example 12-2.

Example 12-4. The awards.yml fixture, populated with semi-real data and links to students

```
#test/fixtures/awards.yml
# instead of computing student_id for each award and giving students
# explicit id fields, we reference the student by the name of their
# fixture

pi:
  name: Private Investigator
  year: 1988
  student: magnum

pilot:
  name: Helicopter Pilot - Island Hoppers
  year: 1990
  student: tc

owner:
  name: King Kamehameha Club
  year: 1989
  student: rick
```

It's important to note that the names of students used to make the connections aren't coming from the given_name field. They're the names that were assigned to each student object in the fixture. The same thing applies to the fixture, only it can actually refer to multiple students, not just one. The original fixture, shown in Example 12-5, doesn't even specify any students for courses. Example 12-6, by contrast, establishes relationships, using the names of the fixtures.

Example 12-5. The generated courses.yml fixture, with very little content

```
one:
  name: MyString

two:
  name: MyString
```

Example 12-6. The courses.yml fixture, populated with sort of real data

```
#test/fixtures/courses.yml
# instead of making us write elaborate and fragile data structures,
# the fixtures engine knows how to turn the 'students' list into a
# collection of records to insert into the courses_students table.

surveillance:
  name: Escape and Evasion
  students: magnum, rick

# it's safest to quote strings, especially if they contain colons
```

```
security:
  name: "Personal and private property security"
  students: magnum, rick

aviation:
  name: "Aviation Safety"
  students: tc
```

The fixtures setup is smart enough to establish the many-to-many connection between courses and students and build the necessary table, when given data like Example 12-6.

Once you have your fixtures set up, try running **rails test**. You'll probably get a lot of errors, because the tests themselves still expect the older nonsense fixtures. A lot of errors is a normal place to start in testing, however—it just means there's a lot to do!

When you run `rails test`, Rails will clone the structure (but not the content) of your development database into the test database. It doesn't run the migrations against the test database directly, but it does check to make sure your database is up-to-date with its migrations. If it isn't, you'll get a warning like:

```
You have 4 pending migrations:
  20080627135838 CreateStudents
  20080627140324 CreateCourses
  20080627144242 CreateCoursesStudents
  20080627150307 CreateAwards
Run "rails db:migrate" to update your database then try again.
```

If you get major error messages that sound like your database can't be found, as noted in the warning earlier, check your fixtures to ensure that every field your migrations said had to be there has an actual value.

Once you have the fixtures set up, it's time to move on to the tests.

Model Testing

Unit testing lets you work with your data on a pretty atomic level—checking validations, data storage, and similarly tightly focused issues. Rails scaffolding gives you only a very simple placeholder file, shown in Example 12-7. Even if it wasn't commented out, that code is definitely not sufficient for any real testing, and you should add unit tests that test validations for each field in your model.

Example 12-7. The mostly useless generated model test file, test/models/award_test.rb

```
require 'test_helper'

class AwardTest < ActiveSupport::TestCase
  # test "the truth" do
  #   assert true
```

```
  # end
end
```

Example 12-7 does show one feature of testing—the `assert` statement, which expects its argument to return `true` and reports a test failure if it doesn't. (You can also use deny to report failure on `true`.)

Model tests are pretty straightforward to write, though they are rarely exciting code. In general, they should reflect the validations performed by the model. Example 12-8 shows a definition for the award model that highlights some easily tested constraints. Add the validations highlighted here if they are not already in your award model.

Example 12-8. An award model with constraints defined

```
#app/models/award.rb
class Award < ApplicationRecord
  # every award is linked to a student, through student_id
  belongs_to :student
  validates_associated :student

  validates_presence_of :name, :year

  # particular award can only be given once in every year
  validates_uniqueness_of :name, scope: :year,
    message: "already been given for that year"

  # we started the award scheme in 1980
  validates_inclusion_of :year, in: (1980..Date.today.year)
end
```

Model tests work on a single instance of a model, so the uniqueness constraint isn't an appropriate test, but it's easy to test for the presence of names and years as well as the year being 1980 or later. Example 12-9 shows a set of tests, stored in *test/models/award_test.rb*, that check to make sure that the year constraint is obeyed.

Example 12-9. Testing to ensure that the year constraint behaves as expected

```
#test/models/award_test.rb
require 'test_helper'

class AwardTest < ActiveSupport::TestCase
  def test_validity_of_year

    # create new student for association in award
    student = Student.create({given_name: "Mark", date_of_birth: "1972-09-05",
                              start_date: "2009-01-18"})

    # test for rejection of missing year
    award = Award.new({name: "Test award", student_id: student.id})
```

```
    assert !award.valid?

    # test under lower boundary
    award.year = 1979
    assert !award.valid?

    # lower boundary
    award.year = 1980
    assert award.valid?

    # top boundary
    award.year = Date.today.year
    assert award.valid?

    # top boundary case, award isn't valid for next year
    award.year = Date.today.year + 1
    assert !award.valid?
  end
end
```

After adding the preceding code, run your model tests. You should see something like:

```
ruby-2.2.2@rails5 marklocklear:students03 marklocklear$ rails test:models
Run options: --seed 25905

# Running:

.

Finished in 0.054994s, 18.1837 runs/s, 90.9183 assertions/s.

1 runs, 5 assertions, 0 failures, 0 errors, 0 skips
```

All of the tests in the test_validity_of_year method call the valid? method of the award object created in the first line. The valid? method checks an object with a set of values against the validations specified in the model definition. In this case, each assertion pushes against a rule about the value for year.

Some test purists prefer to have only one assertion per test. In traditional unit testing, they're completely correct—this ensures that tests are isolated from each other, reducing the odds of missing an error or reporting false errors. Rails model tests are a little different, but it's probably still appropriate to limit tests to a single assertion.

First, a new student is created, and then a newly created award has a name: argument specified along with the required student_id, but no year:. That award object should fail validation because the model checks for the presence of year. Then the method assigns a value that is too low to be acceptable and again looks for a failure. Then it tests right on the minimum value, looking this time for a positive result. The next two assertions test on the top boundary and then just beyond that boundary. The first should work, and the second should not.

 If you ever feel like simply having a test fail, the `fail` method lets you fail with a message.

Awards are relatively simple, however. The many-to-many courses/students relationship is a lot more complicated. It's easier to test from one side, though, rather than trying to test from both, so courses will get the simple test file shown in Example 12-10, just checking that the course has a name, while students get the much more complicated tests shown in Example 12-11.

Before running the following code, be sure to add a validation for the presence of `name`: in the course. Add the following line to *app/models/course.rb*:

```
validates_presence_of :name
```

Example 12-10. Simple tests for the courses model, just examining basic functionality

```
#test/models/course_test.rb
require 'test_helper'

class CourseTest < ActiveSupport::TestCase
  def test_validity
    course = Course.new
    assert !course.valid?
    course.name = "New course"
    assert course.valid?
  end
end
```

For this next set of tests to pass we need to be sure there are validations in the student model for `date_of_birth` and `start_date`. Specifially this addresses the `assert` statement highlighted in Example 12-11 that checks if a student with only a `given_name` and `family_name` is valid. In this case, it is not. Add the following code to *app/models/student.rb*:

```
validates_presence_of :date_of_birth, :start_date
```

Example 12-11. More complicated tests for students, testing validity and whether they can be enrolled in courses

```ruby
#test/models/student_test.rb
require test_helper

class StudentTest < ActiveSupport::TestCase

  fixtures :students, :courses

  def test_validity
    jonathan = Student.new({given_name: "Jonathan", family_name: "Higgins"})
    assert !jonathan.valid?, "Should require date of birth, start date"
    jonathan.date_of_birth = "1989-02-03"
    jonathan.start_date = Date.today
    assert jonathan.valid?, "Failed even with all required info"
  end


  def test_name
    jonathan = Student.new({given_name: "Jonathan",
        family_name: "Higgins"})
    assert_equal jonathan.name, "Jonathan Higgins", "name method screwed up"
  end

  def test_enrolled_in
    tc = students(:tc)
    assert tc.enrolled_in?(courses(:aviation)), "TC not enrolled in surveillance?"
    assert !tc.enrolled_in?(courses(:security)), "TC should stay out of security"
  end

  def test_unenrolled_courses
    magnum = students(:magnum)
    rick = students(:rick)
    assert_equal [courses(:aviation)], magnum.unenrolled_courses
    assert_equal [courses(:aviation)], rick.unenrolled_courses
    jonathan = Student.new({given_name: "Jonathan", family_name: "Higgins"})
    assert_equal Course.all, jonathan.unenrolled_courses
  end
end
```

The first line of the class specifies the fixtures that need to be loaded for these tests:

```ruby
fixtures :students, :courses
```

The first two test methods in the class, `test_validity` and `test_name`, are much like the tests used on awards, simply ensuring that the student model behaves as described. The `test_validity` method creates a new object and first makes sure that it fails when missing required information, then adds the information and makes sure that it passes. (You could, of course, add extra assertions to test each additional field.) These `assert` methods include an extra argument, a message to be reported if the test fails. That may or may not be easier for you to manage than the line number automatically reported.

The `test_name` method creates a student with a given and family name, then tests the `name` method to see if it returns the expected value. It uses a new method, `assert_equal`, that expects the values of its two arguments to be equal. If they aren't, it reports a failure. (There's also `assert_not_equal` for the opposite situation.)

The next two methods, `test_enrolled_in` and `test_unenrolled_courses`, are more complicated and rely on the fixtures heavily. The `test_enrolled_in` method doesn't actually set any values, it just checks to see whether a given student—the one identified as `:tc`—is enrolled in the courses specified:

```
def test_enrolled_in
  tc = students(:tc)
  assert tc.enrolled_in?(courses(:aviation)),
    "TC not enrolled in surveillance?"
  assert !tc.enrolled_in?(courses(:security)),
    "TC should stay out of security"
end
```

According to the courses fixture, which was shown in Example 12-6, TC (`:tc` in the fixtures) should be enrolled in Aviation Safety (`:aviation`), but not enrolled in Personal and Private Property Security (`:security`). This test makes sure that the `enrol led_in?` method reflects that.

The last test method here, `test_unenrolled_courses`, relies on the fixtures and also creates a new record for comparison:

```
def test_unenrolled_courses
  magnum = students(:magnum)
  rick = students(:rick)
  assert_equal [courses(:aviation)], magnum.unenrolled_courses
  assert_equal [courses(:aviation)], rick.unenrolled_courses
  jonathan = Student.new({given_name: "Jonathan", family_name: "Higgins"})
  assert_equal Course.all, jonathan.unenrolled_courses
end
```

The first two lines create student objects from the fixture identifiers. The first `assert_equal` call checks to make sure that the list of classes in which `magnum` is not enrolled is an array containing the Aviation Safety (`:aviation`) class, which corresponds to the fixture. Then, the next call checks that `rick` is not enrolled in that same Aviation Safety class (`:aviation`). Finally, the method creates a new `jonathan` student, and checks to make sure that his list of unenrolled courses is the same as the list of all courses. He hasn't enrolled in anything yet, after all!

If you run these tests, you'll get a brief report. (`rails test:units` lets you run only the unit tests, or you can use `rails test` or just `rails` to run all of the tests.)

```
$ rails test:models
   Loaded suite ...gems/rake-0.9.2.2/lib/rake/rake_test_loader
   Started
   ......
   Finished in 0.758487 seconds.

   6 tests, 15 assertions, 0 failures, 0 errors, 0 skips

   Test run options: --seed 19138
```

The periods under Started each represent a successful test, while an F would represent a failure and E an error, something that interfered with running the test.

If a test fails—maybe the fixtures reported Giles taking Immoral Aesthetics—you'll see something like:

```
$ rails test:models
Run options: --seed 49252

# Running:

F

Should require date of birth, start date

bin/rails test test/models/student_test.rb:10

.....

Finished in 0.077577s, 77.3425 runs/s, 128.9042 assertions/s.

6 tests, 15 assertions, 1 failures, 0 errors, 0 skips
```

You could track it down by line number, but the message can also be meaningful.

After finishing this section, you might think unit tests seem to test things that are too simple. These were just little pokes and prods, checking to see whether something fairly obvious would happen or not. There are a few reasons these (and other kinds of tests) are valuable, however:

- Model tests accumulate over time, and as a project grows, especially when multiple developers work on it, they serve as a warning that something has changed, probably not for the better.

- Most programmers think about creating code and then testing it afterward. A different, perhaps more effective, approach is to write tests first and then write code that answers the tests. There may be more back and forth to it than that, as development often inspires more functionality and more tests, but defining tests first creates a clear target to aim for. This is known as *test-driven development* (TDD) or *behavior-driven development* (BDD).

- Once you've written a test, it'll run every time you tell Rails to perform testing. You don't need to go back through your application by hand to make sure that things that once worked still worked—the test suite will tell you. Tests can become part of a *continuous integration* environment where tests are automatically run against code that is checked into a repository.

These simple tests of models may seem too simple, but they build a critical foundation that other work can build on.

 If you get tired of calling all of your tests and just want to focus on one, try something like `rails test:units TEST=test/unit/ foo.rb`.

Controller Testing

Model testing checks on data validation and simple connections, but there's a lot more happening in the typical Rails application. Controllers are the key piece connecting data to users, supporting a number of complex interactions that need more sophisticated testing than checking validation or data. Controllers need tests that can examine the actions they were supposed to perform. In Rails, these tests are defined in files in the *test/controllers* directory.

Unlike the model tests generated by Rails, which did nothing, the functional tests created by the REST scaffolding at least provide a basic structure that's useful, though it only tests a very basic set of possibilities. (The controller tests are a placeholder like the model tests are.) The *courses_controller_test.rb* file shown in Example 12-12 is capable of calling the REST methods and making sure they work—except, of course, the fixtures generated by the scaffolding will create problems.

Example 12-12. An almost-functional functional test set generated by Rails for the courses controller

```
#test/controllers/course_controller_test.rb
require test_helper

class CoursesControllerTest < ActionController::TestCase
  setup do
    @course = courses(:one)
  end

  test "should get index" do
    get :index
    assert_response :success
  end
```

```
test "should get new" do
  get :new
  assert_response :success
end

test "should create course" do
  assert_difference(Course.count) do
    post :create, params: { course: { name: @course.name } }
  end

  assert_redirected_to course_path(Course.last)
end

test "should show course" do
  get :show, params: { id: @course }
  assert_response :success
end

test "should get edit" do
  get :edit, params: { id: @course }
  assert_response :success
end

test "should update course" do
  patch :update, params: { id: @course, course: { name: @course.name } }
  assert_redirected_to course_path(@course)
end

test "should destroy course" do
  assert_difference(Course.count, -1) do
    delete :destroy, params: { id: @course }
  end

  assert_redirected_to courses_path
end
end
```

You could use these generated tests as a foundation with the new fixtures by making a few changes, highlighted in Example 12-13, which also adds a bit more specific detail to the test.

Example 12-13. An improved functional test for the courses controller

```
#test/controllers/course_controller_test.rb
require test_helper

class CoursesControllerTest < ActionController::TestCase
  def test_should_get_index
    get :index
    assert_response :success
    assert_not_nil assigns(:courses)
```

```
  end

  def test_should_get_new
    get :new
    assert_response :success
  end

  def test_should_create_course
    assert_difference(Course.count) do
      post :create, course: { name: "Cattle Rustling" }
    end

    assert_redirected_to course_path(assigns(:course))
  end

  def test_should_show_course
    get :show, id: courses(:surveillance).id
    assert_response :success
  end

  def test_should_get_edit
    get :edit, id: courses(:surveillance).id
    assert_response :success
  end

  def test_should_update_course
    put :update, id: courses(:surveillance).id, course: { name: "Singing" }
    assert_redirected_to course_path(assigns(:course))
  end

  def test_should_destroy_course
    assert_difference(Course.count, -1) do
      delete :destroy, id: courses(:surveillance).id
    end

    assert_redirected_to courses_path
  end
end
```

 Rails 5 has removed support for the assigns method. If you run the previous test in Rails 5 you should see a NoMethodError. You can regain this functionality by adding the rails-controller-testing gem to your Gemfile. Remember to run bundle after you update your Gemfile. You can read more about the logic behind removing the method online (*https://github.com/rails/rails/issues/18950*).

The changes are relatively minor, shifting from the generic :one to its replacement in the courses fixture, :surveillance, and supporting names for courses when they're created instead of using blank names, which the model forbids. However, creating controller tests, or modifying them as will be necessary to support the nested resource approach awards use, requires understanding a new set of assertions and methods for calling controllers. Both let you test what the controller would have done in response to an HTTP call.

Calling Controllers

Controllers are called via the GET, PUT, POST, and DELETE methods, with the actual method to be called listed as the first argument and any necessary parameters listed as named parameters after that. Controller testing does not actually create an HTTP request and answer it. Instead, it skips over the issues of routing and goes to the controller directly.

If you want to make HTTP requests in your tests, you can—but in the controller testing.

For RESTful calls, you'll want to test all seven of the methods Rails generates, four with `get` and one each with `put`, `post`, and `delete`. For other controllers, you'll want to write calls for each method and address them appropriately. The `get` method as shown here only passes an `id` value, but you can set other parameters as desired. The `put` and `post` methods both need additional parameters to work, however, taking a `:course` that itself contains a `:name`. Think of these as form fields rather than objects. For example, the `post` looks like:

```
post :create, course: { name: "Cattle Rustling" }
```

The `post` method will call the controller's `create` method, giving it parameters for a `:course`. The only parameter here is `:name`, set to `Cattle Rustling`. It works the same as entering `Cattle Rustling` into a form that was fed to this method.

Instead of specifying the method name with a symbol, you can pass these methods a URL fragment as a string. However, you should leave that usage to integration testing, covered later in this chapter.

Testing Responses

The new assertion methods relate to specific controller actions and their effects:

assert_not_nil_assigns
> Allows the test to check on whether the controller set values for the view to use, though the test doesn't actually call the view. This just makes sure that a given variable is not left as nil.

assert_response
> Compares the HTTP response code that the controller sends to its argument. :success is the most common argument (for 200 OK), while :redirect (for 300–399 responses), :missing (404), and :error (500–599) are also common. (If you have a specific response in mind, you can just give the HTTP response code number as the argument.)

assert_redirected_to
> Lets you check not just the response code, but the location to which the controller redirected the request.

assert_difference
> Makes it easy to check on the number of records in the database, taking a method to call and an integer reflecting the difference. An added record would just be +1, the default, while a deleted record would be –1. assert_difference takes a block as its argument and must wrap around the call to the controller with do and end statements. (There's also an assert_no_difference for when you don't want there to be any difference.)

Most of these are fairly readable, but it's worth examining the most complicated test in detail:

```
def test_should_create_course
    assert_difference('Course.count') do
      post :create, course: { name: "Cattle Rustling" }
    end

    assert_redirected_to course_path(assigns(:course))
  end
```

This method tests the creation of a course. It opens with an assert_difference method, which will check the count of courses at the beginning and check again when it encounters the end statement. Between those checks, the post method calls the course controller's create method. As an argument, post sends create what looks like a form for a course, specifying a :name of Cattle Rustling. After that, assert_difference reaches the end and checks to see if the count indeed increased by 1, the default. If the count didn't increase, the assertion reports a failure, but otherwise, it reports success.

The second assertion checks to where the method redirected the visitor. It uses the assigns method to reach into the variables the controller created and get the course object, and checks that the path specified by the redirection is the same as the path to that `course` object created with `course_path`.

Dealing with Nested Resources

Making awards a nested resource under students took some work in Chapter 9, and similar considerations apply in the testing process as well. Example 12-14 shows the functional tests for awards, from *test/controllers/awards_controller_test.rb*, highlighting areas that needed additional information to support the nesting.

Example 12-14. Adding support for a nested resource to functional testing

```
require test_helper

class AwardsControllerTest < ActionController::TestCase
  def test_should_get_index
    get :index, student_id: students(:magnum).id
    assert_response :success
    assert_not_nil assigns(:awards)
  end

  def test_should_get_new
    get :new, student_id: students(:magnum).id
    assert_response :success
  end

  def test_should_create_award
    assert_difference(Award.count) do
      post :create, award: { year: 2008, name: Test award },
                    student_id: students(:magnum).id
    end

  end

  def test_should_show_award
    get :show, id: awards(:pi).id, student_id: students(:magnum).id
    assert_response :success
  end

  def test_should_get_edit
    get :edit, id: awards(:pi).id, student_id: students(:magnum).id
    assert_response :success
  end

  def test_should_update_award
    put :update, id: awards(:pi).id, award: { year: 2008, name: Test award },
    student_id: students(:magnum).id
    assert_redirected_to student_awards_url(students(:magnum))
  end
```

```
  def test_should_destroy_award
    assert_difference(Award.count, -1) do
      delete :destroy,  id: awards(:pi).id,student_id:
                             students(:magnum).id
    end

    assert_redirected_to student_awards_path(students(:magnum))
  end
end
```

All of these echo the changes in Chapter 9 and are necessary for making the tests work with a nested resource that needs a student context for its controller to operate. The method names for paths change, gaining a `student_` prefix, and all of the calls to `get`, `put`, `post`, and `delete` also need a `:student_id` parameter.

For our students controller test let's add the code in Example 12-15.

Example 12-15. Adding support for students controller test

```
require test_helper

class StudentsControllerTest < ActionController::TestCase
  setup do
    @student = students(:magnum)
  end

  test "should get index" do
    get :index
    assert_response :success
  end

  test "should get new" do
    get :new
    assert_response :success
  end

  test "should create student" do
    assert_difference(Student.count) do
      post :create, params: { student: { date_of_birth: @student.date_of_birth,
      family_name: @student.family_name, given_name: @student.given_name,
      grade_point_average: @student.grade_point_average,
      middle_name: @student.middle_name, start_date: @student.start_date } }
    end

    assert_redirected_to student_path(Student.last)
  end

  test "should show student" do
    get :show, params: { id: @student }
    assert_response :success
  end
```

```
test "should get edit" do
  get :edit, params: { id: @student }
  assert_response :success
end

test "should update student" do
  patch :update, params: { id: @student, student:
  { date_of_birth: @student.date_of_birth,
  family_name: @student.family_name, given_name: @student.given_name,
  grade_point_average: @student.grade_point_average, middle_name:
  @student.middle_name,
  start_date: @student.start_date } }
  assert_redirected_to student_path(@student)
end

test "should destroy student" do
  assert_difference(Student.count, -1) do
    delete :destroy, params: { id: @student }
  end

  assert_redirected_to students_path
  end
end
```

Running all the functional tests should produce results such as:

```
$ rails test:controllers
(in /Users/simonstl/Documents/RailsOutIn/current/code/ch12/students005)
/System/Library/Frameworks/Ruby.framework/Versions/1.8/usr/bin/ruby -Ilib:test
"/Library/Ruby/Gems/1.8/gems/rake-0.8.1/lib/rake/rake_test_loader.rb"
"test/functional/awards_controller_test.rb"
"test/functional/courses_controller_test.rb"
"test/functional/students_controller_test.rb"
Loaded suite /Library/Ruby/Gems/1.8/gems/rake-0.8.1/lib/rake/rake_test_loader
Started
.........................
Finished in 0.608977 seconds.

25 tests, 35 assertions, 0 failures, 0 errors
```

Integration Testing

Integration testing is the most complicated testing Rails supports directly. It tests complete requests coming in from the outside, running through routing, controllers, models, the database, and even views. Rails does not generate any integration tests by default, as creating them requires detailed knowledge of the complete application and what it is supposed to do. Integration tests are stored in *test/integration* and look much like the classes for other kinds of tests. The filename must end in *test.rb*. They call similar methods and also make assertions, but the assertions are different and the flow can cover multiple interactions, as Example 12-16 demonstrates.

Integration tests must be explicitly created under the *test/integration* folder, and Rails provides a generator to create them:

```
$ rails g integration_test student
      invoke  test_unit
      create    test/integration/student_test.rb
```

This will create a blank student test for us, but it doesn't do very much. Let's make it do stuff in Example 12-16.

Example 12-16. An integration test that tries adding a student in test/integration/student_test.rb

```ruby
require 'test_helper'

# Integration tests covering the manipulation of student objects

class StudentsTest < ActionDispatch::IntegrationTest

  def test_adding_a_student
    # get the new student form
    get '/students/new' # could be new_students_path

    # check there are boxes to put the name in
    # trivial in our case, but illustrates how to check output HTML
    assert_select "input[type=text][name='student[given_name]']"
    assert_select "input[type=text][name='student[family_name]']"

    assert_difference('Student.count') do
      post '/students', student: {
        given_name: "Fred",
        family_name: "Smith",
        date_of_birth: "1999-09-01",
        grade_point_average: 2.0,
        start_date: "2008-09-01"
      }
    end

    assert_redirected_to "/students/#{assigns(:student).id}"
    follow_redirect!

    # for completeness, check it's showing some of our data
    assert_select "p", /Fred/
    assert_select "p", /2008\-09\-01/
  end

end
```

Instead of calling the `create` method directly, as the functional tests would do, `test_adding_a_student` starts by using the `get` method—with a URI fragment rather than a function name—to retrieve the form needed for adding a student.

Next, the method examines that form with `assert_select`, one of the Rails methods for testing HTML documents to see if they contain what you expect them to contain. In the first of those two statements, `assert_select` tries to match the pattern:

```
input[type=text][name='student[given_name]']
```

That would be an `input` element with a `type` attribute set to `text` and a `name` attribute set to `student[given_name]`. (The single quotes are necessary to keep the [and] from causing trouble with the match pattern syntax.) The form should match that, as it contains:

```
input id="student_given_name" name="student[given_name]" size="30"
  type="text" />
```

Once Rails has performed those assertions, it moves to actually submitting a new student. There's no way for Rails itself to actually fill in the form and press the submit button (though Capybara can do that). The test does the next best thing, issuing a POST request that reflects what the form would have done, from inside of an `assert_difference` call that looks for an added student:

```
assert_difference('Student.count') do
    post '/students', student: {
      given_name: "Fred",
      family_name: "Smith",
      date_of_birth: "1999-09-01",
      grade_point_average: 2.0,
      start_date: "2008-09-01"
    }
  end
```

Again, the call is to a URL, not to a method name, though this POST call includes parameters designed to reflect the structure that would be returned by the form Rails generated. The page showing this student, Fred Smith, should come back from Rails for display through a redirect, so the next assertion watches for that:

```
assert_redirected_to "/students/#{assigns(:student).id}"
```

The assertion can grab the `id` value for the new student, whatever it is, from the controller, using the all-powerful `assigns` method. If it gets sent somewhere other than it expects, it will report failure.

The next call is fairly self-explanatory:

```
follow_redirect!
```

There's one last step needed here: checking that response to see if it reflects expectations. Following the redirect lets the test continue to the final part of the interaction, in which Rails shows off the newly created student. Here, the test uses more `assert_select` statements in a slightly different syntax:

```
assert_select "p", /Fred/
assert_select "p", /2008\-09\-01/
```

When given a string and a regular expression as arguments, `assert_select` will look for elements of the type given in the string (here, p) that contain values matching the expression. Appendix C has more details on regular expressions, but the first of these is just the string `Fred`, while the other is an escaped version of `2008-09-01`. These are, of course, the values that the test set earlier, and they should appear in the document. Will they?

```
$ rails test:integration
Loaded suite .../gems/rake-0.9.2.2/lib/rake/rake_test_loader
Started
.
Finished in 1.036746 seconds.

1 tests, 7 assertions, 0 failures, 0 errors, 0 skips
```

It all worked.

Creating useful integration tests is difficult. It requires plotting a path through your application and deciding which pieces are relevant, and which are not. As your application grows in complexity and interdependence, they may become critical, though smaller applications can often do without them for a long while.

 If `assert_select` isn't enough for your view-testing experiments, Rails offers many more options:

- `assert_tag`
- `assert_no_tag`
- `assert_dom_equal`
- `assert_dom_not_equal`
- `assert_select_encoded`
- `assert_select_rjs`

Beyond the Basics

Testing is central to Rails development, but virtually everyone has a different perspective on what they want from testing. While the tools demonstrated in this chapter provide a common core of functionality, many developers supplement or replace the testing approach built into Rails with other alternatives. If you want to explore further, you should explore RSpec, Cucumber, and the broader world of TDD and BDD.

RSpec (*http://rspec.info*) takes testing to a higher level, letting you create stories with your code, and testing the results of those stories in a way that lets you see what was supposed to happen and what did or didn't happen as well. It makes it much easier in particular to create tests first and then write code to fill them in. For a lot more on RSpec, visit *http://rspec.info/*.

Cucumber (*https://cucumber.io*) pushes further on testing, toward customer acceptance testing. This is commonly referred to in the programming community as *behavior-driven development* (or BDD, as introduced earlier in the chapter). While RSpec tests will likely be tests you write to hold your code accountable, Cucumber tests will likely come from customers, even if you're the one to translate their expectations into a concrete set of tests. You may also be interested in Matt Wynne and Asiak Hellesoy's *The Cucumber Book* (Pragmatic Bookshelf, 2012).

 For more on RSpec, see *Everyday Rails Testing with RSpec* (*http://bit.ly/2aTANVG*) by Aaron Sumner (Leanpub, 2014).

Add Factory Girl to manage test data and Capybara for more advanced integration testing, and you can make sure your applications work. Even if you stick with the basic Rails testing functionality, your applications should prove much more reliable and your need for debugging will be much less.

Test Your Knowledge

Quiz

1. What three modes can Rails run applications under by default?
2. How much data do you need to put into fixtures?
3. Can the results of one test mess up the results of a test that comes later?
4. How do you check to make sure a variable contains an acceptable value?
5. What kind of component gets tested with Rails functional tests?
6. How do you send a controller a fake HTTP POST request?
7. How do you know whether a controller redirected a request?
8. How can you tell whether a response includes a td element containing a particular value?

Answers

1. Rails can run in development mode, test mode, and production mode. You can define your own modes if you want as well.

2. Your fixtures should include all the kinds of data you want to run tests against.

3. Each test should be completely independent, as Rails will reload all of the fixtures between tests. No test should have an effect on any other test. (If you have multiple assertions within a single test, however, they can interact.)

4. The `valid?` method lets you ask a model if its value would pass validation.

5. In Rails, functional tests are tests of controllers.

6. The `post` method lets you see how a controller would respond to a POST request.

7. The `assert_redirected` method lets you test whether the controller sent a simple response or a redirect.

8. The `assert_select` method lets you specify an element name and a match pattern it should contain, and tells you whether an element whose content matches that pattern exists.

## CHAPTER 13

Sessions and Cookies

Fortune cookies are a good idea. If the message is positive,
it can make your day a little better.
  —Yao Ming, retired NBA center

The Web was built to do one thing at a time. Each request is, from the point of view of the client and server, completely independent of every other. A group of requests might all operate on the same database, and there can be clear paths from one part of an application to another, but for the most part, HTTP and scalable web application design both try to keep requests as independent as possible. It makes the underlying infrastructure easier.

Rails balances that simplicity of infrastructure with application developers' need for a coherent way to maintain context. Rails supports several mechanisms for keeping track of information about users. If you want to keep track of users manually, you can work with cookies. If you want to keep track of users for a brief series of interactions, Rails's built-in session support should meet your needs.

If you want to keep track of users on a long-term basis, you'll want to use the authentication tools covered in Chapter 14.

Getting Into and Out of Cookies

Like nearly every web framework, Rails provides support for cookies. Cookies are small pieces of text, usually less than 4 KB long, that servers can set on browsers and browsers will pass back with requests to servers. Browsers keep track of where cookies came from and only report cookies' values to the server where they came from originally. JavaScript code can reach into a cookie from a web page, but Rails itself is more interested in setting and receiving cookies through the HTTP headers for each request and response.

 When cookies first appeared, they were loved by developers, who saw them as a way to keep track of which user was visiting their site, and hated by privacy advocates. Much of that uproar has calmed, because cookies have become a key part of functionality that users expect, but there's still potential for abuse, as various advertising and social networks demonstrate constantly.

To stay on the good side of potentially cranky users, it's best to set cookie lifetimes to relatively brief periods and use longer cookies only when users request them (as in the classic "remember me" checkboxes for logins). Never store sensitive information directly in cookies, either!

In most cases, your application probably doesn't need to access cookies directly. Rails's built-in session support and user authentication tools can together manage all of the overhead of keeping track of users for you. However, if you want to use cookies directly, either because you have specific needs for them or because you're interacting with other code (say, a JavaScript library) that expects a particular cookie to provide it with a key value, then the upcoming examples should give you a clear idea how it works. Figure 13-1 provides an overall picture of how cookies flow through an application.

Because cookies are about storing data on the client, not the server, a really simple example will do. To get started, this example will build on one of the simplest examples in this book so far, the first version of the `entries` controller with its `sign_in` method from Chapter 4. (Code for this example is in *ch13/guestbook11*.)

 If you'd rather create a new blank copy of this application, run **rails new guestbook**, then **cd guestbook** if necessary, and finally **rails generate controller entries**. You'll also need to uncomment the `match ':controller(/:action(/:id))(.:format)'` line at the end of *config/routes.rb* to allow routing to find this controller.

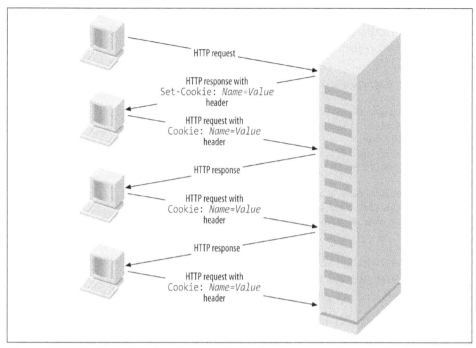

Figure 13-1. The flow of cookies between Rails, the browser, and code in the browser

Example 13-1 shows the new *app/controllers/entries_controller.rb* file, with changes from the Chapter 4 version in bold.

Example 13-1. Keeping track of names entered with a cookie

```
class EntriesController < ApplicationController
  def sign_in
    @previous_name = cookies[:name]
    @name = params[:visitor_name]
    cookies[:name] = @name
  end
end
```

The new first line collects the previous name entered from the cookie and stores it as @previous_name so the view can display it. (The cookie data comes to the server through the HTTP request headers.) The second line, as before, gathers the new name from the :visitor_name field of the form, and the third line stores that name (even if it's empty) as a cookie that will be transmitted to the browser through the HTTP response headers.

The view in *app/views/entries/sign_in.html.erb* just needs three extra lines to show the previous name if there was one, as shown in Example 13-2. (If you made a fresh start, you may need to create the file.)

Example 13-2. Reporting a previous name to the user

```
<h1>Hello <%= @name %></h1>
<%= form_tag action: 'sign_in' do %>
   <p>Enter your name:
   <%= text_field_tag 'visitor_name', @name %></p>
   <%= submit_tag 'Sign in' %>
<% end %>
<% unless @previous_name.blank? %>
  <p>Hmmm... the last time you were here, you said you were
  <%= @previous_name %>.</p>
<% end %>
```

This tests to see whether a previous name was set and, if so, presents the user with what she'd entered. All this really does is demonstrate that the cookie is keeping track of something entered in a past request, making it available to the current request.

The HTTP headers that carry the cookie back and forth are normally invisible, though not that interesting. You can see cookie information in most browsers through a preferences or info setting. At the beginning, this application looks much like its predecessor, as shown in Figure 13-2.

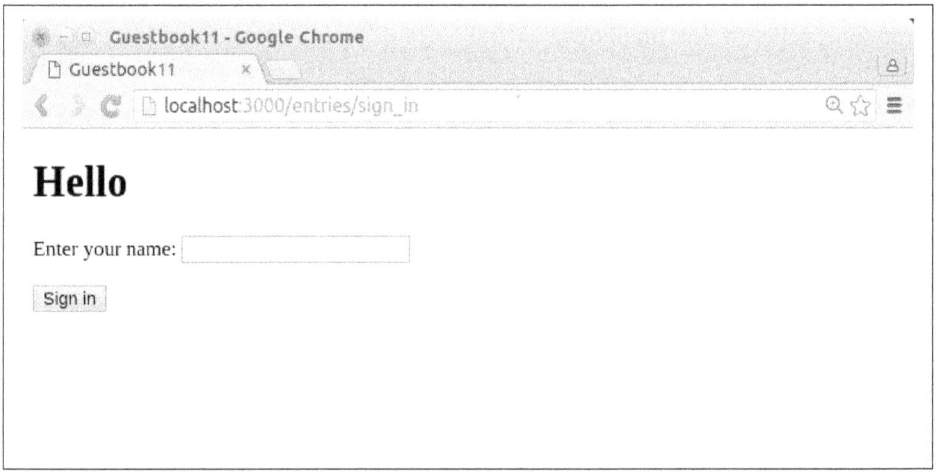

Figure 13-2. A simple name form, though now one with a cookie behind it

In Chrome, you can view cookies by choosing More Tools → Developer Tools, select-ing the Resources tab, clicking the arrow to the left of Cookies, and then choosing localhost. You'll see something like Figure 13-3.

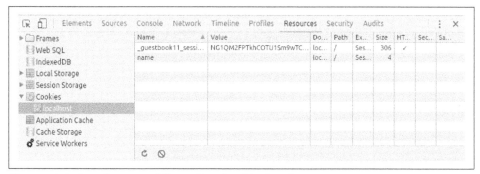

Figure 13-3. A cookie named "name" with a blank value

For now, the :name cookie is the one that matters, and as you can see, its content is blank. It came from localhost, because this is a test session on the local machine. The path is set to /, the Rails default, making it accessible to any page that comes from the localhost server. It gets sent with all HTTP connections and will expire "at end of session"—as soon as the user quits the browser. Users can, of course, delete the cookie immediately. In Chrome you can right-click on the cookie and choose *clear*.

If you enter a name, say "Calba," and click the "Sign in" button, you'll see something like Figure 13-4.

Figure 13-4. The form, with a new name set

Because the :name cookie was previously set to an empty string, the query message still isn't shown, but this time the trigger is set. If you inspect the cookie, you'll see that the :name cookie's value is now "Calba," as shown in Figure 13-5.

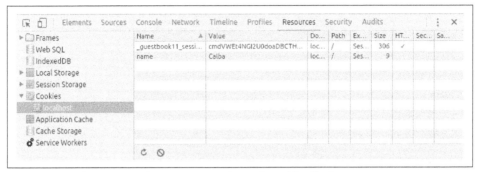

Figure 13-5. The name cookie, now set with a value of "Calba"

If you enter a new name, say "JJ," and click the "Sign in" button, the Rails application will get "JJ" through the form, while still getting "Calba" from the cookie. This time, it will ask why the name has changed, as shown in Figure 13-6.

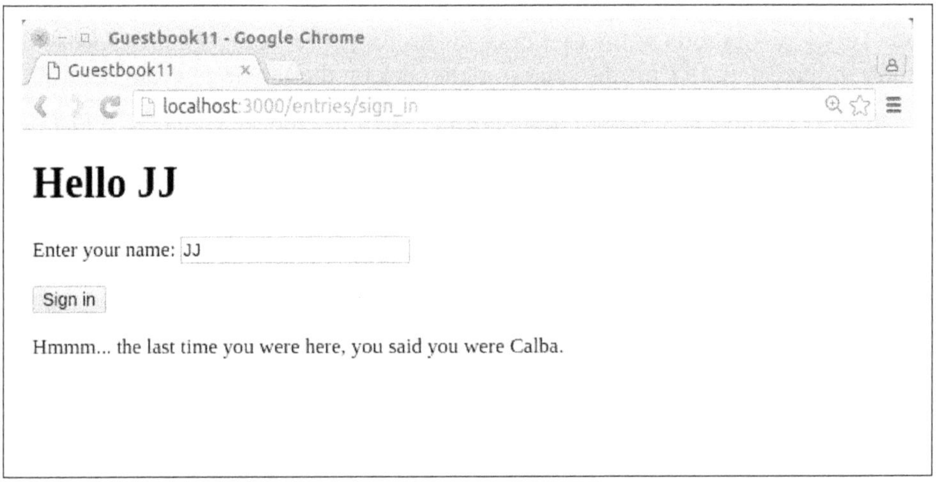

Guestbook11 - Google Chrome

Guestbook11   ×

localhost:3000/entries/sign_in

Hello JJ

Enter your name: JJ

Sign in

Hmmm... the last time you were here, you said you were Calba.

Figure 13-6. Changing names over the session produces a response

Storing the name information in the cookie gives Rails a memory of what happened before so it notices a change.

If you choose to use cookies directly, rather than relying on other Rails mechanisms for keeping track of interactions across requests, there are a few more parameters you should know about when setting cookies. If you set more than just a value for a cookie, the syntax changes. To set both a value and a path for the :name cookie, for example, you would change:

```
cookies[:name] = @name
```

to:

```
cookies[:name] = { value: @name, path: '/entry' }
```

The available parameters include:

`:value`

The value for the cookie, usually a short string. (Typically this is a database key, but make sure not to store anything genuinely secret.)

`:domain`

The domain to which the cookie applies. This has to be a domain that matches the domain at which the application runs. For example, if an application was hosted at *http://myapp.example.com*, `:domain` could be set to *http://myapp.example.com* or *http://example.com*. If it was set to *http://example.com*, the cookie could be read from *http://myapp.example.com*, *http://yourapp.example.com*, or *http://anything.example.com*.

`:path`

The path to which the cookie applies. Like `:domain`, the `:path` must be all or part of the path from which the call is being made. From */entries/sign_in*, it could be set to */*, to */entries*, or to */entries/sign_in*. The cookie can only be read from URLs that could have set that path. (By default, this is */*, making the cookie available to everything at your domain.)

`:expires`

The time at which the cookie will expire. The easiest way to set this is with Ruby's time methods, such as `5.minutes` or `12.hours.from_now`.

`:secure`

If set to `true`, the cookie is reported or sent only over secure HTTP (HTTPS) connections.

`:http_only`

If `true`, the cookie is transmitted over HTTP or HTTPS connections, but is not available to JavaScript code on those pages.

Anytime you find yourself using cookies, especially if you're doing complicated things with them, you should consider using sessions or authentication instead.

Storing Data Between Sessions

Cookies are useful for keeping track of a piece of information between page changes, but as you may have noticed in Figures 13-3 and 13-5, Rails was already setting a cookie, a session cookie, with each request. Rather than manage cookies yourself, you can let Rails do all of that work and move one step further back from the details. (This example is available in *ch13/guestbook12*.)

Sessions are a means of keeping track of which user is making a given request. Rails doesn't know anything specific about the user, except that he has a cookie with a given value. Rails uses that cookie to keep track of users and lets you store a bit of information that survives between page requests.

You can set and retrieve information about the current session from the session object, which is available to your controller and view. Because it's a better idea in general to put logic into the controller, Example 13-3, which is a new version of the *app/controllers/entries_controller.rb* file, shows what's involved in storing an array in the session object, retrieving it, and modifying it to add names to the list. Virtually all of it replaces code that was in Example 13-1, with only the retrieval of the name from the form staying the same.

Example 13-3. Working with an array stored in the session object

```
class EntriesController < ApplicationController
  def sign_in
    #get names array from session
    @names=session[:names]

    #if the array doesn't exist, make one
    unless @names
      @names=[]
    end

    #get the latest name from the form
    @name = params[:visitor_name]

    if @name
      # add the new name to the names array
      @names << @name
    end

    # store the new names array in the session
    session[:names]=@names
  end
end
```

Most of the new code is about working with an array rather than a simple field. It's not a big problem if a string is empty, whereas trying to add new entries to a nonexistent array is a bigger problem. The sign_in method gets the names array from the session object and puts it in @names. If the session object doesn't have a names object, it will return nil, so the unless creates a names array if necessary. Then the method retrieves the latest visitor_name from the form and adds it to the @names array. The very last line puts the updated version of the @names array back into the session object so that the next call will have access to it.

Example 13-3 is more verbose than it needs to be, as you could work on session[:names] directly. However, it's a bit clearer to work with the @names instance variable, and this approach lets the view work strictly with instance variables.

The view requires fewer changes—just a test that the list of names exists and a loop to display the names if it does. The changes to *app/views/entries/sign_in.html.erb* are highlighted in Example 13-4.

Example 13-4. Reporting a set of previous names to the user

```
<h1>Hello <%= @name %></h1>

<%= form_tag action: 'sign_in' do %>
  <p>Enter your name:
  <%= text_field_tag 'visitor_name', @name %></p>

  <%= submit_tag 'Sign in' %>
<% end %>

<% if @names %>
<ul>
  <% @names.each do |name| %>
    <li><%= name %></li>
  <% end %>
</ul>
<% end %>
```

As Figures 13-7 through 13-9 demonstrate, the application now remembers what names have been entered before.

Figure 13-7. The first iteration, where no previous names are recorded in the session object

Figure 13-8. The second iteration, where one previous name has been recorded in the session object

Figure 13-9. The third iteration, where two previous names have been recorded in the session object

If you quit your browser and return, or try a different browser, you'll get the empty result shown in Figure 13-8 again, as the session changes. This application is very different from the application at the end of Chapter 4, which stored names from everyone in the same database. Because this application relies on the `session` object, only the names entered in this browser at this time will appear. That session identifier will vanish when the user quits her browser because the session cookie will be deleted, and those names will no longer be accessible.

The `session` object builds on the cookie functionality described in the previous section, but Rails takes care of all the cookie handling. For simple applications, where you're just going to store something small in the session, you now know everything you need to know and can skip ahead if you'd like.

There are, of course, more details, more things you can tweak. First of all, you can turn sessions off if you have an application that doesn't need them and want a little speed boost. Just add **session :off** at the top of controller classes or, for the whole application, in *app/controllers/application_controller.rb*. (You can turn individual controllers back on with **session :on**, and the documentation for `ActionControl ler::SessionManagement` shows many more options for controlling when sessions are used.)

Just as with cookies, you can limit the use of sessions to secure HTTPS connections. To do so, just start off with **:session_secure => true**. Sessions will stop working over regular HTTP connections and only work when HTTPS is in use.

Find out more about sessions and cookies in the session discussion in the Ruby on Rails guides (*http://bit.ly/2aTCBhp*).

Flashing in Rails

The Rails `flash` mechanism doesn't support state across separate user requests like the other mechanisms in this chapter. (Nor does it have anything to do with Adobe's Flash technology.) It does, however, provide an easy way to maintain state within a user request that gets answered with a redirect.

When a controller calls `redirect_to`, which is common in RESTful PUT and POST handling, the method that gets the redirect starts off with a fresh set of variables. You can't work in one controller method and then pass the rest of the work to another controller method while retaining the variable context.

There's one exception to this context reset—the `flash` mechanism. Most of the time, `flash` just gets used for sending messages from a controller to a view generated by another controller, as in this scaffolding excerpt:

```
flash[:notice] = 'Course was successfully updated.'
format.html { redirect_to(@course) }
```

In the layout for the course views, this line reveals the contents of that `flash`:

```
<p style="color: green"><%= flash[:notice] %></p>
```

Although `:notice` is the most common key used with flash, you could also use `:warn ing`, `:error`, or any other key that seems appropriate to your task. (`:notice`, `:warn ing`, and `:error` work automatically with the templates Rails generates, which is convenient.)

There are only a few catches. First, you should always keep the contents of the `flash` simple and small. It's stored in the session and, like everything else in the session,

---

should be as lightweight as possible. Second, the contents only survive one redirect. If you want to keep the contents across multiple redirects, you'll need to call `flash.keep` before each additional redirect. Similarly, you can call `flash.discard` to get rid of the flash.

You can also use `flash.now`, which makes the values you set available for immediate use, in case, for example, your code has an error and never reaches a redirect.

Test Your Knowledge

Quiz

1. How much information should you store in cookies?

2. How do you specify how long a cookie will last?

3. Where does Rails normally store the information you put in the cookie object?

4. What does calling `flash` do?

Answers

1. You should store as little information in cookies as your application can manage.

2. Cookie lifespans default to expiring when the user quits the browser, but can be set to more specific lengths of time with the `:expires` parameter.

3. By default, Rails stores the cookie objects information directly in the cookie, on the user's browser, but note that you can change this by modifying your *config/ environment.rb* file.

4. The `flash` method lets you set a message to be shown to the user even after a redirect.

## CHAPTER 14

Users and Authentication

If you think technology can solve your security problems, then you don't understand the problems and you don't understand the technology.
—Bruce Schneier

While sessions expand your application-building possibilities, almost any interactive application that will be around for a while needs to be able to keep track of users. You might be a little surprised to hear that Rails itself doesn't include any mechanisms for tracking users, unlike many web frameworks. That isn't so much a failure as an opportunity for developers to create their own authentication approaches. There are many gems available for Rails that make authentication a snap to implement. However, writing code for your own authentication is not terribly difficult, so that is how we will approach authentication in this chapter. The code we will be using is based on an updated version of Ryan Bates's "Authentication from Scratch" Railscast (*http://bit.ly/2aTD2bt*). This screencast was written for Rails 3, but watching it will give you a good sense of what the code is doing. Writing your own authentication gives you much more control over your code, and if you do use a gem you may find yourself quickly overwriting or rewriting many parts of the code provided by the gem.

 Two of the most popular gems for authentication are `Devise` (*http://bit.ly/2aTEqdW*) and `OmniAuth` (*http://bit.ly/2aTEpqz*). While `Devise` is by far the most popular authentication gem in the Rails community, `OmniAuth` has the advantage of providing libraries for third-party authentication like Twitter and Facebook.

As a final note before we get started, new web developers often ask at what point in the development process you should add authentication to an app. It's best to build out the core functionality of your app first, then apply authentication. For this example, we will start with the book code for Chapter 9 (*students03*). Imagine *students03* is a functional application, so now let's add authentication to it.

The Sign-up Process

First let's develop a way for our users to sign up for a user account. To do that, we'll generate a users controller along with a new action.

```
ruby-2.2.3$ rails g resource user email password_digest
      invoke  active_record
      create    db/migrate/20151124123859_create_users.rb
      create    app/models/user.rb
      invoke    test_unit
      create      test/models/user_test.rb
      create      test/fixtures/users.yml
      invoke  controller
      create    app/controllers/users_controller.rb
      invoke    erb
      create      app/views/users
      invoke    test_unit
      create      test/controllers/users_controller_test.rb
      invoke    helper
      create      app/helpers/users_helper.rb
      invoke      test_unit
      invoke    assets
      invoke      coffee
      create        app/assets/javascripts/users.coffee
      invoke      scss
      create        app/assets/stylesheets/users.scss
      invoke  resource_route
       route    resources :users
```

Notice we used g instead of `generate` in the command line: this is just a shortcut in Rails to save you a few keystrokes. Next, we used the `resource` keyword rather than scaffolding with this generator. The `resource` command creates a model and controller similar to scaffolding, but does not automatically create the seven default controller actions and views. This is a good choice for authentication because we want to be very intentional about the controller actions and views we make available within the application. As an example, we would not want a standard index view of all users, as this would be a security vulnerability. Along with the users controller, this code also generated a user model. Our user model will have an email string that will be used as a unique username, and we'll use `password_digest` to allow us to use `has_secure_password` (more on this later). Finally, note that we did not specify a data type on the user and email fields. If you do not specify a type when using generators, Rails will use a string type.

Now run **`rails db:migrate`** to add the users table to our database. In the user model, add the following code:

```
class User < ApplicationRecord
  has_secure_password
end
```

has_secure_password allows for basic authentication in Rails. In addition to adding this method to our user model, we also need to uncomment the bcrypt gem in our Gemfile. bcrypt is an encryption library we'll use to encrypt our users' passwords:

```
gem 'bcrypt', '~> 3.1.7'
```

If your version number is different, that's OK. Be sure to run bundle after uncommenting this line in your Gemfile in addition to restarting your web server.

In our users controller, add the following code:

```
class UsersController < ApplicationController
  def new
    @user = User.new
  end

  def create
    @user = User.new(user_params)
    if @user.save
      session[:user_id] = @user.id
      redirect_to root_url, notice: "Thank you for signing up!"
    else
      render "new"
    end
  end

  private
    # Use callbacks to share common setup or constraints between actions.
    def set_user
      @user = User.find(params[:id])
    end

    # Never trust parameters from the scary internet, only allow the whitelist.
    def user_params
      params.require(:user).permit(:email, :password, :password_confirmation)
    end
end
```

In the new action we are creating a new user object, and in the create action we are creating a new user object with the user parameters. If that user object is successfully saved, we redirect the user to the root URL (be sure to set a root route if it has not been done already), and display the message "Thank you for signing up!"; otherwise, we display the new page. So let's create that new page now. Create the file *app/views/users/new.html.erb* and place the following code in it:

```
<h1>Sign Up</h1>

<%= form_for @user do |f| %>
```

```
<% if @user.errors.any? %>
  <div class="error_messages">
    <h2>Form is invalid</h2>
    <ul>
      <% @user.errors.full_messages.each do |message| %>
        <li><%= message %></li>
      <% end %>
    </ul>
  </div>
<% end %>

<div class="field">
  <%= f.label :email %><br />
  <%= f.text_field :email %>
</div>
<div class="field">
  <%= f.label :password %><br />
  <%= f.password_field :password %>
</div>
<div class="field">
  <%= f.label :password_confirmation %><br />
  <%= f.password_field :password_confirmation %>
</div>
<div class="actions"><%= f.submit "Sign Up" %></div>
<% end %>
```

This should look very similar to other forms we have used. Note that we are using `password_field` rather than `text_field` for our `password` and `password_confirma tion` fields. This ensures that the password does not appear in the browser as plain text. Also, don't be alarmed that we don't have `password` and `password_confirmation` fields in our database. Because we added these fields to our `user_params` action in our controller, the user is able to submit them through this form.

Now in our *app/views/application/_navigation.html.erb* layout file, we'll add a link to allow users to sign up:

```
<p>
  <%= link_to "Students", students_url %> |
  <%= link_to "Courses", courses_url %> |
  <%= link_to "Sign Up", new_user_path %>
</p>

<hr />
```

With this code in place, let's give our authentication a try. Start the server, browse to *http://localhost:3000/students*, and click the Sign Up link. Now create a new user as shown in Figure 14-1.

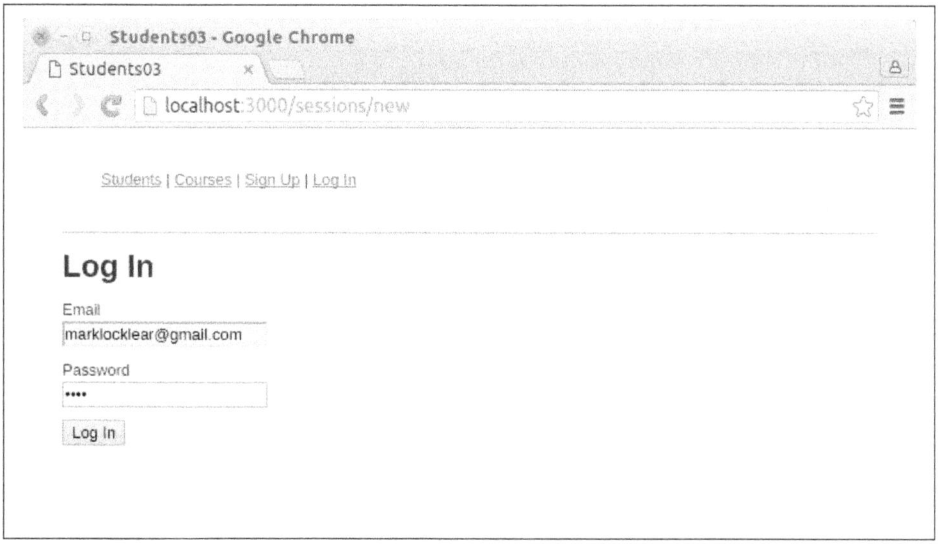

Figure 14-1. A non-admin user

This is nice, but we have not really done any authentication; we've simply created a user record. To apply authentication to our app, we need a way to actually log in. To do this, let's first create a sessions controller to handle this. Execute the following command:

```
rails g controller sessions new
```

Before going forward we need to make an adjustment to our *app/config/routes.rb* file for the sessions controller we just created. Let's delete the GET route for sessions and replace it with resources.

```
resources :sessions
```

Add the following code to *app/views/sessions/new.html.erb*:

```
<h1>Log In</h1>

<%= form_tag sessions_path do %>
  <div class="field">
    <%= label_tag :email %><br />
    <%= text_field_tag :email, params[:email] %>
  </div>
  <div class="field">
    <%= label_tag :password %><br />
    <%= password_field_tag :password %>
  </div>
  <div class="actions"><%= submit_tag "Log In" %></div>
<% end %>
```

Now in our sessions controller, add the following code:

```
class SessionsController < ApplicationController
  def new
  end

  def create
    user = User.find_by(email: params[:email])
    if user && user.authenticate(params[:password])
      session[:user_id] = user.id
      redirect_to root_url, notice: "Logged in!"
    else
      flash.now.notice = "Email or password is invalid"
      render "new"
    end
  end
end
```

This is a lot of code, but it's not really that difficult to understand. In our `create` method, we start by creating a user variable and assigning a user that we find based on an email address the user entered. The next few lines read like this:

```
if user && user.authenticate(params[:password])
```

If we find the user, and the user is authenticated (the `authenticate` method we call on the user object is provided to us by `has_secure_password`):

```
session[:user_id] = user.id
redirect_to root_url, notice: "Logged in!"
```

then we create a session based on the users' ID (`user_id`), redirect the user to the root URL, and display the notice "Logged in!":

```
else
  flash.now.notice = "Email or password is invalid"
  render "new"
end
```

Otherwise, we display the notice "Email or password is invalid" and re-render the new view.

Now that we have a way for our registered users to log in, let's add a link in our navigation partial for them to do so:

```
<p>
  <%= link_to "Students", students_url %> |
  <%= link_to "Courses", courses_url %> |
  <%= link_to "Sign Up", new_user_path %> |
  <%= link_to "Log In", new_session_path %>
</p>

<hr />
```

Give this a try by going to *http://localhost:3000/students*, clicking the Log In link, and logging in with the user you created earlier. While you are at it, try logging in with an invalid username or password. You should see the "Email or password is invalid" notice.

This is great—we can create a login with a user! But something is still not right. Notice that after you log in, you still see the Sign Up and Log In links at the top of the page. It would be nice if, once we are logged in, we display the user's email address along with a Log Out link. For that we need some way of getting the user who is currently logged in. To do this, we'll add a `current_user` method to our application controller. We add this to our application controller so it is available anywhere in our application:

```ruby
class ApplicationController < ActionController::Base
  # Prevent CSRF attacks by raising an exception.
  # For APIs, you may want to use :null_session instead.
  protect_from_forgery with: :exception

  private

  def current_user
    @current_user ||= User.find(session[:user_id]) if session[:user_id]
  end
  helper_method :current_user
end
```

Here we are creating a `current_user` instance variable that holds the current session ID. Also, notice we created a `helper_method` for the current user so it is also available in our views.

Now that we have a way of identifying if a user is logged in, we can update our navigation partial. While we are here let's also add a Log Out link. Update your layout file with the following code:

```erb
<p>
  <%= link_to "Students", students_url %> |
  <%= link_to "Courses", courses_url %> |
  <% if current_user %>
    Logged in as <%= current_user.email %>|
    <%= link_to "Log Out", session_path("current"), method: "delete" %>
  <% else %>
    <%= link_to "Sign Up", new_user_path %> |
    <%= link_to "Log In", new_session_path %>
  <% end %>
</p>

<hr />
```

This code checks if `current_user` is `true` (i.e., if a user is logged in), and if so, then we display the current user's email address and a Log Out link. Otherwise, we display the Sign Up and Log In links.

Finally, we need an action to handle the logout process. We'll create an action in our sessions controller to handle this functionality. Add the following code to your sessions controller:

```ruby
class SessionsController < ApplicationController
  def new
  end

  def create
    user = User.find_by(email: params[:email])
    if user && user.authenticate(params[:password])
      session[:user_id] = user.id
      redirect_to root_url, notice: "Logged in!"
    else
      flash.now.notice = "Email or password is invalid"
      render "new"
    end
  end

  def destroy
    session[:user_id] = nil
    redirect_to root_url, notice: "Logged out!"
  end
end
```

This is pretty simple. All we're doing is setting the user_id session to nil to clear the session and redirecting the user to the root URL with the "Logged out!" notice. Give it a try: reload your page if you are still logged in, and you should see the Log Out link. Clicking that link should log you out of your app, and display the "Logged out!" message.

Give this a try by refreshing your web browser, and click the Log Out link. You should see the "Logged out!" notice along with the Sign Up and Log In lines in the navigation partial.

One more small item before moving on: let's make our routes a little easier to read. In our *routes.rb* file add the following code:

```ruby
get 'signup', to: 'users#new', as: 'signup'
get 'login', to: 'sessions#new', as: 'login'
get 'logout', to: 'sessions#destroy', as: 'logout'
```

Now we can use these routes in our navigation partial:

```erb
<p>
  <%= link_to "Students", students_url %> |
  <%= link_to "Courses", courses_url %> |
  <% if current_user %>
    Logged in as <%= current_user.email %>|
    <%= link_to "Log Out", logout_path %>
  <% else %>
    <%= link_to "Sign Up", signup_path %> |
```

```
    <%= link_to "Log In", login_path %>
  <% end %>
</p>

<hr />
```

Now go to your application and try these updated Log In and Log Out links. Make note of the URLs in the address bar. Rather than seeing */session/new* when logging in, you see */login*. Adding custom routes like these is a nice way to pretty up your URLs and also make them easier to remember and enter into the browser address bar.

Wiring Authentication to Your Application

Now let's take a step back and look at what we have for a moment. We started with a fully functional application (our students app), and separately from all that code and logic we have added authentication logic. This is great, but authentication is not limiting the user in any way, and there is no difference in what an authenticated user can do versus what an unauthenticated user can do. A user who is not logged in can view, add, edit, and create students as well as awards and courses. With this in mind, we might want to proceed by limiting the ability to edit and update records to only authenticated users. Let's apply this to our students model. We'll do this by adding a method called authorize to our application controller, and this will allow us to use it anywhere in our application:

```
class ApplicationController < ActionController::Base
  # Prevent CSRF attacks by raising an exception.
  # For APIs, you may want to use :null_session instead.
  protect_from_forgery with: :exception

  private

  def current_user
    @current_user ||= User.find(session[:user_id]) if session[:user_id]
  end
  helper_method :current_user

   def authorize
     redirect_to login_url, alert: "Not Authorized" if current_user.nil?
   end
end
```

In this method we redirect the user to the login URL and display the alert message Not Authorized if current_user is nil—which means the user is not logged in. Now we can use this method in a before_action in any controller we want to protect. Let's add this to our students controller:

```
class StudentsController < ApplicationController
  before_action :set_student, only: [:show, :edit, :update, :destroy]
  before_action :authorize, only: [:edit, :update, :destroy]
```

```
# GET /students
# GET /students.json
def index
  @students = Student.all
end
...
```

Now go to *http://localhost:3000/students*, making sure to log out, and try the Edit and Destroy links. For each of these actions you should be redirected to the login page. You could easily add the same before filter to the awards and courses controllers to get the same functionality. We might want to also hide the Edit and Destroy links in the view, if users are not logged in. We can do this by adding some conditional logic in the index view for students:

```erb
<tbody>
  <% @students.each do |student| %>
    <tr>
      <td><%= student.given_name %></td>
      <td><%= student.middle_name %></td>
      <td><%= student.family_name %></td>
      <td><%= student.date_of_birth %></td>
      <td><%= student.grade_point_average %></td>
      <td><%= student.start_date %></td>
      <td><%= student.courses.count %></td>
      <td><%= student.awards.count %></td>
      <td><%= link_to 'Show', student %></td>
      <td><%= link_to 'Awards', student_awards_path(student) %></td>
      <% if current_user %>
        <td><%= link_to 'Edit', edit_student_path(student) %></td>
        <td><%= link_to 'Destroy', student, method: :delete,
                    data: { confirm: 'Are you sure?' } %></td>
      <% end %>
    </tr>
  <% end %>
</tbody>
```

Here we are able to take advantage of the `current_user` helper method we created by only displaying the Edit and Destroy links if the user is logged in. This also emphasizes an important point: we need to limit user activity not just in the view, as we are doing here, but also at the controller level as we did previously.

 Never rely solely on hiding links in the view as an authentication method, as we did here. An implementation such as the before filter in the controller should be used to ensure users can't enter a URL in the address bar to get access to an action. If we only hide links in the form, users could still type in `/students/1/edit` to edit a record.

Classifying Users

Most applications have at least two categories of users: administrators and ordinary users. Many applications have finer-grained permissions, but this is a good place to start, and why you created scaffolding instead of just a model when setting up users in the first place. Code for this is available in *ch14/students03*.

The first step toward creating an extra category of users is to create a migration with a suitable name:

```
rails generate migration AddAdminFlagToUsers
```

In the newly created migration, under *db/migrate*, change the migration file with the name ending in *add_admin_flag_to_users* so that it looks like Example 14-1.

Example 14-1. A migration for adding a boolean administration flag to the users table

```
class AddAdminFlagToUsers < ActiveRecord::Migration
  def change
    add_column :users, :admin, :boolean, default: false, null: false
  end
end
```

This adds one column to the users table, a boolean named admin. It defaults to false —most users will not be administrators and can't have a null value. Run **rails db:migrate** to run the migration and add the column.

Now it's time to explore the user scaffolding to make it easy to specify which users are administrators. In *app/views/users*, modify *app/views/users/new.html.erb* so it looks like Example 14-2.

Example 14-2. Adding a checkbox to indicate an administrator

```
<h1>Sign Up</h1>

<%= form_for @user do |f| %>
  <% if @user.errors.any? %>
    <div class="error_messages">
      <h2>Form is invalid</h2>
      <ul>
        <% @user.errors.full_messages.each do |message| %>
          <li><%= message %></li>
        <% end %>
      </ul>
    </div>
  <% end %>

  <div class="field">
    <%= f.label :email %><br />
```

```
      <%= f.text_field :email %>
    </div>
    <div class="field">
      <%= f.label :password %><br />
      <%= f.password_field :password %>
    </div>
    <div class="field">
      <%= f.label :password_confirmation %><br />
      <%= f.password_field :password_confirmation %>
    </div>
    <div class="field">
      <%= f.label :admin %><br />
      <%= f.check_box :admin %>
    </div>
    <div class="actions"><%= f.submit "Sign Up" %></div>
<% end %>
```

In addition we need to add the admin field to our strong params in our users control-ler:

```
...
  def user_params
    params.require(:user).permit(:email, :password,
    :password_confirmation, :admin)
  end
...
```

This is a bit contrived. In the real world we would not allow users to decide whether or not they are admins when they sign up, but it will work for our purposes. For this to be production ready, we would need to build a profile so users could modify their settings, or build an admin console so admins could modify other users' credentials. Another useful option is, rather than adding an Admin checkbox to your view, simply setting the admin flag for users in the console like this:

```
2.2.3 :005 > u = User.find 7
  User Load (0.2ms)
  SELECT "users".* FROM "users" WHERE "users"."id" = ? LIMIT 1  [["id", 7]]
 => #<User id: 7, email: "preston@gmail.com", password_digest: "$2a...",
    created_at: "2015-11-25 11:56:54",
    updated_at: "2015-11-25 11:56:54", admin: false>
2.2.3 :006 > u.admin = true
 => true
2.2.3 :007 > u.save
   (0.1ms)  begin transaction
  SQL (1.0ms)
  UPDATE "users" SET "updated_at" = ?, "admin" = ? WHERE "users"."id" = ?
  [["updated_at", 2015-11-25 11:57:28 UTC], ["admin", true], ["id", 7]]
   (1.4ms)  commit transaction
 => true
2.2.3 :008 > u
 => #<User id: 7, email: "preston@gmail.com", password_digest: "$2a...",
```

```
created_at: "2015-11-25 11:56:54",
    updated_at: "2015-11-25 11:57:28", admin: true>
```

This is great for smaller apps with a limited number of users, or even larger apps where you know the number of admin users is small.

Now give this a try. Sign up with a new user and check the Admin checkbox to make the user an admin, as shown in Figure 14-2.

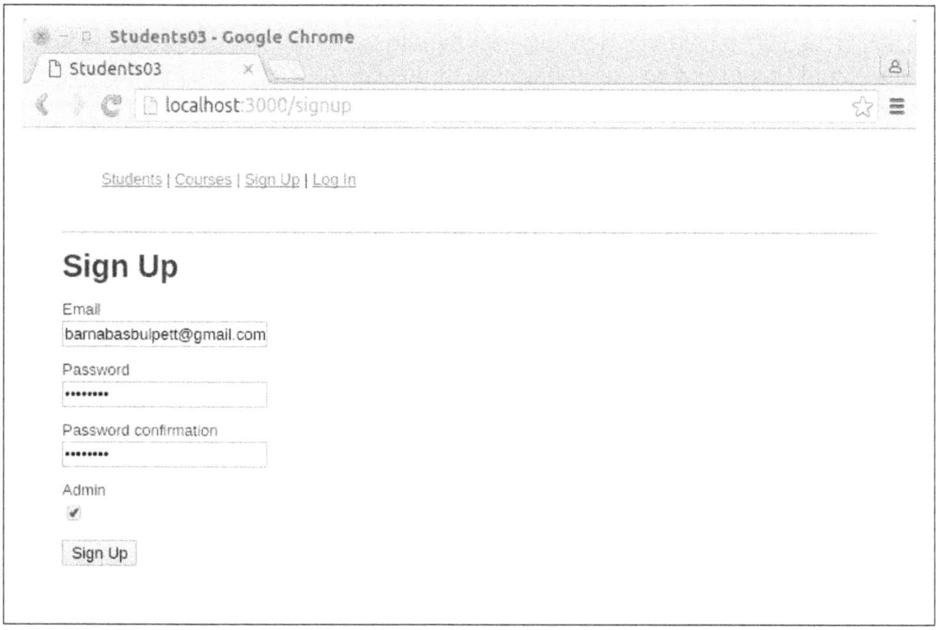

Figure 14-2. An admin user

Now that users have an administrative flag, and now that there is at least one user with the admin flag set to true, it's time to make that flag matter.

Before we get started, let's lay out some requirements for each of our users:

- Unauthenticated users can do nothing.
- Authenticated non-admin users can only view students (index and show actions).
- Admin users can do everything (new, edit, and destroy).

Let's walk through each of these requirements. For the first requirement ("Unauthenticated users can do nothing"), all we need to do is modify our authorize before filter to apply to all actions in the students controller:

```
class StudentsController < ApplicationController
  before_action :set_student, only: [:show, :edit, :update, :destroy]
```

```
before_action :authorize
...
```

Now, if you log out of the application and try to browse to */students, students/new,* or *students/1,* you should be redirected to the login page.

Our next requirement is "Authenticated non-admin users can only view students (index and show actions)," but let's kill two birds with one stone and also look at the final requirement, "Admin users can do everything (new, edit, and destroy)." We can create an `is_admin` before action that will handle both of these requirements for us. We will add this action to our application controller so it is accessible anywhere in our application:

```
class ApplicationController < ActionController::Base
  # Prevent CSRF attacks by raising an exception.
  # For APIs, you may want to use :null_session instead.
  protect_from_forgery with: :exception

  private

  def current_user
    @current_user ||= User.find(session[:user_id]) if session[:user_id]
  end
  helper_method :current_user

  def authorize
    redirect_to login_url, alert: "Not authorized" if current_user.nil?
  end

  def is_admin?
    redirect_to students_path, alert: "Not authorized" if
    current_user.nil? or !current_user.admin?
end
```

This method is very similar to our `authorize` method. In this case we will redirect users to the `students_path` and display a "Not authorized" alert if `current_user` is `nil`, or is not an admin. Now that we have a method in place, let's add a before filter in our controller that references it:

```
class StudentsController < ApplicationController
  before_action :set_student, only: [:show, :edit, :update, :destroy]
  before_action :authorize
  before_action :is_admin, only: [:new, :edit, :update, :destroy]
  ...
```

Now, before the new, edit, or destroy actions are called, the `is_admin` method will be called, and will verify whether a user is an admin. Let's try a few tests to see if this works. First, log in as a non-admin user as shown in Figure 14-3.

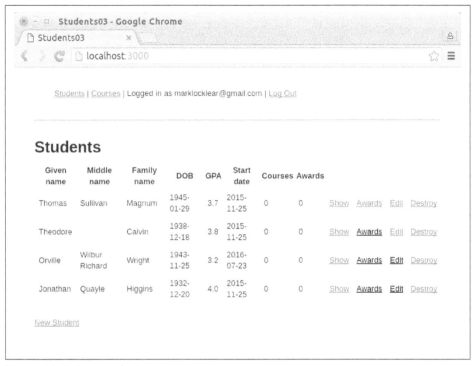

Figure 14-3. A non-admin user

We can see our list of students, and our Show link works, but if we try clicking on the Edit and Destroy links we are simply redirected to the students index view. Rather than tempt users with functionality they don't have, let's remove the Edit and Destroy links from the users' view. To do this we'll check if the `admin` flag is `true` for `cur rent_user` in the students index view. We will also apply this logic to the New Student link since a non-admin user does not have the ability to create a new user:

```
...
<tbody>
    <% @students.each do |student| %>
      <tr>
        <td><%= student.given_name %></td>
        <td><%= student.middle_name %></td>
        <td><%= student.family_name %></td>
        <td><%= student.date_of_birth %></td>
        <td><%= student.grade_point_average %></td>
        <td><%= student.start_date %></td>
        <td><%= student.courses.count %></td>
        <td><%= student.awards.count %></td>
        <td><%= link_to 'Show', student %></td>
        <td><%= link_to 'Awards', student_awards_path(student) %></td>
        <% if current_user.admin? %>
```

```
        <td><%= link_to 'Edit', edit_student_path(student) %></td>
        <td><%= link_to 'Destroy', student, method: :delete,
                data: { confirm: 'Are you sure?' } %></td>
     <% end %>
   </tr>
 <% end %>
</tbody>
</table>

<br>

<% if current_user.admin? %>
  <%= link_to 'New Student', new_student_path %>
<% end %>
```

All we're doing is adding a conditional to the links we want to hide from non-admin users. The statement `if current_user.admin?` will return `false` if the `admin` field is `false` for a user, and as a result the `link_to` statement will not run. Now refresh your browser, and the Edit, Destroy and New Student links should not be displayed.

OK, that takes care of our non-admin user, so now let's test our admin user. Log in as an admin user, and this user should be able to do everything!

The beginning of this user's journey goes as planned. Zoid gets a screen name (Figure 14-4), then visits the students page (Figure 14-5) where all the data is visible.

Figure 14-4. A new user, freshly welcomed

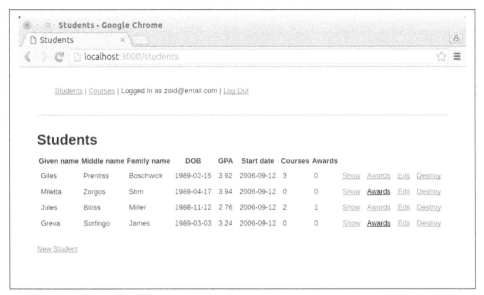

Figure 14-5. The students page works as planned for the new user

Feeling curious, though, Zoid tries the Edit link for one of the students and is rewarded with the editing page (Figure 14-6).

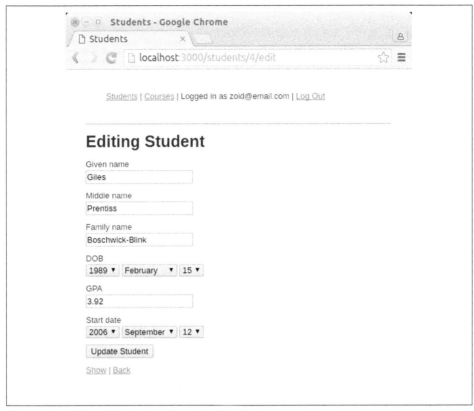

Figure 14-6. The editing page also works for the new user

It's only when Zoid tries to submit the edits that the `authorization?` method decides it's time to lock him out (Figure 14-7).

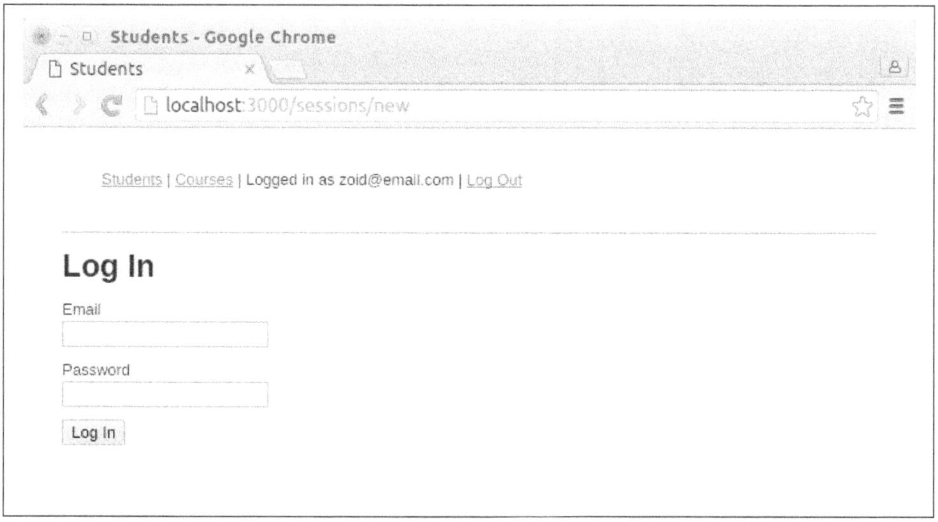

Figure 14-7. The new user's attempt to edit a student is finally blocked and he faces a new login screen

From a strictly data security point of view, this is fine. The user can't change data without proper authorization. From the user's point of view, though, the interface is lying, offering opportunities that look like they should be available. As an interface issue, this is a problem with the views and we can solve it by checking whether the current user is an administrator before presenting those options. This needs to be checked in each of the *index.html.erb* files for students, courses, and awards—a little repetition is necessary. The changes, though, are just a pair of `if` statements, high-lighted in Example 14-3.

Example 14-3. Removing inappropriate choices from a user with limited powers

```
<h1>Listing students</h1>

<table>
  <tr>
    <th>Given name</th>
    <th>Middle name</th>
    <th>Family name</th>
    <th>DOB</th>
    <th>GPA</th>
    <th>Start date</th>
    <th>Courses</th>
    <th>Awards</th>
  </tr>

<% @students.each do |student| %>
  <tr>
```

```
  <td><%= student.given_name %></td>
  <td><%= student.middle_name %></td>
  <td><%= student.family_name %></td>
  <td><%= student.date_of_birth %></td>
  <td><%= student.grade_point_average %></td>
  <td><%= student.start_date %></td>
  <td><%= student.courses.count %></td>
  <td><%= student.awards.count %></td>
  <td><%= link_to 'Show', student %></td>
  <td><%= link_to 'Awards', student_awards_path(student) %></td>
<% if current_user.admin? %>
  <td><%= link_to 'Edit', edit_student_path(student) %></td>
  <td><%= link_to 'Destroy', student, confirm: 'Are you sure?',
                 method: :delete %></td>
<% end %>
  </tr>
<% end %>
</table>

<br />

<% if current_user.admin? %>
<%= link_to 'New student', new_student_path %>
<% end%>
```

This just removes the Edit, Destroy, and New options. (The Awards entry moves up a line, above Edit, to reduce the number of if statements needed.) Now, when Zoid logs in and visits the students page, he'll see just the options he's allowed to use (Figure 14-8).

There are a few other features that need the same treatment, like the link to the form for enrolling students in courses from the *app/views/students/show.html.erb* file. Every reasonably sophisticated application that has moved beyond the basic CRUD interface will have a few of these cases.

 It's convenient to check results by keeping multiple browser windows open, logged into different user accounts (one admin, one non-admin). Remember, though, that Rails is tracking authentication status through sessions, which use cookies, that apply to the whole browser and not just a single window. You can use incognito (Chrome) or private (Firefox) windows for this type of testing.

There's still one leftover that may be worth addressing, depending on your security needs. The authorization? method has secured the data, and the view no longer shows the user options she can't really use, but if a user knows the URL for the edit form, it will still open. It's a GET request, after all. This is a good reason to make sure that these forms don't display any information that isn't publicly available through other means. If this is an issue, it may be worth the effort of adding authorization checks to every controller method that could spring a leak.

Figure 14-8. A more limited array of options appropriate to an ordinary user

More Options

A complete application would support many more tasks around authentication. A few of the most notable include:

- Logging in through Twitter, Facebook, and others (the Railscasts cover this)
- An interface for managing users and privileges
- Letting users stay logged in to their account on a given browser
- Finer-grained permissions for different categories of users (check out Pundit on GitHub (*https://github.com/elabs/pundit*))
- Mechanisms that let users reset their passwords
- Email address verification
- Detailed account settings that let users set preferences

All of these things, however, are projects with details that vary widely across different applications. The OmniAuth gem supports some of these options, such as connecting the password system to email, but most of this is work that's very dependent on what precisely you want to build. The users model is a model like any other: you can extend it, connect tables to it, and build whatever system you'd like behind your application. The `OmniAuth` gem gives you a foundation, and you can build whatever you need on top of it.

Test Your Knowledge

Quiz

1. Where is user and password information stored?
2. How do you tell a controller that users must be logged in to use it?
3. Where do you modify the rules that authorize users to have certain privileges?
4. How do you keep the logs from storing potentially sensitive security-related information?

Answers

1. User and password information is stored in the database, in a model you name when you first generate the authentication mechanisms.
2. The `before_action :authorize` method will block requests by unauthenticated users.
3. You can redefine the `authorized?` method in the `ApplicationController` class in *app/controllers/application_controller.rb*.
4. You can keep sensitive information out of the logs with `filter_parameter_logging`.

## CHAPTER 15

Routing

For me, in songwriting, I have a route I can take. Maybe there's some forks; I can go this way, this way. But I know those roads. I still have the experience behind me.
—Dave Matthews

Rails routing can shock developers who are used to putting their code in files wherever they want to put them. After the directory-based approach of traditional HTML and template-based development, the highly structured Rails approach looks very strange. Almost nothing, except for a few pieces in the *public* folder, is anywhere near where its URI might have suggested it was. Of course, this may not be so shocking if you've spent a lot of time with other frameworks or blogs—there are many applications that control the meanings of URIs through mechanisms other than the filesystem.

 If you prefer to read "URI" as the older and more familiar URL, that's fine. Everything works the same here. (And the core method Rails uses to generate URIs is, of course, url_for, in the UrlMod ule.)

Rails routing turns requests to particular URIs into calls to particular controllers and lets you create URIs from within your applications. Its default routing behavior, especially when combined with resource routes generated through scaffolding, is often enough to get you started building an application, but there's a lot more potential if you're willing to explore Rails routing more directly. You can create interfaces with memorable (and easily bookmarkable) addresses, arrange related application functionality into clearly identified groups, and much, much more.

What's more, you can even change routes without breaking your application's user interface, as the routing functionality also generates the addresses that the Rails view helper methods put into your pages.

 Changing routing can have a dramatic impact on the web services aspect of your applications. Programs that use your applications for JSON-based services aren't likely to check the human interface to get the new address, and won't know where to go if you change routing. Routing is effectively where you describe the API for your projects, and you shouldn't change that too frequently without reason. (It can also break user bookmarks.)

Creating Routes to Interpret URIs

Rails routing is managed through a single file, *config/routes.rb*. When Rails starts up, it loads this file, using it to process all incoming requests.

 If you're in development mode, which you usually are until deployment, Rails will reload *routes.rb* whenever you change it. In production mode, you have to stop and restart the server.

The default *routes.rb* contains a lot of help information that can get you started with the routes for your application, but it helps to know the general scheme first. In routing, Rails takes its fondness for connecting objects through naming conventions and lets you specify the conventions. Doing that means learning another set of conventions, of course!

Specifying Routes

The smallest, simplest place to start figuring out how Rails handles routing is to examine a simple named route. An example looks like:

```
get 'students/:id' => 'students#show'
```

First, we specify the HTTP method we want to use—in this case `get`, followed by the URI `students/:id`, and ending with the controller (`students`) and action (`show`) separated by the # sign.

For example, if your Rails server on localhost, port 3000, had a controller named `students` that had an action named `show`, and you wanted to apply that to the record with the `id` of 20, this rule would let you do that with a call to:

```
http://localhost:3000/students/20
```

When Rails gets this, it checks for a rule that looks like it matches the URI structure. It checks the default rules last, but when it encounters the first default rule, Rails knows from this to set `:controller` to `people`, `:action` to `show`, and `:id` to `20`. The symbols (prefaced with colons) act as matching wildcards for the routing. Rails uses that information to call the `PeopleController`'s `show` method, passing it `20` as the `:id` parameter.

If a request comes in that would match `':controller'` or `':controller/'`, Rails assumes that the next piece would be `index`, much as web servers expect *index.html* to be a default file. The `:action` will be set to `index`. Also, Rails ignores the name of the web server in routing, focusing on the parts of the URI after the web server name.

Routing rules also work in reverse. The `link_to` helper method and the many other methods `link_to` supports can take a `:controller`, an `:action`, and optionally even an `:id`, and generate a link to a URL for accessing them. For example, in your view you could add:

```
<%= link_to 'Student 20', controller: 'students', action: 'show', id: 20 %>
```

which would, working with the default rule, produce:

```
http://localhost:3000/students/20
```

The last parenthetical option in the same rule supports format requests. If a user wanted to request JSON specifically, she could write:

```
http://localhost:3000/students/20.json
```

Rails will set `:controller` to `students`, `:action` to `show`, `:id` to `20`, and `:format` to `json`. Then it uses that information to call the `StudentsController`'s `show` method, passing it `20` as the `:id` parameter and `json` as the `:format` parameter.

If your controller checks the `:format` parameter—Chapter 5 examined `respond_to`, the easiest way to do this—and the value is one you've checked for, your controller can send a response in the requested format. This isn't limited to HTML or JSON— you can specify other formats through the extension. If your controller supports them, visitors will get what they expect. If not, they might be disappointed, but nothing should break.

 You could and probably should also specify the format through the MIME content-type header in the HTTP request, but that doesn't get checked in ordinary Rails routing.

There is another approach that lets you specify URIs quite precisely: explicit specification of the URI and directions for where to send its processing. This looks like:

```
get 'this/uri/exactly'  => 'students#new'
```

Using either of these rules, if a request comes in to a Rails server at *localhost:3000*, looking like:

```
http://localhost:3000/this/uri/exactly
```

then Rails will call the students controller's new method to handle the request. While explicitly declaring mappings from individual URIs to particular controller actions is certainly precise, it's also not very flexible.

 You can get even more parameters through the query string. They aren't mapped by the router specifically, but they still become part of the params collection sent to the controller. This is a feature that creates some risks, as users may be able to inject unexpected additional parameters this way.

Globbing

While it's useful to have the default route retrieve an id value and pass it to the controller, some applications need to pull more than one component from a given URI. For example, in an application that makes use of *taxonomies* (trees of formal terms), you might want to support those tree structures in the URI. If, for example, "floor" could refer to "factory floor" in one context, "dance floor" in another context, and "price floor" in yet another context, you might want to have URIs that look like:

```
http://localhost:3000/taxonomy/factory/floor
http://localhost:3000/taxonomy/dance/floor
http://localhost:3000/taxonomy/price/floor
```

The only piece that the routing tool needs to be able to identify is taxonomy, but the method that gets called also needs the end of the URI as a parameter. A route that can process that might look like:

```
get 'taxonomy/*steps' to: 'taxonomy#show_tree'
```

The asterisk before steps indicates that the rest of the URI is to be "globbed" and passed to the showTree method as an array, accessible through the :steps parameter. The show_tree method might then start out looking like:

```
def show_tree
  steps = params[:steps]
      ....
end
```

If the method had been called via *http://localhost:3000/taxonomy/factory/floor*, the steps variable would now contain ['factory', 'floor']; if called via *http://local host:3000/taxonomy/factory/equipment/mixer*, the steps variable would now contain

['factory', 'equipment', 'mixer']. Globbing makes it possible to gather a lot of information from a URI.

If you put something after a glob and Rails finds a specific match, the globbing will stop there. You can even have multiple globs in a match string, though it's probably not a good idea to get too carried away.

Regular Expressions and Routing

While Rails is inspecting incoming request addresses, you might want to have it be a little more specific. You do so with the `constraints:` option. For example, you might create a route that checks to make sure that the `id` values are numeric, not random text, and presents an error page if the `id` value has problems. To do this, you can specify regular expressions in parameters for your routes:

```
get students/:id, to: students#show, constraints: { id: /\d/ }
get students/:id, to: students#show, to: errors#bad_id
```

The first rule looks like the default rules, but checks to make sure that the `:id` value is composed of digits. (Regular expressions are explained in Appendix C.) If the `id` is composed of digits, the routing goes on as usual to the appropriate `:controller` and `:action` with the `:id` as a parameter. If it isn't, Rails proceeds to the next message, which sends the user to a completely different errors controller (in this case, the `bad_id` action of the errors controller).

A Domain Default with root

Often when prototyping, developers (and especially designers) like to start with the top page in a site, the landing page visitors will see if they just enter the domain name. The vision for this "front door" often sets expectations for other pages in the site, and the front door gets plenty of emphasis because it's often the first (or only) page users see. Even in an age where Google sends users to pages deep inside of a site, users often click to "the top" to figure out where they landed.

There are two ways to build this front door in Rails. The first way, which may do well enough at the outset, is to create a static HTML file that is stored as *public/index.html*. That page can then have links that move users deeper into your application's functionality. It's more likely, however, that projects will quickly outgrow that, as updating a static page in an otherwise dynamic application means extra hassle when things change.

The second approach deletes *public/index.html* and uses routing to specify where to send users who visit just the domain name. The easiest way to do this is to use `root`, which appears (commented out) in the *config/routes.rb* file. If you want visitors to the domain name to receive a page from the entry method of the welcome controller, you could write:

```
root to: "welcome#entry"
```

This can only apply to the top point of your URL hierarchy. Although it appears deep in the *routes.rb* file, it probably makes sense to move the root route to the top, as routes get checked in order and the top page of an application is often a busy place.

Mapping Resources

If you're building REST-based applications, you will become very familiar with resources. It both saves you tremendous effort and encourages you to follow a common and useful pattern across your applications. Chapters 5 through 9 have already explored how REST works in context, but there are a few more options you should know about and details to explore. A simple resources call might look like:

```
resources :people
```

That one line converts into *seven* different mappings from calls to actions. Each REST-based controller has seven different methods for handling requests. Table 15-1 catalogs the many things this call creates.

Table 15-1. Routing created by a single resources call

Name	HTTP method	Match string	Parameters
people	GET	/people	{:action=>"index", :controller=>"people"}
	POST	/people	{:action=>"create", :controller=>"people"}
new_person	GET	/people/new	{:action=>"new", :controller=>"people"}
edit_person	GET	/people/:id/edit	{:action=>"edit", :controller=>"people"}
person	GET	/people/:id	{:action=>"show", :controller=>"people"}
	PUT	/people/:id	{:action=>"update", :controller=>"people"}
	DELETE	/people/:id	{:action=>"destroy", :controller=>"people"}

For all of the routes that use HTTP GET methods, Rails creates a named route. As discussed later in the chapter, you can use these to support _path and _url helper methods with link_to and all of the other methods that need a path or URL for linking.

> If your application contains Ruby singleton objects, you should use resource rather than resources for their routing. It does most of the same work, but supports a single object rather than a set. (Singleton objects have an include Singleton declaration in their class file, which marks it as deliberately allowing only one object of that kind in the application.)

This `resources` call, its seven routes, and the supporting seven controller methods are all it takes to support the scaffolding. However, there will likely be times when you want to add an extra method to do something specific. You can do that without disrupting the existing RESTful methods by using `member`, which lets you specify actions that apply to individual resources. For example, to add the `roll` method to the `courses` resource, Chapter 9 called:

```
resources :courses do
  member do
    get :roll
  end
end
```

In addition to the seven methods, the routing now supports an extra. The named route `roll_course` uses the GET method, as the parameter suggests. It calls the `roll` method on the `courses` controller, which you'll have to create.

If you need multiple extra methods, you just list them in the `member` block:

```
resources :students do
  resources :awards

  member do
    get :courses
    post :course_add
    post :course_remove
  end
end
```

Nesting Resources

Chapter 9 went into extended detail on the many steps necessary to create an application using RESTful nested resources, in which only awards that applied to a given student were visible. Making that change required a shift at many levels, but the change inside of the routing was relatively small. Instead of two routing declarations in *routes.rb*:

```
resources :awards
resources :students
```

they combined into a containing block and a nested block:

```
resources :students do
  resources :awards
end
```

The resulting routes still create seven routes for `:awards`, but they all look a little different. Instead of names such as `award` and `new_award`, they shift to `student_award` and `new_student_award`, highlighting their nested status. Their paths are all prefixed with `/student/:student_id`, as the award-specific parts of their URIs will appear after that, "below" students in the URI hierarchy.

You can also specify multiple resources to nest by placing them in the containing block. If students also have, say, pets, you could make that a nested resource as well in a single declaration:

```
resources :students do
  resources :awards
  resources :pets
end
```

Route Order and Priority

Using wildcards makes it likely—even probable—that more than one routing rule applies to an incoming URI. This could have produced an impenetrable tangle, but fortunately the creators of Rails took a simple approach to tie-breaking: rules that come earlier in the *routes.rb* file have higher priority than rules that appear later. Rails will test a URI until it comes to a match, and then it doesn't look any further.

In practice, this means that you'll want to put more specific rules nearer the top of your *routes.rb* file and rules that use more wildcards further down. That way, the more specific rules will always get processed before the wildcards get a chance to apply themselves to the same URI.

Checking the Map

As your list of routes grows, and especially as you get into some of the more complicated routing approaches, you may want to ask Rails exactly what it thinks the current routes are. The simplest way to do this is to use the `rails routes` command. Sometimes its results won't be a big surprise, as when you run it on a new application with only the default routes:

```
/:controller(/:action(/:id))(.:format) :controller#:action
```

If you run it on a more complicated application, one with resources, you'll get back a lot more detail—names of routes, methods, match strings, and parameters, as shown in Figure 15-1.

```
student_awards     GET    /students/:student_id/awards(.:format)           awards#index
                   POST   /students/:student_id/awards(.:format)           awards#create
new_student_award  GET    /students/:student_id/awards/new(.:format)       awards#new
edit_student_award GET    /students/:student_id/awards/:id/edit(.:format)  awards#edit
student_award      GET    /students/:student_id/awards/:id(.:format)       awards#show
                   PATCH  /students/:student_id/awards/:id(.:format)       awards#update
                   PUT    /students/:student_id/awards/:id(.:format)       awards#update
                   DELETE /students/:student_id/awards/:id(.:format)       awards#destroy
students           GET    /students(.:format)                              students#index
                   POST   /students(.:format)                              students#create
new_student        GET    /students/new(.:format)                          students#new
edit_student       GET    /students/:id/edit(.:format)                     students#edit
student            GET    /students/:id(.:format)                          students#show
                   PATCH  /students/:id(.:format)                          students#update
                   PUT    /students/:id(.:format)                          students#update
                   DELETE /students/:id(.:format)                          students#destroy
```

Figure 15-1. Routing created by a single resources call

And that's just for one resource! (OK, a resource with another nested in it.) Note that Rails lines these routes up on the HTTP method being called, which is not always the easiest way to read it. If you have lots of routes, and especially lots of resources, you'll need some good search facilities to find what you're looking for.

 If you're working on Mac OS X or Linux and just want to find one route in the haystack, you may find it useful to do something like `rails routes | grep root`, piping the output of `rails routes` through the grep search program. In this case, it would be looking for a line with `root` in it. If you try that in *ch14/students08*, you'll get back a response like:

```
root / students#index
```

Alternatively, you can visit *http://localhost:3000/rails/info/routes* on any platform to view routes.

Generating URIs from Views and Controllers

Setting up these routes does more than connect URIs to your application. It also makes it easy for you to build connections between different parts of your application. Code can tell Rails what functionality it should point to, and Rails will generate an appropriate URI. There are many methods that generate URIs (`form_for`, `link_to`, and a host of others), but all of them rely on `url_for`, a helper method in the `UrlModule` class.

Pointing url_for in the Right Direction

The method signature for `url_for` doesn't tell you very much about how to call it:

```
url_for(options = {})
```

 Remember, the parentheses around the method arguments are optional, as are the curly braces ({}) around the options hash.

Early Rails applications often called `url_for` by specifying all of the parts needed to create a URI—`:controller`, `:action`, and maybe `:id`:

```
url_for action: 'bio', controller: 'presidents', id: '39'
```

This would produce a URI like:

```
/presidents/bio/39
```

There's a simpler approach, though, if you just want to point to a particular object, say an `@president` object that has an `id` of 39:

```
url_for @president
```

Rails will check through its naming conventions, looking for a named route that matches the object specified. It will then call the named route's `_path` helper method —in this case, probably `president_path`. The value returned by that helper will end up in the URI, likely as:

```
/presidents/39
```

To point to nested resources, you need to provide a little more information, two arguments in an array:

```
url_for [@student, @award]
```

And the result would be something like:

```
/students/1/awards/2
```

You can also point to a nested resource by calling its `_path` helper methods explicitly. For an award nested under a student, you could produce the same result with:

```
url_for student_award_path(@student, @award)
```

Adding Options

The options array is good for more than just specifying the pieces that will go into the URI. It lets you specify how the URI should appear, and add or override details. The available options include:

`:anchor`

Lets you add a fragment identifier to the end of your URI, separated by a # sign. This can be very effective when you want to point users to a specific item in a long list.

`:only_path`

When `true` (which it is by default), `url_for` will only return the path part of the URI, the part that comes after the protocol, hostname, and port. If you want a complete (absolute) URI, this should be set to `false`.

`:trailing_slash`

When `true`, this adds a slash at the end of URIs. While this may meet your expectations for working with directories (or things that look like directories) on the Web, it unfortunately can cause issues with caching, so use it cautiously. This defaults to `false`.

`:host`, `:port`, *and* `:protocol`

These let you specify a particular host (including port number) and protocol. If these are specified, the full absolute URI will be returned, regardless of what `:only_path` was set to.

Infinite Possibilities

Rails routing is implemented using a DSL—a domain-specific language. Ruby lets developers build all kinds of functionality into a very concise form, but at the same time, DSLs can become pretty mind-bending quickly. Routing in particular can grow extremely complicated if you try to take advantage of too many cool Rails features. There are many more possibilities than a *Learning* book can reasonably cover. Among them are:

- Using `resources` with a block
- Custom parameters and conditions
- Abandoning numeric `id` values in favor of more descriptive unique names
- More precisely defined nested resources with path and name prefixes
- Multiple levels of nesting (possible, though not such a good idea)
- Testing routes with `assert_generates`, `assert_recognizes`, and `assert_rout ing`
- Debugging routes from the console
- Extending routing

Once you've run out of things to do with the possibilities explored in this chapter, and feel confident that you understand how Rails is routing requests, you can take the next steps forward and deeper into Rails.

Test Your Knowledge

Quiz

1. How often does Rails reload the *routes.rb* file?

2. How do you set the routing for the empty URL, which is usually the home or landing page for a site?

3. If there are multiple routes that could match a given URL, how does Rails choose?

4. How do you tell Rails to just "grab the rest of this URL and put it into a parameter"?

5. How many routes does a single plain `resources` call create?

6. What's the fastest way to see Rails's list of routes?

7. How do you add a fragment identifier to the end of a URL created with `url_for`?

Answers

1. In development mode, Rails checks to see if the *routes.rb* file has changed and reloads it if it has. In production mode, Rails doesn't check, and you'll need to stop and restart the server to update routes.

2. The `root` method lets you tell Rails how to handle requests aimed at the top of your site, so `root to: "welcome#entry"` would set the landing page of your app to the entry action of the welcome controller.

3. Rails always applies the first route that matches a given URL, starting from the top of *routes.rb*.

4. Globbing, using an asterisk, lets you halt further processing of a chunk of the URL and send it along to the controller method as a parameter.

5. `resources` creates seven routes, representing seven different methods built on REST, with and without a format.

6. The `rails routes` command will show you the list of routes Rails believes it has.

7. The `:anchor` parameter lets you specify a fragment identifier, which comes after # at the end of the URL.

## CHAPTER 16

From CSS to Sass

I try to apply colors like words that shape poems, like notes that shape music.
—Joan Miro

Chapter 3 showed how to add a small amount of CSS to make a Rails application more visually appealing but only scratched the surface of styling. Rails has a powerful component that will help take some of the pain out of styling your app: Sass.

Sass bills itself as a "meta-language on top of CSS" that allows for greater control over styling. If you've ever built a website and wished you could assign a color as a variable or eliminate repetition in your stylesheet (among other things), Sass comes to the rescue.

 Read more about Sass at the Sass website (*http://sass-lang.com*).

Getting Started

Sass actually has two syntax styles and corresponding extensions: *.sass* and *.scss*. In the early days of Sass, files ending in *.sass* used a syntax with an indented system (called, amazingly enough, "Sass"). Whereas typical CSS like that seen in Chapter 3 would have the styles fall between curly braces such as { and }, code in a *.sass* file would not look the same. For example, CSS code like this:

```
#container {
  background: #FFF;
  color: #000;
```

```
        text-align: left;
    }
```

would look like this in Sass:

```
#container
    background: #FFF
    color: #000
    text-align: left
```

This code is amazingly clean. It's beautiful. Sadly, it's not compatible as straight-up CSS without having Sass generate it as such. Therein lies the power of the newer syntax, *.scss*, also known as "Sassy CSS."

As the world's browsers move to take advantage of the CSS3 spec, SCSS is waiting in the wings. If your stylesheet is a valid CSS3 document, it's also valid SCSS. All you need is the right file extension on your stylesheet coupled with Sass power in the background, and you've got yourself a powerful tool well suited for the rapid development nature of building with Rails.

It's a little bit more complex than that, but not by much.

You don't have to do anything to get started using Sass in your Rails application; your stylesheets are created with the *.scss* extension by default. For example, *layout.scss* is found in *app/assets/stylesheets*.

Sassy Style

Sass adds a lot of components to CSS including variables, mixins, and nesting.

Variables

If you've altered styles of any medium- or large-scale website, you're bound to have run into the problem of repetitious code within the labyrinth of your stylesheets. Now that the Rails "don't repeat yourself" mantra is fully ingrained into your web development philosophy, variables in Sass can help eliminate repetitious code.

You've made your headings, links, bold words, classes, and so on, all the same color to match a client's logo. So, your stylesheet might look something like this:

```
h2 {
  color: #66FF00;
  font-size: 20px;
}

b {
  color: #66FF00;
}

.standout {
```

```
    color: #66FF00;
    font-style: italic;
}

a {
    color: #66FF00;
}
```

Already you can see a problem of repetitious code developing. Yes, it's true that a little refactoring of this code could maybe make things easier. But as the stylesheet grows in size, inevitably it also will grow in complexity. Thanks to Sass, we can make this simpler by assigning the:

```
color: #66FF00;
```

as a variable:

```
$lime-green: "#66FF00;"
$branding-colors: $lime-green;

h2 {
    color: $branding-colors;
    font-size: 20px;
}

bold {
    color: $branding-colors;
}

.standout {
    color: $branding-colors;
    font-style: italic;
}

a {
    color: $branding-colors;
}
```

Uh-oh. The client called and that lime green color you were using ended up getting changed to a bold blue color. In the old days, that might require a little find-and-replace work. But since we're working smarter with our Sass, we simply create a new variable. With one line of code, we change the color throughout our application:

```
$bold-blue: #000066;
$lime-green: #66FF00;
$branding-colors: $bold-blue;

h2 {
    color: $branding-colors;
    font-size: 20px;
}

b {
```

```
  color: $branding-colors;
}

.standout {
  color: $branding-colors;
  font-style: italic;
}

a {
  color: $branding-colors;
}
```

You can now play around with that even more. Do the links need to be green? Then call:

```
color: $lime-green;
```

Should some things be blue and others green? Assign the colors to new variables to your heart's content. Need to add sizes to a variable? Call:

```
$margin: 10px;
```

or use the many functions available in the Sass documentation (*http://bit.ly/2aTGBy6*) to expand your variables even further.

Your days of find-and-replace hell are drawing to a close.

Mixins

It's an exciting time to be a web developer. Browser manufacturers are pushing the envelope, allowing implementation of the ever-evolving specifications for HTML5 and CSS3, and giving web developers an excellent toy box to play in.

All of this progress brings with it a little bit of instability. As of this writing, CSS3's box-shadow property works well in Firefox, Safari, Chrome, Opera, and even (gasp!) Internet Explorer 9. When this property is fully implemented across all modern browsers, all you'll need to do is utilize this code to get subtle shadow evenly around an element, like this coding to shadow an img tag with a shadow class:

```
img.shadow {
  box-shadow: 0 0 5px #888;
}
```

Doesn't that look nice? No more do images need to have shadows applied directly to the image file. Instead, the shadow class can easily bring shadowing to any image on the website. Need the shadow to have a different color or a bigger blur distance? That can easily be adjusted with this style.

There's just one problem: not all the browsers just mentioned support the native coding for box-shadow, even though they still implement this in practice using a vendor prefix like so:

```
img.shadow {
  -moz-box-shadow: 0 0 5px #888;
  -webkit-box-shadow: 0 0 5px#888;
  box-shadow: 0 0 5px #888;
}
```

 Vendor prefixes must come first to work properly.

Mixins allow you to "mix in" code in other areas of your stylesheet to make it reusable. I once had to go through my stylesheet and eliminate the vendor prefixes in multiple places after adoption of the CSS3 property I was using became fairly ubiquitous. If I could have used mixins that day, I would have only needed to change my code once, rather than the multiple places it was scattered throughout my stylesheet.

Instead of this:

```
img.shadow {
  -moz-box-shadow: 0 0 5px #888;
  -webkit-box-shadow: 0 0 5px#888;
  box-shadow: 0 0 5px #888;
}
```

my mixin could have been defined like so:

```
@mixin shadowed-boxes {
  -moz-box-shadow: 0 0 5px #888;
  -webkit-box-shadow: 0 0 5px #888;
  box-shadow: 0 0 5px #888;
}
```

Now all I would need to do is include the mixin name, shadowed-boxes, in my code:

```
img.shadow {
  @include shadowed-boxes;
}
```

And I can keep reusing the mixin in my CSS wherever I want to use the previously specified shadowing:

```
header {
  @include shadowed-boxes;
}

div.topstory {
  @include shadowed-boxes;
}
```

And so on.

Nesting

Sass can help trim the size and increase readability of stylesheet code through the use of nesting. We've already seen nesting quite a bit in our Ruby code, but with CSS?

Yes, it's here, and it's fantastic.

Here's a personal example. Often I'll include an h1 inside of a header. It's a common design convention, one that might look like this:

```
header {
  width: 960px;
  margin: 0 auto;
  border: 1px solid #000;
}

header h1 {
  font-style: italic;
  font-size: 1.5em;
  color: red;
}
```

But with nesting support in Sass, your CSS can be written like this instead:

```
header {
  width: 960px;
  margin: 0 auto;
  border: 1px solid #000;

  h1 {
    font-style: italic;
    font-size: 1.5em;
    color: red;
    }
  }
```

The difference is subtle, but you can see the h1 is nested inside the curly braces for the header.

But wait, there's more! You can also self-reference elements in your stylesheets. In this ever-more-touchscreen-device world, I tend to shy away from using :hover pseudo-classes with my links. But I'm a big believer in keeping my visited links a different color than unvisited ones, which plays out like this in a Sass-powered stylesheet:

```
a {
  color: #03507B;
  text-decoration: none;
  &:hover {
    text-decoration: underline;
  }
}
```

The key thing to notice here is the ampersand. Our code is taking advantage of nesting, but as you know, `a:hover` isn't really nested (it is a pseudoclass, after all); the `a` is the parent of `:hover` in this instance. That's where the ampersand comes in, representing the parent in nested CSS.

Making Everything Work Together

When building the *students* app, we ended up using several scaffolds, and for each one, a corresponding stylesheet in the *app/assets/stylesheets* directory. Using what you've learned about Sass, let's apply it to our students application.

First you'll need to do a bit of housekeeping. It's common practice to break down styles into separate stylesheets for better organization. Having one really long stylesheet can be a pain to manage as a project grows. But you also need to ensure your application knows about all your Sassy stylesheets and includes them for use.

In the students application, navigate to *app/assets/stylesheets*. Find the *application.css* file and rename it *application.scss*. From there, we need to import all the other stylesheets using the `@import` directive:

```
/*
 * This is a manifest file that will automatically include all the stylesheets
 * available in this directory and any subdirectories. You're free to add
 * application-wide styles to this file and they'll appear at the top of the
 * compiled file, but it's generally better to create a new file per style scope.
 *= require_self
 *= require_tree
 */

    @import "awards.scss";
    @import "scaffolds.scss";
    @import "students.scss";
```

There's just one *tiny* little problem with the preceding code: Sprockets, which we'll dive deeper into in the next chapter. For now, all you need to know is that Sprockets uses the code `*= require_tree` to load all the files in the *stylesheets* directory. However, the files are loaded *individually* rather than bundled together in a way that Rails can use to process Sass code from all your stylesheets in the same namespace. This means that variables and mixins defined in one file may not be available to other files.

By removing `*= require_tree` from your *application.scss* file and using the `@import` directive to use the files you specify, you ensure that your app can now share all the variables, mixins, and nested CSS of the imported stylesheets. With your app running, you can see the compiled stylesheet at *http://localhost:3000/assets/application.css*.

This is a good start; all the stylesheets are being brought together in one place thanks to Sass magic. Now we'll open up the *students.scss* file in the *app/assets/stylesheets* directory and get to work on some better style.

Let's style the h1 of the students index page, and also the names of the students:

```scss
$bluish: #0067A1;
$student-color: $bluish;

body h1 {
  background-color: $student-color;
  padding: 10px;
  color: #FFF;
  margin: 0;
}

td.name {
  color: $student-color;
}
```

We'll also modify the table in *app/views/students/index.html.erb* for simplicity:

```erb
<h1>Listing students</h1>

<table>
  <tr>
    <th>Student Name</th>
    <th>Date of birth</th>
    <th>Grade point average</th>
    <th>Start date</th>
    <th>Awards</th>
    <th></th>
    <th></th>
    <th></th>
  </tr>

<% @students.each do |student| %>
  <tr>
    <td class="name">
      <%= student.given_name %>
      <%= student.middle_name %>
      <%= student.family_name %>
    </td>
    <td><%= student.date_of_birth %></td>
    <td><%= student.grade_point_average %></td>
    <td><%= student.start_date %></td>
    <td><%= student.awards.count %></td>
    <td><%= link_to 'Show', student %></td>
    <td><%= link_to 'Edit', edit_student_path(student) %></td>
    <td><%= link_to 'Destroy', student, confirm: 'Are you sure?',
      method: :delete %></td>
  </tr>
<% end %>
```

```
</table>

<br />

<%= link_to 'New Student', new_student_path %>
```

Head over to *http://localhost:3000/students* and check out the changes. The h1 and the
table cell with the name class share the same color, *bluish*. If we decided to play with
other colors, we'd simply need to create a new color variable like $redish: #DB4327;
and assign it to the $student-color like so:

```
$student-color: $redish;
```

It's time to mix in a shadow around the entire body element. We can stay in the *stu-
dents.scss* file, and put this bit of code right above our color variables:

```
@mixin  bodyshadow {
  -moz-box-shadow: 0 0 5px #888;
  -webkit-box-shadow: 0 0 5px #888;
  box-shadow: 0 0 5px #888;
}
body  {
    @include bodyshadow;
    padding: 4px;
    width: 80%;
}
```

A quick refresh of the page, and if your browser supports CSS3, it should look like the
page shown in Figure 16-1.

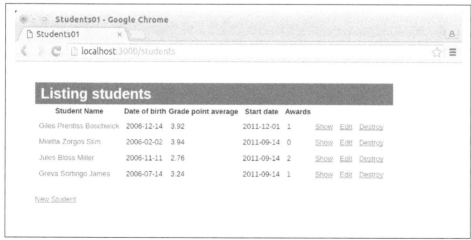

Figure 16-1. Our application begins to show a little style

If there is one thing that makes me nervous, it's the possibility I might accidentally
delete something. Thankfully, if I were to click the Destroy link I'd get a dialog box

asking me if I really wanted to do that, but we can do better. We'll make the link stand out and make it painfully obvious.

In our *students.scss* file, we'll throw this bit of code at the bottom:

```
a {
color: #0B3641;
&:hover {
  background-color: #FFF;
  color: #23C331;
}
&.destroy {
  color: #DB4327;
}
}
```

While this changes the color of the links ever so slightly, it does two more dramatic changes: nesting makes hovered links turn green, and adding a `destroy` class makes that Destroy link stay red (Figure 16-2).

To make this all work, we just need to modify one last bit on our *index.html.erb* file in the students view:

```
<td><%= link_to 'Destroy', student, confirm: 'Are you sure?', method: :delete,
:class => 'destroy' %></td>
```

becomes:

```
<td><%= link_to 'Destroy', student,
  method: :delete, data: { confirm: 'Are you sure?' }, class: :destroy %></td>
```

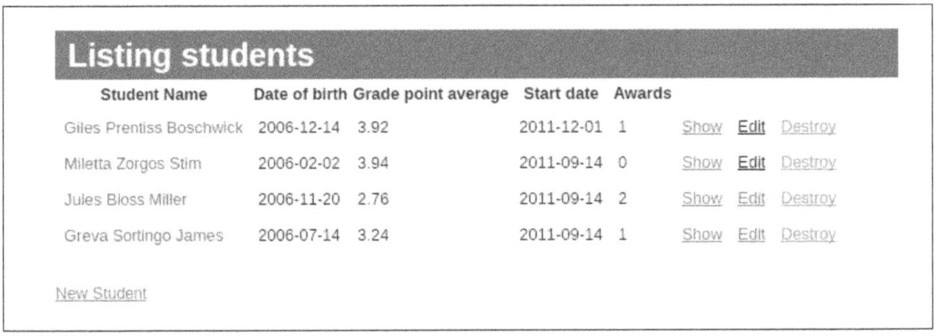

Listing students

Student Name	Date of birth	Grade point average	Start date	Awards			
Giles Prentiss Boschwick	2006-12-14	3.92	2011-12-01	1	Show	Edit	Destroy
Miletta Zorgos Stim	2006-02-02	3.94	2011-09-14	0	Show	Edit	Destroy
Jules Bloss Miller	2006-11-20	2.76	2011-09-14	2	Show	Edit	Destroy
Greva Sortingo James	2006-07-14	3.24	2011-09-14	1	Show	Edit	Destroy

New Student

Figure 16-2. Our app now shows red Destroy links, prompting us to delete with caution

Becoming Sassier

Our look at Sass is a good beginning to satisfy most left-brained developers, but the aesthetically oriented will want to go further. The Sass official website (*http://sass-lang.com*) has documentation, tutorials, and code examples. Be sure to check out the functions page in the documentation (*http://bit.ly/2aTGBy6*) as well.

You may also want to explore the *Pragmatic Guide to Sass* (Pragmatic Programmers, 2011).

Test Your Knowledge

Quiz

1. What file extension do you need to start using Sass?

2. What can you use to assign values in your stylesheet?

3. Is there a way to reuse code with several values assigned to it?

4. How can you refactor your CSS code to make it more readable?

5. You're ready to use Sass through your application. How do you implement it?

Answers

1. Change your stylesheet from *.css* to *.scss*.

2. Like Ruby code, variables can be used to make your CSS code less repetitious.

3. Mixins allow for very reusable code, like when used with the ever-evolving CSS3 specification.

4. Sass can help trim the size and increase readability of stylesheet code through the use of nesting.

5. Change your *application.css* extension to *application.scss*, use the @import directive to import other CSS partials you want available across your application, and remove the code `*= require_tree` from the *application.scss* file.

## CHAPTER 17

Managing Assets and Bundles

If you count all your assets you always show a profit.
—Wilson Mizner

Our journey through Rails so far has been thorough, if not a little exhausting. Generators that build entire application structures. Validations in one line of code. Object-relational mapping that helps make creating a database schema a breeze. Relationships that make sense.

Is it any wonder that companies like Airbnb, Groupon, GitHub, Basecamp, and many more are using Ruby on Rails to build amazing products? It's a web developer's playland, filled with tools to make the process fun and productive.

Much of the joy of building with Rails comes from embracing the limitations it creates. The structure of the framework means you have to figure out how to build your application the way Rails wants you to build it. Unfortunately, for the longest time, JavaScript and CSS were treated as "second-class citizens," shoehorned into the *public* folder to fight for themselves. Because the framework dictates how you'll use it, frontend designers had to live with the status quo.

All of that changed with Rails 3.1. In the final four chapters, we'll examine how changes to the Rails framework finally brought JavaScript and CSS into the framework (literally) and what that means for the future of frontend development in Rails.

The Junk Drawer

Prior to Rails 3.1, the *public* directory served as a "junk drawer" where stylesheets, scripts, images, HTML, text, and other files would live. Got some new pics? Throw them in *public/images*. Need a print stylesheet? That went in *public/stylesheets*. PDFs? Not a problem.

Watch the RailsConf 2011 keynote (*http://bit.ly/2aTGvqf*), where David Heinemeier Hansson (DHH) talks about the junk drawer, the asset pipeline, and more. Should you want to create an app from the start without Sprockets turned on, run `rails new app name --skip-sprockets` when creating a new application.

DHH was right: the *public* directory had become a catch-all for non-Ruby/Rails items and wasn't treated equally to the rest of the framework. There was nothing framework-specific about the *public* directory other than we needed somewhere to put those files, shown in Figure 17-1. After all, we want our application to have style, interactivity, and images, right?

Name	Date Modified	Size	Kind
404.html	Sep 6, 2011 1:05 PM	728 bytes	HTML
422.html	Sep 6, 2011 1:05 PM	711 bytes	HTML
500.html	Sep 6, 2011 1:05 PM	728 bytes	HTML
favicon.ico	Sep 6, 2011 1:05 PM	Zero bytes	Windo
images	Today 10:08 AM	--	Folder
index.html	Sep 6, 2011 1:10 PM	6 KB	HTML
javascripts	Sep 6, 2011 1:05 PM	--	Folder
pdf	Sep 6, 2011 1:05 PM	--	Folder
robots.txt	Sep 6, 2011 1:05 PM	204 bytes	Plain T
stylesheets	Sep 6, 2011 1:05 PM	--	Folder

Figure 17-1. The sad tale of a public directory from an application prior to Rails 3.1

Sprockets

Sprockets is a library for compiling and serving web assets like JavaScript and CSS files. It also serves as a "preprocessor pipeline," which means it can use languages like Sass/SCSS, as we saw in Chapter 16, and CoffeeScript, which we'll learn about in Chapter 18.

Sprockets makes JavaScript and CSS first-class citizens, all because of that preprocessor pipeline it adds to a Rails application. It has fundamentally changed how images, JavaScript, and CSS are handled within the Rails ecosystem, moving them out of the junk drawer and into first-class-citizen status.

Dissecting the Pipeline

When we generated our students application, Rails automatically created a set of subdirectories inside of a directory called *assets* (*app/assets*, shown in Figure 17-2). Those subdirectories—*images*, *javascripts*, *stylesheets*—not surprisingly are the new homes for their respective assets. Now that they're no longer relegated to the *public* directory, Sprockets has plans for them.

 The asset pipeline is turned on by default. If you decide against it, edit *config/application.rb* and place `config.assets.enabled = false` in the file.

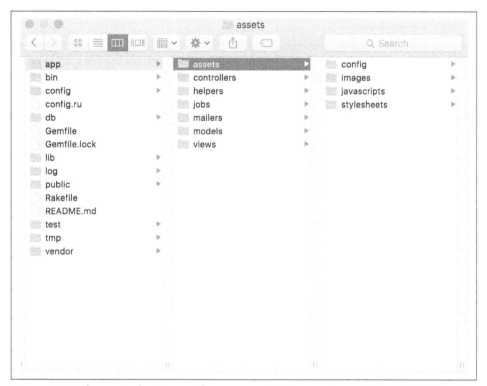

Figure 17-2. The assets directory with our generated images, javascripts, and stylesheets subdirectories on our students application

Putting It All Together

Let's see how all of this works together. Make sure your students app is running. If not, start it in the command line by running `rails server`. In your browser, visit *http://localhost:3000/assets/application.css*. You'll see something like Figure 17-3.

localhost:3000/assets/application.css - Google Chrome
localhost:3000/ass⋮ ×
localhost:3000/assets/application.css

```
/*
 * This is a manifest file that'll be compiled into application.css, which will include all
the files
 * listed below.
 *
 * Any CSS and SCSS file within this directory, lib/assets/stylesheets,
vendor/assets/stylesheets,
 * or any plugin's vendor/assets/stylesheets directory can be referenced here using a
relative path.
 *
 * You're free to add application-wide styles to this file and they'll appear at the bottom
of the
 * compiled file so the styles you add here take precedence over styles defined in any other
CSS/SCSS
 * files in this directory. Styles in this file should be added after the last require_*
statement.
 * It is generally better to create a new file per style scope.
 *
 */
/* ---------- STUDENTS.SCSS ---------- */

body {
  -moz-box-shadow: 0 0 5px #888;
  -webkit-box-shadow: 0 0 5px #888;
  box-shadow: 0 0 5px #888;
  padding: 4px;
  width: 80%; }

body h1 {
  background-color: #0067A1;
  padding: 10px;
  color: #FFF;
  margin: 0; }

td.name {
  color: #0067A1; }
```

Figure 17-3. Our application.css file, compiled and compressed with all our imported stylesheets

As you can see, all of your stylesheets are compiled into one long file. Because we added the @import directive to our *app/assets/application.css* file in the last chapter, Sprockets uses the information in the top of the file, the manifest, to compile the file we see at *http://localhost:3000/assets/application.css*.

This file includes loads of information. As you scroll down the file you'll notice each block of style information is preceded with its location in your application. This is quite handy for debugging. Quickly glance at your CSS to see what you want to modify, and you'll be given the line number and location so you can find it with ease.

The stylesheets are loaded in the order the @import directives are listed in *application.css*. If you have a file like *scaffold.css* that doesn't change much, you could have it load last in the manifest by listing it last in *application.css.scss*. That will save you time and be easier on your eyes when you're sifting through the compiled stylesheet.

Although all this information is handy, it can be a bit hard to decipher if you start loading several different stylesheets. Adding a commented line of code at the top of each individual stylesheet file makes for easier reading.

For example, a simple line of code like this:

```
/* ---------- SCAFFOLDS.SCSS ---------- */
```

translates to a visual break in the page like so:

```
a.destroy {
  color: #DB4327;
}

/* ---------- SCAFFOLDS.SCSS ---------- */
/* line 2, /Users/rumblestrut/Webapps/students01/app/assets/stylesheets/
          scaffolds.css.scss */
body {
  background-color: #fff;
  color: #333;
  font-family: verdana, arial, helvetica, sans-serif;
  font-size: 13px;
  line-height: 18px;
}
```

It should come as no surprise that you can view additional file types in the asset pipeline in a browser by following their path:

- *app/assets/application.js* is accessible at *http://localhost:3000/assets/application.js.*

- *app/assets/places.js.coffee* (we'll discuss CoffeeScript in the next chapter) is accessible at *http://localhost:3000/assets/places.js.coffee.*

The same goes for other files in the pipeline. In fact, you're not limited to only images, stylesheets, or JavaScript files. Create a new folder in the *assets* directory called *text*, and inside of it is a file called *hello.txt*. Open that file, type the word **Hi** in it, and then close and save it.

If you were to try to access *http://localhost:3000/assets/hello.txt*, you'd get a routing error. Restart the app, and Rails will add the new directory and its contents to the load path. Access *http://localhost:3000/assets/hello.txt* now, and you'll see something like Figure 17-4.

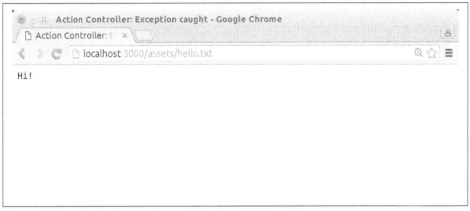

Figure 17-4. Our plain-text file available for all the world to see

You've already seen that the pipeline can be used inside the *app/assets* directory. In addition, there are two other places in your application that can use pipeline assets:

lib/assets
> Perhaps you have code that isn't tied down to this application, but you maintain it. Since you've claimed responsibility for this bit of code, put it here. An example of this would be if a company had assets that were used in-house by a variety of applications. For code that's maintained by a third party, that would be more at home in *vendor/assets*.

vendor/assets
> Got a favorite jQuery plug-in? Fan of Eric Meyer's Reset CSS? Those third-party assets belong here.

Not to leave the *public* directory out: you can put assets there, but they'll be served as static files only—no dynamic action there.

The pipeline uses *app/assets*, *lib/assets*, and *vendor/assets* by reducing the number of requests a browser makes to render your application's web pages. Fewer requests lead to faster loading of web pages, and ultimately lead to a faster application.

This makes sense. We might have multiple stylesheets, but Sprockets works to compile them all into one master CSS (or SCSS) file. The same goes for JavaScript files. Sprockets does the work for us in the background, minimizing and compressing files, removing whitespace and comments.

Lastly, it might be helpful to know how to link to these wonderful files in your application. You've already seen how to link to stylesheets and JavaScript, respectively:

```
<%= stylesheet_link_tag 'application' %>

<%= javascript_link_tag 'application' %>
```

And anywhere in your application, you can link directly to an image by using
`image_tag`:

```
<%= image_tag "rails.png" %>
```

Bundler

One of the more interesting aspects of working on a Rails project is its community. If
you're stuck on a program, mailing lists, forums, books, blogs, and user groups can
help you get over the hump.

Another great addition to the community—a by-product of the open source move-
ment itself—is the prevalence of tools that are widely available, and often free. Such is
the case with *gems*: Ruby libraries written by others in the community to add more
features to your application.

You've already seen gems in action. `OmniAuth` is a gem that provides multiprovider
authentication. Even Rails itself is a gem—you remember running `gem install
rails`, right?

Although many of the gems available are useful, free, and fun to explore, managing
them properly used to be like herding cats—that is, until Bundler came along and
changed everything.

Bundler is a gem management tool for the "cat herding" aspect of your Ruby application's dependencies. When you first created your students application, the last command to run before you could proceed was `bundle install`. That command caused
your computer to run out, grab all the dependencies for a basic Rails app, and then
install them for you, as shown in Figure 17-5.

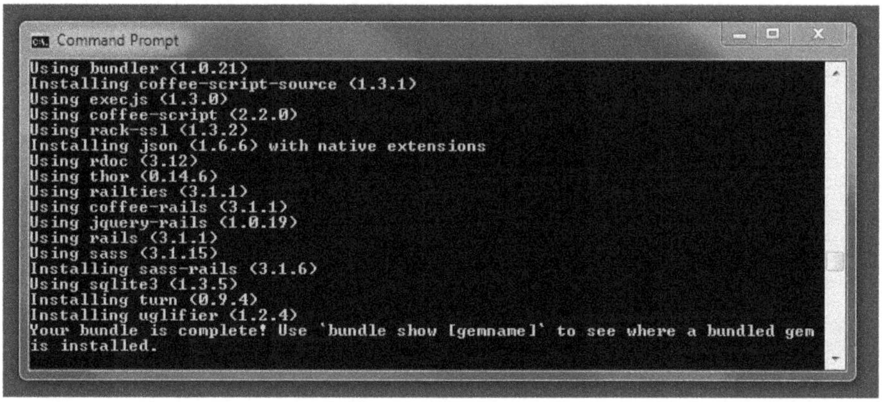

*Figure 17-5. "Your bundle is complete!" means Bundler has taken care of all of your gem
dependencies for you and you're ready to get started building your app*

Adding a gem is as simple as editing a text file. In the root of your application is a file called the *Gemfile*. Say you wanted to add the `Friendly_Id` gem. Open the Gemfile in a text editor and add **gem 'friendly_id'** in the file. Save it, then switch back over to the command line and run **bundle install**. You'll see something like Figure 17-6.

```
gem 'sqlite3'
gem 'friendly_id' # Added the Friendly_ID gem
```

Figure 17-6. Editing the Gemfile so Bundler will fetch the necessary gem and its dependencies when run

There's another important file being modified by Bundler that we'll need to take a look at: *Gemfile.lock*. This file will "lock down" which version of a gem was installed initially (clever name, eh?). If you had created an app using `Friendly_ID` version 3.2.1, you'd still be using that version until you manually updated the gem.

This makes your application more portable: you'll always be using the exact same version of the gem, which protects from future upgrades that could break your app before you're ready. When you are ready to update a specific gem, running the command **bundle update** with the gem name will do that. Of course, your *Gemfile.lock* file will be updated as well, like this: bundle update friendly_id.

But what if you want to just update everything? Run bundle update with no arguments and it'll all be taken care of, but be forewarned: this can become tricky as your application grows.

You'll notice we haven't even really talked about version numbers. In a way, you don't need version numbers when installing gems in your Gemfile, as Bundler will always fetch the latest version by default. There is a way to change that. Adding the version for the gem in your Gemfile will prohibit Bundler from updating the gem, even if bundle update is run, as you can see in Figure 17-7.

```
gem 'sqlite3'
gem 'friendly_id', '3.2.1' # Added the Friendly_ID gem
```

Figure 17-7. With the version number passed as an argument for the Friendly_ID gem installation, it will stop updating even if bundle update is run

You'll need to run the bundle exec command when executing some commands, such as migrating a database: bundle exec rails db:migrate. In doing so, you ensure your application is using the gem specified in your Gemfile.

If you want even more control over which versions of a gem Bundler manages, here are some helpful arguments:

```
gem 'gemname', '2.11.12'
```

As mentioned before, this keeps *Gemfile.lock* at this version for a gem, until you update it manually.

```
gem 'gemname', '~> 2.11.12'
```

The tilde tells Bundler to update the last number only when Bundler is executed. So if a new version, say 2.11.13, comes out, Bundler will update your gem to that version. But if 2.12.2 were available, the gem would not upgrade to 2.12.

```
gem 'gemname', '>= 2.11.12'
```

Bundler will update only if the gem that has been released is greater than or equal to 2.11.12.

It's worth noting that a good practice for adding gems to your Gemfile includes either setting an explicit version number, or using the ~>. Keeping these versions locked down until you've had a chance to fully test them with your application could save you a lot of heartache should the gem have gone through major changes since your last upgrade.

And since we're all fans of rapid development, a neat thing about Bundler is that it can check a gem's dependencies more quickly if a version number is specified in the Gemfile.

If you're looking to update a published gem, head over to *http://www.rubygems.org/* and find the one you want to update. The site has a nifty little feature: click on the clipboard icon and it will copy the exact bit of code needed for your Gemfile, like so:

```
gem 'friendly_id', '~> 4.0.5'
```

Just paste it in and you're ready to run `bundle install` to get updating.

 Episode 45 of the Ruby Rogues podcast (*http://bit.ly/2aTGfry*) discusses how Bundler deals with version numbers and dependencies. This episode is a few years old, but is still very relevant.

The last thing we'll talk about is groups. Back in your Gemfile, you'll notice a section of gems grouped together:

```
group :development, :test do
  # Call 'byebug' anywhere in the code to stop execution and get a debugger
  gem 'byebug', platform: :mri
end
```

In this code, the group is called `development`. Any gems (in this case only one: bye-bug) are not used in the production environment by default. That's because in *config/application.rb*, this line set development and test environments as the default:

```
Bundler.require(*Rails.groups)
```

Groups helps control when a gem should be installed or loaded. In the case of the application we were working on at the beginning of this section, had it been using Bundler, we could have created two groups: one to load the gem for development and another to use for the production environment.

Perhaps using the `twitter-bootstrap-rails` gem was enough to get us started building a layout during development, but when it came time to launch with custom code, it was unnecessary to include it in production. Groups allows me to specify that like so:

```
group :development do
  gem 'twitter-bootstrap-rails'
end

group :development, :test do
  # Call 'byebug' anywhere in the code to stop execution and get a debugger
  gem 'byebug', platform: :mri
end
```

In the case of a default Rails app, the byebug gem is only needed for development and test environments. That is why we see it included in the development and test groups only.

There's much more to Bundler and its capabilities. For more information, run **bundle help** to get a full list of commands, or visit Bundler's official website (*http://gembundler.com*).

Test Your Knowledge

Quiz

1. After Ruby on Rails 3.1, what change made JavaScript and CSS files have the same "status" as Ruby files?

2. What tool manages gems within a Rails application?

3. What resource can you use to find gems and find out about updates?

4. Is it possible to specify different groups of gems for each environment (development, test, production)?

Answers

1. The Sprockets library began shipping with Rails 3.1 for compiling and serving web assets like JavaScript and CSS files. It also serves as a "preprocessor pipeline," which means it can use languages like Sass/SCSS and CoffeeScript.

2. Bundler is for managing gems. It uses your Gemfile to install gems and their dependencies within a project.

3. The Ruby Gems website (*http://www.rubygems.org*) is the home of the RubyGems application. It has lots of information about using, creating, and sharing gems. The site will even provide you with the exact bit of code you need to stick in your Gemfile to install or update gems.

4. Yes. By using groups in your Gemfile, you control when a gem will be installed or loaded. If you were playing around with different types of gems while building your application in development, you could leave out unused ones for production through a group.

## CHAPTER 18

Sending Code to the Browser: JavaScript and CoffeeScript

Once you wake up and smell the coffee, it's hard to go back to sleep.
—Fran Drescher

Rails has had a complicated and tumultuous relationship with JavaScript. It emerged at about the same time that Ajax development was making JavaScript popular again, and Rails eagerly integrated Ajax tools. Remote JavaScript (RJS) templates let developers create JavaScript with Ruby, Rails helped the Prototype library find its footing, and a variety of helper methods provided extra support in view templates.

Those solutions put Rails ahead of the crowd for a while, but developments in Rails and in the larger JavaScript world led to better conclusions. Rails's shift toward REST-based approaches made RJS and the various helper methods seem less necessary, as code in the client could easily request XML and then JSON data from the server. Developers could cleanly separate their client and server logic that way, making it easier to maintain applications. In the JavaScript world, jQuery overtook Prototype to become the dominant JavaScript library. As JavaScript use became more complicated, many developers turned to CoffeeScript to simplify their code.

 Perhaps not surprisingly, CoffeeScript, like Sprockets and Sass, lives outside of the Rails framework independently of what ships with recent versions. You can find the original project's page (*https://github.com/jashkenas/coffeescript*).

Sending JavaScript to the Browser

When you created the awards and students controllers for our application, Coffee-Script files were generated inside of *app/assets/javascripts*: *awards.js.coffee* and *students.js.coffee*, respectively. If you prefer to work with standard JavaScript or jQuery, simply change the file extension and it will work just fine. We will do that in the next example. Code for this is available in *ch18/students0X*.

To use regular JavaScript, rename the file from *students.coffee* to *students.js*. Open *app/assets/javascripts/students.js*. Since we've changed the file type from the default CoffeeScript to plain JavaScript, there is a minor (but very significant) change we must make to the file before we can add our own logic. Notice the block of comments at the top of the file:

```
# Place all the behaviors and hooks related to the matching controller here.
# All this logic will automatically be available in application.js.
# You can use CoffeeScript in this file: http://coffeescript.org/
```

It's great that Rails has provided us with this information, but the comments have been formatted for *CoffeeScript* with the hash (#) symbol. This happens to be an illegal character in JavaScript and will throw an exception if it's in our *.js* file. What's more, Rails will refuse to compile the file if it contains this corrupt syntax. Go ahead and remove the comments so you have a clean, empty file to work with.

All you need is a little JavaScript to play with. Rails provides "out of the box" access to the jQuery library by default, so let's take advantage of that. We'll add a visual cue to those who are putting data into the students application. The code shown in Example 18-1 will do the trick.

Example 18-1. JavaScript for highlighting a form field

```
$(document).on('ready', function() {
    $("input").focus(function() {
        $(this).parent().addClass("curFocus");
    });
    $("input").blur(function() {
        $(this).parent().removeClass("curFocus");
    });
});
```

When used with a form, this little snippet of code will use jQuery to highlight an input field when the cursor is in a text field (focus), and then remove the highlighting when we've moved on (blur). It does this by dynamically adding a class of curFocus to the parent of our input, which is a div in this case.

The code is fairly straightforward. From the second line you could read it like this: when there is a focus on the input, add a class of curFocus to the parent. And then, the second argument says: when there is a blur on the input, remove the `curFocus` from the parent (again, the `div`).

You'll also need to add a little CSS to get our desired effect. In *app/assets/stylesheets/students.css.scss*, add this to the bottom of the file:

```
div.curFocus {
  background: #fdecb2;
  @include bodyshadow;
  width: 250px;
}
```

This stylesheet makes the field stand out, giving it a nice background and a body-shadow mixin, and sets the width of the `div` to 250 pixels so it doesn't stretch the width of the page. Save your file, then load up *http://localhost:3000/students/new* in your browser to see the result in Figure 18-1.

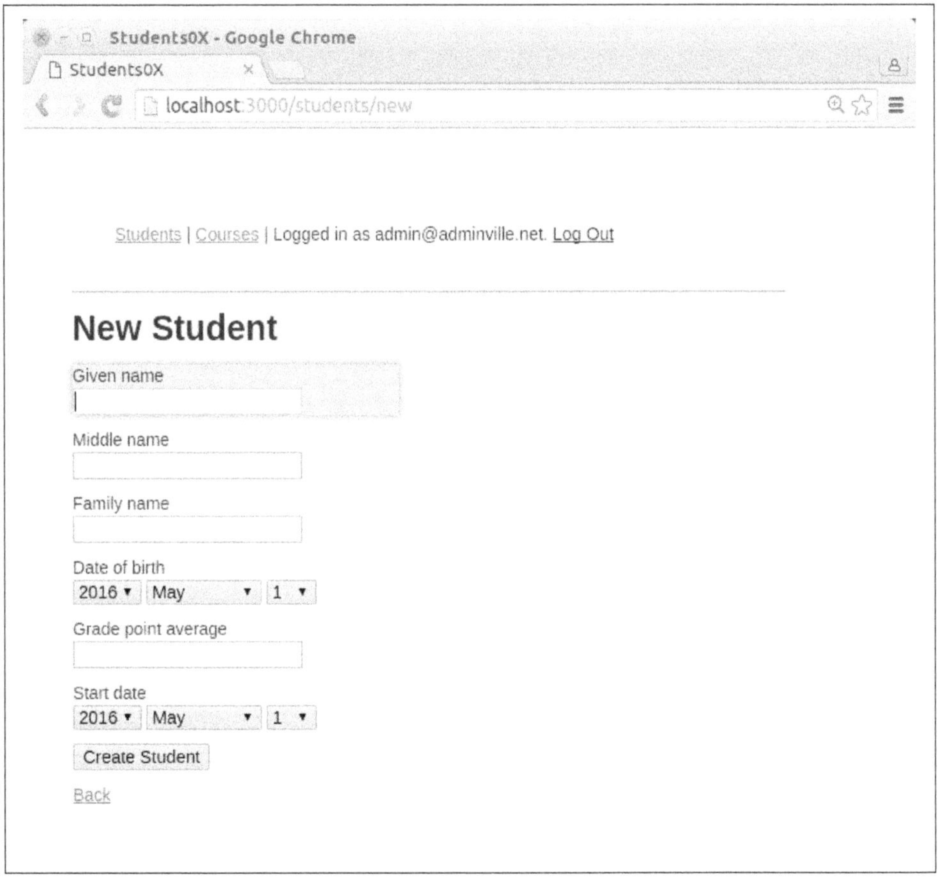

Figure 18-1. Our students application with our JavaScript in place

It's close, but it's off a little bit because of that class that gets added to the div. You can add a little bit of padding to the div itself to help fix this. Back in your stylesheet, add the following to the bottom as well.

```
div.field {
  padding: 10px;
}
```

Now you can refresh the page in the browser and see the finished result in Figure 18-2.

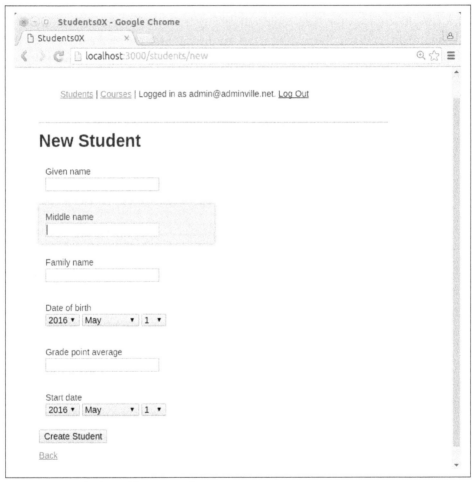

Figure 18-2. A little padding goes a long way

Simplifying with CoffeeScript

We're quickly moving toward a future very similar to that envisioned by *Star Trek*. If you've ever watched the shows, you'll see much of the technology starting to take shape in one way or another in modern times. Perhaps it's the realization of a self-fulfilling prophecy for technology, but handheld communicators, handheld tablet reading devices, and small devices that analyze our world are all becoming real products.

One of the more interesting technologies to me in the *Star Trek* (and other science fiction) universe is that of the universal translator. The remarkable device translates hard-to-understand languages into something familiar, with a small computer doing all the work for you.

In a way, that's how CoffeeScript works.

CoffeeScript is a programming language that compiles into JavaScript. Similar to the universal translator, you can write CoffeeScript code that is "translated" to JavaScript. If you've written JavaScript code, you'll instantly see CoffeeScript's appeal: it can spit out JavaScript with about one-third less code, it runs fast, and the clean syntax is similar to Ruby's beautiful code.

The backstory behind the CoffeeScript parser is available at the Grammer.Coffee site (*http://bit.ly/2aTH9nX*).

As of version 3.1, CoffeeScript ships with Ruby on Rails out of the box.

As with Sass, the quickest way to get started with CoffeeScript is by appending *.coffee* to your *.js* scripts to make them valid CoffeeScript files, such as *example.js.coffee*. Unlike with Sass, however, you'll need to understand CoffeeScript's syntax for it to work correctly.

To really get down into the meat of all that CoffeeScript has to offer, we recommend you check out Alex MacCaw's *The Little Book on CoffeeScript* (O'Reilly, 2012).

Have Some Sugar with Your CoffeeScript

Like the universal translator, CoffeeScript does some amazing work in the background to make its magic known. Unlike in our science fiction example, we need to do a little more to help it achieve our goals.

CoffeeScript borrows from the Python programming language in that it uses syntactic whitespace. This means you'll need to be consistent with your tabs for each line of code. As a Rubyist, you're likely familiar with the practice of two spaces for indentation. This will work fine in CoffeeScript.

 CoffeeScript is much more finicky about whitespace than Ruby. You can be inconsistent with two spaces on one line and three on the next for indentation, and Ruby code will run without a hitch. In CoffeeScript, though, you'll need to keep the same convention throughout your code for it to run.

CoffeeScript changes JavaScript syntax in a few key ways:

Curly braces
> Spend any bit of time with JavaScript, and you'll notice the prominent use of (what some might consider ugly) curly braces, {}. With CoffeeScript, these are a thing of the past. You can safely remove curly braces from your code, but be sure to use consistent indentation.

The `var` *call*
> Used to declare a variable in JavaScript, the `var` call isn't used in CoffeeScript. You'll never need to write `var`; the compiler takes care of that for you.

Return statements
> Return statements are also not necessary. CoffeeScript will automatically return whatever you have at the end of a function call, implying that it is a return.

> Speaking of functions, their definitions have been replaced by the `->` symbol. You can remove parentheses around an argument if you'd like. This isn't required. Sometimes it just feels better to have the parentheses around an argument, but it's your call. There is one exception: if there isn't an argument, you'll need a set of empty parentheses instead.

> You can even put function definitions on one line if you like, provided it's short enough to be a good fit for that. `function show_alert()` would be written as `show_alert() ->`.

Semicolons
> JavaScript's experienced a few controversies over semicolons lately. Most of the time, those aren't needed either. You can safely remove them in CoffeeScript.

Comments
> While the double slash, `//`, might work just fine in JavaScript, you'll need to use the hash character, `#`, to start a comment line in CoffeeScript, just like in Ruby. Multiline comments are encapsulated within a set of three hash characters:

```
# This is a comment

###
  This is a multiline comment.
  How are you doing today?
###
```

if/else *conditionals*

Now we really start to see how elegantly CoffeeScript can reduce the amount of code used. When you can remove parentheses and curly braces, then delimit your conditions through indentations (that whitespace we referenced before), things just get cleaner.

So JavaScript code that looks like this:

```
var d, time;

d = new Date();
time = d.getHours();

if (time < 10) {
  document.write("Good morning");
} else {
  document.write("Good day");
}
```

ends up using a little bit less code in CoffeeScript:

```
d = new Date()
time = d.getHours()

if time < 10
  document.write "Good morning"
else
  document.write "Good day"
```

You also can put if statements on one line, but you'll need to use the then keyword for CoffeeScript to be aware of the beginning of the block:

```
if (time < 10) then document.write "Good morning" else
document.write "Good day"
```

Arrays

You can easily make arrays by using whitespace and square brackets:

```
authors = [Mark, Jonathan, Daryl]
```

Converting to CoffeeScript

We could easily cut and paste Example 18-1 and throw it into our application for use, as is. But we wouldn't be taking advantage of CoffeeScript's syntax, and should the need arise to add more functionality, we wouldn't be harnessing the value of using less code for the same result.

Instead, we'll keep our *.coffee* file intact and go with CoffeeScript instead. Our finished product will look like Example 18-2, available in *ch18/students0Y*.

Example 18-2. CoffeeScript for highlighting a form field

```
$(document).on "ready", ->
    $("input").focus ->
        $(this).parent().addClass("curFocus")
    $("input").blur ->
        $(this).parent().removeClass("curFocus")
```

Run the application, and you'll see the same result as Figure 18-2.

Taking a cue from what we've learned earlier in this chapter, you can see the obvious gains in having less code. There are fewer lines (five compared to eight), no curly braces, no semicolons, and no traditional function calls. Much of it looks the same, just simpler. Now, imagine this times a couple of hundred lines of code as our project scales up, and you'll really start to see what a difference CoffeeScript can make.

As with Sass, you can see all the compiled files rolled up into one by visiting *http://localhost:3000/assets/application.js*. You'll need to scroll all the way to the bottom, but there our newly added JavaScript code will be, ready for use.

A friend of mine who teaches banjo lessons was telling me about his process of introducing new players to the art. Although he could start with teaching his students how to read notation, key changes, flats, and sharps, he has decided on a different route.

Instead, his method has the students begin by learning tablature. In case you're not familiar with the concept, tablature, or tabs, is a way to learn how to play an instrument by learning where your fingers will go on the fretboard of an instrument, rather than going into the weighty details of music theory.

Purists might say this isn't the correct way to learn, that a student should begin with the most rudimentary of music basics and then work from there. As an instructor, my friend's intention is simple: once a student learns how to play a song quickly from the start, it creates a desire to learn more and progress from there.

CoffeeScript shouldn't be the only thing you learn for how to make JavaScript, just as tabs aren't the only way to learn banjo or guitar. CoffeeScript isn't required to have JavaScript code in your application. But it can be an excellent way to get started with JavaScript development, and put you on the path to better frontend development.

As with the complicated nature of JavaScript, this is by no means an exhaustive overview of CoffeeScript's syntax, or its power. There's much more to delve into as you learn how it can be used with your application.

Test Your Knowledge

Quiz

1. What is the default JavaScript framework used by Rails?

2. How can you start using CoffeeScript in your application?

3. CoffeeScript's syntax is more simplified than JavaScript's in several ways—what can you avoid using?

Answers

1. The popular jQuery library replaced the long-used Prototype framework.

2. The quickest way to get started with CoffeeScript is by appending *.coffee* to your *.js* scripts to make them valid CoffeeScript files, such as *example.js.coffee*.

3. Curly braces, the `var` call, return statements, and semicolons are not used by CoffeeScript.

## CHAPTER 19

Mail in Rails

*Prior to email, our private correspondence was secured by a government institution
called the postal service. Today, we trust AOL, Microsoft, Yahoo, Facebook,
or Gmail with our private utterances.*
   —John Battelle

Most of Rails is built around HTTP, but there will be times you also want to send or
receive email messages. Thanks to the ActionMailer system, it's almost as easy to send
and receive mail messages as it is to send and receive information over HTTP.
Because mail systems are separate from Rails, there's still some difficulty in connecting Rails to mail servers, but you can at least get started pretty easily. If you would
like to code along with this chapter, make a copy of *ch09/students03* and start there.

Sending Mail Messages

Telling Rails to send email messages requires putting a little bit of infrastructure in
place, creating views specifying what the messages should say, and telling Rails when
to send what. Except that it's an extra piece that goes outside the usual HTTP context,
it's not very difficult.

First, you need to generate a mailer:

```
$ rails generate mailer AwardMailer
    create  app/mailers/award_mailer.rb
    invoke  erb
    create    app/views/award_mailer
    invoke  test_unit
    create    test/mailers/award_mailer_test.rb
    create    test/mailers/previews/award_mailer_preview.rb
```

Alongside the *assets*, *controllers*, and *models* directories within the *app* directory, Rails
has provided us with the *mailers* directory. Mailers aren't really models, controllers,

or views, so they get a separate place. Inside of that folder, *award_mailer.rb* offers a very basic start:

```
class AwardMailer < ApplicationMailer
end
```

Setting defaults is useful, and the from field is probably the one most likely to be consistent. You can also set default to, subject, cc, and bcc fields if you want. For now, let's set a default from email along with a method that can actually do something, in this case send a notice that an award has been given. (Perhaps this triggers a hand-made award certificate.)

```
class AwardMailer < ApplicationMailer
  default from: "me@barnabasbulpett.com"

  def award_email(award)
    @award = award
    mail(to: 'Barnabas Bulpett <barnabasbulpett@example.com>',
      subject: "Award from Learning Rails")
  end
end
```

There's no actual content there beyond the subject line, though. The content, like the content of a web page delivered by Rails, comes from a view. Unlike web page content, however, mail can include multiple main pieces. Typically, one is HTML, for those who like their email vivid, and one is plain text, for those who just want the basics. ActionMailer now supports this convention automatically. All you have to do is create two views, one for plain text and one for HTML.

The plain-text one is very simple, and goes in */app/views/award_mailer/award_email.text.erb*. (The ERb file gets its name from the method within the mailer.)

```
The <%= @award.name %> award for
<%= @award.year %> has gone to <%= @award.student.name %>.
```

The HTML one in */app/views/award_mailer/award_email.html.erb* has the same content, except of course that it has a lot more markup:

```
<!DOCTYPE html>
<html>
  <head>
    <meta content="text/html; charset=UTF-8" http-equiv="Content-Type" />
  </head>
  <body>
    <h1>Award Notification</h1>
    <p>The <%= @award.name %> award for <%= @award.year %> has gone to
    <%= @award.student.name %>.</p>
  </body>
</html>
```

Rails doesn't yet know that it's supposed to actually send email when an award is assigned. That requires adding a line of code to the awards controller, here placed in the `create` method:

```
def create
  @award = @student.awards.build(award_params)
  # was @award = Award.new(params[:award])

  # Tell the AwardMailer to send a notice Email
  AwardMailer.award_email(@award).deliver
  respond_to do |format|...
  end
end
```

You can tell Rails to send mail from wherever you think it appropriate, but controllers are usually the most logical place to do it.

Rails just needs one more piece of information before it's ready to send a message. What mail server should it use? This information goes in the configuration files (*/config/environments/development.rb* for use in development mode and */config/environments/production.rb* for production mode). It's very likely you'll have a different setting for each of these modes, and in test mode, Rails delivers messages to a queue for inspection rather than sending them out to actual mail servers.

There are two different ways you can send email. You can have Rails deliver to a local sendmail process, which is probably the best approach on a server. If that's not an option, which is likely when you're developing on a laptop, you can have Rails contact an SMTP server to send the message, just as your email client normally would. The default is SMTP.

For testing, you may want to explore the MailCatcher gem (*http://mailcatcher.me*).

To send mail over SMTP, you'll need to specify at least the server address, maybe the port, and maybe a lot more information for authentication. A simple configuration might look like:

```
config.action_mailer.delivery_method = :smtp
  config.action_mailer.smtp_settings = {
    :address              => "mail.example.com",
    :port                 => 25,
  }
```

If you need to do something more complex—which is likely in an age where email is barely trusted—see the detailed configuration for Gmail (*http://bit.ly/2aTHiYd*). We've provided an sample of such a setup in *ch19/students10/config/environments/development.rb* (approximately line 31) in the example code for this chapter.

Now, finally, you can send a message. Start up the server with **rails server**, and go to a page for a student. Then, using the navigation at the bottom of that student page, go to the student's Awards page, shown in Figure 19-1.

Figure 19-1. Awards page for a student

Click on New Award, and you'll be able to enter a new award, as shown in Figure 19-2.

Figure 19-2. Creating a Chemistry Wizard award

When you click the "Create award" button, you'll get the usual response shown in Figure 19-3, but you'll also have an email message like that in Figure 19-4.

Figure 19-3. Award created (web version)

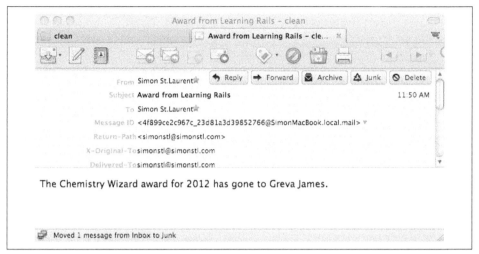

Figure 19-4. Award created (email version)

If you look at the source (or in your logs), you'll see all of the work Rails did for you, assembling the headers and the multipart message:

```
Started POST "/students/2/awards" for 127.0.0.1 at 2016-01-11 18:59:01 -0500
Processing by AwardsController#create as HTML
  Parameters: {"utf8"=>"✓", "authenticity_token"=>"GpDgpVMsNCDSWZ8x9XSj...",
  "award"=>{"name"=>"Chemistry Wizard", "year"=>"2012"},
  "commit"=>"Create Award", "student_id"=>"2"}
  Student Load (0.3ms)
  SELECT  "students".* FROM "students" WHERE "students"."id" = ? LIMIT ?
  [["id", 2], ["LIMIT", 1]]
  Rendered award_mailer/award_email.html.erb (0.6ms)
  Rendered award_mailer/award_email.text.erb (0.3ms)
AwardMailer#award_email: processed outbound mail in 262.5ms
Sent mail to barnabasbulpett@example.com (21.0ms)
Date: Mon, 11 Jan 2016 18:59:01 -0500
From: me@barnabasbulpett.com
To: Barnabas Bulpett <barnabasbulpett@example.com>
Message-ID: <569441c5db444_7a0e103a38030640@barnabas-ThinkPad-L412.mail>
Subject: Award from Learning Rails
Mime-Version: 1.0
Content-Type: multipart/alternative;
 boundary="--==_mimepart_569441c5d8c85_7a0e103a380305d";
 charset=UTF-8
Content-Transfer-Encoding: 7bit


----==_mimepart_569441c5d8c85_7a0e103a380305d
Content-Type: text/plain;
 charset=UTF-8
Content-Transfer-Encoding: 7bit
```

```
The Chemistry Wizard award for 2012 has gone to Greva James.
----==_mimepart_569441c5d8c85_7a0e103a380305d
Content-Type: text/html;
 charset=UTF-8
Content-Transfer-Encoding: 7bit

<!DOCTYPE html>
<html>
  <head>
    <meta content="text/html; charset=UTF-8" http-equiv="Content-Type" />
  </head>
  <body>
    <h1>Award Notification</h1>
    <p>The Chemistry Wizard award for 2012 has gone to
    Greva James.</p>
  </body>
</html>
----==_mimepart_569441c5d8c85_7a0e103a380305d--
```

Rails can do more for you. You can include images (linked or inline), send attachments, send the email to multiple recipients, or add headers to your heart's delight. It's probably safest to start simple, and then add features as your application needs them.

Previewing Mail

Rather than using a third-party gem to view emails, Rails gives you the ability to preview emails using ActionMailer. A preview class was created for you when you generated your award mailer. It is located in *test/mailers/previews/award_mailer_preview.rb*. To see the preview of award_email, add a method with the same name to the preview class and call AwardMailer.award_email, passing it a valid award. In this case, we'll just get the first award in the database:

```
# Preview all emails at http://localhost:3000/rails/mailers/award_mailer
class AwardMailerPreview < ActionMailer::Preview
  def award_email
    AwardMailer.award_email(Award.first)
  end
end
```

In your browser go to *http://localhost:3000/rails/mailers* to see a list of available previews. In this case we only have one (award_email). If you click on it, you should see the preview shown in Figure 19-5.

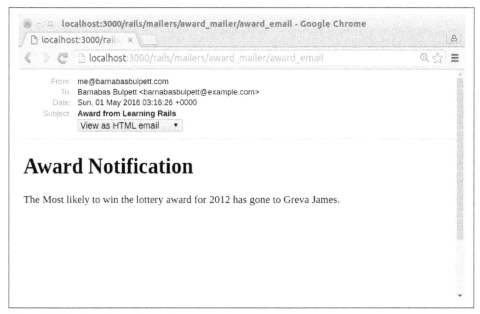

Figure 19-5. Award email preview

Notice that you can choose to view either an HTML or text version of the email with the drop-down box under the subject. By default, these preview classes live in *test/ mailers/previews*. You can configure this using the `preview_path` option. For example, if you want to change it to *lib/mailer_previews*, you can configure it in *config/ application.rb*.

Receiving Mail

While sending email out is probably a more common scenario in most web development, there will also be times when you want your application to process incoming email messages. ActionMailer also supports this, after a setup process that may be more difficult than the Rails-specific part of the work.

Setup

Retrieving email is harder than sending it, because so much depends on the details of how your server delivers it. Servers could use dovecot, getmail, or any of a variety of tools to take mail out of the incoming queue and put it in specific mailboxes. Unfortunately, there's no way for this book to explain configuring mail servers to pass mail to Rails without it growing much longer.

All of the setup variations, though, collect incoming messages and send them directly to a class in the Rails application. While Rails does its own routing for incoming

HTTP requests, the mail server configuration handles the question of which Rails method will get to receive which email message.

Processing Messages

Once the servers are feeding messages to Rails, the Mail library (*https://github.com/ mikel/mail/*) will help your application process them. The easiest way to do this is to create a new mailer with a `receive` method.

For a simple, if not particularly secure, demonstration, *ch19/students11* shows how to make this work. It processes messages formatted like Example 19-1 to adjust the GPA of a student, identified by their `id` number. Run **rails generate mailer Student Mailer** to create a mailer base. Then make it look like the *app/mailers/ student_mailer.rb* file shown in Example 19-2. It will check incoming mail to see if it's from the right person, and parse the message body with regular expressions to see if it should change a student's GPA. Perhaps most important, it logs its results.

Example 19-1. An email message sent to the Rails application to change a student's GPA

```
From: foo@bar.org
Subject: Score

Student: 2
GPA: 3.45
```

Example 19-2. Processing incoming emails to see if they came from an administrator, extracting their content with regular expressions, and then making a change to the student data

```
class StudentMailer < ActionMailer::Base

  def receive(email)
    return unless email.subject =~ /^Score/

    sender = email.from[0]
    user = User.find_by_email(sender)
    unless user == 'edd@example.org'
      logger.error "Refusing scores message from unauthorized sender"
      return
    end

    # we've passed the first test -- email's from an admin user
    # and has a subject starting with 'Score'

    # extract the text content from the message
    content = email.multipart? ? (email.text_part ? email.text_part.body.decoded :
nil) : email.body.decoded

    # search through the content line-by-line for student and GPA
```

```
content.split(/\r?\n/).each do |l|
  if l =~ /Student:\s*(\d+)/i then
    @student = Student.find_by_id($1.to_i)
  end
  if l =~ /GPA:\s*(\d+\.\d+)/i then
    @gpa = $1.to_f
  end
end

# if the data's here, make the change.

if @student and @gpa
  @student.update_attribute('grade_point_average', @gpa)
  logger.info "Updated GPA of #{@student.name} to #{@gpa}"
else
  logger.error "Couldn't interpret scores message"
end
  end
end
```

The first few steps check that the message belongs to this processor. First, it checks for a subject line starting with "Score," and just `returns`, ending this processing, if it doesn't. Then it checks the `from` address, compares it to the list of email addresses for users, and again, `returns` if the user isn't an administrator.

The next part of the method pushes regular expressions hard, first splitting the body of the message on a new line, and then extracting the student's `id` and their new GPA by testing a match pattern and extracting the matched value, if there is one, from `$1`. The last part is much simpler, just setting that student's GPA to the one specified.

When processing email, using `logger.info` and `logger.error` is a good idea. No one's going to be seeing a response come back, unless you extend this to emailing an acknowledgment back. Log messages make these kinds of processing much easier to debug.

To try this out, you can send an email message if you've configured your server. If not, there's a complete test message, with headers and content, in the *test.msg* file at the top level of the *students011* directory, which looks like Example 19-3.

Example 19-3. A test message for trying out Rails's ability to process incoming email

```
Return-Path: <simonstl@simonstl.com>
X-Original-To: simonstl@simonstl.com
Delivered-To: simonstl@simonstl.com
Received: from SimonMacBook.local (cpe-24-59-184-80.twcny.res.rr.com [24.59.184.80])
    by mail.simonstl.com (Postfix) with ESMTPSA id 5384D18C0031
    for <simonstl@simonstl.com>; Sat, 14 Apr 2012 12:48:30 -0400 (EDT)
```

```
Message-ID: <4F89AA5A.4060203@simonstl.com>
Date: Sat, 14 Apr 2012 12:48:26 -0400
From: "Simon St.Laurent" <simonstl@simonstl.com>
User-Agent: Mozilla/5.0 (Macintosh; Intel Mac OS X 10.6; rv:11.0)
Gecko/20120327 Thunderbird/11.0.1
MIME-Version: 1.0
To: "Simon St.Laurent" <simonstl@simonstl.com>
Subject: Score
Content-Type: text/plain; charset=ISO-8859-1; format=flowed
Content-Transfer-Encoding: 7bit

Student: 1
GPA: 3.34
```

 You can create a similar message by sending yourself an email and then looking at it through View Source or something similar.

A shorter message with fewer headers would do, but this certainly shows ActionMailer's ability to cut through the cruft. Run the Rails application with **rails server** and then, if you're in Linux, OS X, or another Unix-like operating system, call (in a separate window if necessary):

```
cat test.msg | rails runner 'StudentMailer.receive(STDIN.read)'
```

Or, if you're in Windows:

```
rails runner 'StudentMailer.receive(STDIN.read) < test.msgs
```

In the log, you'll see:

```
Refusing scores message from unauthorized sender
```

followed by the message it refused. If you change the from line so that it contains an edd@example.org, however, you'll get:

```
  [1m[36mStudent Load (0.3ms)[0m  [1mSELECT "students".* FROM "students"
WHERE "students"."id" = 1 LIMIT 1[0m
        [1m[35m (0.1ms)[0m  begin transaction
        [1m[36m (0.0ms)[0m  [1mcommit transaction[0m
      Updated GPA of Giles Boschwick to 3.34
```

It's a small taste of what Rails can do with email, and it opens up tremendous possibilities beyond the reach of the Web. You'll definitely want to provide more security around this, but it shows how you can take content from email, process it, and integrate it with your application.

The `rails runner` command lets you call pieces of your Rails application directly. It's a convenient way to do things like inject content from a shell script, start a long-running process, or, as in this case, test something out.

Test Your Knowledge

Quiz

1. Where do you tell Rails how to send email?
2. How do you specify which variables fit where in a given mail message?
3. What Rails command-line tool can you use to call pieces of your Rails application directly?

Answers

1. The configuration files in *config/environments/*, such as *development.rb*, *testing.rb*, and *production.rb*, are a good place to specify the settings that Rails should use to send outgoing mail.

2. A model class extending `ActionMailer::Base` containing a method that sets email parameters can handle all of the header information for email messages, and a view (one each for HTML and text) can define their content.

3. The `rails runner` call lets you communicate directly with your Rails application from the command line.

## CHAPTER 20

Pushing Further into Rails

If an expert says it can't be done, get another expert.
—David Ben-Gurion

At this point, Rails should seem much less mysterious. You should understand how to build fairly sophisticated Rails applications, and the magic of assembling applications by naming convention. As much as you've learned, though, you could go much further.

Changing to Production Mode

So far, you've likely been running all of your code in development or testing mode. Shifting to production mode is kind of like graduating. Running your application in production mode means that it runs all of its queries against your production database, and that it loads the Rails configuration from *config/environments/production.rb*. You also should precompile your assets with `bundle exec rails assets:precompile`, as the production environment won't do that automatically. (You can set Rails up to do that, but it will likely create efficiency problems.)

Because of the way Rails is set up by default, the shift in environments to production mode results in changes to the following configuration settings:

`config.cache_classes = true`
    Rails doesn't check to see if any code has changed every request, so everything runs a lot faster in production mode.

`config.action_controller.perform_caching = true`
    Caching is enabled, letting Rails optimize its performance by minimizing redundant processing.

```
config.action_controller.consider_all_requests_local = false
```
Verbose error reporting is disabled, so Rails won't confess all to total strangers. Only users coming in from localhost (on the same machine) will see the full report. Instead, most users will get much briefer error messages, and you'll need to check the logfiles to figure out what's causing those error messages. The logs will also have much more concise reporting, especially of database requests.

```
config.whiny_nils = false
```
In development mode, Rails raises an exception if you try to call a method on an object whose value is nil. In production mode, it doesn't. You have to be responsible for catching this kind of error, likely through formal testing and trying the application out in development mode.

```
config.log_level = :info
```
Development logs are much terser, shifting from :debug-level reporting to recording only items at :info level or more important.

You can, of course, configure production mode however you'd like in *config/environments/production.rb*, but the defaults probably make sense for most applications. For much more on Rails configuration, see the Ruby on Rails guides (*http://guides.rubyon rails.org/configuring.html*).

Finally, although Rails offers just development, testing, and production environments, you don't likely want to leap from development mode to live production. For anything larger than a trivial application, you'll want to try out your app in production mode on a staging server to make sure everything behaves as expected before putting it into real live production on a server your visitors can reach.

Deploying Is Much More Than Programming

Most of this book teaches you to write Rails applications by yourself, on a single machine. You need to have those skills before you can move on to the challenges of deploying applications to the Web (or even to an intranet), but you'll quickly find there's more to learn. Part of the challenge of learning that, though, is that everyone's path will be different. Even as more and more people use Rails, there are more practices, toolsets, and needs that fragment the way people actually use Rails.

Just a few of those divisions include:

Solitary programmers and teams
This book has assumed that a single reader is working with it, exploring what's here, and writing code. You may have shared it with others, but the kinds of instructions given here are broadly meant for individual learners who can try things out and make their own mistakes.

If you're working in a team environment, those rules will change. Some teams do operate as groups of individuals who work separately and have responsibility for their own territory, but many divide responsibilities. The group may decide on data structures and have one person implement the migrations. A designer may create an overall look for the application and the rest of the team just creates views and styles within that approach. You may never have to think about the remaining deployment questions in this list, because someone else handles them —or you may have to deal with all or parts of them.

Source code management

Whether you work by yourself or as part of a team, you'll probably find some kind of source code management helpful. Filesystems with backups are an OK start, but usually when I need to revert code I find it was from the wrong time-frame for the backup to be helpful.

There are lots of choices in source code management, but the current leader seems to be Git (*http://git-scm.com*). Git makes it easy to have your own local copy with branches for whatever changes you want, supports a variety of collaboration styles, and is getting extra support lately from GitHub (*http://github.com*), which adds a layer of social and management functions on top.

Databases

You've probably been using SQLite as you worked through this book. It's the default for Rails development mode, and by far the easiest choice. Unfortunately, easy stops being a virtue when you have thousands or millions of users to serve— you need speed and scale. While you *can* deploy Rails applications with a SQLite database, it only makes sense for tiny ones, and preferably applications that primarily read rather than write to the database.

The obvious choice for deployment has been MySQL, which scales better and gets along well with Rails. However, some developers are starting to look for more powerful relational databases (like PostgreSQL), and many are looking beyond relational databases to the NoSQL world of CouchDB, MongoDB, Cassandra, and many more. MySQL is still a reasonable place to start, but there are a lot more possibilities to consider now.

Servers, or not really

Putting complex applications on the Web used to be all about servers. You'd buy or lease the biggest or smallest box that fit your needs and your budget, and then you had full control of that server to do whatever you needed.

Today, while you certainly still can have your own servers, you're more likely to rent hosting, and in many cases you're renting a virtual server that only looks like a coherent server to you, but is in reality scattered across a farm of servers supporting many virtual servers. If you're tired of managing servers and all of their details, however, you can instead lease hosting services with Rails at their heart rather than Linux or another operating system. Engine Yard (*http://www.engine yard.com*) and Heroku (*http://www.heroku.com*) both offer Rails services where you think in terms of the application, not in terms of which resources you have to provide to run the application.

(Web) Application servers

There was a while when it seemed that nearly everything on the Web was hosted by the Apache server or Microsoft's Internet Information Server. Rails wasn't a comfortable fit with either of those, and developers explored a lot of possibilities, including Mongrel, lighttpd, and more.

If you're choosing tools for a server, rather than using a cloud service, you may have to figure out what works best here. Common choices include nginx or Apache using Phusion Passenger (*https://www.phusionpassenger.com*) and unicorn (*http://unicorn.bogomips.org*), IIS using FastCGI, or (especially if you're hiding Rails in an enterprise environment) various approaches using JRuby to run Rails in a Java environment. (And no, deploying to production using WEBrick is not a good idea, unless you expect a very limited number of users.)

Testing tools and approaches

Chapter 12 introduced you to testing with Rails's own tools, which will certainly get you started. Testing, though, is somewhere between a practice and a religion in the Rails community, with many different sects offering different tools and methodologies.

If you're working on a team, you probably need to learn the approach your team is using. If not, or if you get to decide what the team uses, you have a lot of choices ahead of you. RSpec and Cucumber are among the most popular tools, but different levels of testing—unit, functional, integration, performance, stress, and security—all have toolsets and methodologies.

Deployment tools

There's much more to deploying an application these days than copying over some files, modifying configuration, and maybe restarting a server. It's one thing to run a migration adding fields, copying data into them from old fields, and then deleting the old fields in the quiet of SQLite at your desk, but are you ready to do that on a live public system with real data? Or to switch other supporting tools in and out?

Tools like Capistrano (*https://github.com/capistrano/*) let you manage the Rails part of changes to your application, and you may also want to look into Chef or Puppet for broader provisioning support, especially on multiple machines. For a lot more information on this side of Rails, see *Enterprise Rails* (O'Reilly, 2008).

Monitoring and metrics tools

You've tested your code, deployed it, and made sure it works. How do you know it keeps working? How do you know how well it works? How do you figure out why it works so well—or not so well?

There are all kinds of tools for monitoring your site, working at all kinds of levels. Cloud providers may provide you with their own metrics, and servers have logs, but many different tools can aggregate, visualize, and let you manipulate data. Nagios, Ganglia, Cacti, and many more are available. For a simpler start, you might try the Exception Notification gem (*http://bit.ly/2aTIfA2*).

Update strategies

OK, you have all of those parts. Your app is up and running, and you have happy users.

How often do you update your application? What kinds of updates will you make, and how will you make sure they don't disrupt your user's expectations and experience? This is less about tooling and more about project decisions, but as with everything else, there are a lot of decisions to make.

Joining the Rails Ecosystem

You've done a lot of practical work now, but what can you learn and share?

Keep Up with Rails

Rails 5 was the latest and greatest when this book was updated, but Rails continues to evolve. An easy way to keep an eye on Rails is to visit the Ruby on Rails website (*http://rubyonrails.org*) for core Rails development announcements.

If you'd like to talk rather than read, the #rubyonrails IRC channel (*http://irc.lc/free node/rubyonrails*) is usually busy. Additionally, in email, the rubyonrails-talk list (*https://groups.google.com/group/rubyonrails-talk*) churns through 40 or more messages a day, at all levels of difficulty.

Screencasts and podcasts are another good way to learn more about Rails. For many years Rails Casts (*http://railscasts.com*) was the gold standard for Rails screencasts. However, as of this writing, these screencasts are out of date. That being said, much of the information is still very relevant, and worth taking a look. For more up-to-date screencasts, check out Go Rails (*https://gorails.com*). In addition, you can find sceencasts for most of the chapters in this book at this book's website (*http://learning rails5.com/screencasts*).

Ruby

Ruby is an immensely powerful and flexible language. It makes it possible, even sometimes easy, to perform complicated tasks in a few lines of code. Its metaprogramming capabilities and facilities for creating domain-specific languages (DSLs) allow developers to create frameworks optimized for particular tasks. Rails takes full advantage of these features and offers an opportunity to learn how they can simplify application development.

At the same time, though, these features can be among the most confusing, as they don't look quite like the normal Ruby programming you'd find in an ordinary tutorial. They can make reading documentation and source code difficult when you're not familiar with the techniques being used.

Once you've gotten comfortable in Rails, learning more Ruby is probably the best way to jump-start your learning process. A thorough understanding of Ruby will let you write more efficient and sometimes even more readable code. It will help you to look through the Rails source code when documentation isn't quite clear enough about what something is supposed to do. It will let you repackage your functionality as libraries or plug-ins, making it easier to reuse your code.

Part of the promise of Rails is that you don't need to write a lot of code to get things done, but once you've started applying Rails, you'll want to know a lot more about Ruby. When you're ready to explore more deeply, try *The Ruby Programming Language* (O'Reilly, 2008), *The Well-Grounded Rubyist* (Manning, 2009), *Eloquent Ruby* (Addison-Wesley, 2011), *Programming Ruby* (Pragmatic Programmers, 2009), or the *Ruby Cookbook* (O'Reilly, 2015).

Working with and Around Rails

Rails is a powerful set of tools. What if you don't need that power, though, and want to do a lot less?

One of the best features of Rails is that it runs on top of Rack (*http://rack.github.io*). Rails uses Rack to process HTTP requests, but because it runs on Rack it can be combined with other pieces built on Rack, whether you're in development mode or in production. Most of the tools for hosting and deploying Rails expect Rack as the base, and can work with other applications or frameworks built on Rack.

If you're building a tiny application that needs to do one thing and do it well, you may want to explore writing applications directly on top of Rack. Devise, built on Warden, and described in Chapter 14, is built this way. Because it plays more of a supporting role, it fits neatly lower in the stack than Rails itself. It gains efficiency and isolation, and can rely on callbacks and redirects to communicate its information to Rails.

If the Rack API is too close to the protocol for you, take a look at Sinatra (*http://www.sinatrarb.com*). Sinatra is still extremely small, but provides a DSL for handling HTTP requests. It's still close to the protocol, but automates much of the ordinary HTTP work. It provides a simple routing approach, and can support extensions, helpers, and more. You can even do things like write Sinatra applications that include ActiveRecord, giving you access to parts of Rails that might be convenient while running with much less overhead. If you want to explore Sinatra, take a look at *Sinatra: Up and Running* (O'Reilly, 2011).

Keep Exploring

Rails may not directly meet all of your web development needs, but the community and capabilities are growing fast. At this point, you're probably not yet a Rails expert, but hopefully this book has given you the foundation you need to become one.

An Incredibly Brief Introduction to Ruby

The protean nature of the computer is such that it can act like a machine or like a language to be shaped and exploited.
—Alan Kay

Fortunately, you don't need to know a whole lot of Ruby to get real work done with Rails. The creators of Rails have used many of Ruby's most advanced features to make Rails easy to work with, but you can enjoy the benefits without having to know the details. This appendix explains the basics you'll need to perform typical tasks in Rails and should help you get started. For a lot more detail on Ruby, try *Learning Ruby* (O'Reilly, 2007), *The Ruby Programming Language* (O'Reilly, 2008), *The Well-Grounded Rubyist* (Manning, 2014), or *Head First Ruby* (O'Reilly, 2015). Also check out the tutorials at Try Ruby (*http://tryruby.org*).

 If you've never worked with a programming language before, this appendix may go too fast for you. It's hard to be incredibly brief and cover the basics at the same time. Ruby is a beautiful but sometimes mystifying language. Its syntax is very robust, which means there is a lot of flexibility, but also that it's sometimes difficult to decipher.

Because this is a Rails book, examples will work inside of the Rails framework, in a Rails view and controller, rather than from the command line. If you haven't touched Rails before, it makes sense to read Chapter 1 first and get Rails installed, and then come back here for more instruction.

How Ruby Works

Ruby is an object-oriented language. Although it's often compared to Perl, because Ruby code often looks like Perl, Ruby's object orientation goes much deeper. Practically everything in Ruby is an object.

What does that mean?

Objects are combinations of logic and data that represent a (usually mostly) coherent set of tasks and tools for getting them accomplished. Programming objects aren't quite as concrete as objects in the real world; they're often created and destroyed (or at least abandoned for cleanup later) in fractions of a second. Nonetheless, in those brief moments—or in the hours, days, or years they could also exist—they provide a practical means of getting things done.

In some sense, a program is a big tool chest filled with these objects, and programming is about assembling objects to put into the chest. Ruby provides some starter objects, a means of creating new objects, and, of course, ways to start these objects interacting with each other so that the program actually runs.

There are a few other important things to know about Ruby. They're probably most important if you're coming to Ruby from other programming languages that have different expectations, but they all affect the way you'll write Ruby programs:

- Ruby is an *interpreted* language (rather than being compiled), meaning that it reads through the code and decides how to execute it *while it's running*, rather than reading it and turning it into a highly optimized set of instructions before it actually runs. So, while not as fast as a compiled language like C++ or Java, it also adds a lot of flexibility.

- Ruby also has really *flexible syntax* expectations. Most of the time this makes things easier—you don't need to type parentheses around method parameters most of the time. Other times, however, you'll find yourself facing mysterious error messages because you didn't include parentheses and the situation is slightly ambiguous. (This book tries to warn you about these kinds of situations when they appear in Rails.)

- Ruby uses *dynamic typing*.[1] Some languages (notably Java, C, and C++) expect that the programmer will always know, and always specify, the kind of information he expects to store in a given information container, a *variable*. Locking that down in advance makes it easy to do some kinds of optimization. Ruby has taken another path, leaving variables open enough to contain any kind of information

---

1 Sometimes this is called *duck typing* because when Ruby processes information, "if it looks like a duck and quacks like a duck, it's a duck."

and be created at any time. Again, this allows for a much more flexible approach, in which operations can change what they do based on context. Sometimes, however, it means that things can go wrong in strange and unpredictable ways if something unexpected is in a variable.

- Ruby supports *blocks* and *closures*. You don't need to know how to create methods that work with blocks or closures in order to use Rails, but you definitely do need to know how to call methods that expect a block of code as an argument. At first, your best choice for dealing with these features will be to look at sample code and use it as a foundation rather than trying to step back and figure out how this should work in the abstract.

- Ruby lets advanced developers perform *metaprogramming*, even creating *domain-specific languages* (DSLs), which are kind of like their own miniature programming language focused on a particular task. You don't need to know how to do metaprogramming to use Rails, but you should be aware that Rails uses these techniques. Sometimes you'll encounter something that claims to be Ruby but seems very strange and too specialized to be part of the Ruby language. Odds are good that metaprogramming is involved. As with blocks and closures, it's often best to start out by emulating sample code to work toward figuring it out.

Ruby is a very powerful language. It's not hard to get started in Ruby, but you should at least be aware of these powerful techniques so you can recognize them when you encounter them. Knowing that these possibilities exist may help reduce your frustration when you encounter mysterious difficulties.

How Rails Works

Rails is a set of Ruby objects and naming conventions that together make up a *framework*. Installing Rails is a first step toward building an application, but while it gives you many useful objects that can run happily in a web environment, there's a lot missing, a lot you have to provide.

You can buy a beehive—a set of boxes with frames that the bees will inhabit and fill with honey. It'll have a top, a base, an entrance, a number of useful architectural features, and a nice coat of paint. It looks like a beehive when it's set up. Unfortunately, setting up a beehive is just the first step. To make a beehive work, you have to add bees, who will finish building their home, collect useful nectar and pollen, and make the hive interact with the world.

Rails gives you an empty beehive. You don't add bees, exactly, but you do populate it with your own logic. That logic turns Rails from an empty container into a dynamic application, connected to the outside world and performing the tasks you define.

The rest of this appendix will teach Ruby within the Rails framework, explaining the language in the context you'll likely be using it.

 If you want to stay at the command line, you can also run much of this code in irb, the Ruby command-line interface described in Chapter 11.

Getting Started with Classes and Objects

Most of the Rails files you'll work with and create define classes. (They do so even when they don't have explicit class definitions, as Rails performs some of its magic in the background.) The clearest place to work with objects in Rails is in the controller classes. To get started, therefore, go to the command line and create a new application and a new controller:

```
rails new testbed
...
cd testbed
...
rails generate controller Testbed index
```

For the rest of this appendix, there are only two files that matter: *app/views/testbed/index.html.erb* and *app/controllers/testbed_controller.rb*. For right now, replace the contents of *app/views/testbed/index.html.erb* with:

```
<%= @result %>
```

That will make it easy to see the results of the code in the controller, which is a clearer place to explore Ruby. (@result is a variable whose value various examples will set.)

If you open *app/controllers/testbed_controller.rb*, you'll see the following code. It doesn't yet do anything, except tell the programmer what it is and what it derives from:

```
class TestbedController < ApplicationController
  def index
  end
end
```

The first line, class TestbedController < ApplicationController, tells you two important things. First, it tells you that this file contains a class definition, for a class named TestbedController. Second, it tells you—you can read < as "inherits from"—that this class is descended from ApplicationController. Even though this file is basically empty, it inherits a lot from ApplicationController. Well, actually, even though ApplicationController is almost as empty (see *app/controllers/application_controller.rb* if you're curious), it inherits from ActionController::Base, a key part of the Rails framework that provides a lot of functionality for connecting controllers with requests and data.

 Fortunately, one of the benefits of Rails is that you almost never need to worry about what's actually done in the superclasses, as these ancestors are called. It's strange to say "don't look" in a tutorial—but you really don't have to look, and certainly not at first.

The next two lines define an empty method, index, which the next section will improve on. Finally, the closing end brings the definition of the TestbedController class to its conclusion.

So, this is a class. What's an object?

An object is an *instance* of a class. This class defines what a TestbedController looks like. When Rails gets a request that it thinks requires a TestbedController, it reads the class definition and creates an object that will perform as that class specifies. If necessary, Rails will create places to store the object's data as well as connections to call its methods. Rails may create many different TestbedController objects at the same time (one per request), but all will use the same definition. The process of creating an object from a class definition is called *instantiation*.

Comments

While they don't actually do anything in a Ruby program, comments are critical for making code readable, especially complicated code. Ruby comments start with a # character and continue to the end of that line. If a line starts with #, then the entire line is a comment. If a line starts with code and then includes a # (outside of a quoted string or regular expression), then everything to the right of the # is considered a comment and ignored. For example:

```
# This whole line is a comment
x = 2  # x is assigned the value 2, and the comment is ignored.
```

Comments are useful for humans, especially when you read someone else's code or return to a project after a long while away, but Ruby will just ignore them.

Variables, Methods, and Attributes

TestbedController is a pretty dull class so far. If you start Rails with rails server, and visit *http://localhost:3000/testbed/index*, you'll get a blank page. There's nothing in @result, because TestbedController's index method doesn't actually do anything.

That's easily fixed. Change the definition of index to:

```
class TestbedController < ApplicationController
  def index
    @result = 'hello'
  end
end
```

Now, when you load the page, you'll see "hello" as the result. (This is not exciting enough to deserve a screenshot.)

Variables

@result is a variable, a container for information. Because the name of the variable started with @, it is an *instance variable*, connected to the object in such a way that other objects can see it. That lets the view retrieve it to shows its value. The new line of code assigned (=) an expression to the @result variable, the string hello.

The string was surrounded with single quotes (') to indicate that it was a string, a series of characters, rather than another variable name or something else entirely. If you need to include an apostrophe or single quote inside of a single-quoted string, just put a backslash (\) in front of the quote, as in 'Hello! Ain\'t it a pretty day?'. This is called *escaping* the quote, hiding it from normal processing.

@result could take many different kinds of values; Ruby isn't picky about what goes into its variable containers. You can assign it numbers, objects, boolean values—pretty much anything that comes to mind will work in Ruby. Ruby will do its best to figure out what to do with the values you assign to your variables. For example, you could write:

```
def index
  one = 1
  two = 2
  @result = one + two
end
```

The value of @result would be 3, what you get for evaluating the expression one + two, which leads to adding 1 and 2. (Note that one and two are *local variables*—they don't have an @ in front of their names, and are available only within the index method.) If, however, you'd written:

```
def index
  one = 'one'
  two = 'two'
  @result = one + two
end
```

the value of @result would be onetwo, because the plus operator (+) combines strings sequentially (also called *concatenating* them) instead of adding their numeric values. When Ruby runs that line of code, it checks to see what types are in the values before deciding how the operator will behave.

Ruby isn't as flexible as some other dynamically typed languages. If you set one to 'one' and two to 2, you'd get the error message "can't convert Fixnum into String." Ruby may not keep close track of what types your variables have, but effectively it's your responsibility to do so.

While programmers often think of their code as determining the main flow of logic through an application, from a user's point of view most of what's interesting is what happens to the variables. Does data go to the right place? Is it stored properly? What are the results of calculations on that data?

Variables are the places you store that data as they follow these paths through your applications. You can assign values to variables and change those values. You can perform operations on those values (like +, -, *, /, and much, much more), and pass variables to methods as arguments.

Arrays and hashes

Sometimes a variable should hold more than just one value. It needs to contain a list, a list of lists, or even a collection where values are connected to names. Ruby supports these needs with *arrays*, which are simple lists, and *hashes*, which are collections of named data.

Arrays start out simple. While you can create arrays more programmatically with the Array object, it's easiest to create an array by surrounding a comma-separated list of values with square brackets:

```
my_array = [1, 2, 'tweet']
```

The values can be any Ruby expression. This one happens to mix two numbers and a string. You can reference specific items by number. For example, you might redefine the index method to look like:

```
def index
  my_array = [1, 2, 'tweet']
  @result = my_array[2]
end
```

If you've done a lot of programming, you might not be surprised that the @result variable ends up containing tweet. Why? Because Ruby counts arrays from zero, not from one. my_array[0] is 1, my_array[1] is 2, and, of course, my_array[2] is tweet.

Sometimes you'll want to have lists containing lists. Ruby supports this by letting you put arrays inside of arrays:

```
my_nested_array = [ [1, 2, 'tweet'], [3, 4, 'woof'], [5, 6, 'meow'] ]
```

If you wanted to reach the meow, you'd go to item 2 of the overall array, and then item 2 of the array inside of item 2, as in:

```
def index
  my_nested_array = [ [1, 2, 'tweet'], [3, 4, 'woof'], [5, 6, 'meow'] ]
  @result = my_nested_array[2][2]
end
```

 You can mix arrays of any size you'd like inside of another array, or even mix in ordinary values. There's no requirement that the array structure must be consistent.

Hashes are just a little more complicated. Hashes, also called maps or associative arrays, contain keys and values. Keys are effectively names that correspond to values. Within a given hash, all of the keys have to be unique. (Values can duplicate as necessary, though.) The easiest way to create a hash is with a hash literal:

```
my_hash ={ 'one' => 1, 'two' => 2, 'three' => 'tweet' }
```

To retrieve items from the hash, just call for them by name, as in:

```
def index
  my_hash = { 'one' => 1, 'two' => 2, 'three' => 'tweet' }
    @result = my_hash['two']
  end
```

In this case, @result will contain 2, as that corresponds to the name two. As with arrays, you can also create hashes through the Hash object and its methods.

Both the key and the value can have any type: you can use numbers, strings, or—as Rails often does, especially in method calls—symbols.

Symbols

Rails uses symbols—names preceded by a colon, like :courses or :students—practically everywhere. They get used like variables, to refer to models. They get used as labels for options in method calls. When you're first starting out in Rails, your best option is to study the examples and see where symbols are used and where other kinds of variables are used. Then, just follow the established pattern.

Why does Rails use symbols? The short answer is efficiency. Ruby handles symbols with less processing than strings. The long answer is a lot more complicated than that, involving the metaprogramming glue that holds the framework together. When you're ready to extend the Rails framework yourself, you'll need to learn the details. Until then, you don't need a deep understanding.

Methods

So far, all of the action in these examples has taken place in one method: index. You may have the occasional controller with just one method, but most classes contain more than one method. Methods can call each other, passing each other data, establishing program logic through these many interconnections. A simple demonstration in the same testbed controller shows how this works:

```ruby
class TestbedController < ApplicationController
  def index
    @result = add_them(1, 2)
  end

  def add_them(firstNumber, secondNumber)
    firstNumber + secondNumber
  end

end
```

When index is called, it sets a value for @result. The expression it uses, however, is a call to another method, add_them, which is given two arguments, 1 and 2.

The arguments are shown here in parentheses because most other languages use them, and it's a little easier to imagine what happens. However, the parentheses are optional in Ruby and often omitted.

The add_them method specifies that it takes two parameters, named firstNumber and secondNumber. The expression on the second line, firstNumber + secondNumber, will be evaluated, yielding 3. Ruby methods return the last value they produced, so add_them will tell index that its answer is 3. @result will be set to 3, which will be presented through the view.

If you prefer, you could write return firstNumber + secondNumber, making it explicit that the value is the return value for the method. However, you won't see this done frequently in other people's Ruby code.

Privacy, please

Because of the way Rails routing works, the add_them method could potentially be exposed to the public—though there isn't a view for it, it won't get useful arguments, and we would need to add a route for it. Fortunately, Ruby offers a way to hide such methods from public view while keeping them accessible to other methods in the same class. Just add the keyword private before add_them is defined:

```ruby
class TestbedController < ApplicationController
  def index
    @result = add_them(1, 2)
  end
```

```
    private

    def add_them(firstNumber, secondNumber)
     return firstNumber + secondNumber
    end
   end
```

Methods that follow the private are still available to the other methods in the class, but can no longer be called from outside of it.

 Ruby also offers public and protected keywords for specifying access to methods, but they aren't frequently needed in Rails programming.

super

The methods explicitly listed in the TestbedController class are only a subset of the methods the class actually contains, because of the opening declaration:

```
    class TestbedController < ApplicationController
```

All of the methods that are defined in ApplicationController will also be available in TestbedController. If you want some different behavior in TestbedController, you can *override* methods—defining new methods with the same name and arguments.

Chapter 8 shows how overriding methods can work, but there's frequently one small problem. As often as not, the new method wants to do what the old method did, plus something additional. For example, this was a method overriding the text_field method from ActionView::Helpers::FormBuilder:

```
    class TidyFormBuilder < ActionView::Helpers::FormBuilder
    ....
    def text_field(method, options={})
        label_for(method, options) + super(method, options)
    end
```

The text_field method here wants to create a label, and then call the original method that it was overriding. The call to super isn't to a method called super—it's to the text_field method specified in the ActionView::Helpers::FormBuilder class. This is a common technique when you need to tweak the functionality the framework provides.

Calling methods: advanced options

While you probably won't be writing methods as sophisticated as the ones in the Rails framework itself for a little while, there are a few techniques you should understand for calling those methods.

The first, simpler, one is Rails's frequent use of methods that take an options hash as an argument. While reading the Rails API documentation, you might encounter something like:

```
text_field_tag(name, value = nil, options = {})
```

The method name is `text_field_tag`, and it takes a `name` argument and a `value` argument, which has a default value of `nil`. But what is `options = {}`, especially since most calls to `text_field_tag` don't even use { and }?

`options = {}` provides a way for methods to accept named parameters, taking a hash with named values specified elsewhere in the documentation. In a more formal world, the named parameters would form a hash literal inside of { and }, but Ruby doesn't require that level of formality. You could write:

```
text_field_tag 'Name', 'Jim', {maxlength: 15, disabled: true}
```

but more typically you'll see:

```
text_field_tag 'Name', 'Jim', maxlength: 15, disabled: true
```

In general, named parameters go at the end of the method call, and the curly braces are optional. There are times, however, when the braces are necessary, as noted in the section "Creating Checkboxes" on page 99 in Chapter 6.

The second, harder, one is Rails's use of methods that take an unnamed block of code as an argument. This happens frequently with helper methods as well as in the migration code explored in Chapter 10, but it's a pattern that can appear anywhere. Sometimes, as in the layout issues discussed in Chapter 2, the block passing is just a quiet part of the framework, and you only notice it because of a `yield` call.

The key to recognizing a method that takes a block as an argument is the `&proc` or pair of curly braces at the end of the list of arguments, and examples that show the method wrapping around other code, usually with `do`. The typical form looks pretty similar, whether in straight Ruby code or in ERb view markup. For example, `create_table` in a migration looks like:

```
create_table :awards do |t|
    t.string :name
    t.integer :year
    t.integer :student_id
end
```

A `form_for` call, meanwhile, looks like:

```
<%= form_for([@student, @award]) do |f| %>
  <%= f.error_messages %>
  <p>
    <%= f.label :name %><br />
    <%= f.text_field :name %>
  </p>
  <p>
    <%= f.label :year %><br />
    <%= f.text_field :year %>
  </p>
  <p><%= f.submit "Create" %></p>
<% end %>
```

Each of these calls does something when it is first called. create_table orders the creation of a database table, while form_for creates an HTML form element. They don't just complete and disappear, however—they create a context, using do, that applies until the end statement. The t variable and the f variable provide information that makes it possible for the calls inside of the do to be much shorter (and much less repetitive) than would otherwise be necessary.

When you're working in Ruby code, you'll often use { and } in place of do and end. It's easier to read do and end amidst the < and > of the HTML markup, though.

Rails uses blocks for other purposes as well. Chapter 2 explains how the yield statement lets a method execute code passed to it as a block when it seems convenient. Some helper methods (notably benchmark and cache) use blocks this way.

If you want to become a Ruby pro, studying techniques for using blocks as arguments is a good way to familiarize yourself with ways that Ruby makes amazing things happen in a very compact amount of code.

Attributes

Ruby attributes lie somewhere between methods and variables. Well, actually, attributes are methods, but when used, they feel like variables. Attributes are methods that end in =, and they get called whenever you assign a value to the property with that name. Chapter 8 used a photo= method to capture incoming data when the photo field arrived from a form. You may find use for them eventually in your Rails development, but at the beginning, it's mostly useful to know the technique exists.

Another way to think about it is: attributes are specific properties of an object, while methods are capabilities of an object.

In Ruby all instance variables (attributes) are private by default. This means you don't have access to them outside the scope of the instance itself. The only way to access the attribute is using an accessor method. Fire up irb and give the following example a try:

```ruby
class Foo
  def initialize(color)
    @color = color
  end
end

class Bar
  def initialize(color)
    @color = color
  end

  def color
    @color
  end
end

class Baz
  def initialize(color)
    @color = color
  end

  def color
    @color
  end

  def color=(value)
    @color = value
  end
end

f = Foo.new("red")
f.color # NoMethodError: undefined method 'color'

b = Bar.new("red")
b.color # => "red"
b.color = "yellow" # NoMethodError: undefined method `color='

z = Baz.new("red")
z.color # => "red"
z.color = "yellow"
z.color # => "yellow"
```

In this example the Baz class has a "setter" method that allows you to access (and change or set) the @color variable. Special thanks to Simone Carletti on Stack Overflow (*http://bit.ly/2aTIbAf*) for this example.

Logic and Conditionals

Classes, variables, and simple methods may carry some basic applications a surprisingly long way, but most applications need more logic. This quick tour through Ruby's control structures will give you more tools for building your applications.

Operators

Your program logic will depend on combining variables with operators into expressions. Those expressions then get resolved into results, which may be used to assign values to variables, or to give an answer about whether a test passed or failed. Most Ruby operators should look familiar if you've ever used a programming language before. The following table shows an abbreviated list of operators you're likely to encounter in your first forays into Rails.

Operator	Use(s)
+	Addition, concatenation, making numbers positive
–	Subtraction, removing from collections, making numbers negative
*	Multiplication
/	Division
%	Modulo (remainder from integer division)
!	Not
**	Exponentiation (2**3 is 8, 10**4 is 10,000)
<<	Shift bits left, or add to a collection
<	Less than
<=	Less than or equal to
>=	Greater than or equal to
>	Greater than
<=>	General comparison—less than yields −1, equal returns 0, greater than 1, and not comparable nil
==	Equal to (note that a single = is just assignment and always returns true)
===	Tests to see whether objects are of same class
!=	Not equal to
=~	Tests a regular expression pattern for a match (see Appendix C)
!~	Tests a regular expression pattern for no match
&&	Boolean AND (use to combine test expressions)
||	Boolean OR
and	Boolean AND (lower precedence)
or	Boolean OR (lower precedence)
not	Not (lower precedence)

Operator	Use(s)
..	Range creator, including end value
...	Range creator, excluding end value
defined?	Tests variable definition, returns details

Nearly all of these can take on other meanings, as Ruby lets developers redefine them. Usually they'll behave as you expect, but if they don't, you may need to examine the context you're programming in.

if, else, unless, and elsif

The `if` statement is pretty much at the heart of all computer programming. Though it might be very painful, nearly all code could be rewritten as `if` statements. The basic approach looks like:

```
if expression
  thingsToDo
end
```

To create a simple example again, return to the `TestbedController`:

```
class TestbedController < ApplicationController
  def index
    @result = 'First is greater than or equal to last.'
    first=20
    last=25
    if first < last
      @result = 'First is smaller than last.'
    end
  end
end
```

Because the value of `first` is less than the value of `last`, the `first < last` expression will evaluate to `true`, and `@result` will be set to `First is smaller than last`. For evaluation purposes, anything except for `false` or `nil` will evaluate to `true`. Definitely try changing the values of `first` and `last` and reloading.

The `if` statement has a simple opposite: `unless`. It performs its tasks if the expression returns `false`. While you don't really need it, it can make some code more readable:

```
def index
  @result = 'First is smaller than last.'
  first=20
  last=25
  unless first < last
    @result = 'First is greater than or equal to last.'
  end
end
```

The `unless first < last` statement means exactly the same as `if !(first < last)`.

Sometimes you want to do something more when your first test fails. This calls for the `else` statement, which lets you do things other than what you had planned if your `if` or `unless` succeeded. You could rewrite these two little methods as:

```
def index
  first=20
  last=25
  if first < last
    @result = 'First is smaller than last.'
  else
    @result = 'First is greater than or equal to last.'
  end
end
```

and:

```
def index
  first=20
  last=25
  unless first < last
    @result = 'First is greater than or equal to last.'
  else
    @result = 'First is smaller than last.'
  end
end
```

Using an `else` can both make your code's results more explicit for later developers who have to maintain it, and support your efforts to do different things based on a single test.

There's one last option in regular `if` statements: `elsif`, which combines an `else` and an `if`. You can only use it with `if`, not with `unless`, but you can have as many `elsif`s as you want. A simple example that extends the logic of the previous code is:

```
def index
  first=20
  last=25
  if first < last
    @result = 'First is smaller than last.'
  elsif first == last
    @result = 'First is equal to last.'
  else
    @result = 'First is greater than last.'
  end
end
```

Note that it's `elsif`, not `elseif`, and that the double equals sign (`==`) tests for equality rather than assigning a value. Using a single equals sign in a comparison is a common mistake for new arrivals from other languages. Not only does it assign the value, it always returns `true`, satisfying the conditional test.

There is still one other variation on `if` that you might encounter. Instead of:

```
if expression
  thingsToDo
end
```

it looks like:

```
somethingToDo if expression
```

It's more concise and sometimes more readable, but it can certainly confuse you if you're looking for neatly indented logical statements. If you want, though, you can write:

```
@result = 'First is greater then last' if first > last
```

Shorthand if/else

The `?:` operator isn't precisely a statement, but it works like an abbreviated `if/else` statement. It's mostly used in cases where you need to return a slightly different result for one of two cases. It starts with a test expression, then has a question mark (`?`), then the value returned if the test expression is `true`, then a colon (`:`), and then the value returned if the test expression is `false`. In a previous example we had:

```
def index
  first=20
  last=25
  if first < last
    @result = 'First is smaller than last.'
  else
    @result = 'First is greater than or equal to last.'
  end
end
```

which could be rewritten as:

```
def index
  first=20
  last=25
  @result = (first < last ? 'First is smaller than last.' :
  'First is greater than or equal to last.')
end
```

Again, the message reported would be that `First is smaller than last.`, but you can try changing the values to see what happens.

case and when

If your if statements start sprouting elsifs everywhere, it may be time to switch to case and when statements. These let you specify an expression in the case, and then test it against various conditions. You could rewrite the earlier test as:

```
def index
  first=20
  last=25
  case
    when first < last
       @result ='First is smaller than last.'
    when first == last
       @result ='First is equal to last.'
    when first > last
       @result ='First is greater than last.'
  end
end
```

There are actually many ways to write case statements. If you want to reduce repetition, you might try:

```
def index
  first=20
  last=25
  @result = case
    when first < last
       'First is smaller than last.'
    when first == last
       'First is equal to last.'
    when first > last
       'First is greater than last.'
  end
end
```

This works because case returns a value, and the when clauses just set that value. You can also add an else clause to the end of your case statement, to catch the situation where none of your when clauses matched.

Ruby ignores all when conditions after the first match (also known as a *short circuit*), unlike many C-syntax languages that require break statements to skip over subsequent tests after the first match.

Loops

Evaluations are useful, but sometimes you want to just go around and around until you've tested something a set number of times, a particular condition is met, or you just plain run out of additional data to process. Ruby offers all kinds of ways to go around and around.

while and until

The while and until methods let you create loops that run for as long as the specified condition is true (while) or false (until). Both of these take a do…end block that will be run until the loop decides to stop. A simple example that demonstrates this is counting. With while, counting from 1 to 10 might look like:

```
def index
  count=1
  @result =' '
  while count <= 10 do
    @result = @result + count.to_s + " "
    count= count + 1
  end
end
```

The first time through the loop, count starts out with a value of 1, and the condition count <= 10 evaluates to true, so Ruby proceeds into the loop. The string value of count gets tacked onto the end of @result, with a space for clarity, and then the value of count is increased by one. When the end corresponding to the do is reached, the loop goes back to its start at while and evaluates the condition. If the condition is still true, it goes through the loop again; if not, it ends the loop and goes forward. In this case, it hits the end at the end of the index method, and we're done. The view reports @result, which is "1 2 3 4 5 6 7 8 9 10."

 The to_s method on count converts its numeric value to a string. The to_s method is a general facility for turning Ruby objects into strings. You may want to support this in your own programming, as it is often easier to see the state of something when it can be expressed as a string.

You could write the same thing with until, except that the condition would be reversed:

```
def index
  count=1
  @result =' '
  until count > 10 do
    @result = @result + count.to_s + " "
    count= count + 1
  end
end
```

You will doubtless have more exciting conditions than incrementing variables, but remember: Rails can do many things for you, but it won't protect you from an infinite loop. If your conditions aren't met (or refused for until), your code will go on and on until you halt it or it runs out of resources. Always make sure that the loop will come to a halt by itself, no matter what you feed it.

Just counting

If you know how many times you want something to go around in a loop, you can use the times method on any numeric variable. times takes a block, marked with {}, which it will run that many times. For example:

```
def index
  count=3
  @result =''
  count.times {
    @result = @result + "count "
  }
end
```

will produce "count count count" as the loop goes around three times.

for

A for loop takes a variable and a collection. In its simplest counting approach, the collection is a range, specified with a starting value, then two periods (..), and then an end value. The variable will be set to a value from the range as the loop proceeds, and will advance one step every time the loop hits end until it's done:

```
def index
  count=13
  @result =' '
  for i in 1..count
    @result = @result + i.to_s + " "
  end
end
```

Of course, like most things Ruby, the for loop has greater powers than just this. You can use it to iterate over an array:

```
def index
my_array= [5, 4, 3, 2, 1]
@result =' '
  for i in my_array
    @result = @result + i.to_s + " "
  end
end
```

The loop will go through the array to produce "5 4 3 2 1." You can do even fancier things with hashes, extracting both the key and the value:

```
def index
my_hash= { 'one' => 1, 'two' => 2, 'three' => 3, 'four' => 4 }
@result =' '
  for key,value in my_hash
    @result = @result + "key: " + key + " - value: " + value.to_s + "<br />"
  end
end
```

As of Ruby 2.x hashes keep their order. You'll see a result something like:

```
key: one - value: 1
key: two - value: 2
key: three - value: 3
key: four - value: 4
```

These are a few of the simpler ways to use loops in Ruby. There's much more to explore.

 Ruby offers a vast array of syntax for problem solving. Just because you *can* does not mean you *should* be clever when coding. Be mindful of other developers who may come behind you to interpret something you have written. Sometimes being explicit with an extra line or two of code has more value than composing a clever one-liner that will take more time to decipher later. Or, if you must play mental gymnastics with your code, then be liberal with comments to help others out.

Many More Possibilities

Ruby offers, and Rails can use, a variety of other structures for passing control through a program:

- `return`, `break`, `next`, and `redo` statements for moving through or from loops
- `throw` and `catch` statements for breaking out of code
- Iterators that go beyond loops
- `raise`, `rescue`, `retry`, and `ensure` statements for exceptions

Rails doesn't allow the use of Ruby's `BEGIN` and `END` statements, however.

An Incredibly Brief Introduction to Relational Databases

It's impossible to move, to live, to operate at any level without leaving traces, bits, seemingly meaningless fragments of personal information.
—William Gibson

"I thought the whole point of Rails was that it hid the database and just let me write Ruby code! Why do I need to know about these things?"

Rails has all kinds of features for building web applications, but its foundation component is the way that it lets you get information into and out of relational databases. You *can* build simple applications without knowing much about databases, just telling Rake to do a few things and making sure you gave Rails the right data type for each field. You *don't* need to know Structured Query Language (SQL), the classic language for working with databases.

Building a more complex Rails application, though, really demands at least a basic understanding of how relational databases work. It helps to think about tables and their connections when defining Rails models, at least when you first set them up.

 NoSQL databases are an alternative approach in Rails. Tools like Firebase, CouchDB, MongoDB, and many others have gems available that make them easy to plug into your Rails app. However, traditional SQL databases are still at the heart of Rails, so we will use those examples in this appendix.

Tables of Data

The foundational idea behind relational databases is a simple but powerful structure. Each table is a set of sets, and within a single table all of these sets have the same data structure, containing a list of named fields and their values. For convenience, each set within table is called a *row*, and each field within that row is part of a larger named *column*, as shown in Figure B-1. It looks a lot like a spreadsheet with named columns and unnamed rows.

id	given_name	middle_name	family_name	date_of_birth	grade_point_average	start_date
1	Giles	Prentiss	Boschwick	3/31/1989	3.92	9/12/2006
2	Milletta	Zorgos	Stim	2/2/1989	3.94	9/12/2006
3	Jules	Bloss	Miller	11/20/1988	2.76	9/12/2006
4	Greva	Sortingo	James	7/14/1989	3.24	9/12/2006
...	...	...	...	...	...	...

Figure B-1. The classic row/column approach to tables

The resemblance to a spreadsheet is only superficial, however. Spreadsheets are built on grids, but those grids can have anything in them that any user wants to put in any given place in the spreadsheet. It's possible to build a spreadsheet that is structured like a database table, but it's definitely not required. Databases offer much less of that kind of flexibility, and in return can offer tremendous power because of their obsession with neatly ordered data. Every row within a table has to have the same structure for its data, and calculations generally take place outside of the tables, not within them. Tables just contain data.

You also don't normally interact with database tables as directly as you do spreadsheets, though sometimes applications offer a spreadsheet-like grid view as an option for editing them. Instead, you define the table structures with a *schema*, like that shown in Table B-1, and move data in and out with code.

Table B-1. A schema for the table in Figure B-1

Field name	Data type
id	:integer
given_name	:string
middle_name	:string
family_name	:string
date_of_birth	:date
grade_point_average	:float
start_date	:date

Depending on the database, schemas can be very simple and terse or very complicated and precisely defined. Rails isn't that interested in the details of database schema implementations, however, because its "choose your own database backend" approach limits how tightly it can bond to any particular one. As a result, Rails takes the terse and simple approach, supporting only these basic data types:

```
:string
:text
:integer
:float
:decimal
:datetime
:timestamp
:time
:date
:binary
:boolean
```

In addition to the preceding data types, Postgres also offers the following ones. These are stored as strings if your app is run with a non-Postgres database:

```
:hstore
:json
:array
:cidr_address
:ip_adress
:mac_address
```

Rails won't create a database schema much more complicated than the one shown in Figure B-2, though it will probably add some extra pieces to the schema that you don't need to worry about. There are timestamps, which Rails adds even when you don't ask for them, and IDs, which you don't control but which come up in URLs all the time. The Rails ID serves another function inside the database: it's a *primary key*, a unique identifier for that row in the table. Databases can find information very rapidly when given that key.

id	given_name	middle_name	family_name	date_of_birth	grade_point _average	start_date
1	Giles	Prentiss	Boschwick	3/31/1989	3.92	9/12/2006
2	Milletta	Zorgos	Stim	2/2/1989	3.94	9/12/2006
3	Jules	Bloss	Miller	11/20/1988	2.76	9/12/2006
4	Greva	Sortingo	James	7/14/1989	3.24	9/12/2006
...	...	...	...	...	...	...

id	username	password_hash	role
763	Demetrius	ASVUQP8AZV8	administrator
845	Sharon	8WEROCPA387	class_admin
973	Wilmer	S3DO3VP3A8AS	class_admin
1021	Nicolai	SDF83NC9A2F2J	data_analyst

Figure B-2. Multiple but unconnected tables in a database

Limitations of Tables

There is a huge amount of data out there that doesn't fit neatly into tables. Most of the time, in web applications, you can just put the pieces that do fit into tables, and put the pieces that don't fit easily (like pictures or XML files) in the filesystem somewhere.

If you get into situations where little of the information you're working with fits neatly into tables—lots of hierarchical information, for instance—you may want to go looking for other kinds of tools. You might need a different kind of database, an XML store maybe, and you probably won't find Rails to be your best option. Rails bindings for XML databases *could* be very cool—`ActiveDocument?`—but certainly aren't a mainstream tool at present. NoSQL databases, though, are pioneering this kind of territory.

Connecting Tables

You can build many simple applications on a single-table database, but at some point, working within a single table is just way too constraining. The next step might be to add another table to the application, say for some completely separate set of issues. A users table that identifies users and their administrative roles might be the next thing you add to an application, as shown in Figure B-2.

With these tables, you can write an application that checks to see if users have the rights to make changes to the other table. You could add lots of other disconnected tables to the database as well (and sometimes you'll have disconnected tables), but at the same time, this isn't taking advantage of the real power of relational databases.

They're much more than a place to store information in tables: they're a place to manage related information effectively and efficiently.

So, how does that work? Remember the primary key? Rails uses it to get to records quickly, but the database can also use it internally. That means that it's easy for data in one table to refer to a row in another using that same primary key. That yields structures like the one shown in Figure B-3.

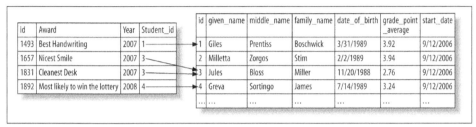

Figure B-3. Connected tables in a database

Establishing connections between tables is simple—one just has to reference the other using its key. When you link to a record in another table by storing the key for that record in your own table, that key is called a *foreign key*. By using foreign keys to connect to primary keys, databases can assemble related information very quickly. Whose "2007 Best Handwriting" award was that? Student 1, whom we can find out is Giles Boschwick by checking the other table.

You can link tables to tables to tables. You might, for example, have a table that lists who presented each award, which links to the award table the same way that the award table linked to the students table, as shown in Figure B-4.

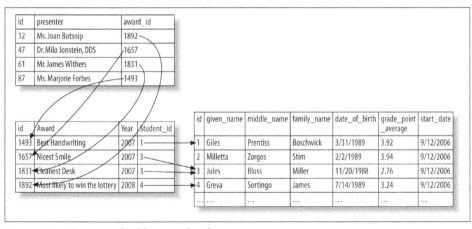

Figure B-4. Connected tables in a database

With tables linked this way, you can ask questions like, "Which presenters gave Jules Bloss Miller awards in 2007?" and get the answer of, "Dr. Milo Jonstein, DDS" and "Mr. James Withers." You—or more likely a program—can follow the IDs and the links to those IDs to come up with the right answer.

Using Tables to Connect Tables

These kinds of links allow the table doing the pointing to establish one connection per row. That might lead to no connections to some rows in the targeted table, one connection to a row, or even many connections to given rows in the targeted table. You can constrain those options, but there's one kind of connection that isn't supported by this simple mechanism. It doesn't allow for many-to-many relationships.

A classic many-to-many relationship is students and classes. Often, each student takes many classes. Each class contains many students. The mechanism shown in Figures B-3 and B-4 isn't very good at this. You *could* create multiple fields for holding multiple links to the same table, but any time you have more than one field pointing at the same table, you're setting yourself up for some complicated processing. It's hard to know how many pointers you'll need, and all of your code would have to look in multiple different places to establish connections. None of this is fun.

It's fine, even normal, to have multiple foreign keys in a table, as long as they all reference different tables.

There is, however, a convenient way to represent many-to-many relationships without creating a tangle. Instead of putting pointers from one table to another inside of the table, you create a third table that contains pointers to the two other tables. This third table is often called a *join table*. If you need to represent multiple relationships between different rows in the two tables to be joined, it's easy—just add another row specifying the connection in the table representing connections.

Figure B-5 shows the students table, a new courses table, and a new table connecting them. (For convenience of drawing, the courses table has its ID values on the right side, and the join table has its mostly useless ID in the middle, but it doesn't really matter. You can leave IDs out of join tables entirely if you want.)

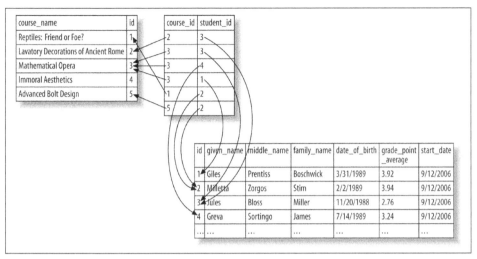

course_name	id		course_id	student_id
Reptiles: Friend or Foe?	1		2	3
Lavatory Decorations of Ancient Rome	2		3	3
Mathematical Opera	3		3	4
Immoral Aesthetics	4		3	1
Advanced Bolt Design	5		1	2
			5	2

id	given_name	middle_name	family_name	date_of_birth	grade_point _average	start_date
1	Giles	Prentiss	Boschwick	3/31/1989	3.92	9/12/2006
2	Milletta	Zorgos	Stim	2/2/1989	3.94	9/12/2006
3	Jules	Bloss	Miller	11/20/1988	2.76	9/12/2006
4	Greva	Sortingo	James	7/14/1989	3.24	9/12/2006
...	...	...	...	...	...	...

Figure B-5. Connected tables in a database

If you work through the connections, you can see that course 5125, Mathematical Opera, is popular, at least in these tiny fragments of what is probably a larger dataset. It has Jules Miller, Greva James, and Giles Boschwick in it. Working the other direction, you can also see that Jules Miller is taking both Mathematical Opera and Lavatory Decorations of Ancient Rome. Using this approach, students can have many courses, and courses can have many students, and all our queries need to do is ask for all of the connections.

Remember, in Rails, you never want to name a table (or other object) "class." Rails has a lot of reserved words that can lead to very strange errors.

Granularity

In addition to linking through keys, there's one other critical aspect of database table design that you should know before embarking on writing applications: data granularity matters! If you read traditional explanations of relational databases, you'll see a lot about *normalization*, which is the process of creating tables that can be easily manipulated through code.

Much of normalization is about reducing duplication, which is usually best done by breaking data into multiple tables, as shown earlier. Another key part, however, is deciding how small (or large) each field in a table should be.

In the students table, shown originally in Figure B-1, each piece of a student's name had a separate field. Why? Well, it's pretty ordinary to want to sort a list of students by last name. It's also normal to leave out middle names in most correspondence. That's much easier to do when the pieces are already broken out, and avoids the problem of figuring out which part of a name is which algorithmically. In the presenter's table in Figure B-4, it probably wasn't worth breaking out those pieces—the name would go on a certificate once and never be examined again.

Doubtless, some purists would want those presenters' titles and names broken into smaller pieces, and you could do that. The question, though, is always going to be what you want to do with the data. If you're not interested in sorting the presenters' names, it may not be worth the extra effort on your part of fragmenting them. Similarly, if you only use street addresses for mailing, it might make sense to keep them as one field rather than separating house number from street number.

Problems, of course, arise when you realize that you really did need to sort a list of addresses by street or presenters by last name. Splitting existing data into smaller pieces once you've already built an application can be extremely annoying. For your first few applications, you may want to err on the side of breaking things up, as it's easier to recombine separate fields than to split them out again.

 Rails makes combining those fragmented fields easier with the com posed_of method.

Once these structures are built, you can write queries that look for those connections —in SQL or in Rails. (Rails will effectively write the SQL query for you.)

Databases, Tables, and Rails

For more than a decade, most web applications that used a database used SQL to move information into and out of databases. SQL is a powerful tool for creating and manipulating database structures, as well as for moving information in and out of those structures, but it's tightly focused on database projects only. You can't build a complete web application using SQL, so historically developers have written the bulk of their applications in another language and then made SQL calls against a database. Developers needed to know both SQL and the other language.

Nearly all modern web frameworks use what are called *object-relational mappers* (ORMs) to interact with the database. Rails takes the position that it's better to manage data and logic in the same language, in this case Ruby. ActiveRecord abstracts the SQL calls away, though they still exist if you look through the development logs. At the same time, Rake and migrations handle the care and feeding of the database, defining and creating (or removing) tables. You define the tables in Ruby, and call `rails db:migrate` to make things happen.

If you already know SQL, you have a bit of an advantage when it comes to debugging Rails applications by checking logs and tinkering inside of the database. You may, however, have a disadvantage in getting started with Rails, as Rails pretty much expects developers to put the SQL toolkit away. There may be times when SQL is still actually necessary, so Rails supports a `find_by_sql` method, but in general, if you find yourself writing SQL, odds are good that you just haven't found a better way to do things in Rails itself.

You do have one critical choice to make regarding databases, however: which database to use with Rails. By default, SQLite is the default database. It's easy to use with minimal configuration, keeps its information in a single (easily transferred) file, and is widely available. However, it is not considered a production database, and should only be used in development environments.

For production you will want to consider heavier-duty options that can handle more simultaneous connections. For many people, MySQL will be the right choice—heftier than SQLite, but not as intimidating as PostgreSQL. Bindings for all three are built into Rails by default, so that part's relatively easy, and bindings for many other databases are available as plug-ins.

You don't need to be a database expert to learn Rails. You will want to have administrators who know how to manage, optimize, and back up whatever database system you choose to use for deployment—but those issues should get addressed after you've finished learning Rails. You may want to pick up *Learning MySQL and MariaDB* (O'Reilly, 2015) if you're new to relational databases and you want to take your knowledge to the next level. If you want details on SQLite, try *Using SQLite* (O'Reilly, 2010).

An Incredibly Brief Guide to Regular Expressions

Music is the soul of language.
—Max Heindel

If music is the soul of language, regular expressions are the soul of text processing. Ruby, like many other languages, contains a powerful text-processing shortcut that looks like it was created by cats walking on the keyboard. Regular expressions can be very difficult to read, especially as they grow longer, but they offer tremendous power that's hard to re-create in Ruby code. As long as you stay within a modest subset of regular expressions, you can get a lot done without confusing anyone—yourself included—who's trying to make sense out of your program logic.

For a more detailed tutorial, see Mike Fitzgerald's *Introducing Regular Expressions* (O'Reilly, 2012). For a much more comprehensive guide to regular expressions, see Jeffrey E. F. Friedl's classic *Mastering Regular Expressions* (O'Reilly, 2006) or Tony Stubblebine's compact but extensive *Regular Expression Pocket Reference* (O'Reilly, 2007). *Regular Expressions Cookbook* (O'Reilly, 2012) by Jan Goyvaerts and Steven Levithan is an excellent compendium of ready-to-use expressions and approaches.

What Regular Expressions Do

Regular expressions help your programs find chunks of text that match patterns you specify. Depending on how you call the regular expression, you may get:

A yes/no answer
Something matched or it didn't.

A set of matches

All of the pieces that matched your query, so you can sort through them.

A new string

If you specified that this was a search-and-replace operation, you may have a new string with all of the replacements made.

Regular expressions also offer incredible flexibility in specifying search terms. A key part of the reason that regular expressions look so arcane is that they use symbols to specify different kinds of matches, and matches on characters that aren't easily typed.

Starting Small

The most likely place that you're going to use regular expressions in Rails is the `vali dates_format_of` method demonstrated in Chapter 7, which is shown here as Example C-1.

Example C-1. Validating data against regular expressions

```
# ensure secret contains at least one number
  validates_format_of :secret, :with => /[0-9]/,
    :message => "must contain at least one number"

# ensure secret contains at least one upper case
  validates_format_of :secret, :with => /[A-Z]/,
    :message => "must contain at least one upper case character"

# ensure secret contains at least one lower case
  validates_format_of :secret, :with => /[a-z]/,
    :message => "must contain at least one lower case character"
```

These samples all use regular expressions in their simplest typical use case: testing to see whether a string contains a pattern. Each of these will test `:secret` against the expression specified by `:with`. If the pattern in `:with` matches, then validation passes. If not, then validation fails and the `:message` will be returned. Removing the Rails trim, we could roughly state the first of these in Ruby as:

```
if :secret =~ /[0-9]/
  #yes, it's there
else
  #no, it's not
end
```

Let's fire up the irb console and give this a try with a clever one-liner. In your console type **irb** and press Return.

```
2.2.3 :001 > secret = "password"
 => "password"
2.2.3 :002 > if secret =~ /[0-9]/ then
```

```
                 puts "yes, it's there" else "no, it's not" end
 => "no, it's not"
2.2.3 :003 > secret = "password1"
 => "password1"
2.2.3 :004 > if secret =~ /[0-9]/ then
                 puts "yes, it's there" else "no, it's not" end
 => yes, it's there
```

The =~ is Ruby's way of declaring that the test is going to compare the contents of the left operand against the regular expression on the right side. It doesn't actually return true or false, though—it returns the numeric position at which the first match begins, if there is a match, and nil if there is none. You can treat it as a boolean evaluator, however, because nil always behaves as false in a boolean evaluation, and other non-false values are the same as true.

There isn't room here to explain them, but if you need to do more with regular expressions than just testing whether there's a match, you'll be interested in the $~ variable (or Regexp.last_match), which gives you access to more detail on the results of the matching. A variety of methods on the String object, notably sub, gsub, and slice, also use regular expressions for slicing and dicing. You can also retrieve match results with $1 for the first match, $2 for the second, and so on—variables created by the match.

There's one other feature in these simple examples worth a little more depth. Reading them, you might have thought that /[0-9]/ was a regular expression. It's a regular expression object, but the expression itself is [0-9]. Ruby uses the forward slash as a delimiter for regular expressions, much like quotes are used for strings. Unlike strings, though, you can add flags after the closing slash, as you'll see later.

If you'd prefer, you can also use Regexp.new to create regular expression objects. (This usually makes sense if your code needs to meet changing circumstances on the fly at runtime.)

The Simplest Expressions: Literal Strings

The simplest regular expressions are simply literal strings. There are plenty of times when it's enough to search against a fixed search pattern. For example, you might test for the presence of the string "Ruby":

```
sentence = "Ruby is the best Ruby-like programming language."
sentence =~ /Ruby/
# => 0 - The first instance of 'Ruby' appears at position 0.
```

Character Classes

Example C-1 tested against letters and numbers, but there are many ways to do that. [a-z] is a good way to test for lowercase letters in English, but many languages use characters outside of that range. Regular expression character classes let you create sets of characters as well as use predefined groups of characters to identify what you want to target.

To create your own character class, use the square brackets: [and]. Within the square brackets, you can either list the characters you want, or create a set of characters with the hyphen. To match all the (guaranteed) English vowels in lowercase, you would write:

    /[aeiou]/

If you wanted to match both upper- and lowercase vowels, you could write:

    /[aeiouAEIOU]/

(If you wanted to ignore case entirely in your search, you could also use the i modifier described earlier: /[aeiou]/i.)

You can also mix character classes in with other parts of a search:

    /[Rr][aeiou]by/

That would match Ruby, ruby, raby, roby, and a lot of other variations with upper- or lowercase R, followed by a lowercase vowel, followed by by.

Sometimes listing all the characters in a class is a hassle. Regular expressions are difficult enough to read without huge chunks of characters in classes. So instead of:

    /[abcdefghijklmnopqrstuvwxyz]/

you can just write:

    /[a-z]/

As long as the characters you want to match form a single range, that's simple—the hyphen just means "everything in between."

There's also a "not" option available, in the ^ character. You can reverse /[aeiou]/ by writing:

    /^[aeiou]/

Regular expressions also offer built-in character classes, listed in Table C-1, that can make regular expressions more readable—at least, more readable once you've learned what they mean.

Table C-1. Regular expression special character classes

Syntax	Meaning
.	Match any character. (Without the m modifier, it doesn't match newlines; with the m modifier, it does.)
\d	Matches any digit. (Just 0–9, not other Unicode digits.)
\D	Matches any nondigit.
\s	Matches whitespace characters: tab, carriage return, newline, form feed.
\S	Matches nonwhitespace characters.
\w	Matches word characters: A–Z, a–z, and 0–9.
\W	Matches all nonword characters.

Escaping

Of course, even in simple strings there can be a large problem: lots of characters you'll want to test for are used by regular expression engines with a different meaning. The square brackets around [0-9] are helpful for specifying that it's a set starting with zero and going to nine, but what if you're actually searching for square brackets?

Fortunately, you can "escape" any character that regular expressions use for something else by putting a backslash in front of it. An expression that looks for left square brackets would look like \[. If you need to include a backslash, just put a second backslash in front of it, as in \\.

Some characters, particularly whitespace characters, are also just difficult to represent in a string without creating strange formatting. Table C-2 shows how to escape them for convenient matching.

Table C-2. Escapes for whitespace characters

Escape sequence	Meaning
\f	Form feed character
\n	Newline character
\r	Carriage return character
\t	Tab character

Modifiers

Sometimes you want to be able to search for strings without regard to case, and you don't want to put a lot of effort into creating an expression that covers every option. Other times you want to search against a string that contains many lines of text, and you don't want the expression to stop at the first line. For these situations, where the underlying rules change, Ruby supports modifiers, which you can put at the end of the expression or specify through the `Regexp` object. A complete list of modifiers is shown in Table C-3.

Table C-3. Regular expression modifier options

Modifier character	Effect
i	Ignore case completely.
m	Multiline matching—look past the first newline, and allow . and \n to match newline characters.
x	Use extended syntax, allowing whitespace and comments in expressions. (Probably not the first thing you want to try!)
o	Only interpolate #{} expressions the first time the regular expression is evaluated. (Again, unlikely when you're starting out.)
u	Treat the content of the regular expression as Unicode. (By default, it is treated the same as the content it is tested against.)
e, s, n	Treat the content of the regular expression as EUC, SJIS, and ASCII, respectively, like u does for Unicode.

Of these, `i` and `m` are the only ones you're likely to use at the beginning. To use them in a regular expression literal, just add them after the closing /:

```
sentence = "I think Ruby is the best Ruby-like programming language."
sentence =~ /ruby/i
# => 8  - "ruby" first appears at character 8.
```

If you want to use multiple options, you can. `/ruby/iu` specifies case-insensitive Unicode matching, for instance.

Anchors

Sometimes you want a match to be meaningful only at an edge: the start or the end, or maybe a word in the middle. You might even want to define your own edge—something is important only when it's next to something else. Ruby's regular expression engine lets you do all of these things, as well as match only when your match is *not* against an edge. Table C-4 lists common anchor syntax.

Table C-4. Regular expression anchors

Syntax	Meaning
^	When at the start of the expression, means to match the expression only against the start of the target (or a line within the target, *when* multiline matching is on).
$	When at the end of the expression, means to match the expression only against the end of the target (or the end of a line within the target, *when* multiline matching is on).
\A	When at the start of the expression, means to match the expression only against the start of the target string, *not* lines within it.

Syntax	Meaning
\Z	When at the end of the expression, means to match the expression only against the end of the target string, *not* lines within it.
\b	Marks a boundary between words, up against whitespace.
\B	Marks something that isn't a boundary between words.
(?=expression)	Lets you define your own boundary, by limiting the match to things next to *expression*.
(?!expression)	Lets you define your own boundary, by limiting the match to things that are *not* next to *expression*.

These make a little more sense if you see them in action. For example, if you only want to match "The" when it's at the start of a line, you could write:

```
/^The/
```

If you wanted to match "1991" when it's at the end of a line, you could write:

```
/1991$/
```

If multiline matching was on, and you wanted to make sure these matches apply only at the start or end of the string, you would write them as:

```
/\AThe/
/1991\Z/
```

The \b anchor is really useful when you want to match a word, not places where a sequence falls in the middle of a word. For example, if you wanted to match "the" without matching "Athens" or "Promethean," you could write:

```
/\bthe\b/
```

Alternately, if you wanted to match "the" *only* when it was part of another word, you could use \B to write:

```
/\Bthe\B/
```

The last two items in Table C-4 let you specify boundaries of your own—not just whitespace or the start or end, but any characters you want.

Sequences, Repetition, Groups, and Choices

Specifying a simple match pattern may take care of most of what you need regular expressions for in Rails, but there are a few additional pieces you should know about before moving on. Even if you don't match something that needs these, knowing what they look like will help you read other regular expressions when you encounter them.

There are three classic symbols that indicate whether an item is optional or can repeat, plus a notation that lets you specify how much something should repeat, as shown in Table C-5.

Table C-5. Options and repetition

Syntax	Meaning
?	The pattern right before it should appear 0 or 1 times.
*	The pattern right before it should appear 0 or more times.
+	The pattern right before it should appear 1 or more times.
{number}	The pattern before the opening curly brace should appear exactly *number* times.
{number,}	The pattern before the opening curly brace should appear at least *number* times.
{number1, number2}	The pattern before the opening curly brace should appear at least *number1* times but no more than *number2* times.

You might think you're ready to go create expressions armed with this knowledge, but you'll find some unpleasant surprises. The regular expression:

```
/1998+/
```

might look like it will match one or more instances of "1998," but it will actually match "199" followed by one or more instances of "8". To make it match a sequence of 1998s, you would write:

```
/(1998)+/
```

If you wanted to specify, say, two to five occurrences of 1998, you'd write:

```
/(1998){2,5}/
```

The parentheses can also be helpful when specifying choices, though for a slightly different reason. If you wanted to match, say, 2013 or 2014, you could use | to write:

```
/2013|2014/
```

The | divides the whole expression into complete expressions to its left or right, rather than just grabbing the previous character, so you don't need parentheses around either 2013 or 2014. Nonetheless, if you wanted to do something like match 2013, 2014, or 2017, you might not want to write:

```
/2013|2014|2017/
```

You could instead write something more like:

```
/201(3|4|7)/
```

 Parentheses also "capture" matched text for later use, and that capturing may determine how you structure parentheses. It's probably not the first place you'll want to start, though.

Greed

There's one last feature of the repetition operators that can cause unexpected results: by default, they're *greedy*. This isn't a question of computing virtue, but rather one of how much content a regular expression can match at one go. This is a common issue in things like HTML, where you might see something like:

```
<a href= "http://example.com" >Example.com</a>
```

You might think you could match the HTML tags simply with an expression like:

```
/<.*>/
```

But instead of matching the opening tag and closing tag separately, that expression will grab everything from the opening < to the closing > of </a>, because it can. If you want to restrain a given expression so that it takes the smallest possible matching bite, add a ? behind any of the repetition operators:

```
/<.*?>/
```

Greed matters more when you use regular expressions to extract content from long strings, but it can yield confusing results even in supposedly simple matching. If you have mysterious problems, greed is a good thing to check for.

More Possibilities

Regular expressions have nearly infinite depth, and this appendix has barely begun to scratch the surface, either of expressions or the ways you can use them in Ruby and Rails. A few of the things this incredibly brief guide hasn't been able to include are:

- Using expressions to fragment a string into smaller pieces
- Referencing earlier matches later in an expression
- Creating named groups
- Commenting regular expressions
- A variety of special syntax forms using parentheses

For more detail on using regular expressions specifically with Ruby, see *The Ruby Programming Language* by David Flanagan and Yukihiro Matsumoto.

Glossary

Speaking in Rails

Understanding is nothing else than conception caused by speech.
—Thomas Hobbes

Rails, like many communities, has developed its own language. You need to know a lot of that language to understand what other people are saying, even when those people are trying to be helpful. This glossary gives you a quick guide to some common terms used in Rails that aren't obvious to outsiders and provides the extra Rails meanings for words used elsewhere that have acquired additional meaning in Rails. Hopefully this will make it easier for you to understand Rails documentation and conversation, but of course, new terms will emerge over time:

ACID

Atomicity, Consistency, Isolation, Durability. A set of principles, usually implemented with relational databases and transactions, that are intended to ensure data reliability. Rails is not designed with ACID as a priority, though transactions are available as a plug-in. (In a different meaning, there are also a variety of "Acid" tests for CSS implementation conformance.)

ActionCable

Introduced in Rails 5, ActionCable extends Rails functionality with real-time message passing with WebSockets.

ActionController

The part of the Rails library that directly interacts with incoming HTTP requests, including routing, parameter passing, session management, and deciding how to render a response. Controller objects are the main way in which Rails developers interact with ActionController.

ActionMailer

The part of the Rails library that manages incoming and outgoing email.

ActionPack

The combination of ActionController and ActionView, which provides a complete package for dealing with and responding to HTTP requests.

ActionView

The part of the Rails library that generates responses to HTTP requests, based on information received from ActionController.

ActiveRecord

The Rails library that handles mappings between the database and Ruby classes. ActiveRecord is pretty much the foundation of Rails, but it can be used outside of Rails as well. ActiveRecord is an implementation of the object-relational mapping (ORM) pattern of the same name described by Martin Fowler.

ActiveSupport

A collection of classes that were developed for Rails, but that can be used in any Ruby environment.

acts_as

A naming convention used in Rails, typically with plug-ins, to indicate that part of a model operates using code provided elsewhere. This convention is not as common as it once was, but still may be seen in legacy Rails apps.

adapter

Code, usually Ruby or Ruby and other languages, that connects ActiveRecord to a specific database.

aggregation

Often used to describe collecting RSS or Atom syndication feeds, but has another meaning in Rails. Aggregation lets you create simpler ways to access combinations of data using the `composed_of` method. You might do this to combine first and last names, or address parts, or other pieces that can be broken down but that are often conveniently used together.

Agile

A variety of software development techniques that tend to focus on smaller-scale iterative development rather than on top-down "waterfall" design and implementation.

Ajax

Originally Asynchronous JavaScript and XML, this former acronym now refers more broadly to web development where methods within a page call back to the server and make smaller changes to a page rather than calling for a complete refresh every time. Ajax applications often resemble desktop applications more closely because of this added flexibility.

assertion

Claims made in test methods whose results will be reported.

assets

In Rails parlance, assets are information outside of your application and its database—images are a classic example—that are incorporated by reference. Assets don't need to be entirely outside of the application, however. Chapter 8 shows how to have Rails manage the arrival of image assets.

association

A relationship between fields in a database.

Atom editor

A common text editor used for developing Rails apps.

Atom format

An XML-based format originally used for syndicating information from blogs, but now moving into many applications where data needs to flow from site to site.

attributes

Attributes are information about an ActiveRecord model class, such as what fields it contains, what types they hold, and so on. Usually, Rails figures out what the attributes are directly from the application database, which knows what they are because they were set by migrations.

authentication

The process of establishing the identity of a user (or of another process) by verifying the validity of some kind of credentials. Using usernames and passwords as credentials is a classic authentication mechanism, but many others are possible.

authorization

The process of granting privileges to an authenticated user. Examples of privileges include rights to execute certain commands and access to specific data. These restrictions can be enforced in the view, in the controller, or in both.

Basecamp (http://www.basecamphq.com/)

A collaboration tool developed by *37signals* and *DHH*. DHH realized while building Basecamp that the underlying framework could be reused for a lot of other projects, and that became the foundation of Rails.

Behavior-driven development (BDD)

An extension of test-driven development (TDD) that leverages a simple, domain-specific scripting language.

benchmark

    Code used to determine and compare performance. Generic benchmarks used to test things like CPU performance are the most common usage, but you could create your own benchmarks to test performance specific to your application.

block

    Chunks of code that can be passed among Ruby methods. Rails uses blocks to implement much of its view functionality, using this technique to connect code from different files into a coherent program.

Bootstrap

    A JavaScript frontend framework developed by Twitter for creating responsive, mobile-first websites. To "Bootstrap an app" means you have added Twitter Bootstrap to an app along with some of its style and responsiveness.

Builder

    An API used to generate XML files from Ruby objects.

business rules

    Logic that is specific to a given application, and often specific to a given business. It specifies rules for data that go beyond the computer-specific "This variable must be a string" to more complex rules like, "This date must be no earlier than x and no later than y" or "All expense reports must come with explicit and authenticated approval before consideration for payment."

CamelCase

    Rails does not do CamelCase, except in class names. CamelCase uses uppercase letters to identify the beginnings of new words. Rails more typically keeps everything lowercase, using underscores (_) to separate the words.

Capistrano

    A Ruby tool for automating running scripts on remote computers, typically used to deploy Rails applications and their updates.

class

    A collection of methods and properties that together provide a definition for the behavior of objects.

component

    A bad idea that disappeared in Rails 2.0, becoming a plug-in. Components mixed rendering and controller logic, and created applications that were both messy and slow.

console

    A command-line interface to Rails applications, which is accessible through `rails console` (also see *irb*).

content type

In HTTP requests (and network requests generally), content types are used to identify the kind of content being sent. Content types are often called MIME types, from their original development as Multipurpose Internet Main Extensions.

controller

The switchboard for Rails applications, controllers connect information coming in from requests to appropriate data models and develop response data that is then presented through views.

cookie

A small (typically less than 4 kilobytes) chunk of text that is stored in a user's browser and sent to the server that created it along with requests. Cookies can be used to track users across multiple requests, making it much simpler to maintain state across requests. In general, however, you should never store any significant information in cookies.

cron

A Unix approach to scheduling tasks that need to run on a regular basis. "Cron jobs" are managed through the crontab configuration file, and the cron daemon makes sure they get executed as requested. (Rails itself doesn't use cron, but you could use cron to manage periodic background housekeeping on a server, for instance.)

CRUD

Create, Retrieve, Update, and Delete (sometimes Destroy). The basic functions needed by most data manipulation programs. *SQL* is very CRUD-like, as is *REST*.

CSS

Cascading Style Sheets, a vocabulary for specifying how precisely web pages should be displayed on screen, in print, or in other media. In a Rails application, a CSS stylesheet is typically an extra file or files kept in the *public/stylesheets* directory, referenced from each view that uses it.

CSV

Comma-separated values, a common if basic method for sharing tabular data.

CVS

Not the American pharmacy/convenience store, but the Concurrent Versioning System, used to manage different versions of programs and related files. In Rails, CVS has typically been replaced by *Subversion* or *Git*.

DELETE

An HTTP verb that means what it says—to delete the resource the DELETE request is addressed to.

deployment
> Putting something out in the "real world," typically moving an application from development to operation.

development
> The mode in which you'll most likely modify and create code. In Rails, development uses a different database and settings from the test or production modes.

DHH
> David Heinemeier Hansson, the creator of Rails and its lead developer. For more DHH, see his blog, *http://www.loudthinking.com/*.

DOM
> Document Object Model, the standard API for manipulating HTML documents in a web browser. (It's also used for XML and HTML outside of the browser.)

DRY
> Don't Repeat Yourself—a central principle of Rails development.

duck typing
> "If it walks like a duck and quacks like a duck, it's a duck." A way of determining what type an object has by looking at what it contains and how it behaves, rather than by looking for an explicit label on it. Duck typing is built into the Ruby language.

dynamic scaffold
> Automatically generated HTML that would let you tinker with a model and the underlying data without actually creating any views. Discontinued in Rails 2.0 in favor of *static scaffolding*.

dynamic typing
> See *duck typing*, described earlier.

Edge Rails
> The latest and (sometimes) greatest version of Rails, Edge Rails lets you develop with the most recent updates to the framework. Exciting for advanced developers, but potentially explosive for beginners. (Note that you can *freeze* Rails versions if one goes by that you really liked or, worse, a new one appeared that broke your code.)

ERb
> Embedded Ruby, the syntax used for Rails views and layouts. ERb lets you mix HTML (or other text-based formats) with Ruby code.

Erubis

An implementation of ERb that is both faster and offers several extensions to ERb. For more information, see Kuwata Lab's Erubis page (*http://www.kuwata-lab.com/erubis/*). You can use Erubis with or without Rails.

exception

A signal sent by a method call as it terminates (using `raise`) to indicate that things didn't go correctly. You can deal with exceptions using `rescue`.

filter

Controller code that lets you wrap your actions with other code that will get run before, after, or around your actions' code.

Firebug

A Firefox plug-in for debugging JavaScript and a wide variety of other aspects of web development.

fixture

Data created for the explicit purpose of testing your Rails applications. Fixtures are specified in YAML and provide a customizable set of data you can use to check the functionality of your Rails code. They are stored in the *test/fixtures* directory.

flash

While you can include Adobe Flash content as external *assets* in your Rails application, `flash` in a Rails context more frequently refers to a method for passing objects between actions. You can set a message in the controller using `flash` and then retrieve and display that message in a view, for example.

form builder

A class containing methods for creating HTML forms. Form builders are typically used to create consistent-looking interfaces across an application and to present complex aspects of your models that need additional interface support.

fragments

Pieces of views that you've asked Rails to cache so that they will be available on subsequent requests.

freezing

Locking your Rails application down so that it runs on a particular version of Rails, no matter what version of Rails you install on your computer more generally. For production applications, this provides a much more reliable running environment. You freeze and unfreeze through the Rake tool.

gem

A package for a Ruby program or library that makes it easy to install across systems. Rails is distributed as a gem.

Gem

A package manager for the Ruby programming language that provides a standard format for distributing Ruby programs and libraries.

generate

Generate, or `rails generate` as it is called from the command line, is a program you can use to have Rails create a wide variety of types of code for you. In general, when creating new functionality, you should let Rails generate much of the code and then customize it, rather than writing from scratch.

GET

The most commonly used HTML request, which has the general meaning of "retrieve content from the specified URL." GET requests are supposed to be *idempotent* and, despite the availability of query parameters, should not be used to change information in an application.

Git

An application for sharing code and code development across many computers and developers. Ruby on Rails itself is now developed using Git to store and manage the code.

GitHub

A website (*http://github.com*) that provides hosting for your Git repositories, version control, and sharing of code and projects.

h

A method commonly used in the past for escaping potentially dangerous content —that is, removing HTML content that could create security problems. Rails now uses h by default.

hash

A collection of name/value pairs. You can retrieve the values by asking for them by name. (You need to know the name to do that, of course!)

HEAD

An HTTP verb that is very similar to GET, but retrieves only the headers, not the body of the request.

helper method

Provides support for commonly performed operations in view code. Helpers are a little less formal than *form builders*, which typically have more understanding of the context in which they work. Rails provides a wide variety of helper meth-

---

ods for common tasks like generating HTML, and you can add your own helper methods as well.

HTML

HyperText Markup Language, a common language used to present information over the Web. HTML files define web pages, including content, formatting, scripts, and references to external resources.

HTML5

A markup language used for structuring and presenting content on the World Wide Web. It was finalized, and published, on 28 October 2014 by the World Wide Web Consortium (W3C). This is the fifth revision of the HTML standard since the inception of the World Wide Web. Its core aims are to improve the language with support for the latest multimedia while keeping it easily readable by humans and consistently understood by computers and devices (web browsers, parsers, etc.).

HTTP

HyperText Transfer Protocol, along with HTML, is the foundation on which the Web is built. HTTP supports requests that include a verb (like GET, POST, PUT, or DELETE) along with a variety of supporting information. Those requests are then answered by a responding server, which reports a [Response Code] and hopefully some information useful to whoever initiated the request. HTTP is itself built on top of TCP/IP, typically using port 80 to receive requests.

HTTPS

Like HTTP, but encrypted. Technically, the HyperText Transfer Protocol over Secure Socket Layer. HTTPS works much like HTTP, except that the web server adds a layer of encryption using public key certificates, it runs on port 443, and browsers are typically much more cautious about caching information that arrived over HTTPS.

id

An identifying value. In Rails, usually the primary key from a table of data, used for quick access to a particular row or object. In HTML, a unique identifier for one element in a document, often used for styling.

idempotent

A fancy word for a specific meaning of "reliable." If an action is idempotent, you can perform that action repeatedly without changing the result.

irb

A command-line shell prompt for interacting with Ruby directly, irb lets you try out code in a much simpler environment than Rails.

IRC

Internet Relay Chat, a key part of the communications that hold the Rails community together. You can find a lot more information on Rails and IRC, including servers, channels, and clients, at the Ruby on Rails wiki (*http://rubyonrails.org/community/*).

iterator

A method that loops through a set of objects, working on each object in the set once.

JavaScript

A high-level, dynamic, untyped, and interpreted programming language traditionally used in client-side programming.

jQuery

The most commonly used JavaScript framework, available at the jQuery website (*http://jquery.com*). Now included in Rails 3.x and newer.

JSON

JavaScript Object Notation, a text-based format for exchanging objects. Douglas Crockford "discovered" it already existing inside of JavaScript and made it a popular interchange format. It's often seen as a more programming-oriented complement or competitor to *XML*. (It's also a subset of *YAML*.)

layout

A file containing the beginning and end of the HTML documents to be returned by views, allowing views to focus on the content of documents rather than on the headers and footers.

linking

Rails supports traditional HTML linking, but in many cases you'll want to use a helper method to create links between the components in your applications.

mass assignment

A convenience feature that turned into a headache. Mass assignment made it easy to pass ActiveRecord a set of parameters and have it assign values based on those parameters automatically. Unfortunately, if the parameters contained unexpected data, perhaps added by a query string, it could assign values you didn't want, opening the door to attackers. These attacks were prevented in Rails 4 and later by requiring strong parameters in controllers specifying which fields can be mass-assigned.

Matz

Yukihiro Matsumoto, creator and maintainer of the Ruby language. "Matz is nice, and so we are nice" (MINASWAN) is a key principle of Ruby culture.

Merb

Originally "Mongrel plus ERb," Merb was a Ruby-based MVC framework that was smaller and more modular than Rails—but was absorbed into Rails 3.x.

method

A unit of code that accomplishes a task.

migration

Instructions for changing a database to add or remove structures that Rails will access. The Rake tool is used to apply or roll back migrations.

mock object

A technique for testing Rails applications that creates objects that expect particular methods to be called, and that exposes more information on the objects for easier debugging.

mod_rails

See Passenger.

model

Code that handles the interactions between Rails and a database. Models contain data validation code—code that combines or fragments information to meet user or database expectations—and pretty much anything else you need to say about the data itself. However, models do *not* contain information about the actual structure or schema of the data they manage—that is kept in the database itself, managed by *migrations*.

Mongrel

A Ruby-based web server now used as the default server for Rails applications when run from the command line. In production, a "pack of mongrels" often runs behind an Apache web server, connecting HTTP requests to Rails.

MVC

Model-View-Controller, an architecture for building interactive applications that lies at the heart of the Rails framework. (See Chapter 3 for a lot more information.)

MySQL

A popular open source relational database, commonly used to store data for larger Rails applications.

naming conventions

The glue that holds Rails together, letting applications figure out which pieces connect to which pieces without requiring a formal mapping table. Rails makes naming conventions feel more natural by supporting features like pluralization.

nginx

> An asynchronous event-driven web server and mail proxy available from the nginx website (*http://nginx.org*).

nil

> A value that means "no value." Nil also evaluates to `false` in comparisons.

nokogiri

> A HTML, XML, SAX, and Reader parser used in Rails to search documents via XPath or CSS3 selectors.

object

> An instance of a class, combining the logic from the methods of the class with properties specific to that particular object.

ORM

> Object-relational mapping, the hard part of getting object-oriented languages and relational databases to work together. Rails addresses this using *ActiveRecord* and makes it (mostly) transparent through *naming conventions*.

pagination

> Chopping up long lists of data into smaller, more digestible chunks. In Rails 2.0, pagination moved out from the core framework into plug-ins, most notably `will_paginate`.

partial

> A piece of view code designed to produce part of a document. Multiple views can then reference the partial so that they don't have to repeat the logic it already contains. Partial names are prefixed with _.

Passenger

> An Apache module, also called *mod_rails*, for deploying Rails applications behind an Apache web server. Also works with *nginx*.

PATCH

> An HTTP method that can be used to update partial resources, unlike PUT, which updates an entire resource.

Pickaxe book

> *Programming Ruby*, the first major book on Ruby, published by the Pragmatic Programmers. Its third edition covers Ruby 1.9.

plug-in

> Additional code, often packaged as a *gem*, that you can use to provide additional functionality to Rails.

pluralization

A feature of *ActiveRecord* that generates much controversy. Models have singular names, like person, while views and controllers use plurals of those names, because they work with many instances of the models. Rails has a set of defaults that handle both standard English pluralization and some common irregulars, like person and people, child and children. There are cases where pluralization doesn't work in English, but fortunately they rarely affect programming.

POST

An HTTP method that sends information to a given URI. POST is mapped to CREATE in REST-based Rails applications, though POST has been used as a general "send-this-stuff-over-there-via-HTTP" method in the past.

Postfix

A commonly used mail server on Unix and Linux computers.

PostgreSQL

A more powerful but somewhat more daunting open source database that is frequently used by developers who want more control than MySQL provides, or access to specific extensions, like the geographic data work in PostGIS.

Pound

A proxying load balancer designed to pass HTTP requests from a web server to other servers in the background.

Pragmatic Programmers

The Pragmatic Programmers, Dave Thomas and Andy Hunt, and their publishing company (*http://www.pragprog.com*). They've written and published a wide variety of books on Ruby and Rails, and run related training courses.

private

Private methods and properties appear in Ruby classes after the `private` keyword, and are only accessible to other code in that same class.

proxy server

Proxy servers (or proxies) receive requests on one end and then resubmit them to other servers. Proxies can be used to manage performance, to provide caching, to hide servers from users (and vice versa), for filtering, or for pretty much anything you want to do with an HTTP request between the request and the response.

Puma

Default development web server as of Rails 5.

PUT

An HTTP method used to send a file to a URI. In Rails RESTful routing, PUT maps to UPDATE, replacing content that was previously there with new content.

quirks mode

A technique used by several browsers to support web pages formatted with older (broken) browsers in mind, while still allowing developers to specify that their pages should be processed using newer and generally more correct standards.

RailsConf

A conference focused on Rails, usually held once a year in North America and once a year in Europe. For more information, see the RailsConf website (*http:// railsconf.com*).

Rake

A command-line tool that originally was Ruby's replacement for the *make* build tool commonly used by Unix applications. Thanks to its scriptable extensibility, it has turned into a one-stop toolkit for applying *migrations* to databases, checking up on routes, *freezing* and unfreezing the version of Rails used by a given application, and many more tasks.

RDoc

The documentation generator used by most Ruby applications, including Rails. The Rails API documentation all gets built through RDoc.

redirect

Responding to a request to one URI by telling the requester to visit a different URI.

regex

Regular expression, a compact if sometimes inscrutable means of describing patterns to match against targeted text.

render

To convert data from one form to another, usually to present it. Web browsers render HTML into readable pages, while Rails views render data from Rails into HTML that gets sent to users' web browsers.

request

In HTTP, a request is a message sent from a client to a server, identifying a resource (a URI) and providing a method—usually GET, PUT, POST, or DELETE.

resource

For Rails development purposes, it's probably easiest to think of a resource as code identified by a URI (or URL). It's the code that will get called once Rails routing has examined the request and decided where to send it. (Outside of Rails, it can be a deeply philosophical notion at the heart of web architecture and infinite debates about web architecture.)

response

In HTTP, a response is a message sent from a server to a client in response to a request. It generally includes a status code as well as headers describing the kind of response, and data to present the client.

REST

Not a vacation. Technically, "Representational State Transfer," but really just a sane way to handle interactions on the Web that takes full advantage of the underlying web architecture instead of chucking it and building something entirely different. Rails 2.0 includes a lot of features designed to make building REST-based applications easier. (See Chapter 5 for a lot more detail.)

REXML

An XML parser built into Ruby.

RJS

An obsolete kind of Rails template used to generate JavaScript, typically for Ajax applications.

RMagick

A *gem* that lets Ruby applications manipulate graphics using the ImageMagick library.

route

To send from one place to another. In Rails, the routing code examines requests coming to the server from various clients and decides based on their URIs which controller should respond to them.

RSS

An acronym of various meanings that refers to several different XML formats for syndicating information from one site (typically weblogs, but also newspapers, periodicals, and other websites) to clients and other servers that might be interested.

rvm

The Ruby Version Manager, which helps you manage both versions of Ruby itself and Ruby resources, notably gems. More information is available at the RVM website (*https://rvm.io*).

scaffold

Code that gets you started, much as scaffolding on a construction project lets workers get to the parts of a building they need to modify. Scaffolding most fre-

quently refers to the REST-based set of models, views, and controllers created by
`rails generate scaffold`.

scale

Scale reflects size. If a program scales, it can survive growing rapidly from serving only a few simultaneous users to serving thousands or even millions of users.

session

A series of HTTP interactions between a single client and the web server. Sessions are usually tracked with *cookies* or with explicit logins.

singleton

An object that has only one instance in a given application. You shouldn't (and
generally can't) create more than one of it.

SOAP

Originally the Simple Object Access Protocol, it proved not very simple, not necessarily bound to objects, and not exactly a protocol. SOAP is the foundation of
most web services applications that don't use REST, taking a very different
approach to communications between applications.

SQL

The Structured Query Language is a common foundation used by databases to
create and destroy structures for holding data, and to place and retrieve data
inside of them. While SQL is extremely useful, Rails actually hides most SQL
interactions so that developers can work with Ruby objects only, rather than having to think in both Ruby and SQL.

SQL injection

A code injection technique, used to attack data-driven applications, in which
malicious SQL statements are inserted into an entry field for execution (e.g., to
dump the database contents to the attacker).

SQLite

A simple database that stores its information in a single file. (In Rails, that file is
kept in the *db* directory.) SQLite is extremely convenient for initial development,
but slows down dramatically as the number of users grows.

Sublime editor

A common text editor used for developing Rails apps.

symbols

Ruby identifiers prefaced with colons that Rails uses for pretty much every variable that gets passed from model to view to controller, as well as for named
parameters. Symbols look and behave like variables for most ordinary programming purposes, but they give Rails tremendous flexibility.

template

Files used to generate output. In Rails, views are written as templates, typically *ERb* or *Builder* templates, though a variety of other template formats are available as extensions.

test

Code designed to put a particular application piece through its paces. Rails comes complete with support for creating your own unit tests (does a model behave predictably?), functional tests (does a method do what it should?), and integration tests (do these methods work together?). You can also create performance tests (how fast does this go, anyway?), and use stubs and mock objects to isolate components for testing.

Test-driven development (TDD)

A software development process that relies on the repetition of a very short development cycle: first the developer writes an (initially failing) automated test case that defines a desired improvement or new function, then writes code to make the test pass.

threads

If you came to Rails from Java or a similar language, you may be looking around for threads. Ruby has threads, after all—why doesn't Rails? Well, Rails is single-threaded, handling requests in a single thread. There are lots of ways around this, including having multiple instances of Rails servers all accessing the same database.

UDDI

Universal Description, Discovery, and Integration, a supposedly magical but now largely forgotten piece of the *web services* picture. It was designed to help developers and programmers find *SOAP*-based web services.

Unicode

The industry-standard way to identify characters. Originally, Unicode mapped one character to each of 65,535 bytes, but as that space filled, it became clear that things were more complicated. Ruby's Unicode support improved substantially in version 1.9, but most things will work fine in 1.8.6.

URI

Uniform Resource Identifier, a slightly polished-up and abstracted version of the old *URL* that can be used to identify all kinds of things, no longer bound to a few protocols. In REST-based Rails applications, URIs connect to applications in a generally unsurprising way.

URL

Uniform Resource Locator, the identifiers that hold together the Web. URLs specify a scheme (like http, ftp, or mailto) that maps to a particular protocol, and the rest of the URL provides information that, used with software supporting the scheme, gets you to the information the URL points to. (Or, if the information is gone, an error message.)

UTC

Coordinated Universal Time, formerly known as Greenwich Mean Time (GMT) or Zulu Time. Time zones are generally expressed as offsets from UTC. (UTC is a "compromise abbreviation" between English and French.)

UTF-8

A common encoding for Unicode characters. Old ASCII files are naturally UTF-8 compliant, but characters outside the ASCII range are encoded into multibyte representations. UTF-16 uses two bytes for most commonly used Unicode characters (on the Basic Multilingual Plane) and encodes characters outside of that range into multibyte sequences.

validate

Checking that something is what it's supposed to be. In Rails, data validation should be performed in the model, though some checks may also be performed in view code—for example, in Ajax applications that do as much on the client as possible.

view

The aspect of a Rails program that presents data and opportunities for interaction to users, whether those are users of web browsers getting HTML or other programs using XML, JSON, or something else entirely.

Web 2.0

What happens when the world finally "gets" the Web instead of treating it as a place to present brochures and catalogs, recognizing that the interactions among millions of people are creating new and (often) useful things.

web developer

A generic term for people who build applications or sites for the Web. Also, a Firefox plug-in that makes it easy to inspect various aspects of client-side website functionality as well as turn them on or off.

web service

Using the Web for program-to-program communication, rather than the classic model of a human at a web browser interacting with a server. Web services development has largely bifurcated into SOAP-based (or WS-*) development and

REST development. Rails 2.0 took a decisive shift toward REST, though you can still write SOAP web services in Rails if you want to.

WEBrick

A Ruby-based web server that is built into standard Ruby distributions from version 1.8.0 to 2.2. Rails 5 introduced Puma as the default web server.

WebSockets

Makes it possible to open an interactive communication session between the user's browser and a server. With this API, you can send messages to a server and receive event-driven responses without having to poll the server for a reply.

why (the lucky stiff)

Author of "Why's (Poignant) Guide to Ruby" (*http://poignantguide.net/ruby/*), why's former very active site (*http://whytheluckystiff.net*) was shut down in 2009. His work has been collected at the whymirror GitHub account (*http://whymir ror.github.com*).

WSDL

The Web Services Description Language, used most frequently by SOAP-based (or WS-*) web service developers, provides a way of describing a web service that programs and humans can use to develop code for interacting with it.

XHTML

Extensible HTML—basically HTML with XML syntax. If you're doing a lot of AJAX work, using XHTML can simplify some of your debugging, but it hasn't exactly caught the world on fire.

XML

Extensible Markup Language is a widely used format for storing information. It insists on precise syntax, but can support a very wide and customizable set of data structures.

XMLHttpRequest

A JavaScript method that lets a program running in a web browser communicate with the server that delivered the page, using the full set of verbs in the HTTP protocol. It is supported by all of the major graphical web browsers, though implementation details are only recently becoming consistent across implementations. `XMLHttpRequest` is at the heart of *Ajax* development.

XML-RPC

An early web services protocol that let developers make remote procedure calls using a particular (and very verbose) XML vocabulary sent over HTTP requests.

XSS

Cross-site scripting is a security hazard that allows crackers to interfere with your program's logic by inserting their own logic into your HTML. The main means of ensuring that your applications don't encounter it is to treat content that might have originated from outside of your immediate control as hostile, accepting as little HTML as your application's needs can tolerate. The h method makes it generally easy to escape any HTML that does come through.

YAML

Yet Another Markup Language, YAML was originally developed as a more programming-centric alternative to XML. Ruby supports YAML for object persistence. Rails uses YAML for configuration information. (And as it turns out, largely by coincidence, JSON is a subset of YAML.)

yield

A sometimes mind-boggling Ruby feature that lets methods take a block of code along with the rest of their parameters and then call that code with yield when needed. Among other things, this is how Rails implements the relationship between views and layouts.

Index

assigns method, 240
associations, 98, 154, 395
Atom editor/Atom format, 395
attributes, 94-104, 136-138, 362, 395
attributions, xxii
authentication
    application of, 263
    classifying users, 273-283
    defined, 395
    options for Rails development, 263
    specifying acceptable actions, 271
    tasks supported, 283
    user account sign-up, 264-271
authenticity_token element, 95
authorization, 395
authorized? method, 284

B

backslash (\\), 356
Basecamp, 309, 395
bcrypt gem, 265
BDD (behavior-driven development), 237, 249, 395
before_action :authorize method, 271, 284
before_actions, 166, 189
BEGIN statements, 371
belongs_to relationship, 155
benchmarks, 396
binstubs, 11
Bitnami, 2
blank fields, 62, 124, 129
blank? method, 55
blocks (Ruby), 33, 353, 361, 396
bookmarks, 84
Bootstrap, 396
box-shadow property, 300
Builder, 396
Bulpett, Barnabas, xxi, xxiii
"bundle install" message, 15
business rules, 396
byebug gem, 219, 223

C

CamelCase, 396
Capistrano, 346, 396
Capybara, 249
case statements, 368
case_sensitive property, 123
change method, 51, 62, 89, 194, 207

checkboxes, for forms, 99-100
class, defined, 354, 396
closures, 353
code
    idiomatic Ruby code, xvi
    troubleshooting examples, xviii
    using examples, xxi
CoffeeScript
    benefits of, 325
    brief history of, 321
    converting to, 327
    hash symbol (#), 322
    JavaScript translations in, 325-327
    original project page, 321
    syntactic whitespace in, 326
collect method, 157, 189
colons (:), 33, 358
columns, adding/removing, 201
command line
    creating Rails applications from, 5
    generating controllers from, 14
    installation instructions, 3
comments, xx, 24
comments (Ruby), 355
components, 396
concatenation, 356
console shell, debugging in, 214-219
constraints: option, 289
content types, 397
continuous integration, 238
controllers
    accessing by default, 39
    adding data to, 18-20
    adding methods to, 45
    basics of, 43
    best practices for, 68-71
    calling, 241
    choosing layouts from, 36
    code access for multiple, 62
    connecting to models, 53-57
    creating layouts for, 34
    defined, 397
    enabling routing for, 46
    error presentation and, 119
    generating from command line, 14
    generating URIs from, 293
    guestbook demonstration, 44-48
    vs. models, 43
    preventing NULLs storage, 54

About the Authors

Mark Locklear is a web developer at the eXtension Initiative and has 20 years of IT experience including network administration, quality assurance, and software development. He is an Adjunct Instructor at Asheville-Buncombe Technical Community College and is passionate about education and teaching students software development.

Barnabas Bulpett is a web developer in North Carolina with full stack, open source experience in frontend, database, and server-side design and development. He is currently employed as a software engineer in the manufacturing sector, creating production, and workflow tools using Ruby on Rails and Ember.js.

Eric J. Gruber makes stuff for the web and is the eGov coordinator for Lawrence, KS.

Colophon

The animals on the cover of *Learning Rails 5* are tarpans (*Equus ferus ferus*). The tarpan was a wild horse that lived in Europe and Asia and died out in the 19th century. Smaller and stockier than a modern domestic horse, it was mouse-gray in color with a dark mane and a black stripe down its back. The breed was known to be intelligent, curious, and independent.

The ancient tarpan ranged from southern France and Spain to central Russia. Its decline was caused by the growth of the European human population in the 17th and 18th centuries, which encroached on the tarpan's natural habitat. Tarpans were also hunted for their meat. The last wild tarpan died in Ukraine in 1879, and the last pure tarpan died in a Russian zoo eight years later, at which point the species officially became extinct.

However, you can still see a tarpan today, thanks to two German zoologists who succeeded in genetically re-creating the breed in the 1930s. Heinz and Lutz Heck began a breeding program while working at a Munich zoo, believing that genes still present in the gene pool of an overall species could be used to re-create extinct breeds. They combined the genes of living horses who showed similar characteristics to the ancient tarpan, and bred the first modern tarpan at the zoo in 1933. This new form of tarpan, known as the Heck horse, is a phenotypic copy of the original wild breed, meaning that it resembles the ancient tarpan but is not exactly the same genetically. Today, there are about 50 tarpans in North America, all of which trace back to the original project in Munich. Most of them are owned by private breeders who are trying to increase the tarpan population. There are not many more than 100 tarpans in the world.

The cover image is from Richard Lydekker's *Royal Natural History*. The cover fonts are URW Typewriter and Guardian Sans. The text font is Adobe Minion Pro; the heading font is Adobe Myriad Condensed; and the code font is Dalton Maag's Ubuntu Mono.

Learn from experts.
Find the answers you need.

Sign up for a **10-day free trial** to get **unlimited access** to all of the content on Safari, including Learning Paths, interactive tutorials, and curated playlists that draw from thousands of ebooks and training videos on a wide range of topics, including data, design, DevOps, management, business—and much more.

Start your free trial at:

oreilly.com/safari

(No credit card required)

9 781491 926192